Business Valuation
Discounts and Premiums

Business Valuation Discounts and Premiums

Shannon P. Pratt, CFA, FASA, MCBA

John Wiley & Sons, Inc.
New York • Chichester • Weinheim • Brisbane • Singapore • Toronto

Library of Congress Cataloging-in-Publication Data

Pratt, Shannon P.
    Business valuation discounts and premiums / Shannon P. Pratt.
        p. cm.
    Includes bibliographical references and index.
    ISBN 0-471-39448-3 (cloth : alk. paper)
    1. Business enterprises—Valuation. I. Title.

    HG4028.V3 P682 2001
    658.15—dc21

                                            2001026448

10 9 8 7 6 5 4 3 2 1

To
Sally Mahedy
my executive assistant at Willamette Management Associates
who manages my (often turbulent) schedule

and

Nancy Ferril
my executive assistant at Business Valuation Resources
who "keeps me connected" with the world

About the Authors

Dr. Shannon P. Pratt is a founder and a managing director of Willamette Management Associates. Founded in 1969, Willamette is one of the oldest and largest independent valuation consulting, economic analysis, and financial advisory service firms, with offices in principal cities across the United States. He is also a member of the board of directors of Paulson Capital Corp., an investment banking firm.

Over the last 30 years, he has performed valuation engagements for mergers and acquisitions, employee stock ownership plans (ESOPs), fairness opinions, gift and estate taxes, incentive stock options, buy–sell agreements, corporate and partnership dissolutions, dissenting stockholder actions, damages, marital dissolutions, and many other business valuation purposes. He has testified in a wide variety of federal and state courts across the country and frequently participates in arbitration and mediation proceedings.

He holds an undergraduate degree in business administration from the University of Washington and a doctorate in business administration, majoring in finance, from Indiana University. He is a Fellow of the American Society of Appraisers, a Master Certified Business Appraiser, a Chartered Financial Analyst, a Certified Business Counselor, and a Certified Financial Planner.

Dr. Pratt's professional recognitions include being designated a life member of the Business Valuation Committee of the American Society of Appraisers, past chairman and a life member of the ESOP Association Advisory Committee on Valuation, a life member of the Institute of Business Appraisers, and the recipient of the *magna cum laude* in business appraisal award from the National Association of Certified Valuation Analysts. He recently completed a six-year term as a trustee-at-large of the Appraisal Foundation.

Dr. Pratt is author of *Business Valuation Body of Knowledge, Cost of Capital,* and *The Market Approach to Valuing Businesses* (all published by John Wiley & Sons, Inc.), and *The Lawyers Business Valuation Handbook* (published by the American Bar Association). He is coauthor of *Valuing a Business: The Analysis and Appraisal of Closely Held Companies,* 4th ed. and *Valuing Small Businesses and Professional Practices,* 3d ed. (both published by McGraw-Hill, Inc.). He is also coauthor of *Guide to Business Valuations,* 11th ed. (published by Practitioners Publishing Company).

He is editor in chief of two monthly newsletters, *Business Valuation Litigation Reporter*™ (formerly *Judges & Lawyers Business Valuation Update,* primarily for the legal community) and *Shannon Pratt's Business Valuation Update*™ (primarily for the professional appraisal community). He oversees *Business Valuation Online Library,* www.BVLibrary.com, which includes papers, regulations, and court case decisions. He also oversees *Pratt's Stats,* the official completed transaction database of the International Business Brokers Association, and www.BVMarketData.com, which includes the online version of *Pratt's Stats* as well as *BIZCOMPS* and *Mergerstat/Shannon Pratt's Control Premium Study.*

Dr. Pratt develops and teaches business valuation courses for the American Society of Appraisers and the American Institute of Certified Public Accountants, and frequently speaks on business valuation at national legal, professional, and trade association meetings. He has also developed and frequently teaches a full-day seminar (sometimes divided into partial days) on business valuation for judges and lawyers.

Curtis R. Kimball, CFA, ASA, is a principal and national director of taxation for Willamette Management Associates, and is director of the firm's Atlanta, Georgia, office. He earned his Bachelor of Arts in Economics from Emory University and his Masters of Business Administration from Duke University.

Mr. Kimball is an Accredited Senior Appraiser (ASA) of the American Society of Appraisers, a Chartered Financial Analyst, a member of the Council of Examiners of the Association for Investment Management and Research, and has been a member of the Grading Staff for the examinations leading to the CFA designation since 1991. He is also a member of The ESOP Association, the American Bankruptcy Institute, the Family Firm Institute, and the National Association of Business Economists.

Linda L. Kruschke, Esq. prepared Appendix A. She is managing editor of *Business Valuation Litigation Reporter™*, court case editor of *Shannon Pratt's Business Valuation Update™*, and publications department manager at Business Valuation Resources. She earned her Bachelor of Arts in Political Science from Whitman College and her J.D. *cum laude* from Northwestern School of Law of Lewis & Clark College.

Z. Christopher Mercer, ASA, CFA, is founder and chief executive officer of Mercer Capital. Mr. Mercer is a member of the Editorial Advisory Board of *Valuation Strategies,* a national magazine published by RIA Group dealing with current business appraisal issues, and a member of the Editorial Review Board of the *Business Valuation Review,* a quarterly journal published by the American Society of Appraisers.

Mr. Mercer is the author of *Quantifying Marketability Discounts* (published in October 1997 by Peabody Publishing, LP) and *Valuing Financial Institutions* (published in 1992 by Business One Irwin (now Irwin Professional Publishing)).

Alina V. Niculita prepared Appendix B. She is the managing editor of *Shannon Pratt's Business Valuation Update™*. She earned her Bachelor of Economics in Banking and Finance from the Academy of Economic Studies in Bucharest, Romania, her Masters in Business Administration from CMC Graduate School of Business (Czech Republic), and her Masters of Business Administration in Finance from the Joseph M. Katz Graduate School of Business at the University of Pittsburgh. She has also completed the departmental curriculum for a Ph.D in Systems Science/Business Administration at Portland State University.

Barry S. Sziklay, CPA/ABV, is a managing member of the accounting and consulting firm of *Cipolla Sziklay Zak & Co., L.L.C.,* which is located in West Orange, New Jersey, and New York, New York. His primary practice emphasis is in the areas of business valuation, forensic accounting and litigation support related to business disputes, economic damages, mergers and acquisitions, matrimonial dissolution, income, gift, and estate taxation of closely held businesses and their principal owners, and estate and trust administration. He graduated from Queens College *cum laude* with a B.A. in Accounting and Economics. Mr. Sziklay is a member of the American Institute of Certified Public Accountants, New York Society of Certified Public Accountants, New Jersey Society of Certified Public Accountants, and the Institute of Business Appraisers.

Daniel R. Van Vleet, ASA, CBA, is a principal and the director of the Chicago office of Willamette Management Associates. He earned his Masters of Business Administration from the Graduate School of Business at the University of Chicago. He is the President of the Board of Directors of the Chicago Chapter of the American Society of Appraisers. Mr. Van Vleet is an adjunct professor of finance at the Kellstadt Graduate School of Business at DePaul University in Chicago, Illinois.

Contents

List of Exhibits

Foreword

Michael J. Bolotsky

When Shannon Pratt first approached me to write the foreword for *Business Valuation Discounts and Premiums,* I was, naturally, grateful and flattered, but also somewhat bemused. After all, I am on record as saying that I personally don't believe that discounts and premiums have any objective reality. [Let me set the record straight here, lest I be skewered on the witness stand at some point in the future: What I mean, of course, is that no one actually trades discounts and premiums. Rather, discounts and premiums are the "fallout" of using less-than-perfect market data to measure value, an effect rather than a cause. If one always had the benefit of perfect guideline transactions, with perfection defined at both the entity level and the shareholder level, then the subject of discounts and premiums would never arise. Stated another way, discounts and premiums are the result, due to a lack of directly applicable data, of valuation experts needing to measure value in one type of market based on the actions of buyers and sellers in a different type of market.]

So I agreed to edit Shannon's manuscript and to make my small contribution, by way of this foreword, to the impressive book that you are about to read. A book devoted entirely to this subject is long overdue; as Shannon indicates, the choice of an appropriate discount or premium is often the single largest element of value in the appraisal process. You will find herein a reference to just about anything you might want to learn about the subject, and if Shannon doesn't touch on it himself you can find extensive bibliographic references to the writings of others. Shannon and I don't always agree on specifics around the subject matter of this book: For instance, he subscribes to the commonly accepted concept of "Levels of Value," while I subscribe to a nonlinear, multivariate conceptual model. However, as always, Shannon presents in this book a survey of all reasonable points of view about a particular subject, and he takes great care to give each point of view its due.

One of the wonderful things about Shannon's dedication to enhancing the profession through his writings is that you can be assured that as soon as enough advances and changes have occurred, Shannon will make sure that a revised edition is available so that you can maintain your knowledge base at the state of the art. Thus, in future editions of this book, I'm sure that we can look forward to expanded sections on using financial option-pricing techniques to price restricted securities, to quantify discounts for lack of marketability, or to quantify blockage discounts, and, who knows, perhaps even the use of "real option" analysis to quantify the value of control. It's a constantly evolving field that we play in, and we should be grateful that Shannon is there to guide us through it.

Michael J. Bolotsky
June 7, 2001

Mr. Bolotsky is a principal in the global accounting and consulting firm, Deloitte & Touche, and he is currently the firm's practice leader for valuation services. The views expressed by Mr. Bolotsky are his personal views and do not necessarily represent those of Deloitte & Touche or of any of the firm's employees or other principals and partners.

Preface

Discounts and premiums is the subject within business valuation where the most disputes occur and where, collectively, the most money is at issue. This book brings together for the first time a comprehensive survey of the collective wisdom and knowledge about all of the major business valuation discounts and premiums:

- Lack of control discounts (e.g., minority, 50/50, and lack of supermajority) and control premiums
- Lack of marketability
  - ♦ For noncontrolling interests
  - ♦ For controlling interests
- Nonvoting versus voting value differentials
- Key person discounts
- Trapped-in capital gains discounts
- Blockage discounts
- Nonhomogeneous assets ("portfolio") discounts
- Contingent liability (e.g., environmental, legal) discounts
- Discounts from net asset value for holding companies, especially family limited partnerships (FLPs) and pass-through entities like limited liability companies (LLCs)
- Discounts from net asset value for undivided direct interests in real assets (e.g., real estate, timber)

For each of these discounts or premiums, this book addresses:

- The conceptual basis for the discount or premium
- Factors affecting the magnitude of the discount or premium
- Empirical evidence of the magnitude of the discount or premium
- Courts' treatments of the discount or premium

The various discounts and premiums are discussed in connection with the purpose of the valuation and what legal mandates may apply:

- Federal gift, estate, and income taxes
- Marital dissolutions

- Dissenting stockholder actions
- Corporate or partnership dissolution (minority oppression) actions
- Employee stock ownership plans (ESOPs)
- Bankruptcy reorganizations

The presentation of divergent viewpoints on important issues will challenge everyone's preconception. Literally hundreds of references to books, articles, and court cases are provided. Every reader will learn something from this book. I certainly did. In selecting quotes, I tried to pick ones that were both typical of consensus positions and typical of minority views.

The book is also enhanced by new and revealing information never before published. For example:

- A table of premiums paid to voting control blocks of stock compared with prices to minority shares
- A table of settlements reached with the Internal Revenue Service across the country on discounts from net asset value for FLPs
- A computation and graph comparing the results achieved by excluding negative premiums (discounts) in the *Control Premium Study* versus including them

Most of the book and article references are provided in the extensive bibliography included as Appendix A. Many of these articles and all of the court cases referenced are available to subscribers at BVLibrary.com, where these references can be searched by keyword and printed as desired.

Other appendixes include:

- Data resources
- A table of cases, organized by type of case (tax, marital, etc.)
- An article on using option-pricing theory to quantify discounts for lack of marketability
- Revenue Ruling 77-287 on using restricted stock data to quantify discounts for lack of marketability
- Securities and Exchange Commission Rules 144 and 144A governing restricted stock

There is also an 8-credit-hour CPE exam.

One thing that is very clear in studying the court cases is that their outcomes are extremely dependent on the quality of expert evidence and testimony presented. I have tried to be comprehensive in cataloging for the reader the relevant empirical evidence that is available for quantification of each type of premium or discount as well as the rationale supporting it.

The book is thoroughly indexed and is designed to be both a tutorial and a reference for

- Business appraisers
- Lawyers
- Certified public accountants
- Fiduciaries, such as trustees and directors
- Investors and intermediaries
- Judges
- Academicians and students
- Government appraisers and reviewers of appraisals

We will be continually building on the material in this book through the BVLibrary.com Web site and our two monthly newsletters, *Shannon Pratt's Business Valuation Update*™ and *Business Valuation Litigation Reporter*™. For a complimentary copy of either or both newsletters, please contact us at the following address. Please also contact us with any questions or comments on the book. And please visit our Web sites for up-to-date information.

Shannon P. Pratt
Business Valuation Resources, LLC
7412 S.W. Beaverton-Hillsdale Highway
Suite 106
Portland, OR 97225

E-mail: *shannonp@BVResources.com*
Phone: (888) BUS-VALU [(888) 287-8258]
Fax: (800) 846-2291 or (503) 291-7955

Web sites:
  BVResources.com (general information)
  BVLibrary.com (articles and text material)
  BVMarketData.com (businesses sold and statistical data)

Acknowledgments

This book has benefited immensely from review by many people with a high level of knowledge and experience in business valuation. The following people reviewed most or all of the entire manuscript, and the book reflects their efforts and constructive counsel.

Mel H. Abraham
Kaplan, Abraham, Burkett & Co.
Wood Ranch, CA

R. James Alerding
Clifton Gunderson, LLP
Indianapolis, IN

Michael J. Bolotsky
Deloitte & Touche
Philadelphia, PA

Stephen Bravo
Apogee Business Valuations, Inc.
Framingham, MA

Rand M. Curtiss
Loveman-Curtiss, Inc.
Pepper Pike, OH

John R. Gilbert
The Financial Valuation Group
Great Falls, MT

Mark Lee
Sutter Securities, Inc.
New York, NY

Howard A. Lewis
Internal Revenue Service
Plantation, FL

Harold G. Martin, Jr.
Keiter, Stephens, Hurst, Gary & Shreaves
Richmond, VA

Gilbert E. Matthews
Sutter Securities, Inc.
San Francisco, CA

Mary McCarter
Columbia Financial Advisors
Portland, OR

Eric W. Nath
Willamette Management Associates
San Francisco, CA

Sarah Nelson
Intellectual Capital Uplink
Chicago, IL

Bonnie O'Rourke
Kroll Lindquist Avey
Philadelphia, PA

John W. Porter
Baker & Botts, LLP
Houston, TX

James S. Rigby
The Financial Valuation Group
Los Angeles, CA

Robert C. Schlegel
Houlihan Valuation Advisors
Indianapolis, IN

Richard M. Wise
Wise, Blackman
Montreal, Quebec, Canada

Robert P. Schweihs
Willamette Management Associates
Chicago, IL

I also very much appreciate the efforts of those who were kind enough to send their comments on the original working papers, which were the foundation for this book: Richard M. Duvall; Jerome H. Lipman of Jerome H. Lipman & Co., Ltd.; Howard A. Port; Carl Steffen, Steffen & Company; Kevin Vannucci; Robert T. Willis, Willis Investment Counsel.

I greatly appreciate the enthusiastic cooperation of the professionals at John Wiley & Sons, John DeRemigis, executive editor, and Judy Howarth, associate editor.

The entire manuscript was typed by Leslie Slavens, whose accuracy and timeliness continue to be outstanding, and Nancy Ferril, my executive assistant at Business Valuation Resources, who contributed to most aspects of the project and kept me organized.

To Linda Kruschke, the project manager on this book, her editorial assistant Tanya Hanson, law clerk Jeff Patterson, and research analysts Jill Johnson, Paul Heidt, and Doug Twitchell, and administrative assistant Janet Marcley, I would like to express my thanks and appreciation for a professional and outstanding job.

Shannon Pratt
Portland, OR

Overview of Business Valuation Discounts and Premiums and the Bases to Which They Are Applied

This chapter calls attention to the high degree of significance of the topic of discounts and premiums in business valuation and provides an overview of various discounts and premiums and the bases of value to which they may be applied.

In general, I will refer to stock when talking about any type of equity interest unless I am talking specifically about partnerships or some other specific ownership form. However, the same concepts as applied to stock, are usually applicable to partnership interests as well as other forms of ownership.

DISCOUNTS AND PREMIUMS REFLECT RELATIVE RISK AND RELATIVE GROWTH

The purpose of a discount or premium is to make an adjustment from some base value. The adjustment should reflect the differences between the characteristics of the subject interest (the interest being valued) and those of the base group on which indications of value are based. These differences in characteristics create differences in risk, either to the entity or to its owners, whether the differences arise from contingent liabilities, lack of control, lack of marketability, or some other factor.

Since discounts decrease value, they have the effect of increasing the expected percentage rate of return over what it would otherwise be if the discount were not applicable. If discounts and premiums are applied correctly, the resulting differential in value should reflect the differential in expected rate of return that an investor would require to compensate for the difference in investment characteristics (risk), given the expected rate of growth of the company.

For example, assume that a publicly traded stock was selling at $10 per share and the market expects the total return on that stock (dividends plus capital appreciation) to be on average 10% per year of which 6% is expected to be from growth and 4% from dividends. Thus, the dividend yield on the stock should be 4% as well. If an investor in an otherwise similar but nonmarketable stock were to require a 12% expected total return to compensate for the lack of marketability, that would mean that the investor would require a $33\frac{1}{3}\%$ discount for lack of marketability from the price at which the stock would sell if it were publicly traded. This would mean that the investor would pay only $6.67 per share for the subject closely held stock in order for the same dollar of return to yield 15% instead of 10% on the price paid. That is, the dividend yield at a 10% required return would be 4% (10% − 6% growth) while the yield at a 12% required return would be 6% (12% − 6% growth). The percentage differential in the yields $(1 - \frac{4\%}{6\%})$ is 33%, which would also be the percentage differential in the price.

Therefore, when estimating the magnitude of a given discount, differences in both risk and expected growth between the subject and the companies used to estimate the base value should also be reflected.

After all discounts and premiums have been applied, it is often a very good idea as a reasonableness or sanity check, to compute the implied expected rate of return on the final concluded value to see if it appears reasonable.

DISCOUNTS AND PREMIUMS ARE BIG-MONEY ISSUES

Often there is more money at stake in determining what discounts or premiums are applicable to some business valuations than there is in arriving at the base value (prediscount valuation) itself. A thorough understanding of (1) the types of discounts and premiums, (2) situations in which each may or may not be applicable, and (3) how to quantify them is a major and indispensable part of the tool kit of any business appraiser or reviewer of business appraisals.

Exhibit 1.1   *Estate of Weinberg v. Commissioner* Experts' and Court's Discounts from Net Asset Value

Minority & Marketability Discounts

	Taxpayer's Expert	IRS Expert	Tax Court
Minority Interest Discount	43%	20%	37%
Marketability Discount	35%	15%	20%
Combined Discount	63%	32%	50%

Source: Robert M. Siwicki of Fleet M&A Advisors. "Tax Court Rejects QMDM and Use of Single Comparable," *Shannon Pratt's Business Valuation Update* (April 2000): 10.

In the dissenting stockholder action of *Swope v, Siegel-Robert, Inc.,* for example, one appraiser testified to a value of $98.40 per share and another testified to a value of $30.90 per share, a difference of well over three to one between the two appraisers' values. However, their base level values were $72.90 and $46.20 per share, respectively. The rest of the difference came from the fact that the first appraiser applied a 35% control premium, which the second did not, and the second appraiser applied a 35% discount for lack of marketability, which the first did not.[1]

There have been many cases in which the parties reached agreement on base values, and the only disputes remaining involved premiums and/or discounts.

In *Estate of Weinberg v. Commissioner,*[2] the parties agreed that the fair market value of an apartment building, the sole asset of a limited partnership, was $10,050,000. The points of disagreement centered on the magnitudes of lack of control and marketability discounts for a 25.32% limited partnership interest. The differences in the experts' positions on the discounts and the court's conclusion are shown in Exhibit 1.1. If the court had accepted the taxpayer's expert's discounts, the concluded value would have been $971,838. If the court had accepted the Internal Revenue Service (IRS) expert's discounts, the concluded value would have been $1,770,103. This magnitude of difference based on combined discounts for lack of control and lack of marketability is not uncommon.

The most famous case dealing solely with the issue of discounts is *Mandelbaum v. Commissioner.*[3] The parties stipulated to freely traded minority interest values, so the only issue was the discount for lack of marketability. After hearing testimony from experts for both the IRS and the taxpayer, the court concluded a discount of 30% for lack of marketability. Some of the court's criteria for reaching its decision are still controversial in the financial community. This case is discussed more fully in Chapter 11.

"ENTITY-LEVEL" VERSUS "SHAREHOLDER-LEVEL" DISCOUNTS AND PREMIUMS

Some categories of discounts apply to the entity as a whole, such as a key person or environmental liability discount; others reflect the characteristics of ownership, such as control versus minority and lack of marketability. These are often distinguished as "entity-level discounts" or "company-level discounts," because they apply to the company as a whole, versus "shareholder-level discounts," which apply to a specific block of stock.

Entity-Level Discounts

Certain discounts apply to the entity as a whole or to all shareholders, individually or as a group, regardless of any individual shareholder's characteristics or attributes. These include, for example:

- Discount for trapped-in capital gains
- Key person discount
- Discount for known or potential environmental liability
- Discount for pending litigation
- "Portfolio," "conglomerate," or "nonhomogeneous assets" discount (for an unattractive assemblage of assets)
- Concentration of customer or supplier base (risk of loss/nonrenewal of significant customers or vendors normally is factored into the multiples in the market approach or the discount rates in the income approach)

These "entity discounts" usually are applied *before* "shareholder discounts," that is, discounts affecting the entity as a whole as opposed to those characteristics affecting the particular share ownership. These entity-level discounts normally are applied to a control-level value. However, in some cases, such as the guideline public company method and sometimes in an income approach, the analysis may lead directly to a minority-level value without ever estimating a control value. In these cases, the entity-level discounts can be applied to those minority values before any shareholder-level adjustments. (The percentage would be the same since entity-level adjustments apply equally to all shareholders.)

Also, in some instances, these "discounts" can be factored into discount or capitalization rates in the income approach or valuation multiples in the market approach to reflect the additional risk that they imply. If this procedure is used, the adjustments to the discount or capitalization rates or market multiples should be clearly explained.

Estate of Mitchell v. Commissioner[4] is a good example of an entity-level discount. The Tax Court first applied a 10% key person discount (for the death of Paul Mitchell) to the $150,000,000 control value for the entity that the court had determined. The court then took the percentage owned by the estate times the remaining $135,000,000 value and applied discounts for lack of control and lack of marketability.

These entity-level discounts usually are applied as a percentage to some measure of value, as in the above example. In some cases, for example, the application of a trapped-in capital gains adjustment, the discount may be quantified as a dollar amount rather than a percentage.

Discounts and Premiums Reflecting Shareholder Characteristics of Ownership

The starting point for any discount or premium has to be a well-defined base to which it is applied. This is especially true of shareholder-level discounts or premiums.

The starting point for discounts relating to characteristics of ownership could be one of the levels defined on the traditional levels-of-value chart (see Exhibit 1.2), such as:

1. Control value, or
2. Minority marketable value (also sometimes called "publicly traded equivalent value" or "stock market value")

If, on the other hand, the analyst believes that publicly traded equivalent value is equal to control value, in accordance with the alternative levels-of-value chart shown in Exhibit 1.3, discounts for both lack of control and for the relative degree of lack of marketability between a control position and a private minority position may be appropriate to derive a private minority value. Further explanation of the concepts embodied in Exhibits 1.2 and 1.3 is included in Chapter 2.

The premiums or discounts reflecting characteristics of ownership fall broadly into two major categories:

1. Degree of control or lack of control. The issue of voting versus nonvoting stock may be regarded as a subcategory of control or as a separate issue.
2. Degree of lack of marketability.

Each of the above has economic bases that must be analyzed in each individual situation.

In a valuation analysis, the degree of control usually is considered before the degree of marketability. This is because, although control and marketability are separate issues, the degree of control or lack of it has a bearing on both the size of the discount for lack of marketability and the procedures that are appropriate to quantify the discount for lack of marketability.

It generally is not practical to use the minority nonmarketable level of value as a starting point because there is no database of arm's length transactions of minority nonmarketable interests and no other empirical data to lead directly to that level of value.

Note that the issue of marketability is usually distinguished from nonmarketability at the minority interest level but not at the controlling interest level. On the minority interest level, "marketable," or "liquid," reflects a stock with an active public trading market that can be sold instantly, with cash proceeds received within three days.[5] Controlling interests are far less liquid than an actively traded security, although in most cases they are more liquid than a private minority position. Therefore, at this point we have no benchmark against which to classify a controlling interest as marketable or nonmarketable. Also, this concept does *not* apply to other types of property, such as real property, where no such liquid market for fractional interests exists.

Exhibit 1.2 "Levels of Value" in Terms of Characteristics of Ownership

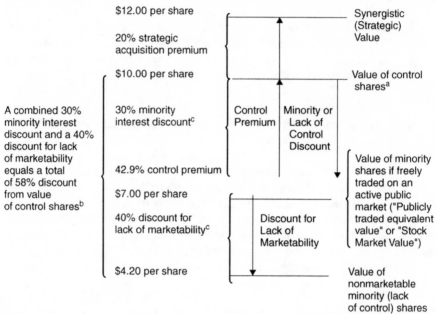

Notes:

[a] Control shares in a privately held company also may be subject to some discount for lack of marketability, but usually not nearly as much as minority shares.

[b] Minority and marketability discounts normally are multiplicative rather than additive. That is, they are taken in sequence:

$10.00	Control Value
- 3.00	Less: Minority interest discount (.30 x $10.00)
$ 7.00	Marketable minority value
- 2.80	Less lack of Marketability discount (.40 x $7.00)
$ 4.20	Per share value of non-marketable minority shares

[c] Note that neither the minority/control nor the marketability issue are all-or-nothing matters. Each covers a spectrum of degrees.

Since we have no such benchmark at the control level, some consider it wise to avoid trying to classify controlling interests as "marketable" or "nonmarketable." (This will be discussed in greater detail in Chapter 9.)

The American Society of Appraisers courses use the term "basis of value" rather than "level of value." They use a chart configured somewhat differently (see Exhibit 1.4). It

Exhibit 1.3 "Levels of Value" in Private Companies Based on Owners' Options for Exit or Liquidity

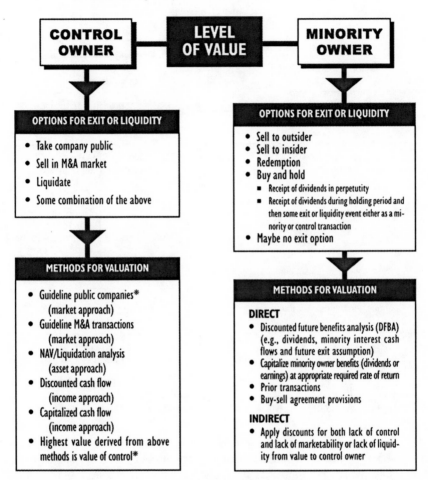

*Guideline public company method—Determine if company could go public. If so, where would it likely trade assuming it was seasoned in the market? If not, is this method applicable? If company could do an IPO, control owners usually cannot cash out, but end up with restricted stock. May need to determine the cash-equivalent value of this restricted stock if public market indicates significantly higher value than the other approaches.

Source: Chart designed by Eric W. Nath.

differs from the levels-of-value chart in that "levels of value" implies a linear process, control being highest, marketable minority next, and unmarketable minority lowest. The American Society of Appraisers chart, developed by Michael Bolotsky, implies a non-linear, multivariate process; it implies that at certain times and for certain companies, marketable minority value can be higher than control value.

Exhibit 1.4   Basis of Value Chart

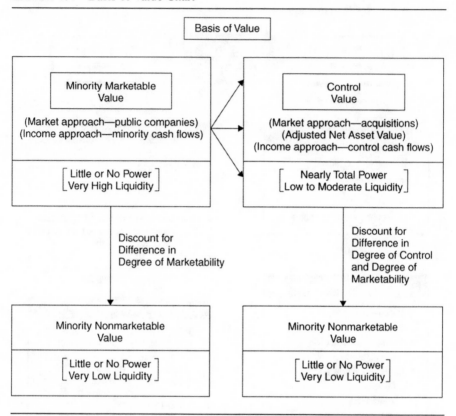

Source: American Society of Appraisers, adapted from chart created by Michael J. Bolotsky.

The American Society of Appraisers Business Valuation Standard VII, shown as Exhibit 1.5, summarizes business valuation discounts and premiums and their application quite succinctly. Appraisers should note Section III, the steps in the application of discounts and premiums.

Degree of Control or Minority

The degree of ownership control covers a wide spectrum, from 100% control ownership to a tiny minority with no control attributes at all. Therefore, discounts for lack of control vary in degree depending on how many and what types of control attributes are present.

It is *vital* to recognize that ownership of stock or a partnership interest does not entail any direct claim on the underlying assets. This is a fundamental concept that those not familiar with business appraisal may not at first grasp. It is the foundation

Exhibit 1.5 American Society of Appraisers Business Valuation Standard VII, Valuation Discounts and Premiums

---

BVS-VII Valuation Discounts and Premiums©

I. Preamble

   A. This standard is required to be followed in all valuations of businesses, business ownership interests, and securities by all members of the American Society of Appraisers, be they Candidates, Accredited Members (AM), Accredited Senior Appraisers (ASA), or Fellows (FASA).

   B. The purpose of this standard is to define and describe the requirements for use of discounts and premiums in the valuation of businesses, business ownership interests, or securities whenever they are applied.

   C. This standard incorporates the general preamble to the Business Valuation Standards of the American Society of Appraisers.

   D. This standard is applicable to appraisals and may not necessarily be applicable to limited appraisals and calculations as defined in BVS-I, Section II.B.

   E. This standard applies at any time in the valuation process, whether within a method, to the value indicated by a valuation method, or to the result of weighing or correlating methods.

II. The Concept of Discounts and Premiums

   A. A discount has no meaning until the conceptual basis underlying the value to which it is applied is defined.

   B. A premium has no meaning until the conceptual basis underlying the value to which it is applied is defined.

   C. A discount or premium is warranted when characteristics affecting the value of the subject interest differ sufficiently from those inherent in the base value to which it is applied.

   D. A premium or discount quantifies an adjustment to account for differences in characteristics affecting the value of the subject interest relative to the base value to which it is being compared.

III. The Application of Discounts and Premiums

   A. The purpose, applicable standard of value, or other circumstances of an appraisal may indicate the need to account for differences between the base value and the value of the subject interest. If so, appropriate discounts or premiums should be applied.

   B. The base value to which the discount or premium is applied must be specified and defined.

   C. Each discount or premium to be applied to the base value must be defined.

   D. The primary reasons why each discount or premium selected applies to the appraised interest must be stated.

   E. The evidence considered in deriving the discount or premium must be specified.

   F. The appraiser's reasoning in arriving at a conclusion regarding the size of any discount or premium applied must be explained.

Source: American Society of Appraisers *Business Valuation Standards.*

of the discount for lack of control. For example, the other day I tried again to back my van up to the local brewery loading dock and swap my stock in the brewery for an equivalent value of beer. I even offered to discount the value of my stock for minority interest and lack of marketability, but still no deal. They said that the stock was not exchangeable for the underlying assets.

I think that the liquidation value of my brewery's assets is a lot greater than what the stock trades for, but I cannot force liquidation or even a partial sale of assets. The profits are good enough that they could at least pay a beer dividend (some distilleries used to pay a whiskey dividend), but they would rather pay outrageous bonuses to the semicompetent chairman of the board (who also happens to have a controlling ownership in the stock).

It is no wonder that the few trades that do take place in the brewery's stock are at a price a great deal lower than a proportionate share of what the whole thing is worth.

Degree of Marketability

Like the degree of control, the degree of marketability can cover a wide spectrum. It can range all the way from active public trading (instant sale with cash in three business days) to no trades at all and severe restrictions on any attempt to sell. For example, most stocks traded on the New York Stock Exchange (NYSE) or the NASDAQ markets have very high liquidity. Partnership interests traded on the secondary market for partnerships registered by the Securities and Exchange Commission (SEC) are marketable, but the liquidity of that market is usually much less than that of the major stock markets.

As alluded to, there can be a distinction between "marketability" and "liquidity." Dictionaries define these terms in various ways, but the general theme seems to be that "marketability" relates to the right to sell something, whereas "liquidity" refers to the speed with which an asset may be converted to cash without diminishing its value. On the other hand, financial texts tend to define these terms somewhat differently. Currently, business appraisers tend to use these terms interchangeably and there is no consensus yet on a distinction between these terms. For the purposes of this book these terms are used interchangeably; however, analysts may wish to define these terms in their report if it is important to the analysis.

Investors cherish liquidity and abhor lack of it. When a stock is not readily marketable (i.e., publicly traded), if it does finally sell, it usually will sell at a significantly discounted price from control value or from an otherwise comparable stock that is publicly traded. This is the conceptual basis for the discount for lack of marketability: one does not know when or for how much one's stock can be sold.

The amount of this discount will vary depending on the degree of liquidity attributes (e.g., occasional trades, potential for a public offering, or sale of the company) to restrictions exacerbating the lack of liquidity.

HOW THE VALUATION APPROACHES USED AFFECT THE LEVEL OF VALUE

Different valuation approaches and methods result in different levels of value. Therefore, in order to understand whether various discounts and/or premiums should be applied to the appropriate base value, the appraiser needs to understand what base value was developed by the valuation method(s) used. This section gives a broad overview, and later chapters discuss more specific detail about how the valuation method(s) impact premiums and discounts.

There is an ongoing debate about whether public stock market multiples, discount rates, and capitalization rates indicate minority or control levels of value. This debate is summarized and examined in more depth in Chapter 2.

Income Approach

Most analysts believe that the question of whether the income approach produces a minority or control value depends for the most part on whether the income or cash flows to be discounted or capitalized represent a minority basis (generally, business as usual) or are adjusted to reflect whatever policies a control owner could implement.

The discount or capitalization rate in the income approach is derived from public stock market data. There are three methods commonly used to derive discount and capitalization rates from public stock market data:

1. The Capital Asset Pricing Model
2. The buildup model
3. The "Discounted Cash Flow method"

(For descriptions of each of these methods, see *Cost of Capital: Estimation and Applications.*[6]) Regardless of what method is used to estimate the discount rate, *the rate developed is from public market data and reflects the assumption of full marketability. Therefore, if minority interest cash flows are used, the result should be the minority, marketable level of value. If control cash flows are used, the result should be control value,* although there may be room for a modest control premium to reflect the ability to exercise the prerogatives of control and gain economic benefit from doing so. For example, most buyers believe that they can improve profitability by better management.

Since there is no market data to benchmark the discount for lack of marketability for controlling interests, it is a matter of the analyst's judgment as to whether a discount for lack of marketability is warranted. Discounts for lack of marketability are covered in detail in future chapters.

Market Approach

Within the market approach, the level of value indicated may depend on whether the guideline publicly traded company method or the merger and acquisition method is used.

Guideline Publicly Traded Company Method. Stock of the guideline public companies are actively traded minority interests. Therefore, the guideline publicly traded company method traditionally has been assumed to produce a marketable minority level of value. However, this assumption has been seriously challenged and there is good reason to believe that such may not always be the case. A full discussion of the debate surrounding this issue is included in Chapter 2.

Guideline Merged and Acquired Company Method. If using merged and acquired guideline companies to derive market multiples, the transactions usually represent controlling interests, so the method is assumed to reflect a control value. Also, this method may reflect synergies, especially in acquisitions of larger companies, which would not be reflected in fair market value.

Asset-Based Approach

Whether the adjusted net asset value or the excess earnings method is used, the general assumption is that asset methods reflect control over the assets and a control value with respect to the levels-of-value chart. This is because, in both methods, individual assets or classes of assets are adjusted to fair market value (often relying on appraisals from other disciplines), and 100% ownership (control), typical market conditions, and no restrictions on transfer are assumed.

USE OF PUBLIC COMPANY DATA TO QUANTIFY DISCOUNTS AND PREMIUMS

The emphasis in this book is on applying discounts and/or premiums in the context of private company valuations, although most of the principles and some examples used are applicable to public companies as well. To illustrate the reality of the discounts and premiums, it is necessary to rely heavily on data from the public markets because this is the only place that actual investor behavior can be observed with respect to most discount and premium issues.

For example, there are virtually no data on prices at which minority interests change hands in private companies compared to the price of a controlling interest in the same company. But we have data on literally thousands of acquisitions of public companies, which relate to exactly that.

Most decision makers, analysts, and courts would rather have an empirical basis for justifying both the reality and the quantification of the premium or discount rather than just an opinion, with nothing to support the analyst's judgment. For the most part, such data are available only in the public market.

HOW THE STANDARD OF VALUE AFFECTS DISCOUNTS AND PREMIUMS

The three primary standards of value that we use for various valuation purposes are:

1. Fair market value
2. Investment value
3. Fair value

While these standards of value are well defined in the appraisal literature, they often are used much more loosely (or ambiguously) in court opinions, especially in family law courts. It is important that the analyst, the attorney, and the court agree on the relevant standard of value, because it may mandate or influence the applicability of certain discounts or premiums, especially with respect to the issue of minority/control and marketability.

Fair Market Value

Fair market value is a concept of value in exchange. It is defined as "the net amount that a willing purchaser, whether an individual or a corporation, would pay for the interest to a willing seller, neither being under any compulsion to buy or to sell and both having reasonable knowledge of relevant facts."[7] It is assumed to be a cash value.

It is important to note that the buyer and seller are "hypothetical," as opposed to any one specific, identified buyer or seller. This is intended to eliminate the influence of one buyer's or seller's specific motivations. However, if there is an active group of competing buyers or sellers with a common set of motivations, this group could constitute the market in which the "hypothetical" buyer and seller might meet to transact, and thus the price that the group would find acceptable could constitute fair market value.

Fair market value is the statutory standard of value for all federal tax cases.[8] It often is the standard of value in bankruptcy proceedings. In some states, precedential case law has established fair market value as the standard of value in property valuations for divorce. The analyst or lawyer must be very careful, however, in the divorce context, because court opinions often use the phrase "fair market value" and then go on to actually apply a standard that is different from the one defined here. Except in Ohio, fair market value is *not* the standard of value in dissenting-stockholder or minority-oppression cases.

Under the standard of fair market value, the focus must be on the specific property (ownership interest) being valued, basically "as is," including control and marketability characteristics. Therefore, minority interests in closely held corporations or partnerships are valued to reflect lack of control and lack of marketability characteristics.

Investment Value

Investment value differs from fair market value as defined in the literature of appraisal in that *investment value* means the value to some *particular* buyer or seller rather than to a *hypothetical* buyer or seller.

Investment value, therefore, might incorporate the synergistic value that some particular buyer may be willing to incorporate into an *acquisition premium* over and above just a control premium that others might pay for the prerogatives of control.[9]

Investment value is often found in legal precedents, especially in the family law courts, where judges often seek "value to the owner" or to the marital community, as opposed to value in exchange. For example, if a company is family owned, there may be no minority discount for a minority owner because, through family attribution, that owner is assumed to be part of a control group.

The analyst and attorney must be extremely careful in studying the relevant case law, because it is quite common to find the phrase "fair market value" in precedential opinions, especially in the family law context, and then find that, in fact, the valuation methodology accepted by the court has actually brought in elements of investment value. Family law courts also sometimes refer to investment value as "intrinsic value."

Fair Value

Fair value is a creature of state legislatures, primarily as the standard of value for dissenting stockholder suits and minority oppression suits. Until 1999 it was defined by the Model Business Corporation Act as "the value of the shares immediately before effectuation of the corporate action to which the dissenter objects, excluding any appreciation or depreciation in anticipation of the corporate action unless exclusion would be inequitable."

This definition clearly eliminates any acquisition premium that would incorporate synergistic value with an acquirer over and above the company's control value on a stand-alone basis. However, the definition does not address the questions of the lack of control or lack of marketability of the shares in question.

In 1999 the Model Business Corporation Act introduced language to the effect that fair value would not incorporate either minority discounts or discounts for lack of marketability. However, as of this writing (mid-2001), no state has yet incorporated that modification into its dissenting stockholder statutes or its shareholder dissolution (minority oppression) statutes.

As of now, there is no clear majority position among the states regarding the interpretation of fair value with respect to the issues of minority/control or lack of marketability, although the trend is toward not applying discounts for these factors in determining fair value. In fact, some treat these issues differently in the context of dissenting stockholder versus corporate dissolution statutes. In each situation, the analyst and the attorney must carefully study the relevant case law. When there is no precedential case law, states often turn to persuasive case law from other states with similar statutory law.

SUMMARY

This chapter has provided a broad overview of business valuation discounts and premiums. I distinguished between those discounts and premiums that affect the whole enterprise and all its owners, called *entity-level* discounts, and those that are specifically a result of ownership characteristics (control and marketability or lack of either), called *shareholder-level* discounts and premiums. Since entity-level discounts impact the whole enterprise, they usually are applied to a control value, derived by any valuation approach or method. However, if the guideline public company method (or some other method producing a minority value) is used without ever reaching a control value, the entity-level discounts are still applicable.

Shareholder-level discounts or premiums, on the other hand, are very specific to the ownership characteristics of the base to which they are applied. Therefore, when dealing with adjustments to value arising from ownership characteristics, the assumptions as to the ownership characteristics of the base to which they are applied must be very clearly defined, or the adjustments are meaningless.

I introduced the traditional levels-of-value chart, which assumes that public market data as applied to a private company, gives a "marketable minority" level of value that is less than control. I also introduced an alternative levels-of-value chart that treats public market value and control value nonlinearly such that public market value could be less than, equal to, or greater than control value. Finally, I have shown how the standard of value (fair market value, fair value, or investment value) has an effect on whether premiums or discounts apply in specific cases.

Following chapters discuss both the concepts and measurement of the various discounts and premiums in detail. They also include details of how various courts have accepted or rejected the application and quantification of these discounts and premiums in contexts such as tax, marital dissolution, dissenting and oppressed stockholder actions, and bankruptcy cases.

Notes

1. *Swope v. Siegel-Robert, Inc.,* 74 F. Supp.2d 876 (E.D. Mo. 1999) *aff'd in part, reversed in part* by 243 F.3d 486 (8th Cir. 2001). (In this case, the district court declined to apply either the control premium or the marketability discount and concluded a value of $63.36 per share, finding them to be discretionary. But the Eighth Circuit reversed, holding that no discounts or premiums should be applied in determining fair value as a matter of law.)
2. *Estate of Weinberg v. Commissioner,* T.C. Memo 2000-51, 79 T.C.M. (CCH) 1507 (2000).
3. *Mandelbaum v. Commissioner,* T.C. Memo 1995-255, 69 T.C.M. (CCH) 2852 (1995), *aff'd,* 91 F.3d 124 (3d Cir. 1996).
4. *Estate of Mitchell v. Commissioner,* T.C. Memo 1997-461, 74 T.C.M. (CCH) 872 (1997), *aff'd in part, vacated in part,* by 2001 U.S. App. LEXIS 7990 (9th Cir. 2001).
5. Mercer, Z. Christopher, *Quantifying Marketability Discounts* (Memphis: Peabody Publishing, LP, 1997), p. 6.
6. For methods to estimate discount and capitalization rates, see Shannon P. Pratt, *Cost of Capital: Estimation and Applications* (New York: John Wiley & Sons, 1998), especially Chapter 8, "Build-up Models," Chapter 9, "The Capital Asset Pricing Model (CAPM)," and Chapter 12, "The DCF Method of Estimating Cost of Capital."
7. 26 CFR 20.2031-3 valuation of interests in businesses.
8. Certain collections matters may differ from the fair market value standard.
9. Some may refer to this standard of value as a form of "value in use," although the appraisal profession considers "value in use" to be a premise of value; that is, the condition of the company when the transaction takes place.

Minority Discounts and Control Premiums

Everyone recognizes that control owners have rights that minority owners do not and that the differences in those rights and, perhaps more importantly, how those rights are exercised and to what economic benefit, cause a differential in the per-share value of a control ownership block versus a minority ownership block. This chapter discusses the differences in those rights and their use or misuse and addresses how to measure the difference in per-share value arising from the ownership and use of those rights.

RELEVANT DEFINITIONS

The value of control depends not only on legal power and rights, but also on economic potential. This is overlooked by some analysts. Of what *additional* value is a control interest in an unprofitable business with no reasonable prospects for profitability? In such a situation, a control owner's rights, to the extent exercised, might produce no value difference. On the other hand, in a situation where significant benefits could be derived from exercising one prerogative (e.g., owner compensation), the value of control might be very large. For those mathematically inclined, the control premium can be conceptualized as the product of two factors: legal power and economic benefit.[1]

Exhibit 2.1 presents relevant definitions. The definitions are fairly good as far as they exist. It is what is missing that is revealing about the state of the business valuation profession. For example, the control premium definition correctly reflects the value of control, but no definition exists for *acquisition premium,* which could reflect the value of both control and synergies. There is also no definition of supermajority, which sometimes is important. Many other important nuances that business apprais-

Exhibit 2.1   Definitions Relating to Minority Discounts and Control Premiums

---

Control   The power to direct the management and policies of a business enterprise.

Control Premium   An amount (expressed in either dollar or percentage form) by which the pro rata value of a controlling interest exceeds the pro rata value of a noncontrolling interest in a business enterprise that reflects the power of control.

Majority Control   The degree of control provided by a majority position.

Majority Interest   An ownership interest greater than 50 percent (50%) of the voting interest in a business enterprise.

Minority Interest   An ownership interest less than 50 percent (50%) of the voting interest in a business enterprise.

Discount   A reduction in value or the act of reducing value.

Discount for Lack of Control   An amount or percentage deducted from the pro rata share of value of 100 percent (100%) of an equity interest in a business to reflect the absence of some or all of the powers of control.

Minority Discount   A discount for lack of control applicable to a minority interest.

Source: International Glossary of Business Valuation Terms.

ers need to consider have not yet found their way into the standard lexicon of business valuation vocabulary (I mentioned the possible distinction between "marketability" and "liquidity" in Chapter 1).

Chapter 18 by Curtis Kimball addresses minority/control differentials where adjusted net asset value is the starting point, especially in the context of family limited partnerships; and Chapter 19 by Daniel VanVleet addresses discounts for undivided interests in assets.

BASIC MINORITY/CONTROL VALUE RELATIONSHIP

In an overly simplistic world, the control premium and the minority discount could be considered to be the same dollar amount. Stated as a percentage, this dollar amount would be higher as a percentage of the lower minority marketable value or, conversely, lower as a percentage of the higher control value. In fact, this is exactly what the simplest form of the traditional levels-of-value chart (Exhibit 1.2) implies.

Let us assume that the average control premium observed for an industry is 35%, and we want to compute the amount of the minority discount this implies. The applicable formula is:

$$\text{Minority Discount} = 1 - \left(\frac{1}{1 + \text{Control Premium}} \right)$$

Substituting the 35% control premium in this formula:

$$\text{Minority Discount} = 1 - \left(\frac{1}{1 + .35} \right)$$
$$= 1 - \left(\frac{1}{1.35} \right)$$
$$= 1 - .74$$
$$= .26 \text{ or } 26\%$$

Thus, a 35% control premium in the context of the levels-of-value chart implies a 26% minority discount.

Unfortunately, as we shall see, the measurement and application of this concept is not as simple as it may appear at first blush. David Simpson sent a warning flag up the pole on this issue in 1991:

> [I]t would seem at first glance that control premiums paid in buyouts of public companies would be ideal indicators of the magnitude of discount necessary for proper valuation of a minority interest. Yet it becomes apparent that such data is compiled from such a diverse field that its usefulness is limited. This diversity is caused by differences in the degree of control obtained, the industry of the acquired company,

the timing of the buyout, the concentration of control among selling shareholders, the perceived benefits or synergies to be obtained by buyers, the receptiveness of management to the offer, and the presence or absence of competitive bids. Finding enough examples from which to draw a valid discount conclusion for a specific degree of control in a specific industry during a given time period is rarely, if ever, possible.[2]

PREROGATIVES OF CONTROL

There are many things a control owner may be able to do that a minority cannot. These include, for example, the abilities to:

- Decide on levels of compensation for officers, directors, and employees
- Decide with whom to do business and enter into binding contracts, including contracts with related parties
- Decide whether to pay dividends and, if so, how much
- Register the stock with the Securities and Exchange Commission for a public offering
- Repurchase outstanding stock or issue new shares
- Make acquisitions or divest subsidiaries or divisions
- Buy, sell, or hypothecate any or all company assets
- Determine capital expenditures
- Change the capital structure
- Amend the articles of incorporation or bylaws
- Sell a controlling interest in the company with or without participation by minority shareholders
- Select directors, officers, and employees
- Determine policy, including changing the direction of the business
- Block any of the above

Depending on state laws, the company's articles of incorporation and bylaws, and agreements with lenders, any of the above prerogatives of control may be exercised by a simple majority control, or they may require some level of supermajority. About half the states require some degree of supermajority, most often two-thirds, for certain major corporate actions such as selling out, merging, or liquidating the company's major assets. If the stock is widely distributed, or if certain contractual rights exist, a block of stock constituting less than a majority may have effective control over some of the above prerogatives.

On the other hand, many states have laws that limit or curb these prerogatives, such as dissenting stockholder and/or minority oppression statutes. State statutes, as well as state court cases, must be studied carefully.

FACTORS AFFECTING DEGREE OF CONTROL

Many factors can affect the degree of control and, consequently, the magnitude of the discount for lack of control (if starting with a controlling interest value) or some premium for elements of control (if starting with a minority interest value).

Anything Less Than 100%

Any proportion of ownership less than 100% leaves room for attacks by minority shareholders on some prerogatives of control. For example, if the company were to sell out or take certain other corporate actions, any minority stockholder might be able to exercise dissenting stockholder rights. There are many ways in which a minority stockholder can create a nuisance for the control stockholder, which could reduce the control premium and the discount for lack of control, thus increasing the minority owner's interest's value.

Supermajority Requirements

About a quarter of the states require something more than a mere 50%-plus-1-share vote to approve certain major corporate actions, such as selling out or merging. Exhibits 2.2A and 2.2B provide tables of the various states' statutory provisions with respect to this issue.

Even in states that do not have statutory requirements of supermajority votes for major corporate actions, any individual company may require supermajority votes for given corporate actions through its articles of incorporation or bylaws.

If a block of stock constitutes control for certain actions but is not large enough to be able to cause other corporate actions, it falls in between a control value and a pure minority value. If starting with a control value, some discount for lack of absolute control usually is warranted. There are no empirical studies available to help quantify the amount of the discount, but such discounts usually fall in the range of 5 to 15%.

In the same vein, if a minority block of stock is large enough to prevent certain corporate actions, this condition is referred to as *blocking power.* Such a block normally is accorded some premium over a pure minority value for blocking power. Because such power is invoked only rarely, the premium tends to be modest, perhaps in the range of 5 to 15%. This premium could be applied to an actively traded minority value (before any discount for lack of marketability) or could be reflected in a smaller discount for lack of control if control value is the base.

In any case, if the size of the block falls into the range where it may have operating but not absolute control, or in the range where it may have blocking power, the analyst should review the relevant state statutes, articles of incorporation, and bylaws to see whether a possible discount or premium for this characteristic should be considered.

Exhibit 2.2A   Summary of State Voting Requirements for Approval of Sale
of Assets as Business Combination

States	Statute Number	Statute Voting Requirements for Approval of Sale of Assets as Business Combination
Alabama	Ala. Code § 10-2B-12.02	Two-thirds of outstanding shares entitled to vote (articles or bylaws may not set requirement at less than a majority)
Alaska	Alaska Stat. § 10.06.568	Two-thirds of the outstanding shares[1]
Arizona	Ariz. Rev. Stat. Ann. § 10-727	Majority of all votes entitled to be cast
Arkansas	Ark. Stat. Ann. §§ 4-27-1202, 4-26-903	Two-thirds of the shares entitled to vote.[1]
California	Cal. Corp. Code §§ 152, 1001	Majority of the outstanding shares entitled to vote
Colorado	Colo. Rev. Stat. § 7-112-102	Majority of all votes entitled to be cast
Connecticut	Conn. Gen. Stat. § 33-831	Majority of the outstanding stock entitled to vote
Delaware	8 Del. C. §§ 271	Majority of all votes entitled to be cast
District of Columbia	D.C. Code § 29-375	Two-thirds of the outstanding shares (but articles may specify a lesser voting requirement but not less than a majority)
Florida	Fla. Stat. § 607.1202	Majority of all votes entitled to be cast
Georgia	Ga. Code Ann. § 14-2-1202	Majority of all votes entitled to be cast
Hawaii	Hawaii Rev. Stat. § 415-79	A simple majority may approve plan of sale of assets for corporations organized after July 1, 1987. For corporations organized before July 1, 1987, at least three-fourths of all the issued and outstanding stock having voting power is required (articles may provide for a lesser voting requirement but not less than a majority)[2]
Idaho	Idaho Code § 30-1-1202	Majority of all votes entitled to be cast
Illinois	805 ILCS 5/11.60	Two-thirds of the votes of the shares entitled to vote[1]
Indiana	Ind. Stat. Code § 23-1-41-2	Majority of all votes entitled to be cast
Iowa	Iowa Code Ann. § 490.1202	Majority of all votes entitled to be cast
Kansas	Kan. Stat. Ann. § 17-6801	Majority of all outstanding stock entitled to vote
Kentucky	Ky. Rev. Stat. Ann. §§ 271B.12-020	Majority of all votes entitled to be cast
Louisiana	La. Rev. Stat. Ann. § 12:121	Two-thirds of the voting power (but articles may provide for a lesser voting requirement but not less than a majority)[1]
Maine	13-A.M.R.S. § 1003	Majority of all the outstanding shares entitled to vote[3]
Maryland	Md. Corps. & Ass'ns Code Ann. §§ 3-105, 3-602, 3-603	Two-thirds of all votes entitled to be cast[4]

Exhibit 2.2A Summary of State Voting Requirements for Approval of Sale of Assets as Business Combination—*continued*

States	Statute Number	Statute Voting Requirements for Approval of Sale of Assets as Business Combination
Massachusetts	Mass. Laws Ann. Ch. 156, §§ 42, 75	Two-thirds of each class of stock outstanding entitled to vote
Michigan	MCL § 450.1753	Majority of the outstanding shares entitled to vote[3]
Minnesota	Minn. Stat. Ann. § 302A.661	Majority of the voting power of all shares entitled to vote
Mississippi	Miss. Code Ann. § 79-4-12.02	Majority of the votes entitled to be cast
Missouri	Mo. Ann. Stat. § 351.400	Two-thirds of outstanding shares entitled to vote
Montana	Mont. Code Ann. §§ 35-1-823	Two-thirds of the votes entitled to be cast (but articles may provide for a majority vote)
Nebraska	Neb. Rev. Stat. §§ 21-20, 136	Two-thirds majority of all votes entitled to be cast
Nevada	Nev. Rev. Stat. §§ 78.565, 78A.130, 82.436	Majority of the voting power
New Hampshire	N.H. Rev. Stat. Ann. § 293-A:12.02	Majority of all votes entitled to be cast
New Jersey	N.J. Stat. Ann. § 14A:10-11	Majority of the votes entitled to be cast.[3] If the corporation was organized before Jan. 1, 1989, then a two-thirds vote is required, however, majority voting requirements may be adopted with a two-thirds vote
New Mexico	N.M. Stat. Ann. § 53-15-2	Majority of the shares entitled to vote[3]
New York	N.Y. Bus. Corp. Law § 903	For corporations organized on or before February 22, 1998 a majority of the votes of all outstanding shares entitled to vote is required. For corporations formed after that date, unless such a corporation amends its articles to provide for a simple majority vote, two-thirds of the votes of all outstanding shares entitled to vote is required
North Carolina	N.C. Gen. Stat. § 55-12-02	Majority of all votes entitled to be cast
North Dakota	N.D. Cent. Code § 10-19.1-104	Majority of the voting power of the shares entitled to vote
Ohio	Ohio Rev. Code Ann. § 1701.76	Two-thirds of the voting power (articles may specify a lesser voting requirement but not less than a majority)
Oklahoma	Okla. Stat. Ann. Tit. 18, § 1092	Majority of the outstanding stock entitled to vote

continued

Exhibit 2.2A Summary of State Voting Requirements for Approval of Sale of Assets as Business Combination—*continued*

States	Statute Number	Statute Voting Requirements for Approval of Sale of Assets as Business Combination
Oregon	Or. Rev. Stat. § 60.534	Majority of all votes entitled to be cast
Pennsylvania	15 Pa. Cons. Stat. Ann. §§ 1924, 1932	Majority of the votes cast by all shareholders entitled to vote
Puerto Rico	14 L.P.R.A. § 3001	Majority of the outstanding stock entitled to vote
Rhode Island	R.I. Gen. Laws § 7-1.1-72	Majority of the shares entitled to vote[3]
South Carolina	S.C. Code Ann. § 33-12-102	Two-thirds of all votes entitled to be cast (articles may specify a lesser voting requirement but not less than a majority)
South Dakota	S.D. Codified Law § 47-6-21	Majority of the shares entitled to vote[3]
Tennessee	Tenn. Code Ann. § 48-22-102	Majority of all votes entitled to be cast
Texas	Tex. Bus. Corp. Act Ann. Art. § 5.10	Two-thirds of outstanding shares entitled to vote[1]
Utah	Utah Code § 16-10a-1202	Majority of all votes entitled to be cast
Vermont	Vt. Stat. Ann. tit. 11A, § 12.02	Majority of all votes entitled to be cast
Virginia	Va. Code § 13.1-724, 13.1-900	More than two-thirds of all votes entitled to be cast (articles may provide for a lesser voting requirement but not less than a majority)[1]
Virgin Islands	13 V.I.C. § 281	A majority of the stock issued and outstanding having voting power (the articles of incorporation may require the vote or written consent of the holders of a larger proportion of the stock issued and outstanding but in no event more than three-fourths thereof)
Washington	Wash. Rev. Code Ann. § 23B.12.020	Two-thirds of all votes entitled to be cast (lesser vote may be provided by each voting class and by total votes)
West Virginia	W. Va. Code § 31-1-121	Majority of the shares entitled to vote[1]
Wisconsin	Wis. Stat. Ann. § 180.1131	Majority of all votes entitled to be cast
Wyoming	Wyo. Stat. § 17-16-1202	Majority of all votes entitled to be cast

Source: Business Valuation Resources, 2001.

[1]If there is voting by class, two-thirds of each class and of total shares outstanding is required.
[2]If there is voting by class, three-fourths of each class and of total shares outstanding is required.
[3]If there is voting by class, a majority of each class and of total shares outstanding is required.
[4]Special voting requirements required in certain circumstances.

Exhibit 2.2B Summary of State Voting Requirements for Approval
of Merger and Share Exchange

States	Code Sections	Statute Voting Requirements for Approval of Merger and Share Exchange
Alabama	Ala. Code § 10-2B-11.03	Two-thirds of the shares entitled to vote (articles or bylaws may not set requirement at less than a majority)
Alaska	Alaska Stat. § 10.06.546	Two-thirds of the outstanding shares[1]
Arizona	Ariz. Rev. Stat. Ann. § 10-1103	Majority of all shares entitled to vote
Arkansas	Ark. Code § 4-27-1103	Majority of all votes entitled to be cast
California	Cal. Corp. Code §§ 152, 1101, 1201	Majority of the outstanding shares entitled to vote
Colorado	Colo. Rev. Stat. § 7-111-103	Majority of all votes entitled to be cast
Connecticut	Conn. Gen. Stat. § 33-817	Majority of the outstanding stock entitled to vote
Delaware	8 Del. C. §§ 251, 255	Majority of all votes entitled to be cast
District of Columbia	D.C. Code § 29-367	Two-thirds of the outstanding shares (articles may not set requirement of less than a majority)
Florida	Fla. Stat. § 607.1103	Majority of all votes entitled to be cast
Georgia	Ga. Code Ann. § 14-2-1103	Majority of all votes entitled to be cast
Hawaii	Hawaii Rev. Stat. § 415-73	A simple majority approval plan of mergers for corporations organized after July 1, 1987. For corporations organized before July 1, 1987, "at least three-fourths of all the issued and outstanding stock having voting power" is required (articles may provide for a lesser voting requirement but not less than a majority)[2]
Idaho	Idaho Code § 30-1-1103	Majority of all votes entitled to be cast
Illinois	805 ILCS 5/11.20	Two-thirds of the votes of the shares entitled to vote[1]
Indiana	Ind. Stat. Ann. § 23-1-40-3	Majority of all votes entitled to be cast
Iowa	Iowa Code Ann. § 490.1103	Majority of all votes entitled to be cast
Kansas	Kan. Stat. Ann. §§ 17-6701, 17-6705	Majority of the outstanding stock entitled to vote[3]
Kentucky	Ky. Rev. Stat. Ann. § 271B.11-030	Majority of all votes entitled to be cast
Louisiana	La. Rev. Stat. Ann. § 12:112	Two-thirds of the voting power (articles may provide for a lesser vote requirement but not less than majority)[1]
Maine	13-A.M.R.S. § 611	Majority of the outstanding shares entitled to vote[4]
Maryland	Md. Corps. & Ass'ns Code Ann. §§ 3-105, 3-106, 3-602, 3-603	Two-thirds of all votes entitled to be cast[5]
Massachusetts	Mass. Law Ann. ch. 156B, §§ 46B, 78	Two-thirds of each class of stock outstanding and entitled to vote

continued

States	Code Sections	**Statute Voting Requirements for Approval of Merger and Share Exchange**
Michigan	MCL § 450.2703	Majority of the outstanding shares entitled to vote[4]
Minnesota	Minn. Stat. Ann. § 302A.613	Majority of the voting power of all shares entitled to vote[4]
Mississippi	Miss. Code § 79-4-11.04	Majority of the votes entitled to be cast
Missouri	Mo. Ann. Stat. § 351.425	Two-thirds of outstanding shares entitled to vote
Montana	Mont. Code Ann. §§ 35-1-815	Two-thirds of votes entitled to be cast (articles may provide for a majority)[1]
Nebraska	Neb. Rev. Stat. §§ 21-20, 130	Two-thirds majority of all votes entitled to be cast
Nevada	Nev. Rev. Stat. §§ 78A.130, 92A.120, 92A.130, 92A.140, 92A.150, 92A.160, 92A.165	Majority of the voting power[3]
New Hampshire	N.H. Rev. Stat. Ann. § 293-A:11.03	Majority of all votes entitled to be cast
New Jersey	N.J. Stat. Ann. § 14A:10-3	Majority of the votes entitled to be cast.[4] If the corporation was organized before Jan. 1, 1989, then a two-thirds vote is required. A corporation organized before Jan. 1, 1989 may adopt the majority voting requirements with a two-thirds vote
New Mexico	N.M. Stat. Ann. § 53-15-2	Majority of the shares entitled to vote[4]
New York	N.Y. Bus. Corp. Law § 903	For corporations organized on or before February 22, 1998 a majority of the votes of the shares entitled to vote is required. For corporations formed after that date, unless such a corporation amends its articles to provide for a simple majority vote, two-thirds of the votes of all outstanding shares entitled to vote
North Carolina	N.C. Gen. Stat. § 55-11-03	Majority of all votes entitled to be cast
North Dakota	N.D. Cent. Code § 10-19.1-98	Majority of the voting power of all ownership interests entitled to vote[4]
Ohio	Ohio Rev. Code Ann. § 1701.78	Two-thirds of the voting power[4]
Oklahoma	Okla. Stat. Ann. tit. 18, §§ 1081, 1082, 1083, 1084, 1086, 1090.2	Majority of the outstanding stock entitled to vote[5]
Oregon	Or. Rev. Stat. § 60.487	Majority of all votes entitled to be cast
Pennsylvania	15 Pa. Cons. Stat. Ann. §§ 1924	Majority of the votes cast by all shareholders entitled to vote[4]
Puerto Rico	14 L.P.R.A. § 3051, 3054, 3055, 3056, 3057, 3058	Two-thirds of the outstanding stock entitled to vote[3]

Exhibit 2.2B   Summary of State Voting Requirements for Approval of Merger and Share Exchange—*continued*

States	Code Sections	Statute Voting Requirements for Approval of Merger and Share Exchange
Rhode Island	R.I. Gen. Laws § 7-1.1-67	Majority of the shares entitled to vote[4]
South Carolina	S.C. Code Ann. § 33-11-103	Two-thirds of the votes entitled to be cast on the plan and two-thirds of the votes entitled to be cast on the plan within each voting group entitled to vote as a separate voting group on the plan (articles may provide for a greater or lesser vote but not less than majority)
South Dakota	S.D. Codified Law § 47-6-4	Majority of the shares entitled to vote[4]
Tennessee	Tenn. Code Ann. § 48-21-104	Majority of all votes entitled to be cast
Texas	Tex. Bus. Corp. Act Ann. art. § 503	Two-thirds of the outstanding shares entitled to vote[1]; shareholder vote may not be needed
Utah	Utah Code § 16-10a-1103	Majority of all votes entitled to be cast
Vermont	Vt. Stat. Ann. tit. 11A, § 11.03	Majority of all votes entitled to be cast
Virginia	Va. Code §§ 13.1-718, 13.1-895	More than two-thirds of all votes entitled to be cast (articles may provide for a greater or lesser vote but not less than a majority)[3]
Virgin Islands	13 V.I.C. §§ 251, 252	Two-thirds of the total number of shares of capital stock
Washington	Wash. Rev. Code Ann. § 23B.11.030	Two-thirds of all votes entitled to be cast (lesser vote may be provided by each voting class and by total votes)
West Virginia	W. Va. Code § 31-1-117	Majority of the shares entitled to vote[4]
Wisconsin	Wis. Stat. Ann. § 180.1103	Majority of all votes entitled to be cast
Wyoming	Wyo. Stat. § 17-16-1103	Majority of all votes entitled to be cast

Source: Business Valuation Resources, 2001.

[1] If there is voting by class, two-thirds of each class and total shares outstanding is required.
[2] If there is voting by class, three-fourths of each class and total shares outstanding is required.
[3] May require a two-thirds vote in certain circumstances.
[4] If there is voting by class, a majority of each class and total shares outstanding is required.
[5] Special voting requirements required in certain circumstances.

Shareholder Oppression Statutes

In some states under certain circumstances, minority shareholders can institute a lawsuit to dissolve the corporation or partnership and be paid their proportionate share of the proceeds from the liquidation. In such states, the controlling stockholder can prevent the dissolution by paying the minority owners the *fair value* of their shares. About half the states now have such statutes, with California Corporation Code 2000 being one of the oldest and most frequently litigated.

The percentage of shares required and the alleged oppressive actions required to trigger such a suit vary from state to state. A future report on discounts and premiums in connection with dissenting stockholder and shareholder oppression actions will contain a summary of states' shareholder oppression statutes, to be published in future editions of *Shannon Pratt's Business Valuation Update*™ and/or *Business Valuation Litigation Reporter*™.

The presence of such a statute might reduce the minority discount slightly if there is a prospect of such an action.

Swing Vote Potential

Depending on the distribution of the stock, a block could have the potential to gain a premium price over a pure minority value because of its potential as a *swing block*. Consider this situation that was recently presented to the financial advisor to an employee stock ownership plan (ESOP). The ESOP in question owned about 35% of the stock, another stockholder owned 35%, and the third largest stockholder owned about 20%. The financial advisor had been conducting annual valuations of the ESOP stock on a minority basis. When the 20% block came up for sale, both the ESOP and the other 35% stockholder would quickly have paid the ESOP minority price to obtain the stock, and a somewhat prolonged series of negotiations ensued. The ESOP ultimately purchased the block at about a 17% premium over the ESOP minority price. The opinion expressed by the financial advisor was that the ESOP did *not* pay more than fair market value for the swing block, considering that it put the ESOP in a control position and otherwise would have put the remaining stockholder in a control position.

Many scenarios could be constructed where a swing block would have the potential to command some premium over a pure minority value. Generally, they arise when a sale of the block could cause a change (e.g., strengthening or weakening) in a control position. However, not all swing vote situations deserve a premium.

Interests of 50%

Interests of 50% are neither control nor minority. A 50% interest usually can prevent corporate actions but cannot cause them to happen. A 50% interest value usually lies about halfway between a controlling interest value and a pure minority value. There is no empirical data for guidance in quantifying 50% interest percentage discounts from control value or premiums over minority value. However, 50% interests sometimes are discounted at about 15% from control value to reflect lack of control.

In some circumstances two 50% interests do *not* have equal lack of control. This situation can arise when one of the 50% interests exercises some prerogatives of control under a contractual arrangement. In this case, the discount from control value should be less for the interest with some control prerogatives and a little greater for the interest without the control prerogatives.

Legal or Regulatory Constraints

Legal or regulatory conditions can prevent a control owner from exercising control prerogatives to the fullest extent. These conditions narrow the gap between control and minority value and reduce the potential minority discount or control premium.

Minority Shareholder Ability to Elect Directors

Some minority blocks of stock have the ability to elect one or more directors. This ability can arise from either of two circumstances: cumulative voting or contractual arrangement. In either case, this right tends to reduce the minority discount. However, there is no body of empirical data to assist in quantifying this factor, so the magnitude of the discount becomes a matter of negotiation in a transaction or of the appraiser's judgment in a non-transaction-related valuation.

Cumulative Voting. In most companies, a majority of the shares can elect all the directors. However, although it is becoming less common, some companies have *cumulative voting*, which enables a minority to elect one or more directors. The concept of cumulative voting is that all the shares may vote for a single director. Thus, if 10 directors are to be elected, the owner of a block of 10% of the stock can cast all of its votes for each share for a single director, thus ensuring the election of one director by the block.[3]

Cumulative voting, however, does *not* automatically assure the minority of representation on the board; the minority must have the minimum shares necessary to elect the director desired and, second, must aggregate its cumulative votes properly.

Cumulative voting may also increase the discount applicable to a control block for lack of full control.

Contractual Appointment. For various reasons, certain blocks of stock may be granted a contractual right to appoint one or more directors. This is often the case in conjunction with venture capital financing. This may reduce the discount for lack of control.

HOW THE VALUATION METHODOLOGY AFFECTS THE MINORITY DISCOUNT OR CONTROL PREMIUM

To reiterate Chapter 1, for a premium or discount to be meaningful, it is necessary to understand the relationship of the discount or premium to the valuation basis to which it is applied. This section discusses the major valuation approaches and methods and what the bases they produce imply regarding the appropriateness of minority discounts or control premiums. In some cases the applicability of a premium or discount is fairly straightforward. In other cases, however, there is substantial controversy about the applicability of a minority discount or a control premium.

Income Approach as Value Basis

Whether the income approach utilized is the discounted cash flow or capitalization of cash flow or earnings, the income approach can produce either a control value or a minority value. Therefore, it is necessary to understand the assumptions used in the income approach implementation to determine whether a minority discount or a control premium is warranted.

Most analysts agree that the extent to which the income approach produces a control or minority value lies primarily in the level of the cash flows or earnings being discounted or capitalized. If the projected cash flows were those that a control owner would expect to receive, a control premium already would be reflected. However, if the projected cash flows used do *not* reflect a control owner's expectation, then a control premium may be warranted.

Some analysts believe that the income approach always produces a publicly traded minority basis of value because both the Capital Asset Pricing Model (CAPM) and the buildup model develop discount and capitalization rates from minority interest transaction data in the public markets. This is a very common and highly flawed conclusion. *There is little or no difference in the rate of return that most investors require for investing in a public, freely tradable minority interest versus a controlling interest.*

As explained in *Cost of Capital*,[4] almost all the difference in the control value versus the minority value in the income approach to valuation is found in the numerator—the expected economic income available to the investor—rather than in the denominator—the discount or capitalization rate.

As Roger Ibbotson has succinctly stated the case: "When you are purchasing a company you are acquiring the ability to potentially control future cash flows. To acquire this option to exercise control, you must pay a premium. Holding all else constant, it should not impact the discount rate."[5]

Generally speaking, investors will not accept a lower expected rate of return for purchase of a controlling interest than for purchase of a minority interest. In fact, there have been many instances in recent years when public minority shareholders appear to require a significantly lower rate of return than control buyers. Control buyers pay premiums because they expect to take action to increase cash flows, not because they are willing to accept a lower expected rate of return. Actions taken to increase cash flows could range anywhere from eliminating nonperforming relatives from the payroll to drastically increasing prices for products or services of both acquirer and target as a result of absorbing a direct competitor.[6]

In adjusting a minority value upward to estimate a control value, some analysts adjust cash flows upward to what a control owner would expect to realize rather than apply a percentage control premium to a minority value. The advantage of this procedure is that it uses case-specific information to quantify the incremental present value of the cash flows that a control owner could generate. Such adjustments could logically include, for example, elimination of excess compensation, elimination of "sweetheart" insider deals, liquidation or utilization of excess assets, and exercise of other prerogatives of control. If cash flows are adjusted for potential synergistic benefits, the result would be investment value or acquisition value, rather than fair market value.

Another possible fundamental adjustment sometimes used in the income approach that is often controversial in disputes over minority versus control value is adjustment of the company's capital structure. The most common such adjustment is to introduce some amount of long-term debt to substitute for an all-equity capital structure, thus lowering the overall cost of capital and raising the present value of projected cash flows. Again, capital structure adjustments are a control prerogative. Also, adjustments in capital structure can result in changes in the cost of components (debt and equity).

Notwithstanding the above, financial buyers still sometimes pay control premiums even if they do not have any opportunities for synergistic benefits or other cash flow improvements, albeit typically much lower premiums than those paid by synergistic buyers. Buyers see certain prerogatives of control as having value. For example, one control prerogative that control owners can implement that minority owners cannot is to register a public offering. Other control prerogatives are to sell interests to employees or to others, to repurchase outstanding minority interests, or to recapitalize. Some will pay a premium simply to be able to call the shots. Some perceive financial or psychological advantages to the control of certain companies. In the discounted cash flow (DCF) method, this could account for a slightly lower discount rate on the part of some buyers.

Market Approach as Value Basis

There are two clearly distinct methods within the market approach:

1. The guideline merged and acquired company method
2. The guideline publicly traded company method

Guideline Merged and Acquired Company Method. The guideline merged and acquired company method usually is based on observing transfers of ownership of an entire company or a controlling interest in a company. These transactions may be of either public or private companies. In either case, a controlling interest was transferred, so usually no control premium is warranted, because it was clearly reflected in the transaction price.

If control transactions are used as a starting point for valuing something less than a controlling interest (e.g., less than absolute control, 50% interest, or minority interest), then usually some discount for lack of control is warranted (and often a discount for lack of marketability as well).

When using available empirical data, the analyst must determine whether the consideration paid was a price for the common equity or a "deal price," that is, total consideration paid for the entire capital structure, including debt assumed and, possibly, preferred stock. If the consideration was a deal price, then the value of the debt and/or preferred stock must be subtracted before applying a discount for lack of control, because such a discount applies only to the common equity, not to the entire capital structure. However, the percentage control premium on equity has the potential to be greater in a highly leveraged company.

If the transaction was structured as an asset sale, then the analyst must determine what assets were sold and what liabilities were assumed, and make adjustments for differences in property transacted. Also, other terms should be compared, such as the inclusion of a noncompete agreement, and the value adjusted for differences before computing multiples.

Guideline Publicly Traded Company Method.   The guideline publicly traded company method is based on applying valuation multiples observed in the day-to-day public stock trading markets to the fundamental data of the subject company. Because the transactions from which the multiples are derived are minority interest transactions, conventional wisdom states that the guideline public company method produces a minority value. Following this line of reasoning, it would not be appropriate to apply a minority discount when the guideline public company method is used as the starting point for valuing a minority interest. Conversely, it often is appropriate to apply a control premium when the guideline public company method is used as a starting point for valuing a controlling interest.

The conventional wisdom prevailed virtually universally among business appraisers until 1990, when Eric Nath introduced what has come to be known as the Nath hypothesis in an article in *Business Valuation Review.*[7] Among other things, Nath suggested that many, if not most, public companies already must be trading at control value, or they would be subject to takeover attempts. This hypothesis and its implications are explored in the next major section.

Asset-Based Approach as Value Basis

Within the asset-based approach, appraisers generally recognize two methods:

1. **The asset accumulation method or net asset value method.** In this method each tangible and intangible asset is adjusted to current values, and the liabilities are subtracted.

2. **The excess earnings method.** In this method all tangible assets are adjusted to current values. The tangible asset value is then multiplied by a reasonable rate of return on tangible assets. If the company's total return is greater than this, the difference is called excess earnings. The excess earnings are capitalized at a rate that reflects the riskiness of those earnings, and the result of this calculation represents the collective value of all intangible assets. The total of the values of the tangible and intangible assets (the latter estimated by capitalization of excess earnings) equals the value of the company.

Both methods produce a control value. Therefore, if valuing a controlling interest by either of the conventional asset-based methods, it usually is not appropriate to add a control premium. If valuing something less than a controlling interest by either of the conventional asset-based methods, it usually is appropriate to apply a discount for lack of control.

DO PUBLICLY TRADED MINORITY STOCK PRICES REFLECT CONTROL VALUE?

The debate over whether publicly traded minority interests represent control or minority values has continued for over 10 years, as has the controversy over the validity of the traditional levels-of-value chart and alternative schematic diagrams to explain minority/control relationships in the market.

In 1990 Eric Nath propounded the hypothesis that most public companies, at least during strong public market conditions, tend to trade at or near their takeover or controlling interest values. If this is true, then valuation based on an analysis of public companies should yield value that is tantamount to a controlling interest value, not a minority interest value. In that case, valuation of a private minority interest using publicly traded stock multiples will require discounts for *both* lack of control and lack of marketability.

Nath noted that takeovers typically represent only 3 to 4% of public equities, implying that most stocks are fully priced. Otherwise, "as blood attracts sharks, a significant difference between the current price of a stock and its value to a controlling owner should trigger some form of takeover attack."[8]

He also pointed out that:

- Many takeovers are strategically motivated, calling into question the applicability of the so-called "control premium" data.
- Control premium statistics can be misleading and unreliable because they exclude negative premiums and because there is such a wide dispersion of premiums.
- There are also premiums paid for minority interests, which lack control.

Nath concluded that the existence of liquidity would tend to eliminate worries about lack of control for public shareholders, thereby allowing value to equilibrate at essentially a control level of value for a given company as long as the company was well-managed and management was communicating effectively with investors.

It was upon this conclusion that Nath also proposed the idea that discount rates developed from public market data should also reflect controlling interest discount rates, in essence implying that as long as there is liquidity, public investors should feel comfortable bidding the price of a company up to the point where their required return is the same as that of a control owner. As mentioned above, Roger Ibbotson agrees with this premise.

In a rejoinder to the Nath hypothesis, Mike Bolotsky recognizes that "[c]ertain public companies are priced at a level roughly equal to what a buyer of the entire company would be willing to offer." Bolotsky points out that this does not change their status as minority interests, which lack prerogatives of control. Therefore, it still is not appropriate to deduct a minority interest discount from publicly traded minority interest values.[9]

Bolotsky also suggests another category of variables that conceptually could be added to the traditional or "prevailing wisdom" levels-of-value chart: information access and information reliability. He notes that limited information access and reliability is "a situation that minority investors in closely held firms face every day, in addition to the lack of liquidity of their shares." Recognizing that there is no empirical basis for measuring the impact of limited information access and reliability, he suggests that, at a minimum, the term "discount for lack of marketability" should be broadened to reflect differences in information access and reliability between public and private firms.

Bolotsky concludes his rejection of the procedure of deducting a minority interest discount from publicly traded stock values with the following elaboration:

a. The price at which a particular publicly traded stock trades represents the consensus price at which *minority blocks* of stock trade. This is true whether that price also *happens to be* the price that a buyer of a 100% control interest would be willing to offer, or whether the minority market price is *below* the offer price for control, or whether it is *above* the offer price for control. Regardless, the market price still represents evidence of the value of the shares to *minority interest* investors.

b. If the public minority price also *happens to be* the price that a typical buyer of a 100% controlling interest would be willing to offer, this obviously means that, in this case, the actively traded minority interest value and the 100% control interest have the same value. However, this does not alter the fact that the public price is based on evidence from minority interest transactions and is therefore a minority interest price that *happens to be* the same as a control price.

c. Yet, the public minority block and the 100% control block clearly have different shareholder-level attributes, whether those differences are stated solely as control attribute differences in the terminology of Prevailing Wisdom or as the net of four different attributes in the framework we introduced earlier. Either way, given that the shareholder-level attributes differ (and we are sure no one would argue that they don't differ), the only way the value of the two interests can be the same is if the value of the differences in shareholder-level attributes is zero. In other words, the premium *must* be zero if the price at which minority blocks trade is equal to the price at which an offer to purchase control would be made, regardless of whether that premium is attributable to control only or is the net of four separate attributes.

d. If a group of public guideline companies having a zero premium is truly comparable to a particular subject company, then the subject company should have similar attributes. That is, it too should have an as-if-freely-traded value that is equal to the price that a typical buyer would be willing to offer for the entire business. If this were not the case, then there must be significant company-level differences between the guideline companies and the subject, differences sufficient to justify a zero premium in one case and a positive premium in the other. If significant company-level differences of this magnitude existed, then the guideline companies would not be similar enough to be usable. Therefore, by definition, if the public guideline company approach is validly used, and if the premium in the public companies is roughly zero, it must also be roughly zero in the subject company.

e.   Therefore, in determining a private company minority interest value in the above scenario, the valuator has only two reasonable choices:

   i.   Begin with the public *minority* price, that is, the as-if-freely-traded value, and adjust for the differences in key attributes between a public *minority* value and a private *minority* value (i.e., differences in liquidity only in the framework of Prevailing Wisdom or differences in liquidity and information in the framework we introduced earlier), or

   ii.   Begin with the control price, which happens to be the same as the public minority price, subtract the value of the appropriate premium between the two prices, which by definition is zero, to derive the as-if-freely-traded value, and then proceed as in "i" above.[10]

The debate continued at the Advanced Business Valuation Conference in Scottsdale in 1991, with Nath pointing out in his speech ("Reconsidering Market Data on Control Premiums") that his original article had already dealt with these potential objections. Bolotsky's theory that a control premium of zero for a public company necessarily implies a control premium of zero in a private company ignores the fact that liquidity eliminates concerns about lack of control for public shareholders. This is not the case for private minority shareholders. Furthermore, private minority shareholders have no more ability to force the controlling owner to take the company public than they do to force its sale in the merger and acquisition market. The meaning of "control" is therefore completely different in a private setting compared with a public setting. So, some additional discount for lack of control must be considered for a private minority interest if guideline public companies are trading at or near their control values.

The American Society of Appraisers' Summer 1995 meeting featured a panel comprised of Nath, Bolotsky, Wayne Jankowske, and Chris Mercer, titled "Is the Levels of Value Concept Still Viable?"

In direct response to the topic question, Mercer said: "[M]y answer is an unqualified 'Yes!' While it does not directly embrace every nuance of value (see particularly Bolotsky's article for an outline of other potential valuation considerations), the Levels of Value model more reasonably and accurately describes the economic and financial reality that I observe every day in our valuation business than any other model I have seen to date."

Michael Bolotsky stated:

More pertinent to this panel is the issue of whether the two attributes, ownership rights and degree of liquidity, as used in the model, adequately describe the behavior of investors under most or all market conditions and time periods. It is my belief, and I believe it can be proved, that the model, as currently constituted, will adequately describe the behavior of investors only under certain market conditions and during certain time periods. The failure of the model to be more universally applicable can be attributed to many factors, including the following:

1. Treating liquidity as if it is an "on" (public companies) or "off" (private companies) factor, rather than a *continuum* from "almost absolute liquidity" (e.g., listed public companies) to "fairly high liquidity" (e.g., OTC pink-sheet companies) to "some liquidity" (e.g., 100% interests in desirable private companies) to "very low liquidity" (e.g., minority interests in most private companies), with any number of intermediate levels of liquidity along the continuum.

2. Treating the ownership rights that lead to *degrees of control* (or, more correctly, degrees of "power") as if they were "on" (controlling interest) or "off" (minority interest) factors, rather than a *continuum* from "absolute power" (e.g., 100% ownership of a company with no debt covenants) to "significant power" (e.g., 51% ownership of a company incorporated in a supermajority-state) to "influence power" (e.g., a 49% ownership in a company where no one else owns more than 1%) to "total lack of power" (e.g., 1% ownership in a company where one person owns the other 99%), with any number of intermediate degrees of power along the continuum.

3. As a corollary of the above two items: Treating liquidity as if it is a line that begins at the "freely-traded value" and ends at the "closely-held minority value," implying that relative degrees of liquidity are irrelevant to buyers of control.

4. Treating empirical market evidence as if it is, by definition, theoretical evidence of the attribute in question, rather than nothing more than the "fallout" of measuring the actions of investors in different types of markets. For example, the unfortunately named "control premium" (better would be "acquisition premium") is not a measure of the value of control simply because people began calling it a control premium instead of an acquisition premium. Objectively, it is nothing more than a measurement of the difference between the price paid for shares in the public market and the price paid for shares in the tender-offer "market." If it measures anything, it measures the *net* of many relevant factors, including but not limited to the perceived benefits of having significant-to-absolute power versus having little-or-no power; and the perceived drawback of having only some liquidity versus having almost absolute liquidity.

Clearly, it would be preferable to have a model that can explain the value behavior of investors in varying market conditions, including the current market where liquid minority interest prices are often at or above the price that a buyer of 100% of the shares would be willing to offer. Such a model can be created by considering the vari-

Exhibit 2.3   Simple Two-Attribute Model

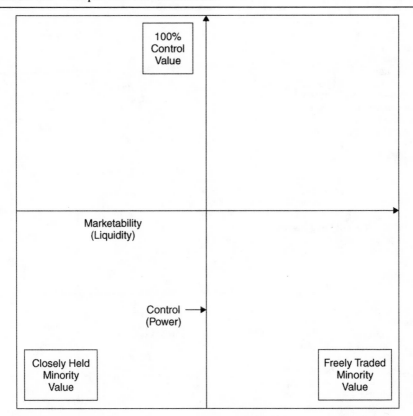

Closely Held Minority
- Very Low Liquidity
- Little or No Power

100% Control Value
- Low to Moderate Liquidity
- Nearly Total Power

Freely Traded Minority
- Very High Liquidity
- Little or No Power

Difference between:

Closely Held Minority and 100% Control
- Very Low vs. Low to Moderate Liquidity
- Little or No Power vs. Nearly Total Power

Freely Traded Minority and 100% Control
- Very High vs. Low to Moderate Liquidity
- Little or No Power vs. Nearly Total Power

Closely Held and Freely Traded Minority
- Very Low vs. Very High Liquidity
- No Differences in Power

Source: Michael J.Bolotsky.

ous ownership attributes as multi-dimensional factors rather than as a one-dimensional line. (See Exhibit 2.3).

At the same time, it is critical to stress the concept that acquisition premiums are the result of the *net* of a *positive* factor (control, or power, in comparison to a freely traded minority) and a *negative* factor (the difference between low-to-moderate liquidity and

Exhibit 2.4 Tradeoff Between Liquidity and Control

1. *This is a representation of typical conditions in the 1970s and early 1980s.*

2. The fact that the perceived benefits of added power outweighed the perceived drawback of lower liquidity caused 100% interests to be perceived as more desirable and hence worthy of a premium.

3. Of course, there were some companies for which the 100% value perception was less than or equal to the freely traded value, but the graph on this page is probably representative of the norm.

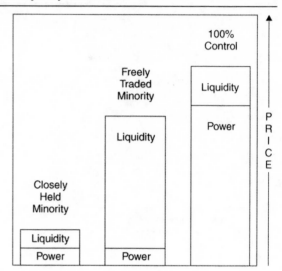

4. *This is a representation of typical conditions more recently.*

5. The fact that the perceived benefits of added power do *not* outweigh the perceived drawback of lower liquidity causes 100% interests to be perceived as equal or even less desirable.

6. Of course, there are still many companies for which the 100% value perception is greater than the freely traded value, but the graph on this page is probably representative of the norm.

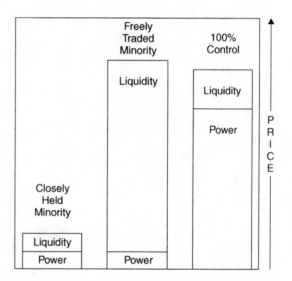

Source: Michael J. Bolotsky.

very high liquidity). It is this issue, not captured in the levels-of-value model, that bridges the gap between the points of view espoused by Nath and by Mercer. It is also the reason why I stated that the term "control premium" was an unfortunate, and misleading, choice of words. (The relative emphasis on these factors changes from time to time and from company to company.) (See Exhibit 2.4.)

In 1995, Mary McCarter and Carla Glass made a presentation to the Advanced Business Valuation Conference of the ASA in Boston. The essence of their presentation was an attempt to reconcile the implied required rate of return for a control owner paying a premium for a public company versus the required rate of return for the public shareholder. Their observation that it makes no sense for a control buyer to accept a lower rate of return than the public shareholder led them to formulate the idea that premiums paid for control must then relate primarily to the ability of the new owner to improve cash flows and earnings.

About the same time, Nath wrote two additional articles: "A Tale of Two Markets," *Business Valuation Review* (September 1994) and "How Public Guideline Companies Represent Control Value for a Private Company," *Business Valuation Review* (December 1997). Together, these two articles formed the basis for the two levels-of-value charts shown in Exhibit 1.3.

At this point, there is still debate over the meaning of public market data and its appropriate location in the levels of value. Nath's alternative levels-of-value chart has some appeal, especially under market conditions such as we have seen in the last few years where public market values have vastly exceeded what any rational buyer ought to pay. On the other hand, if we return to the market conditions of the early- and mid-1980s when financial buyers were taking over public companies at significant premiums and breaking them up to create additional value, the traditional levels-of-value chart would certainly apply.

In my opinion, a strong case could be made that when the share price of a public company is wildly out of line with its intrinsic value (to a financial buyer, and even possibly to a normal strategic buyer), then perhaps the public market value is meaningless and should be disregarded entirely. On the other side of that coin, Nath does not say that the traditional levels-of-value chart never works, so if there arises a situation in which public shares are trading significantly below the mergers and acquisitions market for companies in a given industry, then a single discount for lack of marketability might be appropriate when using the guideline public company method.

In 2001, Mark Lee, a well-known business valuation analyst for over 25 years, went public with his views on the issue. Lee observed as follows:

> The stock market is a market for minority interests in common stock. The principal buyers and sellers are individuals, mutual funds, and financial institutions. The market is highly liquid, individual investment horizons may be short, and risk tolerances can be greater than in illiquid markets. Financing is often readily available from banks and brokers at short-term money rates. Investors are generally passive. Individual investments are usually purchased as part of diversified portfolios, which leads to greater tolerance for risk.
>
> The [mergers and acquisitions] market is a market for whole companies. The principal buyers . . . and sellers are controlling stockholders, corporations, and [leveraged buyout] houses. The market is illiquid; as a result, individual investment horizons tend to be longer. Risk tolerances in the short term tend to be lower than in a liquid market. Transactions are financed using long-term debt from banks, insurance

companies, mezzanine funds, equity of large corporations, and private equity funds. [Mergers and acquisitions] investors take an active role in managing their companies.

The relationship of the two markets is not linear as shown in the single bar [of the levels of value chart]. This linearity presupposes that acquisition premiums apply in all situations; and acquisition premiums are roughly the same amount generally or in each industry.

The relationship of the two markets is better shown as the two overlapping forms as shown in Exhibit 2.5.

Clearly, the existence of an acquisition premium and its magnitude is a "facts and circumstances" test for each individual valuation.

In any case, it is obvious that, given the current state of the debate, one must be extremely cautious about applying a control premium to public market values to determine a control level of value. Conversely, if guideline stocks are trading at or near control value in a given case, valuation of a minority interest by applying a discount for lack of control from the guideline indicators (in addition to a lack-of-marketability discount) might be supported since the minority owner lacks the control prerogative of taking the company public or registering his or her stock in an offering.

Exhibit 2.6 lists the main articles and conference presentations on the foregoing debate.

HOW THE PURPOSE OF THE VALUATION AFFECTS MINORITY DISCOUNTS OR CONTROL PREMIUMS

The treatment of the minority/control issue may vary considerably from one valuation purpose to another, depending on authority in the relevant legal context.

Gift, Estate, and Income Tax

As noted in Chapter 1, all federal tax cases adhere to the standard of *fair market value,* which focuses on the actual characteristics of the specific property being valued. Therefore, if a minority interest is being valued using a methodology that produces a control value, a minority discount usually will be applied. If a control interest is being valued using a methodology that produces a minority value, a control premium may be applied.

Dissenting Stockholder and Shareholder Dissolution Actions

As also noted in Chapter 1, the standard of value for most states' dissenting stockholder and shareholder dissolution statutes is *fair value.* Court treatment of the minority/control issue varies greatly from one state to another, and might not even be the same for dissent versus dissolution actions within the same state.

Exhibit 2.5 Schematic Relationship of Stock Market and M&A Market

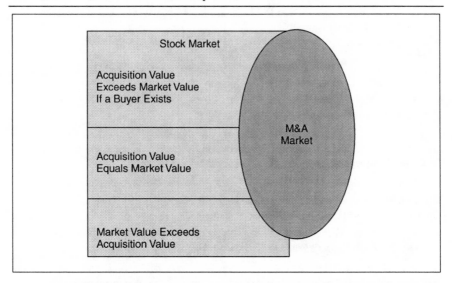

1. The oval in the chart above is the M&A market. The box is the stock market. (The sizes of the two are not proportionate.)

2. If a potential acquirer believes that it can create sufficient added economic benefits, the acquisition value of the company will exceed its market value. The additional economic benefit can pay for the cost of the acquisition premium. These are the transactions reported in the *Control Premium Study* and similar publications.

3. Most publicly traded companies are not taken over in a given year. Generally, there is no market available that can create benefits large enough to justify payment of the premium required for the acquisition of these companies in view of other alternatives.

   If there is no M&A market available to sell a company at a premium to its stock market value, then there is little or no acquisition premium, much less a "theoretical" premium based on an average of acquisitions of dissimilar companies.

4. In emerging industries, such as the Internet in 1998 and 1999, the value of the common stock of a corporation as a whole often is worth less than the aggregate market value of common stock trading as minority interests. While the new industry is viewed as very attractive for investment, individual corporations are perceived as too risky. As a result, individual and institutional investors will pay more for minority interests as part of a diversified industry portfolio than individual acquirers will pay for the entire company.

5. Similarly, many companies spin off units or sell them in an IPO rather than sell the units in the M&A market because a higher price can be obtained in the market than in an M&A transaction.

Source: Mark Lee of Sutter Securities, Incorporated, "Control Premiums and Minority Discounts: the Need for Specific Economic Analysis," *Shannon Pratt's Business Valuation Update* (August 2001):1.

Exhibit 2.6   Articles and Conference Presentations Dealing with the Debate Over
the Question "Do Publicly Traded Minority Stock Prices Reflect
Control Value?"

Articles

Simpson, David W., "Minority Interest and Marketability Discounts: A Perspective, Part I,"
Business Valuation Review, March 1991.

Nath, Eric W., "Control Premiums and Minority Interest Discounts in Private Companies,"
Business Valuation Review, June 1990.

Bolotsky, Michael J., "Adjustment for Differences in Ownership Rights, Liquidity,
Information Access, and Information Reliability: An Assessment of the Prevailing Wisdom
Versus the Nath Hypothesis," *Business Valuation Review,* September 1991.

Nath, Eric W., "A Tale of Two Markets," *Business Valuation Review,* September 1994.

Nath, Eric W., "How Guideline Public Companies Represent Control Value for a Private
Company," *Business Valuation Review,* December 1997.

Lee, M. Mark, "Control Premiums and Minority Discounts: the Need for Specific Economic
Analysis," *Shannon Pratt's Business Valuation Update*™ (August 2001).

Conference Presentations

The full texts of the following conference presentations are available to subscribers on
BVLibrary.com. All conference presentations listed were at the American Society of
Appraisers.

November 1991

Nath, Eric W., "Reconsidering Data on Control Premiums."

June 1995

Nath, Eric W., Z. Christopher Mercer, Michael J. Bolotsky, and Wayne C. Jankowske, "Is the
'Levels of Value' Concept Still Valid?"

November 1995

McCarter, Mary B., "Foundations for Minority and Control Adjustments."

Glass, Carla G., "Foundations for Minority and Control Adjustments, Part 2."

October 2001

Pratt, Shannon P. (moderator), M. Mark Lee, Eric W. Nath, Mary B. McCarter, and Michael
J. Bolotsky, "Levels of Value Revisited."

As will be seen in the dissent and dissolution cases discussed in Chapter 4 on
minority/control issues in the courts, the decisions range all the way from blanket
acceptance of minority discounts to blanket application of control premiums, and
many shades in between. Even when it is clear that a control or a minority value is
appropriate, there have been arguments about appropriate adjustments from both discounted cash flow and guideline public company methodologies.

Marital Dissolutions

There is no standard of value and no statutory or regulatory guidance on the issue of minority or control levels of stock or partnership values for property settlements in marital dissolution proceedings. In general, many courts have tended to avoid applying minority discounts. In a few cases, the courts have reasoned that the minority owner actually has a share of control through family or other operating owners, although this logic generally leads to bad economic decisions and should not form the basis for any valuation adjustment. Virtually no state courts have issued blanket, sweeping precedents on the issue, thus leaving it to be decided on a case-by-case basis.

Pricing for a Synergistic Buyer

If a synergistic buyer can be found, then the seller may be able to obtain some or even all of the synergistic value. In this case, one might apply full "acquisition premiums" as shown at the top of the levels-of-value chart shown as Exhibit 1.2. Data for such acquisition premiums paid historically can be found in the *Control Premium Study,* as described in Chapter 3.

SUMMARY

Virtually no one questions the reality that a minority position in a company lacks valuable prerogatives of control and potential economic benefits that a control owner enjoys. However, the differential in share value between minority and control shares to reflect the presence or absence of these prerogatives and attendant benefits is difficult to measure. Moreover, the differential varies considerably from one set of company-specific and shareholder-specific facts and circumstances to another.

The applicability of a minority discount or control premium depends on the methodology used to arrive at a base value. Both the income approach and the market approach can produce values that may be either minority or control and the analyst must decide which level-of-value model best fits the specific case at hand in order to determine which discounts or premiums should be applied. Exhibit 2.7 summarizes the relationship between methodology used and type of value resulting.

The applicability of discounts and/or premiums often is driven by the legal context. *Fair market value* requires valuing the property in question as it is. Under the standard of *fair value* in dissenting stockholder or shareholder dissolution statutes in some states, however, precedential case law requires valuing minority interests *as if* they were worth a proportionate share of the enterprise value with no lack of control discount, but with no synergistic premium. The minority/control issue for marital dissolution property settlements usually is decided on a case-by-case basis.

Exhibit 2.7 Summary of How the Valuation Methodology Affects the Resulting Value

Approach/Method	Assumptions	Resulting Value
Income Approach	Control cash flows	Control[a]
	Minority cash flows	Minority, marketable
Guideline merged & acquired company method	Control transacted	Control[a]
Guideline publicly traded company method[b]	Trading at or above control value	Control
	Trading below control value	Minority, marketable
Asset accumulation method	Control over assets	Control
Excess earnings method	Control over assets	Control

[a] If synergies involved, could be acquisition value.
[b] As discussed in Chapter 2, this can cover a wide spectrum.

Notes

1. Concept presented by Wayne Jankowske at the 1995 American Society of Appraisers International Conference and at the 1996 Institute of Business Appraisers National Conference.
2. David W. Simpson, "Minority Interest and Marketability Discounts: A Perspective, Part I," *Business Valuation Review* (March 1991): 7.
3. For a formula for computing how many shares are required to elect one or more directors under cumulative voting, see Shannon P. Pratt, Robert F. Reilly, and Robert P. Schweihs, *Valuing a Business,* 4th ed. (New York: McGraw-Hill, 2000), p. 385.
4. Shannon P. Pratt, "Minority Versus Control Implications of Cost of Capital Data," Chapter 15 in *Cost of Capital—Estimation and Applications* (New York: John Wiley & Sons, 1998), pp. 131–136.
5. *Ibbotson Associates Cost of Capital Workshop* (Chicago: Ibbotson Associates, 1998): 12.
6. Pratt, *Cost of Capital,* p. 133.
7. Eric W. Nath, "Control Premiums and Minority Interest Discounts in Private Companies," *Business Valuation Review* (June 1990): 39–46.
8. Ibid.
9. Michael J. Bolotsky, "Adjustments for Differences In Ownership Rights, Liquidity, Information Access, and Information Reliability: An Assessment of 'Prevailing Wisdom' Versus the Nath Hypothesis," *Business Valuation Review* (September 1991): 94–109.
10. Ibid., pp. 106–7.

Chapter 3

Empirical Data Regarding Minority Discounts and Control Premiums

All of the empirical data that we have for guidance in quantifying minority discounts and control premiums come from the public markets for stocks or partnership interests. I know of no studies yet which compare private company minority interest transaction prices with the same company's controlling interest value as measured by a sale of the entire business within a short time.

The empirical data available fall broadly into two categories:

1. Premiums paid for acquisitions of companies compared with public market minority trading prices prior to the acquisition announcement
2. Where net asset value is known or reasonably estimated, the percentage discount observed in minority interest transactions compared with the underlying net asset value

PREMIUMS PAID IN ACQUISITIONS

Prices at which controlling interests in public companies have been sold relative to their previously unaffected trading prices are published in the quarterly

Control Premium Study. This series has been the definitive source for such data for well over a decade.

The introduction to the *Control Premium Study* explains:

> A control premium is defined as the additional consideration that an investor would pay over a marketable minority equity value (i.e., current, publicly traded stock prices) in order to own a controlling interest in the common stock of a company. In this study, the premium is expressed as a percentage of the unaffected marketable minority price per share or the "Mergerstat™ Unaffected Price." This is the price just prior to the point of change in the representative normal pricing of a given security. [*The Control Premium Study*] examines transactions whereby 50.1 percent or more of a company was acquired. A controlling interest is considered to have greater value than a minority interest because of the purchaser's ability to effect changes in the overall business structure and to influence business policies. Control premiums can vary greatly. Factors affecting the magnitude of a given control premium include:
>
> • The nature and magnitude of nonoperating assets
> • The nature and magnitude of discretionary expenses
> • The perceived quality of existing management
> • The nature and magnitude of business opportunities which are not currently being exploited
> • The ability to integrate the acquiree into the acquirer's business or distribution channels
>
> In order to obtain unbiased and accurate pricing information, the scope of this study has been narrowed to completed transactions where the target company was publicly traded.[1]

Exhibit 3.1 presents the definitions of the terms used in the *Control Premium Study*.

Exhibit 3.2 shows announcement and closing dates and equity value of a small group of transactions which is reasonably representative of the wide range of deal size in the database.

Exhibit 3.3 gives the purchase price in dollars per share and the "unaffected" share price and prices one day, one week, one month, and two months prior to the announcement date.

Exhibit 3.4 shows the "control premium" relative to each of the five previous dates for which prices were compiled. The industry and overall average premiums compiled by *Control Premium Study* are based on the "unaffected price."

Note that the "negative premiums" (buyouts at *less than* the Mergerstat unaffected price) are shown with asterisks. They are not included in the *Control Premium Study* industry medians or averages, but the data is there so that the analyst can recompute averages or medians of any group to reflect the "negative premiums" if so desired.

Each quarter's compilation of the control premiums by industry includes data for the trailing 12 months, as shown in Exhibit 3.5. Although "negative premiums" are excluded from the medians and means, the analyst can easily recompute these figures to reflect the "negative premiums." Also, using the online version, the analyst is not

Exhibit 3.1   Definitions of Terms

Consideration Codes	C = Cash D = Debt L = Liabilities S = Stock X = Other (warrants, contingent payments, etc.)
Control Premium	Mergerstat's control premium is computed by comparing the per-share total consideration price for one share of the target company's common stock to the Mergerstat unaffected price. This pre-announcement price is selected by Mergerstat and based on volume and price fluctuations during the period prior to the acquisition announcement.

Guidelines for control premium calculation:
- Determination of announcement data
- Price and volume retrieval prior to announcement date
- Analysis of data for significant fluctuations in price and volume
- Selection of a price just prior to this point of change in representative normal pricing activity
- If no significant price and volume fluctuations occur, selection of the price one day prior to the announcement date
- Determination of the final price that the acquirer offers, per share, to purchase the target company's common stock, per terms of a tender offer
- Computation of the control premium using the following equation:

$$\frac{\text{Purchase Price} - \text{Mergerstat Unaffected Price}}{\text{Mergerstat Unaffected Price}}$$

Mergerstat Unaffected Price	Target company's common stock price per share unaffected by the acquisition announcement. Selected by Mergerstat after analyzing each transaction.
Percentage Common Held After	Percent of the target company's common shares held by the acquiring company following the transaction.
Percentage Common Previously Held	Percent of the target company's common shares owned by the acquiring company prior to the transaction.
Premium 1 Day	Premium computed by comparing the price ultimately paid to the common stock price one day prior to the announcement date.
Premium 1 Week	Premium computed by comparing the price ultimately paid to the common stock price one week prior to the announcement date.

continued

Exhibit 3.1 Definitions of Terms—*continued*

Premium 1 Month	Premium computed by comparing the price ultimately paid to the common stock price one month prior to the announcement date.
Premium 2 Months	Premium computed by comparing the price ultimately paid to the common stock price two months prior to the announcement date.
Price 1 Day	Target company's common stock price per share one day prior to the acquisition announcement date.
Price 1 Week	Target company's common stock price per share one week prior to the acquisition announcement date.
Price 1 Month	Target company's common stock price per share one month prior to the acquisition announcement date.
Price 2 Months	Target company's common stock price per share two months prior to the acquisition announcement date.
Purchase Price Per Share	The total consideration paid per share for the target company's shares.
Target Book Value	Target company's book value, sometimes referred to as shareholder's equity or net tangible assets, is based on the latest reported period prior to the transaction's closing date. Book value is reported in millions and rounded.
Target EBIT	Target company's earnings before interest and taxes (EBIT) based on the latest reported 12-month period prior to the transaction's announcement date. EBIT is reported in millions of dollars and rounded.
Target EBITDA	Target company's earnings before interest, taxes, depreciation, and amortization (EBITDA) based on the latest reported 12-month period prior to the transaction's announcement date. EBITDA is reported in millions of dollars and rounded.
Target Income	Target company's net income (loss), excluding extraordinary items, based on the latest reported 12-month period prior to the transaction's announcement date. Income is reported in millions of dollars and rounded.
Target Market Value of Equity	Target market value of equity based on the purchase price per share times total shares outstanding reported in the period prior to the transaction's announcement date. Market value of equity is reported in millions of dollars and rounded.
Target Price/Book Value Ratio	Purchase price-to-book value ratio for the target company based on the implied market value of equity divided by book value of the target company.

Exhibit 3.1   Definitions of Terms—*continued*

Target Price/Income Ratio	Purchase price-to-net income ratio for the target company based on the implied market value of equity divided by the latest reported 12-month net income prior to the announcement date.
Target Price/Sales Ratio	Purchase price-to-sales ratio for the target company based on the implied market value equity divided by the latest reported 12-month sales prior to the announcement date.
Target Sales	Target company's sales based on the latest reported 12-month period prior to the transaction's announcement date. Sales are reported in millions of dollars and rounded.
Target TIC	Target company's implied total invested capital (TIC) based on the sum of implied market value of equity plus the face value of total interest-bearing debt and the book value of preferred stock outstanding prior to the announcement date.
Target TIC/EBIT Ratio	Target TIC-to-EBIT ratio based on the target TIC divided by the latest reported 12-month earnings before interest and taxes prior to the announcement date.
Target TIC/EBITDA Ratio	Target TIC-to-EBITDA ratio based on the target TIC divided by the latest reported 12-month earnings before interest, taxes, depreciation, and amortization prior to the announcement date.
Total Deal Value	The aggregate purchase price given to shareholders of the target company's common stock by the acquiring company. Shown in millions of dollars and rounded.

Source: Mergerstat/Shannon Pratt's Control Premium Study, 4th Quarter, 2000. Applied Financial Information, LP.

locked in to the 12 trailing months but can compile transactions and averages for any desired time period.

The online study classifies every transaction since 1998 as one of the following:

- Horizontal integration
- Vertical integration
- Conglomerate
- Financial

These classifications enable users to select any subset of type of transaction for summary and/or further analysis. By this means, for example, transactions where premiums are thought to be primarily synergistic can be eliminated.

In mining the data to develop a list of transactions most specifically relevant to the subject being valued, the analyst has the option of selecting any range of SIC

Exhibit 3.2 Announce and Closing Dates, Total Deal Value

Target Name	Announce Date	Closing Date	Target Market Value of Equity ($Mil)	Currency Exchange Rate	Pctg. of Common Previously Held by Acq.	Pctg. of Common Held by Acq. After Trans.
4Front Technologies Inc	08/03/00	10/16/00	231.4	1.00	0.0	100.0
Able Telcom Holding Corp	08/24/00	12/26/00	55.7	1.00	0.0	100.0
Acme Electric Corp	05/30/00	11/22/00	45.7	1.00	0.0	100.0
Acuson Corp	09/27/00	11/10/00	638.3	1.00	0.0	100.0
ADAC Laboratories Inc	11/13/00	12/18/00	402.0	1.00	0.0	100.0
Agritope Inc	09/07/00	12/08/00	30.4	1.00	0.0	100.0
Alteon WebSystems Inc	07/28/00	10/05/00	5,042.1	1.00	0.0	100.0
Anesta Corp	07/17/00	10/10/00	296.1	1.00	0.0	100.0
Aquila Biopharmaceuticals Inc	08/21/00	11/17/00	33.8	1.00	0.0	100.0
Associates First Capital Corp	09/06/00	11/30/00	26,415.5	1.00	0.0	100.0
AXENT Technologies Inc	07/27/00	12/18/00	528.8	1.00	0.0	100.0
Bank of Petaluma	03/21/00	10/16/00	56.6	1.00	0.0	100.0
BankFirst Corp	08/23/00	12/28/00	192.8	1.00	0.0	100.0
Barnett Inc	07/10/00	10/02/00	213.9	1.00	0.0	100.0
BeautiControl Cosmetics Inc	09/13/00	10/18/00	50.6	1.00	0.0	100.0
Bestfoods	05/02/00	10/05/00	20,211.5	1.00	0.0	100.0
BFX Hospitality Group Inc	08/11/00	12/22/00	7.3	1.00	26.0	100.0

Source: Mergerstat/Shannon Pratt's Control Premium Study, 4th Quarter, 2000. Applied Financial Information, LP.

Exhibit 3.3 Purchase Price/Share—Mergerstat Unaffected Price

Target Name	Purchase Price Per Share	Mergerstat Unaffected Price	Price 1 Day	Price 1 Week	Price 1 Month	Price 2 Months
4Front Technologies Inc	18.50	13.75	13.75	14.38	12.25	16.38
Able Telcom Holding Corp	3.40	3.38	3.38	2.50	2.88	2.06
Acme Electric Corp	9.00	6.13	7.44	7.44	7.38	6.00
Acuson Corp	23.00	15.69	15.69	14.69	15.00	12.81
ADAC Laboratories Inc	18.50	18.13	18.13	14.63	11.38	21.75
Agritope Inc	6.26	7.13	7.13	5.44	5.50	7.97
Alteon WebSystems Inc	116.53	89.25	143.00	143.75	95.38	45.19
Anesta Corp	22.01	22.13	22.13	23.88	18.00	14.88
Aquila Biopharmaceuticals Inc	3.91	4.38	4.38	5.13	4.97	2.44
Associates First Capital Corp	36.26	28.00	28.00	26.94	28.00	22.69
AXENT Technologies Inc	18.13	19.06	19.06	22.50	23.75	16.13
Bank of Petaluma	39.19	23.38	23.38	24.75	25.81	22.88
BankFirst Corp	17.42	11.13	11.13	9.88	9.44	8.13
Barnett Inc	13.15	8.50	10.50	9.72	9.75	10.69
BeautiControl Cosmetics Inc	7.00	3.75	3.25	3.25	3.19	4.00
Bestfoods	73.00	48.94	51.31	53.81	46.81	39.75
BFX Hospitality Group Inc	2.25	1.00	1.00	0.94	0.88	0.94

Source: Mergerstat/Shannon Pratt's Control Premium Study, 4th Quarter, 2000. Applied Financial Information, LP.

Exhibit 3.4 Mergerstat Control Premium

Target Name	Mergerstat Control Premium	Premium 1 Day	Premium 1 Week	Premium 1 Month	Premium 2 Months
4Front Technologies Inc	34.5%	34.5%	28.7%	51.0%	13.0%
Able Telcom Holding Corp	0.8%	0.8%	36.1%	18.3%	64.9%
Acme Electric Corp	46.9%	21.0%	21.0%	22.0%	50.0%
Acuson Corp	46.6%	46.6%	56.6%	53.3%	79.5%
ADAC Laboratories Inc	2.1%	2.1%	26.5%	62.6%	−14.9%
Agritope Inc	−12.1%*	−12.1%	15.1%	13.8%	−21.4%
Alteon WebSystems Inc	30.6%	−18.5%	−18.9%	22.2%	157.9%
Anesta Corp	−0.5%*	−0.5%	−7.8%	22.3%	48.0%
Aquila Biopharmaceuticals Inc	−10.6%*	−10.6%	−23.7%	−21.3%	60.4%
Associates First Capital Corp	29.5%	29.5%	34.6%	29.5%	59.8%
AXENT Technologies Inc	−4.9%*	−4.9%	−19.4%	−23.7%	12.4%
Bank of Petaluma	67.7%	67.7%	58.3%	51.8%	71.3%
BankFirst Corp	56.6%	56.6%	76.4%	84.6%	114.4%
Barnett Inc	54.7%	25.2%	35.3%	34.9%	23.0%
BeautiControl Cosmetics Inc	86.7%	115.4%	115.4%	119.6%	75.0%
Bestfoods	49.2%	42.3%	35.7%	55.9%	83.6%
BFX Hospitality Group Inc	125.0%	125.0%	140.0%	157.1%	140.0%

Source: Mergerstat/Shannon Pratt's Control Premium Study, 4th Quarter, 2000. Applied Financial Information, LP.

Exhibit 3.5   Control Premiums by Industry—Trailing 12 Months

SIC Code	Target Category	Closing Date	Target Name	Mergerstat Control Premium
01-09	**Agriculture and Forestry**			
	0742	09/20/00	Veterinary Centers of America Inc	12.1%
10-14	**Mining**			
	Range = 3.5% to 191.1%		*Median = 30.3%*	*Average = 49.0%*
	10 **Metal Mining**			
	Range = 3.5% to 143.9%		*Median = 38.8%*	*Average = 43.2%*
	1041	01/12/00	Acacia Resources Ltd	42.5%
	1041	06/27/00	Australia Gold Resources Ltd	−73.8%*
	1041	05/26/00	Dome Resources NL	3.5%
	1041	06/01/00	Gilt Edged Mining NL	143.9%
	1041	06/22/00	Mindex ASA	10.5%
	1041	08/07/00	Pangea Goldfields Inc	34.6%
	1041	07/31/00	Philippine Gold PLC	56.6%
	1041	07/10/00	Randfontein Estates Ltd	38.8%
	1041	02/24/00	Reef Mining NL	7.7%
	1041	11/29/00	Rio Algom Ltd	50.4%
	1221	05/22/00	Lonmin PLC (Duiker Mining Ltd)	−16.3%*
	13 **Oil and Gas Extraction**			
	Range = 5.7% to 191.1%		*Median = 27.0%*	*Average = 49.1%*
	1311	04/18/00	Atlantic Richfield Co	19.2%
	1311	11/14/00	Beau Canada Exploration	24.3%
	1311	06/05/00	Bellator Exploration Inc	77.6%
	1311	11/14/00	Crestar Energy Inc	5.7%
	1311	08/24/00	Edge Energy Inc	−10.2%*
	1311	12/07/00	Forcenergy Inc	14.5%
	1311	01/04/00	Gaelic Resources	66.5%
	1311	12/12/00	Home-Stake Oil & Gas Co	109.5%
	1311	01/03/00	JET Energy Corp	−14.4%*
	1311	06/15/00	Newport Petroleum Corp	11.8%

Source: Mergerstat/Shannon Pratt's Control Premium Study, 4th Quarter, 2000. Applied Financial Information, LP.

codes, any time frame, any size criteria, and any transaction code or codes. For example, if conditions in the merger market for the industry have been in a steady state for 18 months prior to the valuation date and the analyst wants to eliminate synergies, the analyst might start with financial and conglomerate transactions for a given SIC range for a deal size under $300 million for six quarters prior to (and perhaps surrounding) the effective valuation date.

Descriptions of the businesses of both target and acquiring companies are provided, as shown in Exhibit 3.6. Thus, the analyst is not necessarily committed to the

Exhibit 3.6 Company Descriptions

Target Name	Target Business Description	Acquirer Business Description
4Front Technologies Inc	Provides systems development and integration	Designs, sells, and services information technology products
Able Telcom Holding Corp	Designs, maintains, and integrates communications networks	Provides electrical, mechanical, and other technical management services
Acme Electric Corp	Designs and manufactures power conversion equipment for electronic and electrical systems	Makes custom-engineered essential components
Acuson Corp	Manufactures and provides medical diagnostic ultrasound systems	Provides industrial and building systems
ADAC Laboratories Inc	Designs, develops, manufactures, sells, and services electronic medical imaging and information systems	Makes and distributes lighting products
Agritope Inc	Develops improved plant products and provides technology to the agricultural industry	Researches new targets and proteins for the pharmaceutical, diagnostic, and agricultural industries
Alteon WebSystems Inc	Provides Internet infrastructure solutions	Manufactures fully digital telecommunications switching and communications equipment
Anesta Corp	Develops new pharmaceutical products for oral transmucosal drug administration	Discovers, develops, and markets biopharmaceutical products to treat neurological disorders
Aquila Biopharm-aceuticals Inc	Develops and makes products for the diagnosis, prevention, and treatment of infectious diseases	Discovers and develops novel immunotherapeutic drugs
Associates First Capital Corp	Provides consumer finance, commercial leasing and finance, credit cards, insurance, and related services	National commercial bank
AXENT Technologies Inc	Provides information security solutions designed to manage security policies	Designs, publishes, and supports a diversified line of systems software
Bank of Petaluma	State commercial bank	National commercial bank

Company		
BankFirst Corp	State commercial bank	State commercial bank
Barnett Inc	Markets and distributes plumbing, electrical, and hardware products	Markets and distributes repair and maintenance products
BeautiControl Cosmetics Inc	Manufactures and sells skin care, nutritional supplements, cosmetics, nail care, toiletries, and beauty supplements	Manufactures and sells consumer products for the home including food storage and other containers
Bestfoods	Produces food products and condiments	Produces a variety of consumer products including food, household goods, and chemicals
BFX Hospitality Group Inc	Owns and operates Mexican- and Southwestern-themed restaurants	Private group formed by Robert McLean, Chairman and CEO of BFX, and members of management

Source: Mergerstat/Shannon Pratt's Control Premium Study, 4th Quarter, 2000. Applied Financial Information, LP.

transaction codes, but can make an independent judgment as to classification. Of course, since these companies were all public before the acquisition, one can always go to the SEC filings if more detail is desired.

While this chapter focuses primarily on the *Control Premium Study* for data on minority discounts and control premiums, the studies also contain five fundamental financial figures and the related market value multiples for each transaction:

- Equity multiples
  - ◆ Price/sales
  - ◆ Price/earnings (net income)
  - ◆ Price/book value
- Invested capital multiples
  - ◆ Total invested capital/Earnings Before Interest and Taxes (EBIT)
  - ◆ Total invested capital/Earnings Before Interest, Taxes, Depreciation, and Amortization (EBITDA)

Examples of these are shown in Exhibits 3.7 and 3.8, respectively.

IDENTIFYING INDUSTRIES WITH HIGHER OR LOWER CONTROL PREMIUMS

Often industry control premiums are consistently higher in certain industries, such as technology-based industries where quick reactions and nimbleness are required to achieve bountiful rewards. Exhibit 3.9 shows that trends and control premiums in "Computer Software, Supplies and Services" and "Electronics" are substantially higher than the all-industry average.

These higher-than-average premiums are often seen in specific industries that are rapidly changing, and offer substantially greater opportunities to buyers wishing to penetrate or expand position and momentum in growing markets. Typically, factors seen in such industries include:

- Short reaction time in which to make decisions in order to achieve sales
- Rapidly changing mix of customers and suppliers
- Short duration of "knowledge half-life" such as new discoveries, techniques, and methods constantly outdating "old" concepts
- Scarcities of key talent; rapidly growing salary levels for key personnel
- Murky competitive and regulatory environments
- Exaggerated profit potential due to economies of scale, such as software distribution
- Waves of consolidation among companies representing disparate intellectual property in order to create new markets and emerging consumers

Exhibit 3.7 Target Financials

($ in Millions)

Target Name	Target TIC	Target Sales	Target Income	Target Book Value	Target EBIT	Target EBITDA
4Front Technologies Inc	247.4	253.6	1.5	(0.6)	9.3	17.1
Able Telcom Holding Corp	60.4	458.1	(89.9)	(57.3)	(51.0)	(38.9)
Acme Electric Corp	54.9	79.0	3.1	23.9	5.8	8.0
Acuson Corp	722.7	468.5	(0.3)	224.0	10.5	34.3
ADAC Laboratories Inc	440.9	352.5	(0.2)	75.8	5.1	26.6
Agritope Inc	32.1	7.1	(4.7)	6.7	(4.6)	(3.2)
Alteon WebSystems Inc	5,044.8	66.0	(21.0)	251.4	(20.4)	(17.8)
Anesta Corp	298.1	7.6	(9.4)	70.4	(9.3)	(8.9)
Aquila Biopharmaceuticals Inc	107.3	4.2	(5.5)	10.9	(5.5)	(4.6)
Associates First Capital Corp	99,831.2	12,592.2	1,504.4	10,294.6	6,380.6	6,982.4
AXENT Technologies Inc	529.3	121.7	(0.8)	138.3	1.2	11.4
Bank of Petaluma	56.6	14.8	2.3	14.9	8.3	8.3
BankFirst Corp	195.2	72.9	9.1	86.2	41.5	47.4
Barnett Inc	247.8	278.8	15.9	103.8	28.6	34.3
BeautiControl Cosmetics Inc	57.0	64.2	(7.4)	10.5	(6.1)	(6.1)
Bestfoods	22,595.5	8,637.0	717.0	524.0	1,345.0	1,605.0
BFX Hospitality Group Inc	9.9	17.4	(1.1)	11.7	(1.5)	(0.2)

Source: Mergerstat/Shannon Pratt's Control Premium Study, 4th Quarter, 2000. Applied Financial Information, LP.

Exhibit 3.8 Target Multiples

Target Name	Target P/Sales	Target P/Income	Target P/Book Value	Target TIC/EBIT[1]	Target TIC/EBITDA
4Front Technologies Inc	0.9	155.3	−405.9	26.7	14.5
Able Telcom Holding Corp	0.1	−0.6	−1.0	−1.2	−1.6
Acme Electric Corp	0.6	15.0	1.9	9.4	6.9
Acuson Corp	1.4	−1,994.8	2.8	68.9	21.1
ADAC Laboratories Inc	1.1	−1,914.3	5.3	86.8	16.6
Agritope Inc	4.3	−6.5	4.6	−7.1	−9.9
Alteon WebSystems Inc	76.4	−240.0	20.1	−247.1	−283.1
Anesta Corp	38.8	−31.4	4.2	−32.2	−33.4
Aquila Biopharmaceuticals Inc	8.1	−6.2	3.1	−19.6	−23.1
Associates First Capital Corp	2.1	17.6	2.6	NMF	NMF
AXENT Technologies Inc	4.3	−629.5	3.8	448.6	46.4
Bank of Petaluma	3.8	24.5	3.8	NMF	NA
BankFirst Corp	2.6	21.2	2.2	NMF	NMF
Barnett Inc	0.8	13.4	2.1	8.7	7.2
BeautiControl Cosmetics Inc	0.8	−6.8	4.8	−9.3	NA
Bestfoods	2.3	28.2	38.6	16.8	14.1
BFX Hospitality Group Inc	0.6	−9.3	0.6	−6.6	−55.0

Source: Mergerstat/Shannon Pratt's Control Premium Study, 4th Quarter, 2000. Applied Financial Information, LP.

Exhibit 3.9 Industry Premiums (Percent Premium Offered)

Industry	1996	1997	1998	1999	2000
All Industries	36.6	36.7	35.9	46.1	48.9
Computer Software, etc. (SIC 7371-7379 inclusive)	39.1	37.1	40.3	60.4	57.8
Electronics (SIC 3612-3699 inclusive)	31.0	30.5	43.5	55.5	66.4

Source: Mergerstat Review 2001 (Los Angeles: Applied Financial Information, LP, 2001), as adjusted by Rob Schlegel to include the impact of negative premiums.

CAVEATS REGARDING USE OF CONTROL PREMIUM DATA

Large Dispersion to the Data

There is a tremendous dispersion to the control premiums exhibited by takeover transactions. Using individual industry averages will occasionally narrow the dispersion somewhat, but in most industries the range of premiums is still fairly wide. Furthermore, few industries have enough transactions in any period to reach a conclusion that the observed premiums are a reliable indication of the premium that could be expected in the next ensuing transaction. In any event, after a premium is paid for a company, similar companies' stock may experience a price increase as a reaction, reducing the premium on the next transaction in the industry.

If the *Control Premium Study* data is to be used, I believe that the medians are more reliable measures of central tendency than the means. This is because the means have an upward bias by being distorted by a few very high observations.

Negative Premiums

One would think that if the traditional levels-of-value chart is correct, very few companies would be acquired at a discount. Yet, in the third quarter of 1998, more than one-third of the transactions reported in the *Control Premium Study* were for a price below their pre-merger public market trading prices.[2]

Related to this is another statistical problem with the *Control Premium Study* in that both the means and the medians *exclude* "negative premiums." That is, if a company sold at a discount instead of a premium from its public market price, that discount is not counted in compiling the mean or median premiums. This may also be a significant source of upward bias. When transactions at discounts are included in the aggregate statistics, the mean and median premiums can drop significantly.

Another feature of the revised *Mergerstat/Shannon Pratt's Control Premium Study* is a table that includes the "negative premiums" in the means and medians, but at this point it is only for the overall means and medians. Also, the ability to "mine the data" electronically over at least a three-year period now enables the analyst to zero in on a specific group of the most relevant transactions rather than rely on broad averages.

Many Control Transactions Impound Synergies

A large proportion of the public company mergers and acquisitions in the 1990s were strategic in nature, involving economic benefits of synergies between buyers and sellers. Such synergistic transactions impounded elements of *investment value,* that is, *value to a particular buyer,* as opposed to pure *fair market value,* which is the value of a transaction between *hypothetical willing buyers and sellers.* In other words, the premiums paid in such transactions reflect more than just the prerogatives of control of a company on a stand-alone basis.

Referring back to the traditional levels-of-value chart in Exhibit 1.2, when value for such synergies is included in the premium paid, the total premium takes the price further upward beyond just control value to what might be referred to as *acquisition value.* Consequently, some analysts have suggested that such premiums be labeled *acquisition premiums* or *transactions premiums,* to recognize that they reflect additional values beyond just the value of the elements of control.

Some analysts have suggested that premiums paid by financial buyers are more representative of the pure value of control than premiums paid by strategic buyers. For example, in a 1997 presentation, Chris Mercer explained, "Conceptually, evidence relating to controlling interest transactions involving financial buyers is the best evidence regarding fair market value."[3]

Steve Garber pursued this thought with empirical research presented at the American Society of Appraisers mid-year conference in 1998. He separated out the "going private" transactions over the ten years 1988–1997 and compared the premiums paid compared to the premiums in all transactions. As expected, the average premiums paid in the going private transactions were several percentage points less than the average for all transactions.[4] He attributed this difference to the lack of premium for synergies.

Yet, even "going private" transactions may be based on strategic considerations. For example, an ostensibly financial purchase may be used as a base from which a roll-up or build-up may be commenced.

Most analysts concur that, with the possible exception of industries under consolidation where there are multiple buyers that constitute an effective and relatively predictable market, acquisition premiums observed for public companies generally tend to overstate the pure control premium that could be included in the fair market value of a controlling interest compared with a minority interest. Instead, such premiums usually reflect value to a particular buyer, and therefore reflect elements of investment value over and above fair market value.

Control Premiums Are Specific to a Select Group of Companies

Out of the tens of thousands of public companies only a very small percentage actually are acquired each year. In recent years the companies purchased have often been "best of breed," making them a very unique subset of the market. Statistically, it is unlikely that this small, select group is universally representative of the market as a whole.

The "Hubris Factor"

It is undeniable that some buyers overpay. This may be either because they are swept up in the heat of the action or, as in 1999/2000, they subscribed to the theory that no price could be too high for the hottest new technology because public shareholders would bail them out. When the investment bankers also buy into these ideas you have the necessary conditions for big mistakes to be made. Extremely high premiums in a particular industry, or premiums paid for companies that are already overpriced in the market, are a note of caution.

In fact, in some cases, especially in the 1980s and 1990s, the premium paid, in retrospect, exceeds the value of all of the synergies. Richard Roll observed this phenomenon in the mid-1980s and hypothesized that it was due to the hubris (an exaggerated sense of self confidence) on the part of the acquiring companies' CEOs.[5] Two Columbia University professors tested the hubris hypothesis in the early 1990s and found it valid.[6]

Steven Kaplan, a professor at the University of Chicago, conducted a study of 70 large acquisitions, and concluded that the overpayments continued in the first half of the 1990s. He found an average 13% increase in wealth, accounted for by an average 21% increase in wealth for the target company stockholders and an average 8% loss in wealth for the stockholders of the acquiring companies.[7]

PERCENTAGE DISCOUNTS FROM NET ASSET VALUE

There are certain types of companies for which both underlying net asset value and actual market trading prices for minority interests are publicly available. Most such companies are holding companies of various types, holding real estate, securities, and other investment assets. The percentages below net asset value at which such securities trade are sometimes used as a proxy for minority interest discounts.

A few such sources are the following:

- Prices of publicly traded Real Estate Investment Trusts (REITs) compared with their underlying net asset values, compiled annually by National Association of Real Estate Investment Trusts (NAREIT)
- Prices of SEC-registered limited partnership interests compared with their underlying net asset values, compiled by Partnership Profiles, Inc.
- Prices of publicly traded closed-end mutual fund shares compared with their net asset values, published regularly in the financial press, such as the *New York Times, Wall Street Journal,* and *Barron's,* as well as *Morningstar.*

These various sources and their uses are discussed in Chapters 18 and 19, and Appendix B.

Great care must be exercised in using data from REITs and closed-end funds to avoid over or undervaluation. For instance, REIT shares sometimes trade above and sometimes below net asset value, depending on the state of the markets. The same holds true for closed-end funds where discounts can rapidly become premiums, depending on which sector of the public market happens to be in vogue at the moment. In addition, there are problems currently in using closed-end investment companies as a source for discounts for minority interests. Closed-end investment company managements have begun to use several different techniques to narrow the holding company discount, including: (1) stock buybacks; (2) guaranteed annual distributions as a percentage of net asset value; and (3) liquidating.

With respect to limited partnerships, given the lack of liquidity of these investments (transfers of units and receipt of cash can take several months) there is very likely some element of lack of liquidity in the discounts. So these discounts may be a combination of both lack of control and lack of liquidity.

SUMMARY

Two major and totally different bodies of empirical evidence are often used to estimate minority discounts or control premiums:

1. Prices at which controlling interests are acquired in the public market compared with the preannouncement minority stock trading prices
2. Prices at which holding company interests sell compared with their underlying net asset values
   a. REITs
   b. SEC-registered limited partnership interests
   c. Closed-end mutual funds

As pointed out, there are some shortcomings with the acquisition premium data. Its use to quantify either the value of control in the traditional levels-of-value chart in Exhibit 1.2, or the discount for lack of control in the alternative two-level chart in Exhibit 1.3, must be used with great care. Yet it is all we have at this point until a better tool is devised.

Notes

1. *Mergerstat/Shannon Pratt's Control Premium Study.* Business Valuation Resources, available at BVMarketData.com. Up until 2001, the quarterly studies were available only in print. Starting in 2001, pursuant to a joint venture between Mergerstat™ and Business Valuation Resources™, the study was renamed the *Mergerstat/Shannon Pratt's Control Premium Study,* and is now available online as well as in print. Each quarterly printed book has about 100 pages of data. The online version has the entire book in PDF format, available to print out any or all, plus all the transaction data arranged to sort on any desired field and export to an Excel spreadsheet for analysis. The fourth quarter 2000 data contains 247

transactions, and this is a fairly typical quarter. The 12 quarters of 1998 through 2000 contain a little under 3,000 transactions.

2. See Shannon Pratt, "Control Premiums? Maybe, Maybe Not—34% of 3rd Quarter Buyouts at Discounts," *Shannon Pratt's Business Valuation Update* (January 1999): 1–3.

3. Z. Christopher Mercer, "A Brief Review of Control Premiums and Minority Interest Discounts," Proceedings of the 12th Biennial Business Valuation Conference of The Canadian Institute of Chartered Business Valuators, 1996.

4. Steven D. Garber, "Control vs. Acquisition Premiums: Is There a Difference?" presented at the American Society of Appraisers, Maui, June 1998.

5. Richard Roll, "The Hubris Hypothesis of Corporate Takeovers," *Journal of Business* 59, no. 2 (1986): 212. Reprinted with permission of the University of Chicago Press.

6. Matthew L. A. Hayward and Donald C. Hambrick, "Explaining Premiums Paid for Large Acquisitions: Evidence of CEO Hubris," New York: Columbia University Graduate School of Business (June 1995).

7. Steven Kaplan, "Valuation Issues in Corporate Control Transactions," presented at the American Society of Appraisers Advanced Business Valuation Conference (1995).

Chapter 4

Minority Discounts and Control Premiums in the Courts

Gift, Estate, and Income Tax Cases
    Minority Discount Accepted
        Estate of Barudin v. Commissioner
        Estate of Weinberg v. Commissioner
        Gow v. Commissioner
        Estate of Smith v. Commissioner
        Estate of Jones v. Commissioner
    Control Premium Rejected
        Estate of Wright v. Commissioner
    Minority Discount from "Market Value" Rejected
        Estate of Freeman v. Commissioner
Discounts for Lack of Control in Employee Stock Ownership Plan Cases
    Minority Discount Accepted
        Howard v. Shay
        Reich v. Hall Holding Co.
Dissenting Shareholder Cases
    Cases Denying Minority Discount
        Blitch v. Peoples Bank (Georgia)
        Friedman v. Beway Realty Corp. (New York)
        Hansen v. 75 Ranch Co. (Montana)
        HMO-W, Inc. v. SSM Health Care System (Wisconsin)
        Arnaud v. Stockgrowers State Bank (Kansas)
        Bomarko, Inc. v. International Telecharge, Inc. (Delaware)
        Swope v. Siegel-Robert, Inc. (Missouri)
    Cases Applying Control Premium
        Hintmann v. Fred Weber, Inc. (Delaware)
        In re 75,629 Shares of Common Stock of Trapp Family Lodge, Inc.
          (Vermont)
        Nebel v. Southwest Bancorp (Delaware)
    Applicability of Discounts to Be Determined on Case-by-Case Basis
        Weigel Broadcasting Co. v. Smith (Illinois)
Shareholder Oppression Cases
    Cases Denying Minority Discount

The term "minority discount" is used in this chapter because it is the most commonly used phrase. The reader should be aware, however, that the professional business appraisal community now prefers the term "discount for lack of control." This distinction reflects the possibility that such a discount may apply in certain circumstances, such as a 50% interest, or where the stockholder has a majority interest but less than absolute control when a supermajority is required. (In about half the states, a supermajority vote is required for certain major corporate actions.)

The chapter is organized by type of case in various courts because of differing rules of law:

- Gift, estate, and income tax
- Employee stock ownership plan (ESOP)
- Dissenting shareholder
- Shareholder oppression
- Marital dissolution
- Bankruptcy

The majority of business appraisers and courts treat discounts for lack of control and discounts for lack of marketability as separate items. Nevertheless, appraisers and courts sometimes lump the two factors into a single discount.

This chapter does not purport to be an exhaustive treatise of the many court cases involving minority versus control issues. That would be too great a task for the scope of this book; moreover, this book does not give legal advice. What I have tried to do is select a representative sample that will show the diversity of opinions in each of the several areas of litigation listed earlier. The reader should consult a lawyer for a legal opinion if one is needed.

Although only minority/control issues are discussed in this chapter, most of the cases also involved other valuation issues and frequently another discount or premium issue.*

GIFT, ESTATE, AND INCOME TAX CASES

All gift, estate, and income tax valuations fall under the legal standard of *fair market value*. As such, any time a minority interest is being valued, a minority discount is normally applied in any valuation method that results in a control value. The magnitudes of the minority discounts vary widely and usually are based on expert testimony, supported by empirical evidence presented.

Minority Discount Accepted

Estate of Barudin v. Commissioner.[1] The expert for the taxpayer testified to a combined 67.5% minority and marketability discount based on a single prior transaction in units of a partnership that owned two commercial office buildings. The IRS's expert testified to 15% minority and 15% marketability discounts. The minority discount was based on "market studies" that were unidentified in the written opinion but showed an average of 19%, which is the figure decided on by the court. (As to marketability, studies cited showed averages of 26 to 45%, and the court found a 26% discount.)

Estate of Weinberg v. Commissioner.[2] Both experts and the court agreed that minority and marketability discounts were applicable to this minority limited partnership interest, but there were diverging opinions as to their magnitudes. Both appraisers used data from *The Partnership Spectrum* to quantify discounts using net asset value (NAV) as the basis. The taxpayer's expert used a single strongly comparable guideline partnership and testified to a minority discount of 43%. The IRS's expert used 16 guideline partnerships and testified to a minority discount of 20%. The judge rejected the use of a single comparable, preferring the use of the group of 16. However, the court preferred other aspects of the taxpayer's expert's methodology and concluded a minority discount of 37%. (The judge also determined a discount for lack of marketability of 20%, for a combined discount, taken in sequence, of about 50% from NAV.)

---

*The full texts of all case decisions discussed in this chapter and many more are available at BVLibrary.com. In addition, the case summaries on BVLibrary.com contain the names of the testifying experts in most cases, even if the written opinion does not.

Gow v. Commissioner.[3]   The issue in this case was whether a minority discount was applicable, given that the base value was derived by the discounted cash flow (DCF) method. The taxpayer's expert argued that the DCF value was a control value, and thus a minority discount was applicable. The IRS's expert argued that the DCF value was a minority value, and therefore no minority discount should be applied. The court agreed with the taxpayer's expert and accepted a minority discount.

The DCF method can produce either a minority or control valuation result. It depends primarily on whether the cash flows used are ones a control owner would expect or ones that would accrue to the benefit of a minority owner. The written opinion in this case does not provide enough information for me to decide whether I agree with the court's decision.

Estate of Smith v. Commissioner.[4]   In valuing a minority interest in this farm subchapter S corporation that did not make distributions, the taxpayer's expert used market price to net asset value (P/NAV) ratios for nondistributing real estate investment trusts (REITs) to quantify the minority interest discount. The median P/NAV for the 15 selected guideline REITs was 41.3%, or a 58.7% discount from NAV. The expert chose a discount of 50%. The court agreed that the spread between market price of the shares and NAV was a minority discount and accepted the taxpayer's expert's conclusion.

The same case also involved the valuation of a bank stock. The expert for the taxpayer developed a minority interest discount of 32% based on the inverse of the control premium data derived from the *Control Premium Study*. The judge applied the 32% minority discount so derived.

Estate of Jones v. Commissioner.[5]   In this case valuing partnership interests, one expert used a minority discount of 45% based on the latest full published *The Partnership Spectrum* compilation, and the other used 38% based on the following year's compilations, which covered the period of the valuation date. The court compromised at 40%.

Of perhaps greater interest, the court denied the taxpayer's further 20% discount for lack of marketability. I disagree with this. While the partnership secondary market is thin, the units *are* registered with the SEC, and there *is* a market. But there is no organized market for private partnership interests of which we are aware, and they are therefore far less liquid.

Control Premium Rejected

Estate of Wright v. Commissioner.[6]   At issue was the value of a 23.8% interest in a very thinly traded over-the-counter (OTC) stock. The market price was $50 per share, with only very small blocks traded. The taxpayer's experts applied a blockage discount and concluded a $38 value. The IRS's expert relied on the hypothesis that a single group of investors might purchase the entire block of stock and further use this block to force other minority stockholders to sell, thus acquiring at least 51%, and therefore opined to a 33% control premium and a value of $67.34 per share. The court found the hypothetical scenario unlikely and rejected the control premium. It reduced the blockage discount to 10%, resulting in a value of $45 per share.

Minority Discount from "Market Value" Rejected

Estate of Freeman v. Commissioner.[7] The taxpayer's expert estimated a market value for the minority shares and then applied a 20% minority interest discount and also a discount for lack of marketability. In rejecting the minority discount the court explained:

> [Taxpayer's expert] applied a 20-percent discount to reflect what he believed would be the minority position that a purchaser of the shares would have. We think that that is inappropriate. [He] did not arrive at a value for the corporation and then try to determine the value of minority interest. He arrived at a market equivalent value for a share of the corporation and then multiplied to arrive at the value of the shares. We assume that, in valuing a single share of stock, the market would recognize the minority position of that share, and that no further minority discount would (or could) be demanded.

DISCOUNTS FOR LACK OF CONTROL IN EMPLOYEE STOCK OWNERSHIP PLAN CASES

Most ESOP stock is valued on a minority basis, whether the ESOP owns a controlling interest in the stock or not. If the ESOP clearly has control, the trustees can elect to have the stock valued on a control basis. As in tax cases, the legal standard of value for ESOP cases is *fair market value.*

Minority Discount Accepted

Howard v. Shay.[8] This was a class action suit in which ESOP participants sued for undervaluation on termination of the ESOP and sale of its 38.6% stock interest to a trust controlled by the controlling stockholder. One of the many issues was whether a series of minority interest discounts should have been taken and, if so, their magnitude.

The first discount applied was 60% from NAV on a 50% interest in a Japanese real estate holding company, in which the Japanese partner was the managing partner. It is not clear exactly how much of this 60% was for lack of control because other factors were included, such as the confiscatory Japanese real estate capital gains structure, adverse changes in the Japanese real estate market, and questionable confidence in the real estate appraisal.

The appraiser then applied a 45% minority discount to the stock held by the ESOP. This was based partly on REIT discounts from NAV at the time plus lack of dividend distributions. The appraiser then applied a 50% discount for lack of marketability. The case was heavily litigated, but in the end the appraiser's value was upheld.

Reich v. Hall Holding Co.[9] The ESOP owned a 9.96% interest in Hall Holding Co. stock. One expert had considerable experience in the industry. The court accepted his conclusion of company value based on DCF, comparable acquisitions, and the guideline public company method, but the court did not accept his opinion that there should be no minority interest discount. The other expert had considerable experience in valuing stock for ESOP purposes. The court concluded that a 13% minority discount should be applied to the industry expert's discounted cash flow value and comparable acquisitions value, because the ESOP held only 9.96% of Hall Holding stock. The court also held that the minority discount should not apply to the value derived from the guideline public company method, because that analysis yielded a minority interest value.

DISSENTING SHAREHOLDER CASES

In almost all states, the legal standard of value for dissenting stockholder cases is *fair value*. The statutes are silent, however, as to what this standard implies in the context of control/minority interests, thus leaving the issue of discounts to be determined by the courts through case law. The courts have been widely divergent in their stances on the minority/control issue:

- Precedential opinions (i.e., binding case law) in some states have held that value will be on a proportionate share of control basis.
- Precedential opinions in other states have said that value will be on a minority basis.
- Precedential opinions in yet other states have held that there will be no universal rule and that the determination must be made on the facts and circumstances of each case.
- Some states do not yet have any precedential rule on the minority/control valuation basis issue.

In states that have no precedential case law, courts often look to the case law of other states for guidance, often choosing those states with similarly worded statutory law. To complicate matters even further, courts in states that have precedential case law on the matter occasionally find reasons to reverse the precedent or to make an exception to it. Adding one more wrinkle is a 1999 amendment to the Model Business Corporation Act, which adopted language stating that neither marketability nor minority discounts should be applied in dissenting stockholder suits. At this writing, no state has yet adopted that amendment. However, an appellate court in Georgia made reference to it in rejecting a minority discount.

The lesson for appraisers is clear: Work closely with the client's legal counsel to understand the statutory context and case law implications of each dissenting shareholder matter.

Cases Denying Minority Discount

On balance, there are more state courts on record denying minority discounts than approving them. Even so, this does not constitute a majority of all states, because some have said that it must be decided on a case-by-case basis, and others have no precedential case law on the issue.

Blitch v. Peoples Bank (Georgia).[10]   The trial court allowed a minority discount, but the court of appeals reversed. Only one prior appellate case in Georgia had addressed this issue. In *Atlantic States Const. v. Beavers*, the Georgia Court of Appeals had determined that minority and marketability discounts could be considered in the fair value calculation but should not be overemphasized.[11] The court did not follow this case because it was not binding precedent and because it found authority to the contrary to be more persuasive. (The case of *Atlantic States* was not binding on the *Blitch* decision because it interpreted a prior dissenters' rights statute, and also because the judgment was not fully concurred in by all judges ruling on that case—a requirement by Georgia Court of Appeals rules.)

The court noted that the current Georgia dissenting shareholder statute was based on the Model Business Corporation Act. The court also pointed out that legislative comments to the Georgia statute specifically provide that the official comments to the Model Act were relevant to any interpretation of the Georgia statute. In looking at the official comments, the 1999 amendments to the Model Act, and case law from other jurisdictions holding that minority and marketability discounts should not be applied, the court of appeals concluded that these authorities were more persuasive than *Atlantic States* and adopted a rule rejecting the discount.

Friedman v. Beway Realty Corp. (New York).[12]   The corporation's expert opined to a 9.8% minority discount, based on differences between NAV and market prices for REITs. The court rejected the minority discount. (The court did, however, accept a discount for lack of marketability.)

Hansen v. 75 Ranch Co. (Montana).[13]   The court prohibited the consideration of a minority discount when establishing fair value, despite a stockholders' agreement that reflected such a discount. This decision overruled the same court's 1996 decision in *McCann Ranch, Inc. v. Quigley-McCann*,[14] a shareholder oppression suit in which the court held that nothing in section 35-1-826(4), Model Corporation Act, prohibited consideration of a minority shareholder's lack of control and lack of marketability for minority shares when establishing fair value.

HMO-W, Inc. v. SSM Health Care System (Wisconsin).[15]   The Wisconsin Supreme Court upheld a trial court's ruling that a minority discount would not be allowed in a case under a dissenters' appraisal rights statute. In a footnote, the supreme court defined both minority and marketability discounts and discussed their respective purposes. The court then stated that it was not addressing the issue of whether a marketability discount should be applied because that was not at issue in this case.

Arnaud v. Stockgrowers State Bank (Kansas).[16]   In a case of first impression before the Kansas Supreme Court, it rejected both minority and marketability discounts in a dissenters' suit where a reverse stock split forced out almost all of the shareholders. This result should not be construed too broadly, because the issue put to the Kansas Supreme Court focused very narrowly on the case-specific facts: "Is it proper for a corporation to determine the 'fair value' of a fractional share pursuant to K.S.A. § 17-6405 by applying minority and marketability discounts when the fractional share resulted from a reverse stock split intended to eliminate the minority shareholder's interest in the corporation?"

***Bomarko, Inc. v. International Telecharge, Inc.* (Delaware).**[17] Plaintiff's expert used the guideline public company method and applied a 30% control premium to account for the minority discount inherent in the comparable companies analysis. The court rejected defendants' argument against the control premium, stating "Plaintiffs are entitled to be paid the fair value of their shares without a minority discount."

***Swope v. Siegel-Robert, Inc.* (Missouri).**[18] The U.S. District Court reached its decision consistent with the Missouri Court of Appeals case of *King v. F.I.J., Inc.,* 765 S.W.2d 301 (Mo. Ct. App., 1989). That case held that the question of whether minority and marketability discounts are applicable in Missouri dissenting stockholder cases is to be determined on a case-by-case basis, weighing the individual facts and circumstances. In this case, the court determined that the shares should be valued on a minority basis but that there should be no discount for lack of marketability. The Eigth Circuit reversed, holding that no minority or marketability discounts should be applied in dissenters' rights cases as a matter of law.

Cases Applying Control Premium

The control premium comes into play when a guideline public company valuation method is used and the objective is to reach a control value result. The *Control Premium Study* usually is cited as empirical evidence to quantify this premium.

Some have argued that the full premium paid in acquisitions is too high, on average, to represent the value of control because it often contains elements of synergistic value, which should not be a part of either fair value or fair market value. Resources are now available that give analysts the ability to adjust for these factors.*

***Hintmann v. Fred Weber, Inc.* (Delaware).**[19] Experts valued the subsidiaries of a holding company by a combination of the DCF and guideline public company methods. The Court of Chancery of Delaware held that, because the companies were con-

---

*Beginning in 2001, Business Valuation Resources™ assumed control of the distribution of the *Control Premium Study* and renamed them *Mergerstat/Shannon Pratt's Control Premium Study.* In conjunction with this transfer, each transaction from 1998 forward was assigned a code as either vertical integration, horizontal integration, conglomerate, or financial. With this new information, an analyst using the data can eliminate the synergistic transactions where it is appropriate.

trolled subsidiaries, a control premium was appropriate. The expert for the plaintiff testified that control premiums paid in the industry in the 12 months prior to the valuation were at a mean of 45% and a median of 55%. Because a portion of those premiums reflected postmerger values expected from synergies, the plaintiff's expert arbitrarily adjusted the premium down to 20%, which the court accepted.

***In re 75,629 Shares of Common Stock of Trapp Family Lodge, Inc.* (Vermont).[20]** In this 1999 case of first impression since Vermont's Business Corporation Act was amended in 1994, the Vermont Supreme Court upheld a trial court ruling that applied a 30% control premium. The dissenters' expert testified that "in applying the discounted cash flow (DCF) method, he relied on figures derived from publicly traded companies and that the per share value of a share on the public market is a minority interest value." He testified that the average control premium for the hotel and motel industry was 46% (apparently obtained from the *Control Premium Study*). In applying a 30% premium, he asserted that this figure "was on the conservative side."

The validity of this decision is suspect. It is one thing to apply a control premium to a result derived from the guideline public company method. In the DCF method, though, the only figure to be derived from public companies is the discount rate. As discussed in detail in *Cost of Capital*,[21] and previously in this book, the discount rate is the same or nearly the same for both control and minority interests, and all or most of the difference between control and minority values is accounted for by the expected cash flows, which the expert certainly could not have derived from public companies. Therefore, I question the validity of always applying a control premium to a result reached by the DCF method.

***Nebel v. Southwest Bancorp* (Delaware).[22]** Plaintiff's expert applied a control premium, which the court accepted. Defendant's expert used the DCF and guideline public company methods, with no premium or discount applied. The court rejected defendant's expert's appraisal "because it had a built-in minority discount." (As noted above, the guideline public company method begets a marketable minority value, and the DCF method could reach either a minority or control value.)

Applicability of Discounts to Be Determined on Case-by-Case Basis

***Weigel Broadcasting Co. v. Smith* (Illinois).[23]** The defendants' expert applied both minority and marketability discounts, which the trial court accepted. The appellate court, citing earlier Illinois cases, confirmed that "applying such discounts, therefore, is left to the trial court's discretion." In upholding the discounts in this case, the appellate court also offered the following observations: "The trial court, we think, was justified in finding the illiquidity and minority factors had a significant bearing on the intrinsic value of the stock, especially in the absence of any claim of oppressive corporate conduct."

SHAREHOLDER OPPRESSION CASES

In most states, the standard of value for shareholder oppression cases is *fair value*, the same as for dissenting stockholder cases. However, case law in shareholder oppression matters in a given state does not necessarily parallel the dissenters' cases regarding the minority/control valuation issue.

There is not yet a great deal of case law on minority oppression cases, because statutory remedies are fairly new in most states. This area of litigation is rapidly growing.

Cases Denying Minority Discount

***Brown v. Allied Corrugated Box Co.* (California).**[24] This California case is often cited for the general rule that, under the California shareholder dissolution statute, the oppressed shareholder is entitled to a proportionate share of the enterprise value with no minority discount.

The remedy for oppression under the California statute is to dissolve the corporation and distribute the proceeds to the stockholders. Dissolution can contemplate selling the business of the dissolving company to a third party as a going concern. The controlling shareholders can avoid the dissolution by paying the oppressed stockholders *fair value*. This is interpreted to mean not less than the proceeds that would be realized if the corporation were dissolved, including proceeds if the business of the corporation were sold as a going concern, if that would be the most valuable option.

California corporate attorney Arthur Shartsis explains this process thoroughly in a 1999 article and takes the position that courts often overvalue because they fail to take into account all the costs and risks of dissolution.[25]

***Ronald v. 4-C's Electronic Packaging, Inc.* (California).**[26] Another frequently cited California dissolution case quotes *Brown* and confirms the position:

> [T]he Brown court held that where a decision is made to buy the plaintiffs' shares to avoid a dissolution of the corporation, the shares are not to be devalued even though they represent a minority interest in the corporation. (91 Cal. App. 3d at pp. 485–487.) The court then emphasized that "there is no question but that the lack of control inherent in plaintiffs' minority shares would substantially decrease their value if they were placed on the open market." (Id., at p. 486.) The court reasoned that "[had] plaintiffs been permitted to prove their case and had the corporation then been dissolved, it is clear that upon distribution of the dissolution proceeds each of the shareholders would have been entitled to the exact same amount per share, with no consideration being given to whether the shares had been controlling or noncontrolling. [Fn. Omitted.]"
>
> We agree with the Brown court that the lack of control inherent in plaintiff's minority shares should not be devalued under the statutory "buy-out" procedure of section 2000.

Cooke v. Fresh Express Foods Corp. **(Oregon).**[27]   The court of appeals affirmed prior Oregon case law holding that no minority or marketability discount should be applied in determining fair value in a shareholder oppression action where the oppressors were ordered to buy out the oppressed shareholder.

Tifft v. Stevens **(Oregon).**[28]   The appellate court affirmed the trial court's order compelling the majority to buy out Tifft's stock at appraised fair value, excluding any minority or marketability discounts.

Barnes Ellis, an Oregon corporate attorney who wrote the abstract of the above case for both *Shannon Pratt's Business Valuation Update*™ and also the *Judges & Lawyers Business Valuation Update*™, made these observations:

> Under *Chiles v. Robertson,* 94 Or App 604, 767 P2d 903 (Or. Ct. App. 1989), a court-ordered buy-out for oppression is to be valued without either minority or marketability discounts. By contrast, a valuation under the dissenter's appraisal statute, while excluding a minority discount, will include a marketability discount. *See Columbia Management Co. v. Wyss,* 94 Or App 195, 765 P2d 207 (Or. Ct. App. 1989).[29]

MARITAL DISSOLUTION CASES

Not one state has a statutory standard of value for divorce cases, much less any statutes regarding minority or control issues. Some states have adopted a standard of value through case law. Even in those states, however, the standard is not always consistently followed. When a spouse who is active in the business owns a minority interest, the courts are divided as to whether a minority interest discount should be applied.

Far more business valuation cases at the trial level are for marital property division purposes than for any other area of business valuation litigation. In spite of this, there is very sparse precedential case law in this area. This is partly because the bulk of the cases are relatively small and partly because there often is an inadequate evidentiary record made at trial from which to appeal.

Minority Discount Rejected

Ferraro v. Ferraro **(Virginia).**[30]   The husband in this case owned a 34% interest in various sporting goods stores. The court adopted the husband's expert's valuation using the excess earnings method, which produces a control value. On the other hand, the trial court rejected the husband's expert's application of a minority interest discount, and the appellate court upheld, explaining: "[N]o other person owned a majority interest. . . . Although husband testified that other minority shareholders routinely voted together . . . the trial court was free to reject husband's testimony and conclude that husband's minority ownership did not diminish the value of this asset."

Oatey v. Oatey (Ohio).[31]   The husband contended on appeal that the trial court erred in not applying a minority interest discount. The appellate court upheld the trial court's reasoning that the husband had effective control through family ownership. (This is akin to the IRS's old family attribution rule which Revenue Ruling 93-12 eliminated.)

Howell v. Howell (Virginia).[32]   The court rejected a minority discount for an interest in a law practice. In upholding the trial court, the appellate court found the discounts (both marketability and minority) inappropriate because no transfer of the partnership interest was foreseeable and no one in the firm, nor any group within it, exercised majority control.

Verholek v. Verholek (Pennsylvania).[33]   Pennsylvania is one of the states that, through its case law, clearly has adopted fair market value as the standard of value for divorce. Nevertheless, the court denied a minority interest discount from a value arrived at by the capitalization of earnings method. The court's explanation was that "the expert testified that a minority discount was not needed because the company was not valued as a whole." The opinion lacked sufficient details about the capitalization of earnings method used to enable me to assess the validity of the expert's statement on that point.

Minority Discount Accepted

DeCosse v. DeCosse (Montana).[34]   The husband owned a minority interest, with other family members owning the balance. Every year a Certified Public Accountant valued the stock by the income approach and applied a 20% minority discount. At trial, the CPA testified to the value, net of the 20% discount, which the court accepted. The Montana Supreme Court upheld the lower court's ruling.

Stayer v. Stayer (Wisconsin).[35]   In this case the wife's expert valued the family company as a whole and valued the husband's minority interest as a proportionate share of the total. The husband's expert valued the minority interest based solely on a hypothetical sale of only his minority interest, recognizing both the minority position and also the lack of marketability due to a stockholder agreement. (The decision did not break down the relative effect of minority and lack of marketability.) The court of appeals upheld the trial court's acceptance of the husband's expert's valuation.

BANKRUPTCY CASE

Case Accepting Minority Discount

In re Frezzo.[36]   A Chapter 7 trustee sought to sell debtor's 50% interest in a company. An appraisal by an expert using the income approach yielded a value of

$1,290,000, net of a 10% discount for lack of control and 30% for lack of marketability. The court granted the trustee's motion to sell at that price, despite an objection from the debtor that the interest was worth $2,500,000, but with no expert testimony or evidence to substantiate that position.

SUMMARY

Court decisions on minority/control issues are heavily influenced by the particular legal context. Gift, estate, and income tax issues and also ESOP valuations all fall under the *fair market value* standard, as defined in U.S. Treasury regulations. In this context, minority interests are always valued as such, and minority discounts are applied if the base value for a minority interest is developed by appraisal methodology resulting in a control value.

In almost all states, both dissenting stockholder and stockholder oppression cases fall under the respective state's statutory standard of *fair value*. At this writing, none of the state statutes specifies whether fair value means valuing on a minority basis or on the basis of a proportionate share of the total enterprise value. The case law decisions on this issue have been greatly mixed.

States' marital dissolution statutes provide no guidance on valuation. Court decisions on issues such as minority/control vary considerably.

In the area of bankruptcy, the decisions on the issue of minority/control also differ widely.

Even where precedent seems to be established, it often changes. Any time a valuation potentially contains a minority/control issue, the attorney and/or appraiser should thoroughly search the current case law relevant to the particular valuation.

Notes

1. *Estate of Barudin v. Commissioner,* T.C. Memo 1996-395, 72 T.C.M. (CCH) 488 (1996).
2. *Estate of Weinberg v. Commissioner,* T.C. Memo 2000-51, 79 T.C.M. (CCH) 1507 (2000).
3. *Gow v. Commissioner,* T.C. Memo 2000-93, 79 T.C.M. (CCH) 1680 (2000).
4. *Estate of Smith v. Commissioner,* T.C. Memo 1999-368, 78 T.C.M. (CCH) 745 (1999).
5. *Estate of Jones v. Commissioner,* 116 T.C. No. 11 (2001).
6. *Estate of Wright v. Commissioner,* T.C. Memo 1997-53, 73 T.C.M. (CCH) 1863 (1997).
7. *Estate of Freeman v. Commissioner,* T.C. Memo 1996-372, 72 T.C.M. (CCH) 373 (1996).
8. *Howard v. Shay,* 1993 U.S. Dist. LEXIS 20153 (C.D. Cal. 1993), *rev'd* and *remanded by,* 100 F.3d 1484 (9th Cir. 1996), *cert. denied,* 520 U.S. 1237 (1997).
9. *Reich v. Hall Holding Co.,* 60 F. Supp. 2d 755 (1999).
10. *Blitch v. Peoples Bank,* 246 Ga. App. 453, 540 S.E.2d 667 (Ga. Ct. App. 2000).
11. *Atlantic States Const. v. Beavers,* 169 Ga. App. 584, 314 S.E. 2d 245 (Ga. Ct. App. 1984).
12. *Friedman v. Beway Realty Corp.,* 87 N.Y.2d 161, 661 N.E.2d 972, 638 N.Y.S.2d 399 (N.Y. 1995).
13. *Hansen v. 75 Ranch Co.,* 1998 Mont. 77, 957 P.2d 32 (Mont. 1998).

14. *McCann Ranch, Inc. v. Quigley-McCann,* 276 Mont. 205, 915 P.2d 239 (Mont. 1996).
15. *HMO-W, Inc. v. SSM Health Care System,* 234 Wis.2d 707, 611 N.W.2d 250 (Wis. 2000), aff'g 228 Wis. 2d 815, 598 N.W.2d 577 (Wis. Ct. App. 1999).
16. *Arnaud v. Stockgrowers State Bank,* 268 Kan. 163, 992 P.2d 216 (Kan. 1999).
17. *Bomarko, Inc. v. International Telecharge, Inc.,* 1999 Del. Ch. LEXIS 211 (Del. Ch. 1999), *aff'd, International Telecharge, Inc. v. Bomarko, Inc.,* 766 A.2d 437 (Del. 2000).
18. *Hintmann v. Fred Weber, Inc.,* 1998 Del. Ch. LEXIS 26 (Del. Ch. 1998).
19. *In re 75,629 Shares of Common Stock of Trapp Family Lodge, Inc.,* 169 Vt. 82, 725 A.2d 927 (Vt. 1999).
20. Shannon Pratt, *Cost of Capital: Estimation and Applications* (New York: John Wiley & Sons, 1998).
21. *Nebel v. Southwest Bancorp,* 1999 Del. Ch. LEXIS 30 (Del. Ch. 1999).
22. *Swope v. Siegel-Robert, Inc.,* 74 F. Supp. 2d 876 (E.D. Mo. 1999), *aff'd in part, reversed in part by,* 243 F.3d 486 (8th Cir. 2001).
23. *Weigel Broadcasting Co. v. Smith,* 289 Ill. App. 3d 602, 682 N.E.2d 745 (Ill. App. Ct. 1996).
24. *Brown v. Allied Corrugated Box Co.,* 91 Cal. App. 3d 477 (Cal. Ct. App. 1979).
25. Arthur J. Shartsis, "Dissolution Actions Yield Less than Fair Market Enterprise Value," *Judges & Lawyers Business Valuation Update* (January 1999): 5–7.
26. *Ronald v. 4-C's Electronic Packaging, Inc.,* 168 Cal. App. 3d 290 (Cal. Ct. App. 1985).
27. *Cooke v. Fresh Express Foods Corp.,* 169 Or. App. 101, 7 P.3d 717 (Or. Ct. App. 2000).
28. *Tifft v. Stevens,* 162 Or. App. 62, 987 P.2d 1 (Or. Ct. App. 1999), *rev. denied,* 330 Or. 331, 6 P.3d 1101 (Or. 2000).
29. Barnes Ellis, "Oregon Court of Appeals Finds No Minority Discount Applies in Buy-out of Oppressed Shareholder," *Shannon Pratt's Business Valuation Update* (February 2000): 6.
30. *Ferraro v. Ferraro,* 2000 Va. App. LEXIS 164 (Va. Ct. App. 2000).
31. *Oatey v. Oatey,* 1996 Ohio App. LEXIS 1685 (Ohio Ct. App. 1996).
32. *Howell v. Howell,* 31 Va. App. 332, 523 S.E.2d 514 (Va. Ct. App. 2000).
33. *Verholek v. Verholek,* 1999 Pa. Super. 282, 741 A.2d 792 (Pa. Super. Ct. 1999).
34. *DeCosse v. DeCosse,* 282 Mont. 212, 936 P.2d 821 (Mont. 1997).
35. *Stayer v. Stayer,* 206 Wis.2d 675, 558 N.W.2d 704 (Wis. Ct. App. 1996).
36. *In re Frezzo,* 217 B.R. 985 (Bankr. E.D. Pa. 1998).

Discounts for Lack of Marketability for Minority Interests: Concept and Evidence

Lack of marketability, more often than not, is the largest dollar discount factor in the valuation of a business interest, particularly a minority interest.

PUBLIC MARKET BENCHMARK FOR MARKETABILITY

The United States has the most liquid markets in the world for equity interests. All observers agree that this condition vastly facilitates the formation of equity capital raised from millions of minority equity investors. U.S. equity markets are the benchmark for marketability: Sell your stock instantly over the phone, at or very close to a known public price, and receive cash in your pocket within three business days. Anything short of that standard of liquidity forms the basis for a discount for lack of marketability.

Investors love liquidity and are willing to pay a high premium for it. Conversely, relative to otherwise similar highly liquid securities, investors demand a high discount for lack of liquidity. The market price differential between otherwise comparable, readily marketable and unmarketable interests is greater than most people realize. The incident described in the following narrative helps to drive home the point. Nothing was changed regarding the securities themselves, but even short-term jeopardy of their marketability had a sudden and dramatic impact on their market prices.

> The concept of marketability, or the relative ease and promptness with which a security can be bought or sold, is an underlying assumption of an efficient market. When this assumption is challenged, the results can be severe.
>
> **WS Clearing,** a clearinghouse in Glendale, California, closed its doors on March 6, 1997 because of a net capital deficit of at least $1.1 million.
>
> **Euro-Atlantic Securities,** a brokerage firm in Boca Raton, one of two dozen clients of WS Clearing, stopped making a market in several stocks, because it had relied on WS Clearing's ability to complete transactions in those securities and had no alternative clearinghouse.
>
> The stock of **Hollywood Productions,** a company in the movie and bathing-suit businesses, fell from $7.50 per share to $3.25 (a 57% loss) before closing at $5.25. (Euro-Atlantic had been a market maker in the stock of Hollywood Productions.)
>
> **Metropolitan Health Networks, Inc.** (another stock for which Euro-Atlantic was a market maker) fell from $7 to $4.125 before closing at $5 on the NASDAQ small cap market. Both stocks closed down about 30%, reflecting the discount for lack of marketability. This sequence of events shows that even in liquid markets like NASDAQ, if marketability becomes impaired even temporarily, investors quickly revise their expectations and demand compensation for lack of marketability.[1]

Many factors affect the extent to which the marketability of a given business ownership interest that is not actively traded may differ from the marketability found in active, freely traded securities markets:

- "Put" rights
- Dividends or distributions
- Size of potential market of buyers
- Prospects for going public or being acquired
- Restrictive transfer provisions
- Size and financial strength of company
- Size of interest in question

These factors and others are discussed in subsequent chapters.

EMPIRICAL EVIDENCE TO QUANTIFY DISCOUNTS FOR LACK OF MARKETABILITY

Two series of studies are widely recognized to provide market evidence of the difference between the price of a publicly traded stock and the price of a stock that is otherwise the same or similar but not eligible for public trading as of the valuation date.

These two series of studies are known as the *restricted stock studies* and the *pre-IPO studies*.

RESTRICTED STOCK STUDIES

Many companies whose stocks are publicly traded have outstanding shares that are not registered for public trading or are subject to restrictions on public trading. These shares are identical to the publicly traded shares in all respects except for the lack of registration or the restrictions on trading.

How Restricted Shares of Public Companies Arise

Unregistered or restricted shares can arise in a variety of ways, for example:

- **Shares not registered at the time of IPO.** Underwriters of initial public offerings often are not willing to have all of the outstanding stock registered for public trading at the time of the offering. They are concerned about the risk that insiders may bail out and depress the market. Alternatively, shares might be registered but restricted from trading by a "lockup agreement" for some negotiated period of time.
- **Shares issued in an acquisition.** Companies often use stock to acquire other companies. The stock issued in an acquisition in many cases is unregistered or subject to restrictions on its sale.
- **Private placements.** Companies often sell unregistered shares privately to raise capital without incurring the delay or expense of registering the shares at the time of the placement.

In any of the above scenarios, the owners of the restricted stock may or may not have contractual rights to register the stock at some point in the future or when certain conditions are met.

Nature and Results of Restricted Stock Studies

In any case, *although the unregistered or restricted shares cannot be sold on the open market, blocks of shares may be sold in private transactions.* Thus, the restricted stock studies compare the prices of the restricted stock sales to the public market trad-

Exhibit 5.1 Summary of Restricted Stock Transaction Studies

Time Period	Study	Number of Transactions	Average Discount
1/66–6/69	SEC Institutional Investor	398	25.8%[1]
1/68–12/70	Milton Gelman	89	33.0%
1/68–12/72	Robert Trout	60	33.5%
1/68–12/72[2]	Robert Moroney	148	35.6%
1/69–12/73	Michael Maher	33	35.4%
10/78–6/82	Standard Research Consultants	28	45.0%[3]
1/81–12/88	William Silber	69	33.8%
1/79–4/92	FMW Opinions, Inc.	>100	23.0%
1/80–12/96	Management Planning, Inc.	53	27.1%
1/91–12/95	Bruce Johnson	70	20.0%
1/96–4/97	Columbia Financial Advisors	23	21.0%[4]
5/97–12/98	Columbia Financial Advisors	15	13.0%[5]

[1]The average was 32.6% for OTC companies not required to file reports with the Securities and Exchange Commission.
[2]The exact ending month is not specified.
[3]Median.
[4]Median was 14.0.
[5]Median was 9.0.

ing prices on the same day. Since the shares are identical in every respect except for their trading status, the difference is solely due to marketability and thus serves as empirical evidence of and a benchmark for the amount of discount that the market requires for the lack of marketability.

There have been many independent studies of such transactions. The studies have covered hundreds of transactions from 1966 through the present time. Details of the various studies are included in Chapters 6 and 7.

In 1977 the IRS issued Revenue Ruling 77-287, which recognized the restricted stock studies as empirical data useful for guidance in quantifying discounts for lack of marketability. Exhibit 5.1 summarizes the restricted stock studies. At least up until 1990, the average or median discounts hovered around 33 to 35%.

Results of the Securities and Exchange Commission's Loosening of Restrictions

In 1990 the SEC eliminated the requirement that all restricted stock transactions be registered with it. It issued Rule 144A, which allows qualified institutional investors to trade unregistered securities among themselves without filing registration statements. This created a somewhat more liquid market for the unregistered securities, thus starting a significant trend of reducing the average discounts observed in restricted stock transactions because of the looser restrictions.

In February 1997 the SEC announced that, effective April 29, 1997, the required holding period for securities restricted pursuant to Rule 144 would be reduced from two years to one year. This significantly increased the liquidity of restricted securities. As can be seen from the only restricted stock studies covering the post-1997 period as of our publication date (the Columbia Financial Advisors studies included in Exhibit 5.1), this change significantly reduced the average discount that the market requires for holding restricted securities.

Restricted stocks, by definition, are stocks of companies that already have established public markets. When the restrictions are lifted, an active public market will be available to the owners of the shares. Private companies enjoy no such market or imminently prospective market. Therefore, it is reasonable to expect that the discount for lack of marketability for minority shares of private companies would be greater than that for restricted stocks.

As can be seen from Exhibit 5.1, prior to 1990 the discounts for smaller public company restricted stocks clustered in the area of 33 to 35%. (Size of the company is a factor impacting the magnitude of the discount for lack of marketability, as will be discussed further in Chapter 8.) Since 1990, apparently because the restrictions have been progressively loosened, the discounts have been lower, and the restricted stock study average discounts have become even less relevant as a proxy for private company minority interest discounts for lack of marketability, especially since the holding period was reduced to one year.

This turn of events does, however, provide a good illustration of the effect that higher marketability, higher liquidity, and shorter holding periods have on the relative magnitude of the discount. Extrapolation of these data to private company situations with longer holding periods and less marketability may provide another tool for analyzing the discount.

For example, suppose a stock were absolutely prohibited from sale in a lockup situation, but the lockup expired the next day. Buyers would feel fairly comfortable paying nearly full price for the stock because the next day they would have completely liquid shares just like everyone else. Therefore, one could start with a data point of approximately zero discount for a one-day holding period until the stock became liquid.

The data from the various restricted stock studies have shown that, as the holding period for relatively marketable restricted stock is reduced from two years to one, the discount is reduced from the 20s into the teens. The discount for very restricted stock with a two-year holding period (i.e., pre-1990) versus the discount for relatively restricted stock (post-1990, but pre-1997) is the difference between approximately 33 to 35% and something in the low 20s. These relationships could be used to construct fitted curves that would quantify the discount for completely unmarketable stock with, for example, an expected 5- or 10-year holding period (see Appendix D for some additional considerations in this type of analysis).

This approach is enhanced by another series of studies that comes closer to providing a direct proxy for private company minority interest discounts for lack of marketability: the pre-IPO studies will be discussed next.

PRE–INITIAL PUBLIC OFFERING DISCOUNT FOR LACK OF MARKETABILITY STUDIES

Starting in 1975, another series of studies addressed the quantification of discounts for lack of marketability for minority shares of privately held companies. These studies observed transactions in privately held companies that eventually completed initial public offerings (IPOs). In each transaction, the private transaction price was compared to the public offering price, and the percentage discount from the public offering price was considered a proxy for the discount for lack of marketability.

These discounts still may understate true average discounts for lack of marketability for minority shares of most privately held companies, because in many cases the buyers and sellers knew about the possibility of future liquidity through a public offering. However, the studies do represent actual trades in closely held company shares and, as such, embody another source of direct empirical evidence on the topic of discounts.

The following elements of uncertainty are embodied in the pre-IPO discounts:

- It is not known for sure if the IPO will happen. Market conditions can change rapidly.
- The price of the IPO cannot be known.
- Because the company is private at the time of the transactions, there may be uncertainty as to the current value of the firm.
- Once the company does go public, officers, employees, affiliates, and others still may own restricted stock subject to lockup provisions, which further extends the expected holding period and exposes the owner to market volatility.

There are two series of pre-IPO studies and one new study. One series was originated by and still is updated by Willamette Management Associates, a national business valuation consulting firm. The other series was originated by Robert W. Baird & Co., Incorporated (Baird & Co.), an investment banking firm headquartered in Milwaukee. John Emory headed the Baird & Co. studies and continues to update them through Emory Business Vaulation, LLC, a business valuation firm in Milwaukee, which he and his associates started in 1998. One new pre-IPO study, conducted by Valuation Advisors, LLC, was published in 2000.

Subsequent sections explain the respective methodologies and results of the two series of studies and the one new study.

Although the results of the two series of studies are quite similar, with the average discounts clustering in the 45 to 50% range, the studies are totally independent of one another. In fact, each set of studies had been conducted for several years before either firm learned of the other's work. The new study also shows similar results.

Willamette Management Associates Pre–Initial
Public Offering Studies

Willamette began its series of studies specifically to help quantify the discount for lack of marketability in the *Estate of Gallo v. Commissioner* case.[2]

When a company registers an IPO, it is required by the SEC to disclose all transactions in its stock within three years prior to the IPO as well as the past year's financial results. Willamette obtains registration statements for all nonfinancial operating companies listed in the *IPO Reporter.* Willamette then eliminates all insider transactions (i.e., officers, directors, and employees) and focuses only on those transactions of an arm's-length nature.

For each transaction, Willamette then compares the private transaction price with the IPO price. Because some of the private transactions go back as far as three years, certain adjustments are necessary. The most important adjustment is to recognize the change in the company's earnings from the time of the private transaction to the time of the IPO. Therefore, the studies use price/earnings (P/E) ratios (price to latest 12 months' reported earnings) rather than raw prices. For example, if the private transaction price were at six times the latest 12 months' earnings and the IPO price were at 10 times the latest 12 months' earnings, the discount would be 40% ([10 − 6]/10 = .40). (This requires eliminating those companies that report losses at either the private transaction date or the IPO date.)

Since companies tend to go public when the market for stocks in their industry is relatively good, an adjustment is also made for changes in Standard & Poor's industry average P/E ratios. For example, if the industry average P/E ratio were 15 times at the time of the public offering but only 12 times at the time of the private transaction, the implied discount would be reduced proportionately, in this case to 80% of the implied discount (12/15 = .80). Thus, in the prior example where the implied discount was 40% before adjustment for changes in market conditions, it would be reduced to 32% (.40 × .8 = .32).[3]

Exhibit 5.2 shows the results of the series of Willamette studies as of this writing. Because of the very high cost of these detailed studies, Willamette has not published the complete lists of stocks involved in each year's study. Willamette publishes a summary of the studies but not the underlying data. The relevant data have, however, been provided to courts and opposing experts under confidentiality agreements in many cases involving disputed discounts for lack of marketability so that opposing experts could conduct effective cross-examination.

Some critics have suggested that the studies tend to understate the true discounts because underwriters try to price public offerings at about 15% below market value in order to help ensure a successful offering. However, Willamette has conducted studies of prices six months following the IPOs and found no consistent upward or downward bias in the first six months' performance relative to the market. Further research may shed additional light on this point.

Exhibit 5.2   Summary of Discounts for Private Transaction P/E Multiples
Compared to Public Offering P/E Multiples Adjusted for Changes
in Industry P/E Multiples

Time Period	Number of Companies Analyzed	Number of Transactions Analyzed	Standard Mean Discount	Trimmed Mean Discount*	Median Discount	Standard Deviation
1975–78	17	31	34.0%	43.4%	52.5%	58.6%
1979	9	17	55.6%	56.8%	62.7%	30.2%
1980–82	58	113	48.0%	51.9%	56.5%	29.8%
1983	85	214	50.1%	55.2%	60.7%	34.7%
1984	20	33	43.2%	52.9%	73.1%	63.9%
1985	18	25	41.3%	47.3%	42.6%	43.5%
1986	47	74	38.5%	44.7%	47.4%	44.2%
1987	25	40	36.9%	44.9%	43.8%	49.9%
1988	13	19	41.5%	42.5%	51.8%	29.5%
1989	9	19	47.3%	46.9%	50.3%	18.6%
1990	17	23	30.5%	33.0%	48.5%	42.7%
1991	27	34	24.2%	28.9%	31.8%	37.7%
1992	36	75	41.9%	47.0%	51.7%	42.6%
1993	51	110	46.9%	49.9%	53.3%	33.9%
1994	31	48	31.9%	38.4%	42.0%	49.6%
1995	42	66	32.2%	47.4%	58.7%	76.4%
1996	17	22	31.5%	34.5%	44.3%	45.4%
1997	34	44	28.4%	30.5%	35.2%	46.7%

*Excludes the highest and lowest deciles of indicated discounts.
Source: Willamette Management Associates. Used with permission.

John Emory Pre–Initial Public Offering Studies

The Emory studies (also known as the Baird & Co. studies) observe private transactions up to five months prior to the IPO. Because of the shorter time frame, no adjustments are made; the private transaction price is simply compared with the IPO price. For example, if the IPO price were $20 and the private transaction price $11, the implied discount would be 45% ([20 − 11]/20 = .45).

There is no screening to eliminate insider transactions. As Emory explains,

> In order to provide a reasonable comparison of prices before and at the IPO, I felt it necessary both for the company to have been reasonably sound and for the private transaction to have occurred within a period of five months prior to the offering date.
> The transactions primarily took one of two forms: (1) the granting of stock options with an exercise price equal to the stock's then fair market value; or (2) the

Exhibit 5.3   Value of Marketability as Illustrated in Initial Public Offerings of
Common Stock

Study	Number of IPO Prospectuses Reviewed	Number of Qualifying Transactions	Discounts %	
			Mean	Median
*1997–2000	92	53	54	54
1995–1997	732	91	43	42
1994–1995	318	46	45	45
1991–1993	443	54	45	44
1990–1992	266	35	42	40
1989–1990	157	23	45	40
1987–1989	98	27	45	45
1985–1986	130	21	43	43
1980–1981	97	13	60	66
All 9 Studies	2333	363	47%	44%

*1997–2000 study was for dot-com companies—not comparable to other studies (see text).
Source: John D. Emory, "The Value of Marketability as Illustrated in Initial Public Offerings of Common Stock (Eighth in a Series) November 1995 through April 1997," *Business Valuation Review,* vol. 16, no. 3 (September 1997): 125; John D. Emory Sr., F. R. Dengel, III and John D. Emory Jr., "The Value of Marketability as Illustrated in Dot.Com IPOs: May 1997–March 2000, *Shannon Pratt's Business Valuation Update,* vol. 6, no. 7 (July 2000): 1–2. © Emory Business Valuation, LLC.

sale of stock. . . . In most cases, the transactions were stated to have been, or could reasonably be expected to have been, at fair market value. All ultimately would have had to be able to withstand SEC, IRS or judicial review, particularly in light of the subsequent public offering.[4]

The latest Emory study as of this writing is a specialized study on "dot-com" stocks. This study shows an average discount of a little over 50%, slightly higher than the long-term average covering stocks of all types.

In contrast to Willamette, Emory publishes the complete list of stocks used in each of the time periods studied. Exhibit 5.3 gives a summary of all the Emory studies. Chapter 7 shows all the individual transactions in each of the Emory studies.

The characteristic of marketability is a major positive component of the prices of stocks in U.S. public markets, and these markets are regarded as a benchmark for full marketability. For any lack of this characteristic, investors demand a deep discount in price from an otherwise comparable fully marketable stock. The lack of marketability imposes a high degree of risk compared with an investment that can be liquidated virtually instantly. In other words, investors demand a much higher expected rate of return in order to accept the additional risk attendant to lack of marketability.

Exhibit 5.4   Valuation Advisors 1999 Pre-IPO Discount Study

No. Days Before IPO	Average Discount	No. of Transactions
1–90	32.45%	166
91–180	52.06%	163
181–270	65.84%	99
271–365	73.69%	84
366–730	77.19%	167

Source: Adapted from Brian K. Pearson, "1999 Marketability Discounts as Reflected in Initial Public Offerings," *CPA Expert* (Spring 2000): 3. © 2000 by American Institute of Certified Public Accountants, Inc., reprinted with permission.

Valuation Advisors Pre–Initial Public Offering Study

Valuation Advisors conducted a study of 679 transactions of common stock and options of 336 private companies that ultimately completed IPOs in 1999. Using data from prospectuses, they included stock and option transactions up to two years prior to the IPOs.

Although the research design was somewhat different from either the Willamette or Emory studies, the results were similar, with average discounts slightly higher. The total average discount was 48.97%.

The study broke down the transactions by the length of time intervening between the private company transaction and the IPO. As one might expect, the longer the holding period prior to the IPO, the greater the average discount. The results are shown in Exhibit 5.4.

Companies in the study included a high proportion of "new economy" dot-com companies. Fully 73% of them had no earnings at the time of the IPO, and 57% were founded less than five years prior to the IPO. The slightly higher discounts shown in the Valuation Advisors' study is consistent with the higher discounts shown in Emory's study of dot-com stocks.

REGULATORY AND COURT RECOGNITION OF EMPIRICAL MARKETABILITY DISCOUNT STUDIES

The IRS and the courts have recognized the two series of empirical studies discussed in this chapter as guidance in quantifying discounts for lack of marketability.

Revenue Ruling 77-287

In 1977 the Internal Revenue Service published Revenue Ruling 77-287, which recognized the restricted stock studies as valid empirical evidence for quantifying discounts for lack of marketability. The full text of Revenue Ruling 77-287 is included as Appendix E.

The restricted stock studies are also discussed in the *IRS Valuation Training for Appeals Officers Coursebook* at pages 11-2 through 11-7.[5]

Recognition of Pre–Initial Public Offering Studies

The first of the pre-IPO studies had not yet been published at the time of Revenue Ruling 77-287. The IRS discusses the pre-IPO studies briefly in the *IRS Valuation Training for Appeals Officers Coursebook* at pages 9-3 through 9-6.

In *Mandelbaum v. Commissioner,* the only issue was the size of the discount for lack of marketability. Judge David Laro stated that he used the restricted stock studies and pre-IPO studies as his starting point and adjusted upward or downward based on a variety of factors.[6] (The factors are discussed in Chapter 8.)

In *Estate of Davis v. Commissioner,* expert witnesses for the taxpayer considered both restricted stock and pre-IPO studies, while the expert for the IRS used only restricted stock studies.[7] The court chose a discount for lack of marketability closer to the opinions of the taxpayer's experts, explaining that the IRS expert should have considered both lines of studies to have a more comprehensive basis for his opinion.

SUMMARY

Marketability or liquidity is the ability to convert ownership interests to cash quickly, with minimum transaction costs and at a price very close to a known market price. This attribute is very important to investors. It means they can get their money whenever they want or need it. They do not risk being unable to sell during changing internal company or market conditions. Their proceeds are not diluted by high costs of finding a buyer and effecting a transaction. Because of the current active market, quoted regularly, they do not risk overestimating expected proceeds from sale. Investors demand a much higher expected rate of return if they incur these risks, not infrequently an amount double or triple the rate of return they would expect from a fully liquid investment. They demand this return in the form of a substantially discounted price compared with the price of an otherwise comparable but fully liquid investment.

A large amount of empirical data is available to help quantify this discount for minority interests in closely held companies. The data fall into two major categories:

1. Trades in restricted stocks of publicly traded companies
2. Trades in stocks of privately held companies prior to an IPO

Because of the loosening of restrictions on transactions in restricted public stocks and the resulting increase in their marketability, the restricted stock studies show that transactions since 1990 generally have lower discounts than pre-1990 transactions. This makes current restricted stock transactions somewhat less useful in determining private minority discounts. However, changes in the discount during the 1990s have shed light on the relative magnitude of marketability discounts as a function of the holding period and the degree to which the shares are restricted from resale.

The pre-IPO studies more closely represent the actual circumstances of a closely held company stockholder and thus are generally regarded as a better direct proxy for closely held company minority stock discounts for lack of marketability.

This chapter has addressed only the concept and importance of marketability (and the penalties for lack of it) and data quantifying average discounts for lack of marketability for minority interests. Subsequent chapters address:

- Factors influencing the magnitudes of the discount for lack of marketability
- Quantifying the discount when net asset value is the starting point
- Discounts for lack of marketability for controlling interests
- Courts' treatment of discounts for lack of marketability

The IRS has recognized the restricted stock studies as empirical evidence of lack of marketability in Revenue Ruling 77-287. The U.S. Tax Court and U.S. District Courts have recognized both the restricted stock studies and pre-IPO studies on many occasions.

Notes

1. Jim Jordon, "Clearinghouse Debacle Illustrates Value of Marketability," *Shannon Pratt's Business Valuation Update* (April 1997): 9 (as modified).
2. *Estate of Gallo v. Commissioner,* T.C. Memo. 1985-363, 50 T.C.M. (CCH) 470 (1985).
3. The mathematical procedure is explained slightly differently in Shannon P. Pratt, Robert F. Reilly, and Robert P. Schweihs, *Valuing a Business,* 4th ed. (New York: McGraw-Hill, 2000): 408–409. The result, however, is the same.
4. John D. Emory, "The Value of Marketability as Illustrated in Initial Public Offerings of Common Stock (Eighth in a Series) November 1995 through April 1997," *Business Valuation Review,* vol. 16, no. 3 (September 1997): 124.
5. Internal Revenue Service, *IRS Valuation Training for Appeals Officers Coursebook* (Chicago: Commerce Clearing House, Incorporated, 1998).
6. *Mandelbaum v. Commissioner,* T.C. Memo. 1995-255, 69 T.C.M. (CCH) 2852 (1995).
7. *Estate of Davis v. Commissioner,* 110 T.C. 530 (1998).

Chapter 6

Synopsis of Restricted Stock Studies

This chapter summarizes all available published restricted stock studies and, in addition, includes tabular material from several of the studies.

Quite clearly, discounts on restricted stocks were lower compared to freely traded stock prices starting in 1990 when the SEC issued Rule 144A relaxing the Rule 144 restrictions, and a further trend toward lower discounts began in 1997, when the required holding period under Rule 144 was reduced from two years to one year. This demonstrates that the perceived holding period is a major factor affecting the size of the discount for lack of marketability.

Several of the studies include analyses of other factors affecting the size of the discount, and these results are summarized within the synopsis of each study. The results are generally consistent from study to study, but not universally so. Chapter 8 analyzes these influences by factor rather than by study. The most important factor, dividend payouts, does not show up in the restricted stock studies because very few of the companies in which restricted stock transactions were involved paid any dividends. Chapter 8 brings the payout factor into perspective by reference to data other than the restricted stock transactions.

SECURITIES AND EXCHANGE COMMISSION INSTITUTIONAL INVESTOR STUDY

To this day, the SEC Institutional Investor Study[1] is the most comprehensive restricted stock study, encompassing 398 transactions from January 1, 1966, through June 30, 1969. The SEC broke down the transactions by several criteria:

- Trading market
- Type of institutional purchaser
- Sales of issuer
- Earnings of issuer

The results of the above breakdowns are shown in Exhibits 6.1 through 6.6.

The differences in discounts among different trading markets were significant, as shown in Exhibit 6.1. The smallest discounts were found among stocks listed on the New York Stock Exchange (NYSE). Next were American Stock Exchange (ASE) and over-the-counter (OTC) reporting companies. Most significantly, the largest discounts were found among OTC nonreporting companies, with well over 50% of the transactions showing discounts in excess of 30%. These are companies that are public but, because of the asset size or number of stockholders, do not have to file the annual 10-K or other reports with the SEC. *These are the companies that come closest to resembling privately held companies.*

The differences by type of purchasing institution, as shown in Exhibit 6.2, are not especially significant. The transaction size, illustrated in Exhibit 6.3, did not seem especially important either. The size factor, however, measured by sales as shown in Exhibit 6.4, was significant. Blocks of stock of companies with smaller sales tended to sell at larger discounts.

Exhibit 6.1 Discounts on Purchase Price of Restricted Common Stock Classified by Trading Market

January 1, 1966, to June 30, 1969

DISCOUNT

Trading Market	-15.0% to 0.0%		0.1% to 10.0%		10.1% to 20.0%		20.1% to 30.0%		30.1% to 40.0%		40.1% to 50.0%		50.1% to 80%		Total	
	No. of Trans-actions	Value of Purchases (Dollars)	No. of Trans-actions	Value of Purchases (Dollars)	No. of Trans-actions	Value of Purchases (Dollars)	No. of Trans-actions	Value of Purchases (Dollars)	No. of Trans-actions	Value of Purchases (Dollars)	No. of Trans-actions	Value of Purchases (Dollars)	No. of Trans-actions	Value of Purchases (Dollars)	No. of Trans-actions	Value of Purchases (Dollars)
Unknown	1	1,500,000	2	2,496,583	1	205,000	0	-	2	3,332,000	0	-	1	1,259,995	7	8,793,578
New York Stock Exchange	7	3,760,663	13	15,111,798	13	24,503,988	10	17,954,085	3	11,102,501	1	1,400,000	4	5,005,068	51	78,838,103
American Stock Exchange	2	7,263,060	4	15,850,000	11	14,548,750	20	46,200,677	7	21,074,298	1	44,250	4	4,802,404	49	109,783,432
Over-the-Counter (Reporting Co.)	11	13,828,757	39	13,613,676	35	38,585,259	30	35,479,946	30	38,689,328	13	9,284,047	21	8,996,406	179	178,477,419
Over-the-Counter (Non-reporting Co.)	5	8,329,369	9	5,265,925	18	25,122,024	17	11,229,155	25	29,423,584	20	11,377,431	18	13,505,545	112	104,253,033
TOTAL	26	34,681,849	67	52,337,982	78	102,965,021	77	110,863,863	67	123,621,711	35	22,105,728	48	33,569,418	398	480,145,572

Source: SEC Institutional Investor Study.

Exhibit 6.2 Discounts on Purchase Price of Restricted Common Stock Classified by Institution

January 1, 1966, to June 30, 1969

DISCOUNT

Class of Institution	−15.0% to 0.0%		0.1% to 10.0%		10.1% to 20.0%		20.1% to 30.0%		30.1% to 40.0%		40.1% to 50.0%		50.1% to 80%		Total	
	No. of Trans-actions	Value of Purchases (Dollars)	No. of Trans-actions	Value of Purchases (Dollars)	No. of Trans-actions	Value of Purchases (Dollars)	No. of Trans-actions	Value of Purchases (Dollars)	No. of Trans-actions	Value of Purchases (Dollars)	No. of Trans-actions	Value of Purchases (Dollars)	No. of Trans-actions	Value of Purchases (Dollars)	No. of Trans-actions	Value of Purchases (Dollars)
Banks	6	10,803,050	17	15,021,358	31	35,624,259	26	44,586,199	18	44,581,008	9	3,838,055	12	3,047,068	119	157,500,99
Investment Advisors	7	6,012,188	13	24,429,493	27	50,390,544	26	37,654,718	32	60,149,780	16	13,630,681	16	20,695,041	137	212,962,44
Property and Liability Insurance Companies	1	1,500,000	2	1,438,375	3	2,418,279	3	7,342,061	0	-	3	1,850,000	2	1,659,995	14	16,208,710
Life Insurance Companies	5	6,909,369	2	2,029,500	8	7,735,412	13	9,720,627	8	10,174,527	2	999,993	5	3,631,414	43	41,200,842
Self-Administered Employee Benefit	4	3,109,932	29	3,733,256	2	3,653,133	3	1,748,856	0	-	0	-	2	2,000,000	40	14,245,177
Foundations	0	-	2	3,140,000	1	429,000	0	-	0	-	0	-	0	-	3	3,569,000
Educational Endowments	1	284,250	1	2,500,000	2	600,000	1	1,300,000	0	-	2	1,000,000	1	207,000	8	5,891,250
Venture Capital	2	6,063,060	1	46,000	4	2,114,394	5	8,511,402	9	8,716,396	3	786,999	10	2,328,900	34	28,567,151
TOTAL	26	34,681,849	67	52,337,982	78	102,965,021	77	110,863,863	67	123,621,711	35	22,105,728	48	33,569,418	398	480,145,572

Source: SEC Institutional Investor Study.

Exhibit 6.3 Discounts on Purchase Price of Restricted Common Stock Classified by Size of Transaction and Sales of Issuer

January 1, 1966, to June 30, 1969

DISCOUNT

Sale of Issuer (Thousands of Dollars)	50.1% or More		40.1% to 50.0%		30.1% to 40.0%		20.1% to 30.0%		10.1 to 20.0%		0.1% to 10.0%		Total	
	No. of Trans-actions	Size of Transactions (Dollars)	No. of Trans-actions	Size of Transactions (Dollars)	No. of Trans-actions	Size of Transactions (Dollars)	No. of Trans-actions	Size of Transactions (Dollars)	No. of Trans-actions	Size of Transactions (Dollars)	No. of Trans-actions	Size of Transactions (Dollars)	No. of Trans-actions	Size of Transactions (Dollars)
Less than 100	11	2,894,999	7	2,554,000	17	19,642,364	16	12,197,394	6	12,267,292	9	12,566,000	66	62,122,049
100–999	7	474,040	2	1,221,000	0	–	1	500,000	1	1,018,500	2	3,877,500	13	7,091,040
1,000–4,999	8	4,605,505	13	8,170,747	12	10,675,150	15	9,865,951	10	9,351,738	3	2,295,200	61	44,964,291
5,000–19,999	6	1,620,015	4	1,147,305	13	25,986,008	25	27,238,210	24	21,441,347	47	12,750,481	119	90,183,366
20,000–99,999	3	605,689	3	4,372,676	6	11,499,250	8	11,817,954	18	22,231,737	17	36,481,954	55	87,009,260
100,000 or More	2	1,805,068	0	–	2	2,049,998	3	7,903,586	10	24,959,483	7	10,832,925	24	47,551,060
TOTAL	37	12,005,316	29	17,465,728	50	69,852,770	68	69,523,095	69	91,270,097	85	78,804,060	338	338,921,066

Source: SEC Institutional Investor Study.

94

Exhibit 6.4 Average Discounts on Purchase Price of Restricted Common Stock Classified by Sales of Issuer

SALES OF ISSUER
(Thousands of Dollars)

Year	Less than 100 No. of Transactions	Average Discount (Percentages)	100 to 999 No. of Transactions	Average Discount (Percentages)	1,000 to 4,999 No. of Transactions	Average Discount (Percentages)	5,000 to 19,999 No. of Transactions	Average Discount (Percentages)	20,000 to 99,999 No. of Transactions	Average Discount (Percentages)	100,000 or More No. of Transactions	Average Discount (Percentages)	Totals No. of Transactions	Average Discount (Percentages)
1966	0	–	0	–	1	61.4	7	23.8	10	9.3	3	.2	21	15.3
1967	1	17.2	3	79.4	11	37.4	36	9.5	6	6.2	6	11.2	63	17.7
1968	2	25.6	5	30.0	36	32.6	47	18.7	26	23.9	11	21.1	127	24.5
1969 (first half)	3	41.4	5	45.5	13	26.9	29	27.1	13	21.4	4	25.8	67	27.9
TOTAL	6	32.1	13	47.4	61	32.7	119	18.3	55	18.7	24	16.8	178	23.1

Note: Averages of discounts are weighted by the number of transactions in each range of sales.
Source: SEC Institutional Investor Study.

Exhibit 6.5 Discounts on Purchase Price of Restricted Common Stock Classified by Earnings of Issuer

January 1, 1966, to June 30, 1969
DISCOUNT

Earnings of Issuer (Thousands of Dollars)	50.1% or More		40.1% to 50.0%		30.1% to 40.0%		20.1% to 30.0%		10.1% to 20.0%		0.1% to 10.0%		Totals	
	No. of Trans-actions	Size of Trans-actions (Dollars)	No. of Trans-actions	Size of Trans-actions (Dollars)	No. of Trans-actions	Size of Trans-actions (Dollars)	No. of Trans-actions	Size of Trans-actions (Dollars)	No. of Trans-actions	Size of Trans-actions (Dollars)	No. of Trans-actions	Size of Trans-actions (Dollars)	No. of Trans-actions	Size of Trans-actions (Dollars)
Deficit	0	–	0	–	0	–	0	–	0	–	0	–	0	–
0–99	27	6,901,243	19	11,003,559	28	37,681,014	31	32,796,968	19	25,122,042	46	29,553,418	170	143,058,244
100–999	8	3,299,005	10	6,462,169	19	26,121,758	24	20,344,492	25	16,790,565	16	12,480,144	102	85,498,133
1,000–9,999	0	–	0	–	3	6,049,998	12	16,313,549	17	27,948,007	15	16,955,530	47	67,267,084
10,000 or More	2	1,805,068	0	–	0	–	1	68,086	8	21,409,483	8	19,814,968	19	43,097,605
TOTAL	37	12,005,316	29	17,465,728	50	69,852,770	68	69,523,095	69	91,270,097	85	78,804,060	338	338,921,066

Source: SEC Institutional Investor Study.

96

Exhibit 6.6 Average Discounts on Purchase Price of Restricted Common Stock Classified by Earnings of Issuer Year by Year

EARNINGS OF ISSUER
(Thousands of Dollars)

Year	Deficit		0 to 99		100 to 999		1,000 to 9,999		10,000 or More		Totals	
	No. of Trans-actions	Average Discount (Percentages)	No. of Trans-actions	Average Discount (Percentages)	No. of Trans-actions	Average Discount (Percentages)	No. of Trans-actions	Average Discount (Percentages)	No. of Trans-actions	Average Discount (Percentages)	No. of Trans-actions	Average Discount (Percentages)
1966	0	–	8	14.7	5	25.6	4	10.7	4	8.4	21	15.3
1967	0	–	35	21.8	12	19.2	12	8.1	4	4.9	63	17.7
1968	0	–	48	27.1	49	26.0	21	15.5	9	23.2	127	24.5
1969 (first half)	0	–	19	33.3	36	26.6	10	23.8	2	19.3	67	27.9
TOTAL	0	–	110	25.6	102	25.4	47	15.0	19	15.8	278	23.1

Note: Averages of discounts are weighted by the number of transactions in each range of earnings.
Source: SEC Institutional Investor Study.

Even more significant than size of sales was size of earnings, as shown in Exhibits 6.5 and 6.6. Blocks of stock of companies with lower earnings tended to sell at greater discounts than those with larger earnings; this is shown especially clearly in Exhibit 6.5.

GELMAN STUDY

Milton Gelman studied the transactions through the end of 1970 by four mutual funds established in 1968 specifically for the purpose of investing in restricted stocks.[2] He reported that both the mean and median discount for 89 stocks studied was 33%.

The distribution of discounts observed by Gelman is shown in Exhibit 6.7. Significantly, 36% of all the transactions were at discounts greater than 40%. Nevertheless, to this date, the U.S. Tax Court has recognized only a few discounts of 40% (and only one of 45%) strictly for marketability not combined with any other factors. (The case of *Howard v. Shay* concluded a 50% discount for lack of marketability, but that was an ESOP case, not a tax case, and the ESOP did not have a put option, as required of ESOPs formed more recently.[3])

TROUT STUDY

Like Gelman, Robert Trout studied purchases of restricted stocks by mutual funds.[4] His time frame was 1968 to 1972. He used three of the same funds studied by Gelman plus three others. Although he used more funds and a longer time period than Gelman, he made some eliminations, resulting in a total of 60 transactions studied.

Trout used a multiple linear regression analysis to study the impact of several factors on the size of the discount. The effects of each of these factors, from a multiple regression intercept of 43.53, was as follows, controlling for other variables:

Exhibit 6.7   Distribution of Discounts in Gelman Study

Size of Discount	No. of Common Stocks	% of Total
Less than 15.0%	5	6%
15.0–9.9	9	10
20.0–24.9	13	15
25.0–29.9	9	10
30.0–34.9	12	13
35.0–39.9	9	10
40.0 and over	32	36
Total	89	100%

Source: Milton Gelman, "An Economist-Financial Analyst's Approach to Valuing Stock of a Closely-Held Company," *Journal of Taxation* (June 1972): 353–354. © 1972 Warren, Gorham + Lamont, of RIA, 395 Hudson Street, New York, NY 10014, reprinted with permission.

- **Listed on exchange.** Discount averaged 8.39% less for those listed than for unlisted stocks.
- **Shares outstanding** (a proxy for overall marketability of the company's shares). Discount averaged 4.08% less for each 1 million shares outstanding over the study's average of 1.51 million outstanding.
- **Size of transaction.** This was measured in two dimensions, which were somewhat offsetting:
  - ♦ **Percent of outstanding stock** (voting control). The average discount was .87% less for each percentage point of outstanding stock above the study's average of 7.41%.
  - ♦ **Value of transaction.** The average discount was 4.75 percentage points higher for every $1 million above the study's average of $1.08 million.

MORONEY STUDY

Robert Moroney, an investment banker in Houston, studied 148 restricted stock purchases by 10 mutual funds from 1968 through 1972.[5] He found a range from one 30% premium up to a 90% discount, with an average discount of 35.6%. The results are shown in Exhibit 6.8.

The Moroney article also gives details of discounts concluded by the U.S. Tax Court up to the time of his study.

MAHER STUDY

J. Michael Maher, an insurance company officer and former IRS gift and estate tax agent, studied purchases of restricted stocks by four mutual funds from 1969 through 1973.[6] He found discounts ranging from a low of 2.79% to a high of 75.7%, with an average of 35.4%. His article includes a complete list of the 33 transactions included in the study.

STANDARD RESEARCH CONSULTANTS STUDY

William Pittock and Charles Stryker, then of the Standard Research division of American Appraisal Associates, analyzed 28 private placements of restricted common stock from October 1978 through June 1982.[7] They found discounts ranging from 7 to 91%, with a median of 45%. The U.S. equity markets were quite depressed during the latter part of this period, which may explain why the discounts were unusually high for block sales of illiquid stock.

The sample size used in the study is relatively small to make meaningful analyses of factors influencing the size of the discounts. There was some correlation, however, showing that stocks of companies with larger revenues tended to have lower

Exhibit 6.8 Original Purchase Discounts, Moroney Study
(Discounts from the quoted market value of the same corporation's
"free" stock of the same class)

Investment Company	Original Purchase Discount	Number of Blocks
Bayrock Growth Fund, Inc., New York City (formerly Fla. Growth Fund)	4 blocks bought at discounts of 12%, 23%, 26%, 66%, respectively	4
Diebold Venture Capital Corp., New York City	6 blocks bought at discounts of 16%, 20%, 20%, 23%, 23%, 50%, respectively	6
Enterprise Fund, Inc., Los Angeles	10 blocks bought at discounts of 31%, 36%, 38%, 40%, 49%, 51%, 55%, 63%, 74%, 87%, respectively	10
Harbor Fund, Inc., Los Angeles	1 block bought at a discount of 14%	1
Inventure Capital Corp., Boston	At acquisition dates all blocks were valued at cost	—
Mates Investment Fund, Inc., New York City	1 block bought at a discount of 62%	1
New America Fund, Inc., Los Angeles (formerly Fund of Letters, Inc.)	32 blocks bought at discounts of 3%, 3%, 14%, 14%, 16%, 21%, 25%, 26%, 27%, 33%, 33%, 33%, 35%, 36%, 36%, 37%, 37%, 39%, 40%, 40%, 43%, 44%, 46%, 47%, 49%, 51%, 53%, 53%, 56%, 57%, 57%, 58%, respectively	32
Price Capital Corp., New York City	7 blocks bought at discounts of 15%, 29%, 29%, 32%, 40%, 44%, 52%, respectively	7
SMC Investment Corp., Los Angeles	12 blocks bought at 30% premium, discounts 4%, 25%, 26%, 32%, 33%, 34%, 38%, 46%, 48%, 50%, 78%, respectively	12
Value Line Development Capital Corp., New York City	35 blocks bought at discounts of 10%, 15%, 15%, 15%, 15%, 15%, 20%, 23%, 28%, 28%, 28%, 30%, 30%, 30%, 30%, 30%, 32.5%, 35%, 40%, 40%, 40%, 40%, 40%, 40%, 45%, 50%, 50%, 50%, 50%, 53%, 55%, 55%, 65%, 70%, 90%, respectively	35
Value Line Special Situations Fund, Inc., New York City	38 blocks bought at discounts of 10%, 13%, 15%, 15%, 17%, 17%, 20%, 20%, 20%, 23%, 25%, 25%, 25%, 25%, 26.5%, 27%, 27%, 30%, 30%, 30%, 30%, 30%, 30%, 30%, 30%, 33%, 37.5%, 40%, 40%, 40%, 40%, 45%, 55%, 55%, 56%, 56%, 60%, 81%, respectively	38

Source: Robert E. Moroney, "Most Courts Overvalue Closely Held Stocks," *Taxes—The Tax Magazine* (March 1973): 144–156. Published and copyrighted by CCH Incorporated, 2700 Lake Cook Road, Riverwoods, IL 60015, reproduced with permission.

discounts. While profitability in the latest year was not a significant factor, those companies with only one or two years of profitability out of the last five sold at the highest average discounts, while the two companies in the study that were profitable in each of the last five years showed the lowest discounts.

SILBER STUDY

William Silber analyzed 69 private placements from 1981 through 1989.[8] He found a range from a 12.7% premium to an 84% discount, with an average discount of 33.75%.

Silber investigated several factors that might help explain the different levels of discount. He found that private placements of companies with higher revenues tended to sell at lower discounts, but this accounted for only a few percentage points.

Silber's results regarding transaction size were in direct contrast to those of Trout (although he did not reference the Trout study):

- **Percent of outstanding stock.** "Discounts are larger when the block of restricted stock is large relative to the total shares outstanding."
- **Value of transaction.** ". . . [T]he dollar size of the issue is inversely related to the discount."

FMV OPINIONS STUDY

FMV Opinions, Inc., a business valuation firm, examined over 100 restricted stock transactions from 1979 through April 1992.[9] The mean discount was reported as 23%, but there was no description of the criteria for selection of the transactions over the 13-year period.

The authors offered several generalizations about factors affecting the size of the discount for lack of marketability:

- Discounts were lower for companies with higher revenues and those with higher earnings.
- Discounts were lower for those companies whose unrestricted stocks were traded on the larger exchanges.
- The discounts were *highest* for blocks of stock valued at under $10 million and decreased as the size of the block exceeded $10 million.
- However, discounts were higher for blocks exceeding 10% of ownership than for blocks representing smaller percentages.
- Discounts for lack of marketability were higher as the capitalization of the corporation decreased.
- Discounts tended to range from 30 to 40% for companies with capitalizations under $50 million.

Importantly, they also noted that the discounts in the 17 transactions from May 1991 through April 1992 (after Rule 144A relaxed some restrictions) were smaller on average than those for the earlier years.

MANAGEMENT PLANNING STUDY

Robert Oliver and Roy Meyers studied private placements for the 17-year period from January 1, 1980, through December 31, 1996.[10] They started with 231 transactions, which represented all that were published in *Investment Dealers Digest, Private Placement Letter,* and *Private Equity Week* at the time of the study.

Oliver and Meyers ended up with 53 transactions without registration rights and 27 with registration rights after eliminating the following:

• Market price under $2 per share
• Less than $3 million sales volume
• Companies characterized as "startup" or "developmental stage"
• Companies lacking adequate information

They studied separately those with and without registration rights. Company names and details of each transaction are included with the full text of the study on BVLibrary.com and in Chapter 5 of *Handbook of Advanced Business Valuation.*[11]

The authors offered the following broad observations about the 53 transactions in stocks without registration rights:

• The average discount for lack of marketability was about 27%.
• The median discount for lack of marketability was about 25%.
• These median and average discounts for lack of marketability are slightly lower than the median (28%) and the average (29%) discounts of the entire prescreen group of 231 transactions.
• Only one of the 53 transactions occurred at a price equal to the market price.
• The remaining 52 transactions all reflected discounts for lack of marketability ranging from a low of 3% to a high of 58%.

The 27 stocks *with* registration rights had a median discount of 9.1% and an average discount of 12.8%. This dramatically demonstrates the difference between guaranteed liquidity in a short time versus a longer and perhaps somewhat uncertain holding period until liquidity will be available.

The authors also analyzed the relationships of specific factors and the size of discounts. Following are some of their possibly more important findings.

Factors with the Most Explanatory Power

Certain factors were found to be well correlated with the size of discounts.

Size of Revenues.   Companies with higher revenues tended to have lower discounts.

Size of Earnings.   Companies with higher earnings were clearly associated with lower discounts.

Market Price Per Share.   Companies with higher prices per share tended to have lower discounts.

Price Stability.   Companies with lower standard deviations of trading price tended to have lower discounts.

Trading Volume.   Transactions where the size of the block represented a higher percentage of average trading volume tended to have higher discounts.

Value of Block.   Larger dollar value blocks tended to have lower discounts.

Factors with Some Explanatory Power

Several factors were found to be somewhat correlated with the size of discounts.

Revenue Growth.   There was some tendency for companies with higher 10-year compound revenue growth rates to have lower discounts.

Revenue Stability.   Higher revenue stability was somewhat correlated with lower discounts.

Earnings Growth.   The two quartiles with higher earnings growth rates had lower average discounts than the two quartiles with lower earnings growth rates.

Earnings Stability.   The most stable earnings were associated with lower discounts.

Factors with Minimum Explanatory Power

Some factors had little correlation with the size of discounts.

Debt Ratio.   There appeared to be no relationship between discounts seen in the four quartiles.

State of Market.   The data showed no significant relationship between the discounts during rising versus falling market conditions.

Exhibit 6.9 Relationship Between Earnings and Discount, Management Planning Study

Company	Earnings ($000)	Discount	Median	Average
Presidential Life Corporation	23,967	15.9%		
Crystal Oil Co.	9,113	24.1%		
Integrated Transportation Network Group, Inc.	7,869	54.9%		
AirTran Corp.	6,740	19.4%		
Telepictures Corp.	6,057	11.6%		
Starrett Housing Corp.	5,195	44.8%		
Medco Containment Services, Inc.	3,931	15.5%		
Nobel Education Dynamics, Inc.	3,906	19.3%	18.0%	21.1%
Ryan's Family Steak Houses, Inc. (11/20/85)	3,345	8.7%		
Ryan's Family Steak Houses, Inc. (3/21/85)	3,345	5.2%		
Angeles Corp.	3,095	19.6%		
ICN Pharmaceuticals, Inc.	2,967	10.5%		
North American Holding Corporation (a)	2,921	30.4%		
Gendex Corp.	2,901	16.7%		
50-Off Stores, Inc.	2,816	12.5%		
Sahlen & Associates, Inc.	2,064	27.5%		
REN Corporation-USA (10/1/92)	1,830	17.9%		
REN Corporation-USA (3/17/92)	1,830	29.3%		
Electro Nucleonics	1,791	24.8%		
Dense Pac Microsystems, Inc.	1,698	23.1%		
Sudbury Holdings, Inc.	1,635	46.5%		
Esmor Correctional Services, Inc.	1,543	32.6%		
Max & Erma's Restaurants, Inc.	1,371	12.7%	29.3%	28.8%
Total Research Corporation	1,124	39.0%		
ARC Capital	942	18.8%		
Ragen Precision Industries, Inc.	861	15.3%		
Velo-Bind, Inc.	841	19.5%		
Rentrak Corp.	822	32.5%		
Sym-Tek Systems, Inc.	780	31.6%		
Reuter Manufacturing, Inc.	749	38.5%		
Photographic Sciences Corporation	729	49.5%		
Western Digital Corp.	678	47.3%		
Newport Pharmaceuticals, Intl., Inc.	647	37.8%		
Unimed Pharmaceuticals, Inc.	625	15.8%		
Choice Drug Systems, Inc.	555	28.9%		

continued

Exhibit 6.9 Relationship Between Earnings and Discount, Management Planning Study—*continued*

Company	Earnings ($000)	Discount	Median	Average
Byers Communications Systems, Inc.	546	22.5%		
Pride Petroleum Services, Inc.	544	24.5%		
Interlink Electronics, Inc.	515	23.9%	28.9%	28.6%
Quality Care, Inc.	514	34.4%		
Noble Roman's, Inc.	491	17.2%		
Centennial Technologies, Inc.	464	2.8%		
Black Warrior Wireline Corp.	447	27.3%		
North Hills Electronics, Inc.	439	36.6%		
Anaren Microwave, Inc.	428	34.2%		
Chantal Pharmaceutical Corporation	406	44.8%		
Bioplasty, Inc.	399	31.1%		
Davox Corporation	385	46.4%		
Edmark Corp.	364	16.0%		
AW Computer Systems, Inc.	354	57.3%		
Quadrex Corp.	347	39.4%		
Superior Care, Inc.	336	41.9%		
HORIZON Pharmacies, Inc. (6/16/98)	327	19.1%		
Cucos, Inc.	272	18.8%	31.4%	32.0%
Besicorp Group, Inc.	265	57.6%		
Del Electronics Corporation	240	41.0%		
Harken Oil & Gas, Inc.	204	30.4%		
HORIZON Pharmacies, Inc. (10/23/97)	196	28.0%		
Air Express International Corp.	184	0.0%		
Biopool International, Inc.	141	12.4%		
Ion Laser Technology, Inc.	123	41.1%		
Blyth Holdings, Inc.	99	31.4%		

Note: (a) Class A common stock.
Source: Management Planning, Inc.

As this book went to press, we received a partial update of the Management Planning study. It included 61 transactions, with a low discount of 0% to a high of 58%. Exhibit 6.9 shows the relationship between the level of earnings and the size of the discount. Exhibit 6.10 shows the relationship between earnings stability and the size of the discount.

Exhibit 6.10 Relationship Between Earnings Stability and Discount, Management Planning Study

Company	Earnings Stability	Discount	Median	Average
Gendex Corp.	0.99	16.7%		
Integrated Transportation Network Group, Inc.	0.97	54.9%		
Esmor Correctional Services, Inc.	0.95	32.6%		
Centennial Technologies, Inc.	0.94	2.8%		
AirTran Corp.	0.90	19.4%		
Byers Communications Systems, Inc.	0.90	22.5%		
Ryan's Family Steak Houses, Inc. (11/20/85)	0.90	8.7%	16.7%	19.3%
Ryan's Family Steak Houses, Inc. (3/21/85)	0.90	5.2%		
Max & Erma's Restaurants, Inc.	0.87	12.7%		
HORIZON Pharmacies, Inc. (6/16/98)	0.85	19.1%		
Medco Containment Services, Inc.	0.84	15.5%		
North Hills Electronics, Inc.	0.81	36.6%		
Telepictures Corp.	0.81	11.6%		
50-Off Stores, Inc.	0.80	12.5%		
Cucos, Inc.	0.77	18.8%		
Ion Laser Technology, Inc.	0.71	41.1%		
Chantal Pharmaceutical Corporation	0.70	44.8%		
Electro Nucleonics	0.68	24.8%		
Quality Care, Inc.	0.68	34.4%		
Sudbury Holdings, Inc.	0.65	46.5%		
Velo-Bind, Inc.	0.65	19.5%		
Reuter Manufacturing, Inc.	0.64	38.5%	30.4%	29.8%
Biopool International, Inc.	0.63	12.4%		
North American Holding Corporation (a)	0.63	30.4%		
Ragen Precision Industries, Inc.	0.61	15.3%		
Rentrak Corp.	0.60	32.5%		
Edmark Corp.	0.57	16.0%		
Sahlen & Associates, Inc.	0.54	27.5%		
Crystal Oil Co.	0.42	24.1%		
Quadrex Corp.	0.41	39.4%		
Bioplasty, Inc.	0.38	31.1%		
Nobel Education Dynamics, Inc.	0.34	19.3%		

continued

Exhibit 6.10 Relationship Between Earnings Stability and Discount, Management Planning Study—*continued*

Company	Earnings Stability	Discount	Median	Average
Sym-Tek Systems, Inc.	0.34	31.6%		
Pride Petroleum Services, Inc.	0.31	24.5%		
Choice Drug Systems, Inc.	0.29	28.9%		
Interlink Electronics, Inc.	0.26	23.9%		
Anaren Microwave, Inc.	0.24	34.2%	24.5%	24.9%
Superior Care, Inc.	0.21	41.9%		
Total Research Corporation	0.15	39.0%		
Harken Oil & Gas, Inc.	0.13	30.4%		
ICN Pharmaceuticals, Inc.	0.11	10.5%		
Unimed Pharmaceuticals, Inc.	0.09	15.8%		
Air Express International Corp.	0.08	0.0%		
Angeles Corp.	0.08	19.6%		
Dense Pac Microsystems, Inc.	0.08	23.1%		
Del Electronics Corporation	0.08	41.0%		
Noble Roman's, Inc.	0.06	17.2%		
Photographic Sciences Corporation	0.06	49.5%		
Blyth Holdings, Inc.	0.04	31.4%		
ARC Capital	0.03	18.8%		
Besicorp Group, Inc.	0.03	57.6%		
REN Corporation-USA (10/1/92)	0.02	17.9%	37.8%	36.0%
REN Corporation-USA (3/17/92)	0.02	29.3%		
Starrett Housing Corp.	0.02	44.8%		
Davox Corporation	0.01	46.4%		
Black Warrior Wireline Corp.	0.00	27.3%		
AW Computer Systems, Inc.	0.00	57.3%		
Newport Pharmaceuticals, Intl., Inc.	0.00	37.8%		
Presidential Life Corporation	0.00	15.9%		
Western Digital Corp.	0.00	47.3%		
HORIZON Pharmacies, Inc. (10/23/97)	N.M.	28.0%		

Notes: (a) Class A common stock.
     N.M. Not meaningful.
Source: Management Planning, Inc.

Exhibit 6.11   Johnson Study

Total Net Income	Avg Discount
Negative	22.5%
$0 to $1M	26.0%
$1M to $10M	18.1%
+ $10M	6.3%

Total Sales	Avg Discount
$0 to $10M	23.5%
$10M to $50M	19.4%
$50M to $200M	17.7%
+$200M	13.0%

Transaction Size	Avg Discount
$0 to $5M	26.7%
$5M to $10M	20.9%
$10M to $25M	17.0%
+$25M	10.8%

Net Income Margin	Avg Discount
Negative	22.5%
0% to 5%	23.7%
5% to 10%	15.2%
+10%	11.6%

Source: Bruce Johnson, "Quantitative Support for Discounts for Lack of Marketability," *Business Valuation Review* (December 1999): 152–155.

JOHNSON STUDY

Bruce Johnson, of the firm Munroe, Park & Johnson, studied 72 private placement transactions that occurred in 1991 through 1995.[12] This was the first half decade after the Rule 144 restrictions were relaxed. The range was a 10% premium to a 60% discount with an average discount for these 72 transactions of 20%.

The study analyzed four factors that might influence the size of the discount: (1) positive net income, (2) sales volume, (3) transaction value, and (4) net income strength. The results of his study are shown in Exhibit 6.11.

COLUMBIA FINANCIAL ADVISORS STUDY

As of this writing, the only restricted stock study undertaken since the Rule 144 holding period was reduced to one year in 1997 is the one headed by Kathryn Aschwald at Columbia Financial Advisors, Inc. (CFA).[13]

Their study was divided into two parts: January 1, 1996, through April 30, 1997 (before the reduction in the Rule 144 holding period), and May 1, 1997, through December 31, 1998 (after the one-year holding period became effective, April 29, 1997).

They identified 23 transactions for the 1996–April 1997 period, with discounts ranging from .8 to 67.5%, with a mean of 21%. For the May 1997–December 1998 period, they identified 15 transactions, with a range of 0 to 30%, and a mean of 13%, and a median of 9%.

As explained by Kathryn Aschwald, author of the CFA study:

> Many "rumblings" in the appraisal community have centered around the fact that discounts for restricted stock have been declining, and many appear to be concerned about what this might mean in valuing privately held securities. It makes perfect sense that the discounts for restricted securities have generally declined since 1990 as the market (and liquidity) for theses [sic] securities has increased due to Rule 144A and the shortening of restricted stock holding periods beginning April 29, 1997. Thus, while the newer studies are specifically relevant for determining the appropriate discounts for restricted securities, the studies conducted after 1990 are not relevant for purposes of determining discounts for lack of marketability for privately held stock, because they reflect the increased liquidity in the market for restricted securities. Such increased liquidity is not present in privately held securities.[14]

SUMMARY

The many independent restricted stock studies, encompassing hundreds of transactions, are remarkably consistent over time. They indicate discounts in the 33 to 35% range, up until the SEC started loosening the restrictions in 1990. After that, discounts dropped, reflecting greater liquidity, especially after the holding period was reduced from two years to one year in 1997.

The studies do not address the most important factor influencing the magnitudes of discounts, that is, the level of dividends or cash distributions. This is because almost none of the companies involved in the studies paid dividends. (*The Partnership Spectrum* studies described in Chapter 8 make the point, however, that distributions are a major factor.) Nonetheless, the restricted stock studies are helpful in identifying several other factors that do and do not impact the size of discounts for lack of marketability. Chapter 8 examines the impact of various factors in some detail.

Notes

1. "Discounts Involved in Purchases of Common Stock (1966–1969)," *Institutional Investor Study Report of the Securities and Exchange Commission,* H.R.Doc.N.64, part 5, 92nd Cong., 1st Session, 1971, 2444–2456, available at BVLibrary.com.

2. Milton Gelman, "An Economist-Financial Analyst's Approach to Valuing Stock of a Closely-Held Company," *Journal of Taxation* (June 1972): 353–354.

3. *Howard v. Shay,* 1993 U.S. Dist. Lexis 20153 (C.D. Cal. 1993), *rev'd* and *remanded by,* 100 F.3d 1484 (9th Cir. 1996), *cert. denied,* 520 U.S. 1237 (1997).

4. Robert R. Trout, "Estimation of the Discount Associated with the Transfer of Restricted Securities," *Taxes—The Tax Magazine* (June 1977): 381–385.

5. Robert E. Moroney, "Most Courts Overvalue Closely Held Stocks," *Taxes—The Tax Magazine* (March 1973): 144–156.

6. J. Michael Maher, "Discounts for Lack of Marketability for Closely Held Business Interests," *Taxes—The Tax Magazine* (September 1976): 562–571.

7. William F. Pittock and Charles H. Stryker, "Revenue Ruling 77-287 Revisited," *SRC Quarterly Reports,* vol. 10, no. 1 (Spring 1983): 1–3.

8. William L. Silber, "Discounts on Restricted Stock: The Impact of Illiquidity on Stock Prices," *Financial Analysts Journal* (July–August 1991): 60–64.

9. Lance S. Hall and Timothy C. Polacek, "Strategies for Obtaining the Largest Valuation Discounts," *Estate Planning* (January/February 1994): 38–44.

10. Robert P. Oliver and Roy H. Meyers, "Discounts Seen in Private Placements of Restricted Stock: The Management Planning, Inc. Long-Term Study (1980–1996)," Chapter 5 in *Handbook of Advanced Business Valuation,* Robert F. Reilly and Robert P. Schweihs, eds. (New York: McGraw-Hill, 2000). Used with permission.

11. Ibid.

12. Bruce Johnson, "Restricted Stock Discounts, 1991–95," *Shannon Pratt's Business Valuation Update* (March 1999): 1–3; "Quantitative Support for Discounts for Lack of Marketability," *Business Valuation Review* (Dec. 1999): 152–155.

13. Kathryn F. Aschwald, "Restricted Stock Discounts Decline as Result of 1-Year Holding Period," *Shannon Pratt's Business Valuation Update* (May 2000): 1–5.

14. *Ibid.,* pp. 4–5.

Chapter 7

John Emory Pre–Initial Public Offering Discount for Lack of Marketability Studies—Complete Underlying Data

Study #1: January 1980–June 1981
Study #2: January 1985–June 1986
Study #3: August 1987–January 1989
Study #4: February 1989–July 1990
Study #5: August 1990–January 1992
Study #6: February 1992–July 1993
Study #7: January 1994–June 1995
Study #8: November 1995–April 1997
Study #9: Dot-Com Companies, May 1997–March 2000
Summary
Notes

Chapter 5 described three sets of "pre-IPO" marketability studies:

1. Willamette Management Associates
2. John Emory (Baird & Co.)
3. Valuation Advisors

Of these, only the John Emory series releases the complete details of the actual transactions. This chapter brings all of the transactions for the series of nine studies together in one place. For the convenience of subscribers who wish to perform various statistical analyses across the data in the nine studies, the data are also accessible electronically at BVLibrary.com.

John Emory Sr. originated the studies while at Baird & Co., a Milwaukee investment banking firm, where for many years he served as vice president in the corporate finance department, in charge of appraisal services. He has continued the studies after leaving Baird & Co. through his business valuation firm, Emory Business Valuation, LLC, also in Milwaukee. He is joined there by his son, John Emory Jr., and F. R. Dengel III, both of whom also participate in updating the studies.

A complete list of the articles accompanying each of the studies, most of which were published in *Business Valuation Review,* is contained in the bibliography at Appendix A.

The essential methodology for the studies, as explained in Chapter 5, has remained the same across the entire series of the first eight studies. In summary, the company had to be financially sound, and the private transaction had to occur within five months prior to the IPO date. In the first eight studies, the following were eliminated:

- Development-stage companies
- Companies with a history of operating losses
- Companies with an IPO price under $5 per share

The criteria were relaxed and some additional analyses were included in the ninth study involving dot-com companies from May 1997 through March 2000.

Sources for the transactions were prospectuses in which Baird & Co. was a member of the underwriting syndicate or transactions for which Emory had otherwise obtained prospectuses.

The data are presented in chronological order, from the earliest through the latest.

STUDY #1: JANUARY 1980–JUNE 1981

The final two paragraphs of the article accompanying the first study summarize its conclusions:

> The final question to be answered is that if these kinds of discounts are appropriate for promising situations where marketability is probable, but not a certainty, how much greater should discounts be for the typical company's stock that has no marketability, little if any chance of ever becoming marketable, and is in a neutral to unpromising situation? The inability to get out of a once promising investment that has turned sour is something to be avoided. A minority investor cannot control the destiny of his investment and may well be reduced to watching its value decline to nothing. I speak from personal experience.
>
> It is apparent that lack of marketability is one of the more important aspects to value, and the marketplace itself emphasizes this point. The size of discount for lack of marketability depends on the individual situation and is governed by the promise of the company and the likelihood of future marketability.[1]

The basic theme has not changed since.

The data for the first study is contained in Exhibit 7.1. Ninety-seven prospectuses were reviewed, resulting in 13 qualifying transactions.

STUDY #2: JANUARY 1985–JUNE 1986

The text accompanying the second study is similar to that accompanying the first. Details of the transactions are shown in Exhibit 7.2. This study encompassed 130 prospectuses, this time yielding 21 qualifying transactions.

The average discounts, a mean and median of 43%, are significantly lower than those shown in the first study. As the article points out, the first study was conducted at a time of very depressed market conditions, while the second study was done at a time of record market highs and a more active IPO market.

STUDY #3: AUGUST 1987–JANUARY 1989

The third study encompassed the October 1987 stock market crash. Nevertheless, the average discount of 45% was very close to the 43% discount found in the second study.

The article accompanying this study observes that for several months after the crash there was little IPO activity and that the postcrash IPOs were of significantly increased quality and size. Emory also notes that there was little difference in discounts from the pre- versus post-October 19, 1987 periods. In addition, he remarks that they found little difference in discounts based on the equity size of the issuer. The transactions data are shown in Exhibit 7.3. A review of 98 prospectuses produced 27 qualifying transactions.

STUDY #4: FEBRUARY 1989–JULY 1990

In this study, the average discount again was 45%. Market conditions had not changed drastically. After eliminations from 157 IPO prospectuses studied, only 23 qualifying transactions remained. The qualifying transactions are detailed in Exhibit 7.4.

STUDY #5: AUGUST 1990–JANUARY 1992

This study covered 35 qualifying transactions out of 266 IPO prospectuses reviewed. The mean discount was 42% and the median 40%. Transactions are listed in Exhibit 7.5.

In the accompanying article, Emory comments that, after his eliminations, all the companies were promising in nature, and their securities had good potential for becoming readily marketable. Why else would a bona fide investment banker pursue an underwriting commitment?

The point, again, of course, is the question of how much greater the discount should be for the typical privately held minority block with little or no marketability and little or no chance of ever attaining any marketability.

Exhibit 7.1 Fair Market Value Transactions Which Occurred Within Five Months Prior to an Initial Public Offering as Disclosed in the Prospectus, January 1, 1980–June 30, 1981

Company	Principal Business	Date and Price of Last Transaction Prior to Offering Date (1)	Offering Date Price to Public	Premium from Prior Transaction
Alpha Microsystems	Microcomputer systems systems	2/81 56.00	6/18/81 $15.00	−150%
Anthem Electronics, Inc.	Semiconductor distributor	1/80 6.00	3/04/80 13.50	−125
Apple Computer, Inc.	Personal computer systems	8/80 5.44	12/12/80 22.00	−304
Computer Magnetics Corporation	Transformer mfg.	1/81 3.90	4/14/81 8.00	−105
Diagnostic/Retrieval Systems, Inc.	Military computer systems	9/80 1.28	1/22/81 10.00	−681
Emulex Corporation	Disk/tape controllers	1/81 1.73	3/26/81 12.00	−594
Intergraph Corporation	Computer graphic systems	1/81 4.17	4/07/81 18.00	−332
Inter-Tel	Key phone systems	12/80 12.00	2/05/81 12.50	−4
Kimbark Oil & Gas Company	Oil & gas exploration & production	3/81 10.44	6/04/81 13.00	−25
Monolithic Memories	Computer circuits; bipolar	3/80 4.80	8/06/80 21.00	−338
Management Science America, Inc.	Computer software packages	2/81 7.75	4/08/81 16.00	−106
Network Systems Corporation	Ultra high-speed computer networks	9/80 5.00	2/25/81 14.62	−192
SEI Corporation	Services to bank trust departments	1/81 4.01	3/25/81 17.00	−324
Average				
Median				

(1) In all cases, the fair market value was determined by the Board of Directors on or near the date of the last transaction prior to the offering.

(2) Offering price divided by fair market value on date of last transaction.

(3) 1 minus (last transaction price divided by offering price).

(4) (Book value after offer, minus book value before offer), divided by book value after offer.

Offer Multiple (2)	Percent Discount From Public Offer (3)	Offer Contribution to Equity (4)	Book Value Before Offer (Millions)	Book Value After Offer (Millions)	Nature of Transaction Prior to Public Offering
2.50x	60%	84%	1.963	12.050	Sale at F.M.V
2.25	56	26	5.233	7.064	F.M.V. of options.
4.04	75	76	25.949	108.087	Sale-arm's length negotiations.
2.05	51	56	2.768	6.290	F.M.V. of sold shares.
7.81	87	56	1.951	4.391	Option price at least 100% of F.M.V.
6.94	86	70	1.925	6.429	Option price at least 100% of F.M.V.
4.32	77	63	14.678	39.683	Sale of shares at fair value.
1.04	4	76	2.174	8.875	Option price at least 100% of F.M.V.
1.25	20	47	5.731	10.713	Option price at least 100% of F.M.V.
4.38	77	57	14.380	33.611	Sale of shares at F.M.V.— valuation at unspecified date in 1980.
2.07	52	56	10.979	24.766	F.M.V. determined for tax purposes.
2.92	66	61	7.003	17.803(5)	Option price at F.M.V.—
4.24	76	90	1.757	11.960(6)	Option price at F.M.V.
	60%				
	66%				

(5) Assumes net proceeds to the company of $13.50 per share.
(6) Assumes net proceeds to the company of $16.13 per share.
F.M.V. Fair Market Value.
Source: John D. Emory, Sr., *ASA Valuation* (June 1986): 64–65.

Exhibit 7.2 Fair Market Value Transactions Which Occurred Within Five Months Prior to an Initial Public Offering as Disclosed in the Prospectus, January 1, 1985–June 30, 1986

Company	Principal Business	Offering Date	Price to Public (1)	Last Transaction Date	Price
Bridge Communications Inc.	Local Area Network Systems	18-Apr-85	$12.000	01-Feb-85 (2)	$2.000
Sbarro Inc.	Italian Restaurants	08-May-85	$10.375	01-Mar-85 (2)	$8.000
Carver Corporation	Audio System Components	09-May-85	$11.000	01-Jan-85 (2)	$7.440
Central Sprinkler Corp.	Sprinkler Heads	17-May-85	$12.750	01-Dec-84 (2)	$10.800
VM Software Inc.	Software Products	29-May-85	$16.000	01-Jan-85 (2)	$5.750
Reebok International Ltd.	Athletic Footwear	26-Jul-85	$17.000	06-Jun-85	$5.560
Home Club, Inc.	Membership Warehouses	29-Oct-85	$9.000	10-Sep-85	$6.300
Sandy Corporation	Media-Based Programs	19-Nov-85	$13.000	01-Oct-85 (2)	$6.000
Mercury General Corp.	Seall Auto Insurance	20-Nov-85	$19.000	08-Oct-85	$10.000
Gemcraft Inc	Family Residential Units	13-Dec-85	$8.000	15-Aug-85	$2.000
Century Communications Corp	Cable Systems	11-Feb-86	$12.500	05-Dec-85	$12.000
General Computer Corp	Integrated Computer Systems	04-Mar-86	$13.000	08-Dec-85	$7.800
Poly-Tech Inc	Trash Bags	11-Mar-86	$11.000	01-Dec-85 (2)	$7.500
Capital Wire and Cable Corp	Wire and Cable	29-Apr-86	$13.000	01-Mar-86 (2)	$5.000
Sterling Inc	Fine Jewelry Retailer	14-May-86	$15,500	01-Mar-86 (2)	$10.400
Sigma Designs Inc	IBM Enhancement Products	15-May-86	$5.750	25-Mar-86	$ 2.790 (7)
Modular Technology Inc.	Nonresidential Structures	29-May-86	$7.250	01-Apr-86 (2)	$7.000
Hana Biologics Inc	Cell Biology	05-Jun-86	$10.000	01-Jan-86 (2)	$6.250
Marietta Corporation	Guest Amenity Programs	11-Jun-86	$11.500	01-Mar-86 (2)	$6.600
Cytogen Corporation	Biochemical Systems	18-Jun-86	$13.000	01-Mar-86 (2)	$7.000
Health Management Assoc. Inc.	Health Care Services	20-Jun-86	$10.000	26-Feb-86	$4.500
	Average Values				
	Median				
Study January 1, 1980 to June 30, 1981:					
	Average				
	Median				

F.M.V. Fair Market Value.

(1) In all cases, the fair market value was determined by the Board of Directors on or near the date of the last transaction prior to the offering.

(2) No day indicated in prospectus, only month.

Premium from Prior Trans.	Offer Multiple (3)	Percent Discount From Public Offer (4)	Offer Contri- bution to Equity (5)	Book Value Prior to Offering (Millions)	Book Value After Offering (Millions)	Nature of Transaction Prior to Public Offering
500%	6.00 X	83%	64%	13.076	35.837	Options granted
30%	1.30	23%	66%	3.865	11.249	Shares sold
48%	1.48	32%	69%	2.578	8.377	Options granted
18%	1.18	15%	64%	2.877	7.948	Shares sold
178%	2.78	64%	85%	1.425	9.359	Options granted
206%	3.06	67%	69%	18.843	60.840	Shares issued
43%	1.43	30%	33%	34.337	50.978	Options granted
117%	2.17	54%	13%	9.778	11.300	Shares sold
90%	1.90	47%	39%	54.800	89.978	Options granted
300%	4.00	75%	39%	9.566	15.666	Options granted
4%	1.04	4%	77%	7.223	31.409	Options granted
67%	1.67	40%	58%	2.787	6.671	Options granted
47%	1.47	32%	76%	3.166	13.198	Shares purchased
160%	2.60	62%	61%	7.339	18.879	Option granted
49%	1.49	33%	75%	5.56	22.309	Options granted
106%	2.06	51%	76%	1.523	6.323	Options exer- cised at NRV
4%	1.04	3%	78%	2.398	10.746	Options granted
60%	1.60	38%	86%	2.119	14.827	Performance units
74%	1.74	43%	74%	2.934	11.206	Options granted
86%	1.86	46%	72%	13.87	49.331	Options granted
122%	2.22	55%	56%	10.468	23.668	Options exercised at FMW
	2.10 X	43%				
	1.74 X	43%				
	3.60 X	60%				
	2.92 X	66%				

(3) Offering price divided by fair market value on date of last transaction.

(4) 1 minus (last transaction price divided by offering price).

(5) (Book value after offer, minus book value before offer), divided by book value after offer.

(6) Net Realized Value = Fair Market Value less Price Paid.

(7) Computed from (6).

Source: John D. Emory, Sr., *Business Valuation Review* (December 1986):14.

Exhibit 7.3 Fair Market Value Transactions Which Occurred Within Five Months Prior to an Initial Public Offering as Disclosed in the Prospectus, August 1987–January 1989

Company	Principal Business	Last Transaction Date	Last Transaction Price	Public Offering Date	Public Offering Price	(1) % Discount From Public Offering Price	Book Value Prior To Offering (Millions)	(2) Type of Transaction	Underwriter (Lead)
American Power Conversion Corp.	Power Supply Products	4/88	$3.08	7/88	$7.50	59%	$2.3	Sale	Josepthal
ARIX Corp.	Computer Systems	7/88	$5.25	10/88	$7.50	30%	$23.8	Options	Bear S.
BMC Softwear, Inc.	Software Products	7/88	$7.50	8/88	$9.00	16%	$10.5	Sale	Alex. B.
Cetex Teleman-agement, Inc.	Telecom Man. Ser.	11/87	$5.25	4/88	$9.50	45%	$17.2	Options	Alex. B.
Conner Periphals, Inc.	Winchester Disc. Dr.	4/88	$7.00	4/88	$8.00	13%	$45.6	Options	Shearson
Dell Computer Corp.	Mfg. Personal Computers	1/88	$6.45	6/88	$8.50	24%	$32.4	Sale	Goldman
Egghead, Inc.	Retail Computer Software	4/88	$12.50	6/88	$17.00	26%	$38.0	Options	Donaldson L.
Flextronics, Inc.	Electronics Contract Mfg.	4/88	$5.00	9/87	$10.00	50%	$21.2	Options	Goldman
Genus, Inc.	Semiconductor Equipment	6/88	$2.50	11/88	$5.00	50%	$17.7	Options	Alex. B.
Gitano Group, Inc.	Apparel	8/88	$10.00	9/88	$20.50	51%	$62.3	Sale	Goldman
Gaylord Container Corp.	Paper Pack. Prod.	3/88	$3.71	6/88	$20.50	82%	$68.4	Options	Salomon
H.H.B. Systems, Inc.	Electric Prod. Equipment	6/87	$8.00(3)	10/87	$12.00	33%	$8.6	Sale	Alex. B.
ISOETEC Commu-nications, Inc.	Microprocessor Systems	4/87	$6.00	10/87	$10.00	40%	$23.4	Options	Smith B.
Kinetic Concepts, Inc.	Rent Medical Beds	2/88	$8.00	6/88	$10.50	24%	$12.2	Sale	Morgan S.

Company	Business	Date	Price	Date	Price	%	$ Value	Type	Underwriter
Maxim Integrated Products, Inc.	Mfg. Integr. Circuits	10/87	$2.67	2/88	$5.50	51%	$12.5	Options	Montgomery
Multicolor Corporation	Printer	4/87	$6.32	8/87	$13.25	52%	$2.0	Options	Bradford
Norton Enterprises, Inc.	Trucking	5/87	$8.00	9/87	$12.00	33%	$5.6	Options	Alex. B.
Nuwest Industries, Inc.	Fertilizers	5/88	$2.80	10/88*	$13.50	80%	$53.1	Sale	Dillon Reed
The Office Club, Inc.	Retailer	7/88	$5.00	12/88	$9.00	45%	$8.2	Options	Salomon
Phoenix Technologies, Inc.	Systems Softwear	3/88	$4.64	6/88	$15.00	69%	$8.2	Sale	Montgomery
Selfix, Inc.	Mfg. Home Products	7/88	$6.75	10/88	$7.00	4%	$8.2	Options	Landenburg T.
Silk Greenhouse, Inc.	Retailer	11/87	$2.55	5/88	$11.00	73%	$2.0	Options	Robertson
Synoptics Communications, Inc.	LAN Systems	4/88	$4.06	8/88	$13.50	70%	$8.1	Sale	Morgan S.
Timberjack Corp.	Logging Equipment	2/88	$5.00	5/88	$12.00	58%	$10.0	Options	Kidder P.
Weitek	Supply Circuits	4/88	$2.75	9/88	$10.00	72%	$10.5	Options	Morgan S.
Winston Furniture Company, Inc.	Mfg. Furniture	6/87	$8.00	8/87	$14.00	43%	$3.9	Options	Thomson Mc.
Wainwright Bank & Trust	Bank	8/88	$12.50	10/88	$15.75	21%	$19.3	Options	Landenburg T.
Average	: Mean					45%	$19.4MM		
	: Median					45%	$12.2		
Study January 1, 1985 to June 30, 1986	: Mean					43%	$9.2		
	: Median					43%	$5.6		
Study January 1, 1980 to June 30, 1981	: Mean					60%	$7.4		
	: Median					66%	$5.2		

(1) 1 Minus (last transaction price divided by offering price).
(2) All Options granted were stated to be at the Common Stock's fair market value.
(3) Effective.
*Started trading Oct. 24 under an exclusion. $13.50 is lowest price in subsequent month.
Source: John D. Emory, Sr., *Business Valuation Review* (June 1989): 57.

Exhibit 7.4 Fair Market Value Transactions Which Occurred Within Five Months Prior to an Initial Public Offering as Disclosed in the Prospectus, February 1989–July 1990

Company	Principal Business	Last Transaction Date	Last Transaction Price	Public Offering Date	Public Offering Price	(1) % Discount from Public Offering Price	Book Value Prior to Offering (millions)	(2) Type of Transaction	Underwriter (lead)
Allied Clinical Laboratories, Inc.	Clinical testing labs	4/90	$ 3.34	7/90	$13.00	74%	$ 19.6	Options	Alex. Brown
BE Avionics, Inc.	Mfg passenger control units	1/90	0.81	4/90	7.00	88	3.4	Options	PaineWebber
Bird Medical Technologies, Inc.	Respiratory care	6/90	7.50	8/90	8.00	6	7.6	Options	Smith Barney
BTi-Biomagnetic Technologies	Biomagnetic imaging	5/89	5.40	7/89	9.00	40	7.4	Options	PaineWebber
BTU International, Inc.	Thermal processing equip.	10/88	3.50	2/89	8.00	56	10.4	Sale	Smith Barney
Crest Industries, Inc.	Dist. home impr. products	1/90	4.80	6/90	6.75	29	2.6	Options	Raymond James
Fingerhut Companies, Inc.	Direct mail marketer	11/89	10.91	4/90	16.50	34	295.8	Sale	Smith Barney
Gehl Company	Mfg. ag. & const. equipment	8/89	9.10	11/89	14.00	35	46.1	Options	RW Baird
Goal Systems International, Inc.	Software	4/89	8.00	5/89	9.75	18	31.3	Options	Morgan Stanley
Hologic, Inc.	X-Ray systems	1/90	8.50	3/90	14.00	39	1.6	Options	Hambrecht & Quist
KnowledgeWare, Inc.	Engineering software	8/89	10.35	10/89	12.50	17	10.8	Options	Montgomery Sec.
Lechters, Inc.	Specialty retailer	6/89	13.30	7/89	20.50	35	27.5	Options	Goldman Sachs
Martech USA, Inc.	Pollution & env. services	11/89	5.00	12/89	10.00	50	4.4	Options	PaineWebber
Modtech, Inc.	Modular pre-fab classrooms	4/90	6.00	7/90	10.00	40	6.9	Options	Seidler Amdec

Company	Description								
Neogen Corporation	Agricultural biotech	6/89	0.32	8/89	5.00	94	1.7	Options	Roney & Co.
Neurogen Corporation	Genetic engineering prod.	7/89	4.00	10/89	6.00	33	6.4	Options	Allen & Co.
Newbridge Networks Corporation	Telecommunications prod.	2/89	4.75	7/89	10.50	55	51.0	Sale	Smith Barney
O'Charley's, Inc.	Restaurants	5/90	5.00	7/90	9.00	44	3.4	Options	Alex. Brown
Pharmacy Management Services	Medical containment serv.	12/89	9.00	4/90	12.00	25	3.4	Options	Rbrtsn Stephens
Sequoia Systems, Inc.	Computer systems	9/89	6.50	3/90	9.50	32	25.8	Options	Merrill Lynch
Sierra Tucson Companies, Inc.	Drug rehab facilities	8/89	7.00	10/89	12.00	42	2.2	Options	Oppenheimer
Staples, Inc.	Office prod. superstores	1/89	9.00	4/89	19.00	53	20.6	Options	Goldman Sachs
TETRA Technologies, Inc.	Recycling services	12/89	1.40	4/90	10.00	86	13.8	Options	PaineWebber
Study February 1, 1989 to July 31, 1990 (3)	:Mean					45	26.2		
	:Median					40	7.6		
Study August 1, 1987 to January 31, 1989 (4)	:Mean					45	19.4		
	:Median					45	12.2		
Study January 1, 1985 to June 30, 1986 (5)	:Mean					43	9.2		
	:Median					43	5.6		
Study January 1, 1980 to June 30, 1981 (6)	:Mean					60	7.4		
	:Median					66	5.2		

(1) 1 Minus (last transaction price divided by offering price).
(2) All Options granted were stated to be at the Common Stock's fair market value or reasonably should have been.
(3) 23 Companies.
(4) 27 Companies.
(5) 21 Companies.
(6) 13 Companies.

Source: John D. Emory, Sr., *Business Valuation Review* (December 1990):116.

121

Exhibit 7.5 Fair Market Value Transactions Which Occurred Within Five Months Prior to an Initial Public Offering as Disclosed in the Prospectus, August 1990–January 1992

Company	Principal Business	Last Transaction Date	Last Transaction Price	Public Offering Date	Public Offering Price	(1) % Discount from Public Offering Price	Book Value Prior to Offering (Millions)	(2) Type of Transaction	Underwriter (Lead)
AG Services of America	Supplies farm inputs	5/91	$ 7.00/sh.	8/91	$ 8.25/sh.	15%	$ 4.5	Options	Josephthal
American Dental Laser	Dental laser systems	3/91	7.48	6/91	13.00	42	3.9	Options	Dain Bosworth
Applied Extrusion Tech	Thermoplastic nets	4/91	7.00	6/91	9.50	26	8.0	Options	PaineWebber
Au Bon Pain Co, Inc	Bakery cafe chain	1/91	7.00	6/91	9.00	22	22.2	Options	Morgan Stanley
Brooktree Corp	Integrated circuits	12/90	9.00	4/91	12.00	25	40.9	Sale	Smith Barney
Coastal Healthcare Grp	Physician management	1/91	2.125	6/91	11.50	82	10.5	Options	Smith Barney
Computer Petrol Corp	Energy information	1/91	3.50	5/91	5.00	30	1.3	Options	Kinnard
Crest Industries Inc	Home improvement dist	1/90	4.80	6/90	6.75	29	2.6	Options	Raymond James
Danek Group Inc	Spinal implant devices	3/91	7.73	5/91	15.00	48	7.5	Options	Smith Barney
Diversicare Inc	Health care services	10/91	7.50	11/91	11.50	35	7.4	Sale	Bear Stearns
Duracell Inter Inc	Batteries	3/91	8.50	5/91	15.00	43	342.3	Options	Merrill Lynch
The Failure Grp Inc	Consulting firm	6/90	9.22	8/90	13.00	29	19.3	Options	Prudential Bache
Haemonetics Corp	Blood collection	1/91	11.11	5/91	22.00	49	67.5	Options	First Boston
Hi-Lo Automotive Inc	Auto aftermarket parts	12/90	6.00	5/91	13.00	54	27.1	Options	Dillon Reed
IDEXX Laboratories Inc	Mfg biotech systems	4/91	13.00	6/91	15.00	13	14.5	Options	Lehman
Little Switzerland Inc	Specialty retailer	6/91	10.00	7/91	12.00	17	27.0	Options	First Boston
Liuski International Inc	Microcomputer distributor	5/91	5.25	8/91	7.00	25	4.6	Options	Vantage

Company	Business	Date	Price	Date	Value	(6)*	Prem/(Def)	Type	Underwriter
Lunar Corporation	Bone disease products	5/90	12.75	8/90	12.00		5.9	Options	Smith Barney
Menley & James Inc	Mfg pharmaceuticals	11/91	7.89	1/92	13.00	39	(14.1) d	Options	Smith Barney
Meris Laboratories Inc	Clinical laboratory	6/91	6.00	7/91	9.25	35	4.3	Sale	Robertson Stevens
NAMIC USA Corp	Medical products	8/91	5.00	11/91	18.00	72	12.6	Options	First Boston
OESI Power Corp	Geothermal projects	1/91	8.00	5/91	14.00	43	9.0	Options	Kidder Peabody
Perrigo Co.	Mfg pharmaceuticals	7/91	3.00	12/91	16.00	81	39.0	Options	Morgan Stanley
Platinum Technology	Software products	2/91	7.15	4/91	15.00	52	4.1	Options	Hambrecht & Quist
Sun TV and Appliance	Retailer	2/91	3.20	7/91	10.00	68	25.6	Options	Montgomery
TakeCare Inc	HMO	1/91	10.00	3/91	19.00	47	20.5	Options	First Boston
Tanknology Envrnmntl	Environmental services	1/91	3.00	6/91	11.00	73	15.3	Options	First Boston
Target Therapeutics Inc	Disposable med devices	12/91	8.75	1/92	18.00	51	5.8	Options	Alex. Brown
Thermo Electron Tech	High tech R & D	4/91	8.33	7/91	12.00	31	13.0	Options	Lehman
Trimble Navigation	Satellite navigation	2/90	2.00	7/90	10.00	80	5.7	Options	Smith Barney
TRM Copy Ctrs Corp	Self-serve copiers	10/91	6.00	12/91	8.50	29	5.0	Options	Montgomery
Valley Systems Inc	Industrial cleaning	1/91	3.00	6/91	5.00	40	2.9	Options	Laidlaw
Video Lottery Tech	Video lottery products	2/91	.77	7/91	14.00	94	7.9	Payment	Montgomery
Wellfleet Commun	Internetworking products	6/91	9.75	8/91	17.00	43	12.1	Options	Goldman Sachs
Zilog Inc	Integrated circuits	1/91	8.00	2/91	11.00	27	29.0	Options	Alex. Brown
Mean						42 %			
Median						40 %			

* premium
d deficit

(1) 1 Minus (last transaction price divided by offering price).
(2) All options granted were stated to be at the Common Stock's fair market value or reasonably should have been.
Source: John D. Emory, Sr., *Business Valuation Review* (December 1992):210.

STUDY #6: FEBRUARY 1992–JULY 1993

In this study, the number of qualifying transactions jumped to 54, out of 443 prospectuses reviewed. The mean discount was 45% and the median 44%.

In the article accompanying this study, Emory points out that 32 of the 173 transactions in the first six studies were actual sales, most of the rest being options granted at fair market value. In general, actual sales transaction occurred at greater discounts than options. The six-study average discount for the 32 sales transactions was 49%, and the median was 52.5%. Details are shown in Exhibit 7.6

The article also includes an anecdotal example of the reality of sales of closely held stock at significant discounts from IPO prices:

> As an example of the value of marketability, on July 21, 1993, Robert W. Baird & Co. Incorporated, my employer, was the managing underwriter in an initial public offering of 2,150,000 shares of Starcraft Automotive Corporation at a price of $10.00 per share. On March 29, 1993, about four months before the IPO and with full knowledge of the IPO, in a disclosed and arms-length negotiated transaction, a principal holding 50% of the voting stock, which represented 42% of the economic interest of Starcraft, negotiated a sale of 738,400 shares of his Starcraft stock to Starcraft for a price of $5.42 per share, a discount of 46% from the offering price. This same individual also sold another 486,000 shares less than four months later in the IPO at $10.00 per share and then he retired.[2]

STUDY #7: JANUARY 1994–JUNE 1995

The seventh study covered 314 prospectuses, yielding 46 qualifying transactions. The mean and median discounts were 45%. Details are shown in Exhibit 7.7.

STUDY #8: NOVEMBER 1995–APRIL 1997

This study covered 732 prospectuses and found 91 qualifying transactions in a strong stock market and a market for IPOs that could be considered hot.

Again, the actual sales transactions were at slightly larger discounts than the group as a whole. The total group of transactions is shown in Exhibit 7.8, and a separate table showing only the sales transactions is presented as Exhibit 7.9.

Because more companies were arriving at the IPO market with no earnings, and in some cases with no revenues, the 91 transactions tabulated are net after a final cut of 38 transactions that otherwise would have met the study's criteria. This was done to keep the companies used comparable in quality to those in prior studies. The mean and median discounts for the 38 transactions eliminated were 48% and 47%, respectively, versus the 43% and 42% found in the primary study.

STUDY #9: DOT-COM COMPANIES, MAY 1997–MARCH 2000

The latest study differed from its predecessors in four major respects:

1. Only companies with "com" in their names were included.
2. The study covered a 35-month period as opposed to the 18-month periods of each of the eight earlier studies.
3. All transactions were actual sales, whereas the earlier studies also included options issued.
4. Most of the companies did not have earnings.

There were 53 sales transactions used in the study. These included 42 convertible preferred stock transactions and 11 common stock transactions. Many of the transactions involved private equity funds, where the use of convertible preferred stock rather than straight common stock is the typical practice. Most such stocks automatically converted to common at the IPO date. The overall mean and median discounts for the group of 53 were 54%, as detailed in Exhibit 7.10A.

The study also compiled and tabulated transactions and average discounts by SIC code. These results are shown in Exhibit 7.10B.

A phenomenon of this group of dot-com IPOs was the tendency of their stocks to experience significant price increases following the IPO. Consequently, in addition to the pre-IPO transaction price relative to the IPO price, the study also related the transaction price to the stock price at the close of the IPO date and the stock prices 90 days and 180 days after the IPO. The average results are shown below. The details for each transaction are shown in Exhibit 7.10C.

Pre-IPO Discounts From[3]

	IPO Price	IPO Date Close	Price 90 Days After IPO	Price 180 Days After IPO
Mean	54%	67%	66%	56%
Median	54%	70%	79%	77%

If there were multiple sale transactions within the five-month period prior to the IPO, the earliest transaction within that time frame was used and subsequent transactions were detailed in footnotes, as shown in Exhibit 7.10D. As would be expected, the discount tended to drop as the transaction occurred closer to the IPO.

To determine how the discounts changed relative to revenues, equity, offer size, market capitalization, or loss size, the study examined the average of the top and bottom

Exhibit 7.6 Fair Market Value Transactions Which Occurred Within Five Months Prior to an Initial Public Offering as Disclosed in the Prospectus, February 1992–July 1993

Company	Principal Business	Last Transaction		Public Offering		(1) % Discount from Public Offering Price	Prior to Offering (Millions)		Type (2)	Lead Underwriter
		Date	Price	Date	Price		Equity	Sales		
Absolute Entertainment	Mfg interactive software	12/92	$ 4.80/sh.	4/93	$10.00/sh.	52%	$1	$13	O	Needham & Co.
Access Health Marketing	Info retrieval service	9/91	3.00	2/92	7.00	57	6	10	O	Alex. Brown & Sons
Antrol Inc	Mfg plumbing/ heating prod	12/92	$11.55	3/93	$15.00	23	17	148	S	Smith Barney
Auspex Systems, Inc	Mfg semiconductors	2/93	6.00	5/93	12.00	50	27	51	O	Goldman Sachs
BHC Financial Inc	Provide data processing	12/92	8.00	4/93	14.00	43	27	43	O	Montgomery Sec.
Back Bay Restaurant Grp	Restaurants	12/91	14.00	3/92	17.00	18	4	56	O	Tucker Anthony
Banyan Systems Inc	Mfg software	5/92	6.00	8/92	10.50	43	32	100	O	Robertson Stephens
BioSafety Systems, Inc	Healthcare gloves/ masks	11/92	1.60	2/93	6.00	73	2	11	O	Stonegate Securities
biosys	Mfg pharmaceutical prod	12/91	7.65	3/92	12.00	36	5	1	S	Kemper Securities
Brauns Fashions Corp	Women's clothing stores	11/91	1.88	3/92	7.00	73	5	64	O	Piper Jaffray
Brookstone	Own/operate novelty stores	1/93	8.00	3/93	10.50	24	6	118	O	Robertson Stephens
Brooktrout Technology	Integrated voice/ fax sys	8/92	8.50	10/92	10.00	15	2	10	O	Tucker Anthony
The Buckle	Women's clothing stores	9/91	9.00	5/92	13.50	33	20	87	O	William Blair

Company	Business									Underwriter
CDW Computer Centers	Discount software	12/92	6.77	5/93	12.50	46	1	155	O	William Blair
Calif Culinary Academy	Culinary academy/school	3/93	4.18	6/93	6.50	36	(1)d	10	O	Paulson Investment
Catalina Marketing Corp	Mrktng consulting serv	1/92	10.00	3/92	20.00	50	10	33	O	PaineWebber
Catalytica	Mfg indl process catalysts	12/92	1.80	2/93	7.00	74	5	10	O	Lehman Brothers
Chico's	Women's clothing stores	12/92	8.16	3/93	14.00	42	5	33	O	Robert W. Baird
ChipSoft	Publish tax software	12/91	2.04	4/92	12.50	84	2	33	O	Robertson Stephens
Cmmnty Hlth Computing	Healthcare info sys	11/92	3.00	3/93	10.00	70	12	43	O	Montgomery Sec.
Compuware Corporation	Develop/retail software	7/92	8.64	12/92	22.00	61	33	175	O	Morgan Stanley
Cygne Designs, Inc	Women's clothing	4/93	4.00	7/93	10.00	60	3	145	O	PaineWebber
Delta Queen Steamboat	Operate river cruise	1/92	3.25	3/92	13.50	76	9	51	O	Stephens, Inc.
Discovery Zone, Inc	Children's playgrounds	4/93	15.00	6/93	22.00	32	23	13	O	Merrill Lynch
ERO, Inc	Children's products	1/92	6.46	4/92	16.50	61	(1)d	88	O	Donaldson, Lufkin
Electronics for Imaging	Mfg imaging equipment	8/92	4.33	10/92	12.75	66	8	18	S	Robertson Stephens
GBC Technologies	Computers, periph equip	11/92	6.00	12/92	11.00	45	4	80	O	Raymond James
Gibraltar Packaging Grp	Mfg paperboard	1/92	9.00	3/92	10.00	10	2	18	SD	William Blair
Glacier Water	Water vending machines	10/91	5.78	3/92	11.00	47	1	23	O	Sutro & Co. Inc.
Hampshire Group, Ltd	Mfg sweaters & hose	3/92	$9.90/sh.	6/92	$9.50/sh.	(4) %*	$12	$88	O	Legg Mason

continued

127

Exhibit 7.6 Fair Market Value Transactions Which Occurred Within Five Months Prior to an Initial Public Offering as Disclosed in the Prospectus, February 1992–July 1993—*continued*

Company	Principal Business	Last Transaction		Public Offering		(1) % Discount from Public Offering Price	Prior to Offering (Millions)		Type (2)	Lead Underwriter
		Date	Price	Date	Price		Equity	Sales		
Hook-SupeRx, Inc	Own/operate drug stores	12/91	4.23	6/92	13.00	67	13	1,995	S	Goldman Sachs
ICU Medical, Inc	Mfg medical equip	10/91	7.00	3/92	11.00	36	2	7	O	Sutro & Co.
Intermedia Commun of FL	Telecommunications serv	3/92	6.60	4/92	8.00	18	4.4	5	O	Bear Stearns
Kenfil, Inc	Distributes software	10/92	5.00	1/93	7.00	29	(3)d	167	O	Piper Jaffray
LCI International	Telecommunication serv	3/93	11.33	5/93	18.25	38	(32)d	260	S	Bear Stearns
Liberty Technologies	Diagnostic systems	12/92	6.00	3/93	9.00	33	5	17	O	Robertson Stephens
Molten Metal Technology	Environmental tech	1/93	10.56	2/93	14.00	25	20	3	O	Oppenheimer & Co.
Mothers Work	Womens' clothing stores	1/93	4.62	3/93	13.00	64	6	23	S	Wheat First Butcher
Nathan's Famous	Fast food restaurants	12/92	7.00	2/93	9.00	22	13	21	O	Ladenburg Thalman
Norwood Promotional Prod	Hats, caps, printing prod	6/93	5.25	6/93	11.00	52	(5)d	47	O	Allen & Company
Peak Technologies Grp	Computers, peripherals	6/92	5.95	8/92	8.50	30	6	85	O	William Blair
Platinum Software	Dev modular software	7/92	3.33	10/92	14.00	76	3	16	O	Hambrecht & Quist
RHI Entertainment, Inc	Own film & TV library	4/92	7.50	7/92	10.00	25	17	33	O	Donaldson Lufkin
Rexall Sundown, Inc	Produce vitamins	3/93	9.50	6/93	14.00	32	13	74	O	Raymond James

Company	Business	Date 1	Price 1	Date 2	Price 2	Discount (1)				Underwriter
Rocky Shoes & Boots	Mfg men's footwear	12/92	9.50	2/93	10.00	5	6	32	O	J. C. Bradford & Co.
St Mary Land & Explor	Oil & gas exploration	9/92	4.26	12/92	11.00	61	44	35	O	Hanifen, Imhoff Inc.
Starcraft Automotive Corp	Mfg motor homes	4/93	5.42	7/93	10.00	46	7	84	S	Robert W. Baird
Starter	Sports clothing, uniforms	1/93	11.50	4/93	21.50	47	32	283	O	Merrill Lynch
Syratech Corporation	Mfg silver flatware	8/92	10.00	12/92	17.00	41	63	167	O	Allen & Company
Taco Cabana	Mexican patio cafes	5/92	4.71	10/92	13.50	65	14	54	O	Montgomery Sec.
3CI Complete Compliance	Medical waste	1/92	4.00	4/92	6.00	33	6	5	O	Laidlaw Equities
Trident Microsystems	Mfg chips, circuit boards	7/92	8.00	12/92	17.00	53	20	70	O	Alex. Brown & Sons
Wall Data	Network integration sys	10/92	1.92	3/93	20.00	90	9	32	O	Bear Stearns
Wind River Systems	Develop software	2/92	6.00	4/93	9.50	37	7	25	O	Hambrecht & Quist

Study February 1992 through July 1993 (3):   MEAN DISCOUNT 45%   MEDIAN DISCOUNT 44%
Study August 1990 through January 1992 (4):   MEAN DISCOUNT 42%   MEDIAN DISCOUNT 40%
Study February 1989 through July 1990 (5):   MEAN DISCOUNT 45%   MEDIAN DISCOUNT 40%
Study August 1987 through January 1989 (6):   MEAN DISCOUNT 45%   MEDIAN DISCOUNT 45%
Study January 1985 through June 1986 (7):   MEAN DISCOUNT 43%   MEDIAN DISCOUNT 43%
Study January 1980 through June 1981 (8):   MEAN DISCOUNT 60%   MEDIAN DISCOUNT 60%

* Premium	S Sale	SD Stock Dividend
d Deficit	O Option	

(1) 1 Minus (last transaction price divided by offering price).
(2) All options granted were stated to be at the Common Stock's fair market value or reasonably should have been.

(3) 58 Companies   (5) 23 Companies   (7) 21 Companies
(4) 35 Companies   (6) 27 Companies   (8) 13 Companies

Source: John D. Emory, Sr., Business Valuation Review (March 1994):6–7.

Exhibit 7.7 Fair Market Value Transactions Which Occurred Within Five Months Prior to an Initial Public Offering as Disclosed in the Prospectus, January 1994–June 1995

Company	Principal Business	Last Transaction		Public Offering		(1) % Discount from Public Offering Price	(2) Prior to Offering (Millions)		(3) Type of Transaction	Underwriter (Lead)
		Date	Price	Date	Price		Equity	Sales		
ABR Information Services, Inc.	Healthcare benefits administration	3/94	$ 5.16	5/94	$ 9.75	47%	$4	$ 8	S	Robert W. Baird & Co
AccuStaff, Inc.	Temporary help	4/94	7.50	8/94	10.50	29	5	106	S	JC. Bradford
AD Flex Solutions Inc.	Flexible circuit based instruments	6/94	10.00	9/94	13.50	26	13	60	O	Robertson Stephens
Alternative Resources Corporation	Temporary help	1/94	5.43	5/94	14.00	61	5	62	O	Montgomery
American Oncology Resources, Inc.	Physician management	2/95	8.25	6/95	21.00	61	51	67	S	Alex. Brown
CRA Managed Care, Inc.	Cost containment services	1/95	5.89	5/95	16.00	63	(28) d	128	O	Alex. Brown
CATS Software Inc.	Supplies software	1/95	8.00	3/95	12.00	33	5	18	O	Hambrecht & Quist
Cascade Communications Corp.	Manufactures network switches	3/94	8.00	7/94	15.00	47	12	13	S	Morgan Stanley
Centennial Technologies Inc.	Manufactures font cartridges	1/94	3.60	4/94	6.00	40	2	6	S	Schneider Securities
Central Tractor Farm & Country Inc.	Specialty retailer	5/94	5.59	10/94	15.50	64	28	215	O	Donaldson Lufkin
Cole Taylor Financial Group	Bank holding company	1/94	8.25	5/94	13.00	37	91	N/A	O	Chicago Corp.
Corporate Express	Supplies office products	5/94	11.00	9/94	16.00	31	89	638	O	Alex. Brown
Creative Computers, Inc.	Direct marketer of PCs	11/94	5.50	4/95	17.00	68	1	164	O	William Blair
Datalogix International Inc.	Software solutions	1/95	3.50	6/95	17.00	79	10	37	O	Robertson Stephens

Company	Description									Underwriter
Dialogic Corporation	Signal computing products	11/93	6.67	4/94	11.00	39	20	85	O	Hambrecht & Quist
Digital Link	Digital access products	10/93	3.33	1/94	14.00	76	10	23	O	Bear Stearns
Eagle Finance Corp.	Financial services company	3/94	3.39	7/94	9.00	62	4	N/A	O	Chicago Corp.
Eagle Point Software Corp.	Develops application software	1/95	8.00	6/95	13.00	38	2	14	S	William Blair
Happiness Express Inc.	Popular characters	5/94	7.00	7/94	10.00	30	4	40	O	Rodman & Renshaw
Harmonic Lightwaves, Inc.	Fiber optic systems	1/95	7.20	5/95	13.50	47	10	24	O	Bear Stearns
Hello Direct Inc.	Sells telecommunications products	2/95	8.00	4/95	11.50	30	4	26	O	Alex. Brown
Lazer-Tron Corporation	Games	3/94	7.50	5/94	8.00	6	4	13	O	Von Kasper & Co.
Microtech Research, Inc.	Software tools	8/94	3.38	12/94	8.00	58	10	40	O	Lehman Brothers
Micro Linear Corp.	Integrated circuits	6/94	2.75	10/94	8.50	68	27	36	S	Robertson, Stephens
National Micro Systems Corp.	Telephone products	9/93	4.95	2/94	9.75	49	2	11	O	First Albany
Number 9 Visual Tech Corp.	Visual technology	1/95	7.37	5/95	15.00	51	11	82	S	Robertson, Stephens
OccuSystems, Inc.	Physician management	1/95	7.00	5/95	14.00	50	24	100	O	Donaldson Lufkin
Orbit Semiconductor, Inc.	Design & support	6/94	3.80	11/94	7.50	49	7	38	O	Robertson, Stephens
Physician Reliance Network, Inc.	Physician management	9/94	8.63	11/94	14.00	38	30	59	S	Smith Barney
Physician Sales and Service	Distribution to physicians	1/94	6.94	5/94	11.00	37	12	169	O	Alex. Brown
Piercing Pagoda, Inc.	Jewelry retailer	6/91	8.00	10/94	11.00	27	2	72	O	Wheat First Butcher
Reptron Electronics, Inc.	Integrated electronics	12/93	5.00	3/94	13.00	62	7	127	O	Prudential
Rouge Steel Co.	Steel manufacturing	12/93	10.25	3/94	22.00	53	80	1,076	S	Morgan Stanley
Serologicals Corp.	Antibody products	1/95	6.88	6/94	11.50	40	8	46	O	Smith Barney
Shiva Corporation	Remote connectivity	9/94	11.25	11/94	15.00	25	7	38	S	Goldman Sachs

(continued)

Exhibit 7.7 Fair Market Value Transactions Which Occurred Within Five Months Prior to an Initial Public Offering as Disclosed in the Prospectus, January 1994–June 1995—*continued*

Company	Principal Business	Last Transaction Date	Last Transaction Price	Public Offering Date	Public Offering Price	(1) % Discount from Public Offering Price	(2) Prior to Offering (Millions) Equity	(2) Prior to Offering (Millions) Sales	(3) Type of Transaction	Underwriter (Lead)
Sitel Corp.	Telemarketing	2/95	11.64	6/95	13.50	14	23	93	O	Alex. Brown
Speedway Motorsports, Inc.	Owns speedways	12/94	7.89	2/95	18.00	56	10	32	S	Wheat First Butcher
Spyglass, Inc.	Web technologies	3/95	7.50	6/95	17.00	56	3	7	O	Alex. Brown
Telematic Corporation	Telephone services	6/94	5.50	11/94	9.50	42	2	11	S	Hambrecht & Quist
TheraTx, Incorporated	Rehabilitation programs	3/94	7.50	6/94	12.00	37	36	114	O	Robertson, Stephens
Thompson PBE, Inc.	Distributes auto parts	6/94	7.39	11/94	11.00	33	(4.0) d	92	O	William Blair
Tower Automotive, Inc.	Metal stamping	5/94	6.55	8/94	11.50	43	16	195	O	Kidder Peabody
TRISM, Inc.	Special trucking	10/93	3.95	2/94	14.00	72	6	200	O	Alex. Brown
Truck Components, Inc.	Wheel-end components	5/94	3.16	8/94	10.00	68	22	285	O	Dillon Read
Tylan General, Inc.	Mass flow controllers	10/94	6.31	1/95	7.00	10	11	48	O	Needham
Wandel & Goltermann Tech.	Analysis products	1/94	10.00	4/94	11.00	9	7	27	O	Robinson-Humphrey
Mean						45%				
Median						45%				

d Deficit

N/A Not Available

(1) 1 minus (transaction price divided by offering price).

(2) As close to transaction as data available.

(3) All options granted were stated to be at the Common Stock's fair market value or reasonably should have been; S = Sale transaction, O = Options.

Source: John D. Emory, Sr., *Business Valuation Review* (December 1995):159–160.

Exhibit 7.8 Fair Market Value Transactions Which Occurred Within Five Months Prior to an Initial Public Offering as Disclosed in the Prospectus, November 1995–April 1997

Company	Principal Business	Last Transaction		Public Offering		(1) % Discount from Public Offering Price	(2) Prior to Offering (Millions)		(3) Type of Transaction	Total IPO Offer (Millions)	Market Cap. (Millions)	Underwriter (Lead)
		Date	Price	Date	Price		Equity	Sales				
99 Cent Only Stores	Deep-discount retailer	5/96	$10.99	5/96	$14.50	24%	$2	$162	O	$62	$206	EVEREN Securities
Aavid Thermal Technologies	Provider of thermal mngt products	1/96	9.00	1/96	9.50	5	4	87	O	22	58	Montgomery
Abacus Direct	Marketing research services	5/96	4.20	9/96	14.00	70	2	12	O	71	133	Robertson, Stephens
Advanced Fibre Communications	Mfg digital loop carrier system	6/96	12.50	9/96	25.00	50	(8)	89	O	113	732	Morgan Stanley
Alternative Living Services	National assisted living comp	5/96	4.62	8/96	13.00	64	18	13	S	78	169	NatWest Securities
American Medserve	Provider of pharmacy services	9/96	9.10	11/96	15.00	39	23	60	S	80	173	William Blair
American Residential Services	Residential services	4/96	10.80	9/96	15.00	28	17	124	O	63	127	Smith Barney
Applied Analytical Industries	Pharmaceutical products	4/96	8.35	9/96	16.00	48	23	39	O	43	254	Goldman, Sachs
Biosite Diagnostics	Mfg diagnostic products	9/96	5.50	2/97	12.00	54	21	27	O	29	148	Cowen & Co.
Cal-Maine Foods	Mfg egg products	10/96	4.33	12/96	7.00	38	49	292	O	15	82	Paulson Investment
Catalyst	Warehouse mngt software systems	7/95	10.00	11/95	13.00	23	(1)	18	O	34	106	Robertson, Stephens
CB Commercial Real Estate	Commercial real estate services	9/96	10.00	11/96	20.00	50	(107)	534	O	87	265	Merrill Lynch
Cost Plus	Home living, entertainment products	11/95	11.31	4/96	15.00	25	36	183	O	42	121	Alex. Brown

continued

133

Exhibit 7.8 Fair Market Value Transactions Which Occurred Within Five Months Prior to an Initial Public Offering as Disclosed in the Prospectus, November 1995–April 1997—*continued*

Company	Principal Business	Last Transaction Date	Last Transaction Price	Public Offering Date	Public Offering Price	(1) % Discount from Public Offering Price	(2) Prior to Offering (Millions) Equity	(2) Prior to Offering (Millions) Sales	(3) Type of Transaction	Total IPO Offer (Millions)	Market Cap. (Millions)	Underwriter (Lead)
DAOU Systems	Computer network sys. for hospitals	11/96	4.28	2/97	9.00	52	1	19	O	18	92	Alex. Brown
Data Processing Resources	Provides info tech staffing services	1/96	9.00	3/96	14.00	36	(2)	54	O	37	98	Montgomery
Deltek Systems	Develops integrated bus software	9/96	4.00	2/97	11.00	64	11	35	S	32	186	Montgomery
Diamond Home Services	Home improvement products	6/96	13.00	9/96	29.00	55	32	140	O	22	263	William Blair
Document Sciences	Document automation software	7/96	10.00	9/96	12.00	17	1	13	O	28	12	Deutsche Morgan
Dunn Computer	Customer computer systems	1/97	4.15	4/97	5.00	17	2	17	O	5	25	Network 1 Financial
E*TRADE	Online discount brokerage services	3/96	2.33	8/96	10.50	78	22	43	O	59	309	Robertson, Stephens
Essex	Dev electrical wire and cable products	12/96	10.00	4/97	17.00	41	146	1,332	S	98	491	Goldman, Sachs
Factory Card Outlet	Party supplies, greeting cards	7/96	3.30	12/96	9.00	63	26	103	O	24	60	Alex. Brown
Firearms Training Systems	Simulation systems for arms training	9/96	3.25	11/96	14.00	77	(87)	77	S	84	286	Montgomery
Forrester Research	Independent research firm	9/96	13.00	11/96	16.00	19	4	22	O	32	128	Goldman, Sachs
Gateway Data Sciences	Develops software products	10/95	5.09	3/96	6.75	25	(2)	26	O	8	19	National Securities

Company	Description													Underwriter
Hambrecht & Quist Group	Investment banking	3/96	6.52	8/96	16.00	59		170	396	S	56	355	Hambrecht & Quist
Hamilton Bancorp	Global trade finance	11/96	9.23	3/97	15.50	40		40	25	O	37	147	Oppenheimer
Hibbett Sporting Goods	Full-line sporting goods store	8/96	8.48	10/96	16.00	47		(7)	77	O	32	93	Smith Barney
HomeSide	Residential mortgage banking	11/96	10.29	1/97	15.00	31		388	262	S	110	634	Merrill Lynch
Hot Topic	Music licensed, influenced apparel	6/96	8.80	9/96	18.00	51		297	31	O	23	79	Montgomery
Impath	Provides information on cancer	10/95	9.50	2/96	13.00	27		6	14	O	25	64	Salomon Brothers
Infinity Financial Technology	Develops financial software	8/96	10.50	10/96	16.00	34		8	31	S	43	288	Goldman, Sachs
INS	Complex enterprise network svcs	6/96	8.00	9/96	16.00	50		(3)	44	O	40	495	Morgan Stanley
Intelligroup	Info tech services	6/96	8.00	9/96	10.00	20		(2)	35	O	25	107	Cowen & Co.
Intevac	Static sputtering systems	6/95	2.18	11/95	6.00	64		13	33	O	12	72	Robertson, Stephens
Isocor	Dev elec info exch software	1/96	8.00	3/96	9.00	11		12	17	O	18	76	Hambrecht & Quist
JDA Software Group	Software for retail orgs	11/95	5.25	3/96	13.00	60		(5)	30	O	35	158	Hambrecht & Quist
Kentek Information Systems	Supplier of laser printers	2/96	6.49	4/96	8.00	19		30	68	O	20	55	Janney Montgomery
Kitty Hawk	Air freight charter services	6/96	8.62	10/96	12.00	28		23	142	O	36	125	Smith Barney
Lumisys	Laser-based film digitizers	8/95	6.00	11/95	8.00	25		(4)	15	O	20	50	Hambrecht & Quist
Meta Group	Market assessment company	8/95	6.13	12/95	18.00	66		(4)	27	S	43	92	Robertson, Stephens
Metzler Group	Consulting services	6/96	12.00	10/96	16.00	25		3	19	O	56	165	Donaldson, Lufkin
Millennium Pharmaceuticals	Genomics industry	4/96	6.00	5/96	12.00	50		13	23	O	54	274	Goldman, Sachs

continued

Exhibit 7.8 Fair Market Value Transactions Which Occurred Within Five Months Prior to an Initial Public Offering as Disclosed in the Prospectus, November 1995–April 1997—*continued*

Company	Principal Business	Last Transaction Date	Last Transaction Price	Public Offering Date	Public Offering Price	(1) % Discount from Public Offering Price	(2) Prior to Offering (Millions) Equity	(2) Prior to Offering (Millions) Sales	(3) Type of Transaction	Total IPO Offer (Millions)	Market Cap. (Millions)	Underwriter (Lead)
MIM Corporation	Pharmacy mgmt organization	5/96	7.50	8/96	13.00	42	(11)	278	O	52	156	PaineWebber
Molecular Devices	Mfgs bioanalytical measurement systems	9/95	5.25	12/95	11.00	52	6	25	O	25	95	UBS Securities
NCS HealthCare	Ind. provider of pharmacy services	9/95	10.06	2/96	16.50	39	12	87	S	70	190	Smith Barney
Northwest Pipe Company	Mfg welded steel pipe	8/95	4.78	11/95	9.00	47	15	96	O	15	45	Hanifen, Imhoff
NuCo$_2$	Supplies liquid carbon dioxide	7/95	4.40	12/95	9.00	51	1	7	O	20	48	Raymond James
ONSALE	Sell computers via Internet	12/96	5.00	4/97	6.00	17	2	14	S	15	98	Montgomery
OrCAD	Develops software products	12/95	7.88	2/96	11.00	28	6	14	O	35	67	Wessels, Arnold
Overland Data	Magnetic tape data storage sys	9/96	3.66	2/97	10.00	63	7	51	O	30	99	Jeffries & Co.
PIA Merchandising Services	Routed merchandising systems	12/95	9.81	2/96	14.00	30	6	105	O	33	76	PaineWebber
Pixar Animation Studios	Digital animation Studio	10/95	9.60	11/95	22.00	56	4	12	O	132	823	Robertson, Stephens
Planet Hollywood	Theme restaurants	3/96	14.00	4/96	18.00	22	31	296	O	194	1914	Bear, Stearns
PowerCerv	Client/server development tools	11/95	4.00	3/96	14.00	71	(16)	28	S	46	186	Robertson, Stephens
Printware	Designs computer plates	4/96	3.00	7/96	6.00	50	5	8	O	10	29	RJ Steichen

Company	Description											Underwriter
Procom Technology	Provider of CD-ROM servers	7/96	5.17	12/96	9.00	43	7	83	O	27	99	Montgomery
Q.E.P.	Mfg. specialty tools	6/96	7.23	9/96	8.50	15	4	27	O	10	21	Cruttenden Roth
Qualix Group	Software for UNIX and Windows NT	10/96	5.62	2/97	8.00	30	4	25	O	24	81	Hambrecht & Quist
Raster Graphics	Large format color printing systems	5/96	7.00	8/96	8.00	13	8	33	O	24	67	Hambrecht & Quist
Renal Care Group	Nephrology services	1/96	7.50	2/96	18.00	58	20	71	O	70	157	Equitable Securities
Restrac	Dev human resource staffing software	4/96	4.67	7/96	11.00	58	3	19	O	28	87	Montgomery
RMH Teleservices	Outbound teleservices	5/96	1.91	9/96	12.50	85	(17)	31	S	35	96	Smith Barney
RockShox	Mfg bicycle suspension products	5/96	4.69	9/96	15.00	69	(38)	86	O	72	204	Merrill Lynch
Rogue Wave Software	Prvdr of sftwr parts, related tools	6/96	6.75	11/96	12.00	44	1	19	O	29	91	Hambrecht & Quist
SCB Computer Technology	Information technology services	10/95	9.75	2/96	15.50	37	3	40	S	34	106	Morgan Keegan
SeaChange International	Digital video products	6/96	7.33	11/96	15.00	51	1	36	O	30	191	Morgan Stanley
Segue Software	Dev software for automated testing	12/95	9.00	3/96	18.00	50	1	8	O	50	108	Alex. Brown
Signature Resorts	Developer, operator of timeshare resorts	6/96	12.00	8/96	14.00	14	48	79	O	74	232	Montgomery
SkyMall	In-flight catalogue company	9/96	5.56	12/96	8.00	31	(14)	40	O	16	69	Josephthal Lyon
Smart Modular Technologies	Mfg memory modules, PC card	8/95	7.00	11/95	12.00	42	21	237	O	36	212	Donaldson, Lufkin
Specialty Care Network	Physician practice mgmt co.	10/96	3.00	2/97	8.00	63	11	34	S	26	112	Credit Suisse
Sykes Enterprises	Info technology support systems	12/95	7.50	4/96	18.00	58	10	63	O	59	224	Robert W. Baird

continued

Exhibit 7.8 Fair Market Value Transactions Which Occurred Within Five Months Prior to an Initial Public Offering as Disclosed in the Prospectus, November 1995–April 1997—*continued*

Company	Principal Business	Last Transaction Date	Last Transaction Price	Public Offering Date	Public Offering Price	(1) % Discount from Public Offering Price	(2) Prior to Offering (Millions) Equity	(2) Prior to Offering (Millions) Sales	(3) Type of Transaction	Total IPO Offer (Millions)	Market Cap. (Millions)	Underwriter (Lead)
Synthetic Industries	Mfg polypropylene products	5/96	10.72	11/96	13.00	18	61	289	O	33	108	Bear, Stearns
Template Software	Provides software solutions	9/96	6.00	1/97	16.00	63	10	14	O	34	68	Volpe, Welty
The O'Gara Company	Armor provider for vehicles	8/96	6.11	11/96	9.00	32	4	62	S	18	60	Dillon, Read
The Registry	Provides info tech. consultants	3/96	11.00	6/96	17.00	35	2	131	O	37	168	Adams, Harkness
Titanium Metals	Titanium sponge and mill products	3/96	16.13	6/96	23.00	30	140	251	S	334	723	Salomon Brothers
Trex Medical	Mfg mammography equipment	2/96	10.75	6/96	14.00	23	63	134	O	35	358	NatWest Securities
Trident	Mfg impulse ink jet subsystems	9/95	12.00	2/96	16.00	25	(2)	20	O	48	111	Prudential Securities
Trusted Information Systems	Security solutions for computers	8/96	7.04	10/96	13.00	46	5	19	O	44	142	J. P. Morgan
United Natural Foods	Distributes natural foods	7/96	9.64	11/96	13.50	29	18	381	O	39	167	Smith Barney
USCS International	Provider of customer mgmt software	4/96	12.50	6/96	17.00	26	49	237	O	82	378	Merrill Lynch
Versatility	Provider of client/ server software	9/96	10.50	12/96	15.00	30	2	21	O	33	108	Merrill Lynch
ViaSat	Digital satellite telecomm	7/96	4.09	12/96	9.00	55	6	36	O	20	68	Oppenheimer

VitalCom	Communication networks	10/95	5.72	2/96	12.50	54	7	24	S	25	95	Wessels, Arnold
Vivid Technologies	Mfg automated inspection systems	7/96	3.00	12/96	12.00	75	0	16	S	24	107	Lehman Brothers
Workgroup Technology	Develops software solutions	11/95	3.90	3/96	15.00	74	(4)	9	S	53	111	Alex. Brown
Xionics Document Technologies	Technology for office devices	5/96	4.50	9/96	12.00	63	(7)	24	S	36	121	Adams, Harkness
XLConnect Solutions	Professional services for computing	9/96	9.35	10/96	15.00	38	6	95	O	44	243	Alex. Brown
Xylan	High-bandwidth switching systems	12/95	5.25	3/96	26.00	80	16	30	S	109	1025	Morgan Stanley

Total Transactions	Mean	43%	$19	$94		$47	$198
	Median	42%	$6	$35		$35	$112
	Count	91					

Sale Transactions	Mean	54%	$38	$131		$66	$259
	Median	61%	$8	$32		$45	$171
	Count	22					

Option Transactions	Mean	39%	$13	$82		$40	$178
	Median	40%	$6	$36		$33	$108
	Count	69					

(1) 1 minus (transaction price divided by offering price).

(2) As close to transaction as data available.

(3) All options granted were stated to be at the common stock's fair market value or reasonably should have been.

( ) Negative

O Option Transaction

S Sale Transaction

Source: John D. Emory, Sr., *Business Valuation Review* (September 1997):128–130.

Exhibit 7.9 Discounts for Lack of Marketability Arising from Sales Transactions, November 1995–April 1997

Company	Principal Business	Last Transaction		Public Offering	
		Date	Price	Date	Price
Alternative Living Services	National assisted living comp	5/96	$4.62	8/96	$13.00
American Medserve	Provider of pharmacy services	9/96	9.10	11/96	15.00
Deltek Systems	Develops integrated bus software	9/96	4.00	2/97	11.00
Essex	Dev electrical wire and cable product	12/96	10.00	4/97	17.00
Firearms Training Systems	Simulation systems for arms training	9/96	3.25	11/96	14.00
Hambrecht & Quist Group	Investment banking	3/96	6.52	8/96	16.00
HomeSide	Residential mortgage banking	11/96	10.29	1/97	15.00
Infinity Financial Technology	Develops financial software	8/96	10.50	10/96	16.00
Meta Group	Market assessment company	8/95	6.13	12/95	18.00
NCS HealthCare	Ind. provider of pharmacy services	9/95	10.06	2/96	16.50
ONSALE	Sell computers via Internet	12/96	5.00	4/97	6.00
PowerCerv	Client/server development tools	11/95	4.00	3/96	14.00
RMH Teleservices	Outbound teleservices	5/96	1.91	9/96	12.50
SCB Computer Technology	Information technology services	10/95	9.75	2/96	15.50
Specialty Care Network	Physician practice mgmt co.	10/96	3.00	2/97	8.00
The O'Gara Company	Armor provider for vehicles	8/96	6.11	11/96	9.00
Titanium Metals	Titanium sponge and mill products	3/96	16.13	6/96	23.00
VitalCom	Communication networks	10/95	5.72	2/96	12.50
Vivid Technologies	Mfg automated inspection systems	7/96	3.00	12/96	12.00
Workgroup Technology	Develops software solutions	11/95	3.90	3/96	15.00
Xionics Document Technologies	Technology for office devices	5/96	4.50	9/96	12.00
Xylan	High-bandwidth switching systems	12/95	5.25	3/96	26.00

(1) 1 minus (transaction price divided by offering price).
(2) As close to transaction as data available.

( ) Negative
S   Sale Transaction
Source: John D. Emory, Sr., *Business Valuation Review* (September 1997): 131.

(1) % Discount from Public Offering Price	(2) Prior to Offering (Millions)		Type of Trans- action	Underwriter (Lead)	Size of Transaction in Shares	Description of Transaction
	Equity	Sales				
64%	$ 18	$ 13	S	NatWest Securities	2,007,049	Issued to purchase a Co.
39	23	60	S	William Blair	310,208	Sold to Directors
64	11	35	S	Montgomery	102,000	Exchanged for a business
41	146	1,332	S	Goldman, Sachs	437,709	Sold to management
77	(87)	77	S	Montgomery	232,333	Sold to management
59	170	396	S	Hambrecht & Quist	169,428	Redemption from President
31	388	262	S	Merrill Lynch	11,461,400	Partial payment for Co.
34	8	31	S	Goldman, Sachs	9,524	Sold to Director
66	(4)	27	S	Robertson, Stephens	339,368	Purchase by investors
39	12	87	S	Smith Barney	787,773	Purchase of companies
17	2	14	S	Montgomery	20,000	Sold to a Director
71	(16)	28	S	Robertson, Stephens	230,000	Consideration for Co. sale
85	(17)	31	S	Smith Barney	2,000,000	Purchase by investors
37	3	40	S	Morgan Keegan	125,948	Granted to employees
63	11	34	S	Credit Suisse	100,000	Sold to Director
32	4	62	S	Dillon, Read	2,730	Sale of shares
30	140	251	S	Salomon Brothers	93,000	Granted to employees
54	7	24	S	Wessels, Arnold	34,965	Sold to President
75	0	16	S	Lehman Brothers	15,000	Issued in lieu of fees
74	(4)	9	S	Alex. Brown	666,666	Purchase by investor
63	(7)	24	S	Adams, Harkness	1,000,000	Redemption from investor
80	16	30	S	Morgan Stanley	952,382	Purchased by investors

Mean	54	38	131
Median	61	8	32
Count	22		

Exhibit 7.10A   Pre-IPO Dot-Com Discount Study, May 1997–March 2000

Company	Principal Business	SIC	Transaction Date	Transaction Price	Preferred/Common	IPO Date	IPO Price
Amazon.com, Inc.	Retailer; books	7375	2/97	$ 6.67	P	5/97	$18.00
Ashford.com, Inc.	Retailer; luxury goods	5945	4/99	4.21	P	9/99	13.00
Autobytel.com, Inc.[4]	Vehicle purchasing svcs	7375	10/99	13.20	P	3/99	23.00
Autoweb.com, Inc.	Automotive svcs	7549	10/98	2.37	P	3/99	14.00
Bamboo.com, Inc.[a]	Virtual tours of real estate	7379	3/99	2.07	P	8/99	7.00
Biznessonline.com	Internet access, related svcs	7375	2/99	5.71	P	5/99	10.00
Buy.com[5]	Wholesaler/retailer	5734	10/99	9.07	P	2/00	13.00
COMPS.COM, Inc.[b]	Commercial real estate	7375	2/99	3.68	C	5/99	15.00
Deltathree.com	Telephone communication	4813	10/99	7.98	C	11/99	15.00
Drkoop.com, Inc.[6]	Healthcare network	7375	1/99	4.78	P	6/99	9.00
drugstore.com, Inc.[7]	Retailer; drugstore	5912	3/99	7.83	P	7/99	18.00
Exactis.com	Various business svcs	8900	8/99	6.50	P	11/99	14.00
Fashionmall.com	Retailer; apparel	7375	3/99	4.44	C	5/99	13.00
Garden.com, Inc.	Gardening E-commerce	5961	4/99	7.15	P	9/99	12.00
GoTo.com, Inc.	Online advertising	7379	4/99	6.89	P	6/99	15.00
Healthcentral.com	Information retrieval svcs	7375	8/99	5.20	P	12/99	11.00
Homegrocer.com	Electronic grocery stores	5411	11/99	5.80	P	3/00	12.00
HomeStore.com, Inc.[8]	Real estate	6531	3/99	6.50	C	8/99	20.00
HotJobs.com, Ltd.	Recruiting solutions	7361	5/99	4.12	P	8/99	8.00
ImageX.com	Commercial printing	2752	4/99	4.20	P	8/99	7.00
InfoSpace.com, Inc.	Integrator of content svcs	7375	7/98	8.00	C	12/98	15.00
Iprint.com	Commercial printing	2750	9/99	3.36	P	3/00	10.00
Lifeminders.com	Advertising agencies	7311	9/99	6.74	P	11/99	14.00
Loislow.com, Inc.	Legal information databases	7374	5/99	2.91	P	9/99	14.00
Mail.com, Inc.[9]	Provider of email svcs	7375	3/99	5.00	P	6/99	7.00
MiningCo.com, Inc.[c][10]	News, information svcs	7379	11/99	5.48	P	3/99	25.00
Mortgage.com, Inc.	Mortgage svcs	6162	5/99	8.00	P	8/99	8.00
MP3.com, Inc.[11]	Music provider	3652	4/99	1.33	P	7/99	28.00
Multex.com, Inc.	Invstmnt research provider	7375	12/98	5.00	C	3/99	14.00
Musicmaker.com, Inc.	Music provider	5961	4/99	5.71	C	7/99	14.00
MyPoints.com, Inc.	Direct marketing	7311	3/99	5.00	P	8/99	8.00
Neoforma.com	Catalog, mail-order houses	5961	10/99	5.68	P	1/00	13.00
Onvia.com[12]	Information retrieval svcs	7375	9/99	1.72	P	2/00	21.00
Partsbase.com	Computer related svcs	7379	11/99	2.50	P	3/00	13.00

Discount from IPO Price[1]	Prior to IPO (Mil)			Total IPO Offer (Mil)	At Offer Market Cap. (Mil)	Lead Underwriter
	Equity[2]	Sales[3]	Net Loss[3]			
63%	$ 2.80	$30.90	($8.50)	$ 54	$ 429	Deutsche Morgan
68%	30.3	9.3	(4.3)	81	479	Goldman
43%	25.9	23.8	(19.4)	104	411	BT Alex. Brown
83%	(11.7)	13.0	(11.5)	70	328	CS First Boston
70%	13.0	0.6	(16.7)	28	143	Prudential Securities
43%	0.1	6.2	(2.7)	29	69	Joseph Stevens
30%	23.0	596.8	(130.2)	182	1,679	Merrill
75%	7.9	13.1	(2.4)	68	182	Volpe Brown Whelan
47%	3.8	4.9	(6.1)	90	414	Lehman
47%	(23.2)	0.4	(12.7)	84	248	Bear, Stearns
57%	72.6	8.4	(39.5)	90	762	Morgan Stanley
54%	(23.1)	8.8	(8.3)	53	169	Thomas Weisel
66%	1.5	2.4	0.1	39	98	Gruntal & Co.
40%	21.9	5.4	(19.1)	49	203	Hambrecht & Quist
54%	11.1	2.2	(20.7)	90	666	Donaldson, Lufkin
53%	27.4	0.7	(12.1)	83	217	Lehman
52%	112.1	21.6	(84.0)	264	1,498	Morgan Stanley
68%	65.0	33.2	(57.5)	21	1,341	Morgan Stanley
49%	(5.1)	3.5	(2.2)	24	212	Deutsch Banc Alex. B
40%	(15.1)	4.0	(10.2)	21	113	Volpe Brown Whelan
47%	20.7	7.2	(4.8)	75	302	Hambrecht & Quist
66%	(15.7)	3.3	(13.4)	45	289	CS First Boston
52%	(17.0)	8.0	(19.3)	59	275	Hambrecht & Quist
79%	(18.3)	5.7	(11.2)	56	293	Prudential Securities
29%	12.3	2.6	(17.9)	48	295	Salomon Smith Barney
78%	(24.7)	3.7	(15.6)	75	290	Bear, Stearns
0%	11.0	42.1	(8.9)	57	332	CS First Boston
95%	10.4	1.8	(1.8)	346	1,866	CS First Boston
64%	(37.2)	13.2	(9.7)	42	296	BancBoston Robertson
59%	(2.2)	0.1	(5.2)	118	424	Ferris, Baker, Watts
38%	5.9	4.9	(21.5)	40	190	BancBoston Robertson
56%	(18.8)	0.6	(34.2)	91	733	Merrill
92%	26.6	27.2	(42.8)	168	1,656	CS First Boston
81%	1.5	0.4	(5.9)	46	183	Roth Capital

continued

Exhibit 7.10A   Pre-IPO Dot-Com Discount Study, May 1997–March 2000
               —*continued*

Company	Principal Business	SIC	Transaction Date	Transaction Price	Preferred/Common	IPO Date	IPO Price
Pets.com[13]	Retail; pet related	5999	11/99	9.44	P	2/00	11.00l
Phone.com, Inc.[14]	Wireless telephone software	3661	3/99	7.24	P	6/99	16.00
PlanetRx.com, Inc.	Healthcare E-commerce	5912	6/99	8.68	P	10/99	16.00
Priceline.com Inc.	E-commerce svcs	7375	12/98	3.20	P	3/99	16.00
PurchasePro.com, Inc.	E-commerce svcs	7389	6/99	3.50	P	9/99	12.00
Quepasa.com, Inc.[15]	Spanish portal	7379	3/99	7.00	C	6/99	12.00
Sciquest.com	Nondurable goods	5199	7/99	7.46	P	11/99	16.00
ShopNow.com, Inc.[16]	Wholesaler/retailer	7374	4/99	7.00	P	9/99	12.00
Shopping.com	Wholesaler/retailer	5963	9/97	3.00	C	11/97	9.00
SmarterKids.com	Hobby, toy, game shops	5945	7/99	4.18	P	11/99	14.00
Snowball.com[17]	Information retrieval svcs	7375	11/99	6.33	P	3/00	11.00
Software.com, Inc.	Messaging software	7373	4/99	6.15	P	6/99	15.00
Stamps.com, Inc.	Purchasing, printing postage	5961	2/99	5.49	P	6/99	11.00
TheStreet.com, Inc.	Financial news, commmentary	7374	2/99	12.00	C	5/99	19.00
Varsitybooks.com	Retailer, books	5942	9/99	6.72	P	2/00	10.00
VitaminShoppe.com, Inc.	Nutritional information	5961	7/99	9.15	P	10/99	11.00
Webstakes.com, Inc.[d]	Promotional marketing	7311	6/99	6.00	P	9/99	14.00
Xoom.com, Inc.[e][18]	Direct marketing	7311	7/98	10.80	C	12/98	14.00
Yesmail.com, Inc.[f]	Email direct marketing	7319	5/99	1.75	P	9/99	11.00

Note: See Exhibit 7.10D for footnotes.
Source: © Emory Business Valuation, LLC *Dot-Com Pre-IPO Study*
(2000):A-1–A-3, D-1.

10 transactions in each of those categories. Only one of the 53 companies had positive earnings. The results were as follows:

	Mean Size of Discount from IPO Price	
	10 at Top of Category	10 at Bottom of Category
Revenue	55%	57%
Equity	52%	61%
IPO Size	59%	56%
Market Capitalization at IPO	63%	51%
Loss Size	63% (smallest net loss)	52% (largest net loss)

Discount from IPO Price[1]	Prior to IPO (Mil)			Total IPO Offer (Mil)	At Offer Market Cap. (Mil)	Lead Underwriter
	Equity[2]	Sales[3]	Net Loss[3]			
14%	51.1	6.3	(67.4)	83	290	Merrill
55%	32.0	8.0	(16.9)	64	488	CS First Boston
46%	79.0	0.8	(24.1)	96	813	Goldman, Sachs
80%	55.3	35.2	(112.2)	160	2,277	Morgan Stanley
71%	(10.9)	2.8	(10.0)	48	216	Prudential Securities
42%	0.7	0.0	(10.2)	48	165	Cruttenden Roth
53%	(62.8)	1.7	(20.2)	120	395	Donaldson
42%	36.7	9.1	(25.4)	87	402	Dain Rauscher Wessels
67%	0.0	0.1	(1.3)	12	36	Waldron & Company
70%	(19.0)	1.5	(18.9)	63	271	Hambrecht & Quist
42%	34.7	6.7	(34.8)	69	410	Goldman, Sachs
59%	(11.8)	28.8	(6.8)	90	610	CS First Boston
50%	(7.2)	0.0	(7.5)	55	382	BancBoston Robertson
37%	(2.8)	5.7	(19.9)	105	446	Goldman, Sachs
33%	22.1	11.8	(25.5)	41	156	Robertson
17%	(8.1)	6.7	(7.2)	50	224	Thomas Weisel
57%	(23.3)	5.6	(5.6)	50	199	Bear, Stearns
23%	3.8	5.6	(7.4)	56	183	Bear, Stearns
84%	1.9	6.2	(6.7)	37	224	Deutsch Banc Alex. B

Mean	54%	$8.8	$19.9	($20.9)	$78	$477
Median	54%	$2.8	$5.7	($12.1)	$63	$295
Count	53					

There seemed to be little correlation among revenues, equity, or IPO offer size and the size of the discount.

SUMMARY

The John Emory pre-IPO studies cover a span of 20 years and hundreds of transactions. This chapter has documented every single transaction that was recorded in the studies in that two-decade span.

The results are extremely consistent over time, documenting average discounts around 45% over varying market conditions, with the average discounts for the recent dot-com study a little higher. (Readers are cautioned not to include the dot-com

Exhibit 7.10B Discounts by SIC Code, Pre-IPO Dot-Com Discount Study, May 1997–March 2000

SIC Code	SIC Code Description	Company	Discount From IPO Price[1]
2750	Printing and Publishing	Iprint.com	66%
2752	Commercial Printing, Lithographic	ImageX.com	40%
3652	Phonograph Records, Prerecorded Audio Tapes, Disks	MP3.com, Inc.	95%
3661	Telephone, Telegraph Apparatus	Phone.com, Inc.	55%
		Smarterkids.com	70%
		Mean	**63%**
4813	Telephone Communications, Except Radiotelephone	Deltathree.com	47%
5199	Nondurable Goods, Not Elsewhere Classified	Sciquest.com	53%
5411	Grocery Stores	Homegrocer.com	52%
5734	Computer, Computer Software Stores	Buy.com	30%
5912	Drug, Proprietary Stores	drugstore.com, Inc.	57%
		PlanetRx.com, Inc.	46%
		Mean	**52%**
5942	Book Stores	Varsitybooks.com	33%
5945	Hobby, Toy, Game Shops	Ashford.com, Inc.	68%
5961	Catalog, Mail-Order Houses	Garden.com, Inc.	40%
		Musicmaker.com, Inc.	59%
		Neoforma.com	56%
		Stamps.com, Inc.	50%
		VitaminShoppe.com, Inc.	17%
		Mean	**44%**
5963	Direct Selling Establishments	Shopping.com	67%
5999	Miscellaneous Retail Stores, Not Elsewhere Classified	Pets.com	14%
6162	Mortgage Bankers, Loan Correspondents	Mortgage.com, Inc.	0%
6531	Real Estate Agents, Managers	HomeStore.com, Inc.	68%
7311	Advertising Agencies	Lifeminders.com	52%
		MyPoints.com, Inc.	38%
		Webstakes.com, Inc.	57%
		Xoom.com, Inc.	23%
		Mean	**43%**
7319	Advertising, Not Elsewhere Classified	Yesmail.com, Inc.	84%
7330	Business Services	Exactis.com	54%
7361	Employment Agencies	HotJobs.com, Ltd.	49%
7373	Computer Integrated Systems Design	Software.com, Inc.	59%
7374	Computer Processing, Data Preparation	Loislaw.com, Inc.	79%
		ShopNow.com, Inc.	42%
		TheStreet.com, Inc.	37%
		Mean	**53%**

Exhibit 7.10B   Discounts by SIC Code, Pre-IPO Dot-Com Discount Study, May 1997–March 2000—*continued*

SIC Code	SIC Code Description	Company	Discount From IPO Price[1]
7375	Information Retrieval Services	Amazon.com, Inc.	63%
		Autobytel.com, Inc.	43%
		Biznessonline.com	43%
		COMPS.COM, Inc.	75%
		Drkoop.com, Inc.	47%
		Fashionmall.com	66%
		Healthcentral.com	53%
		InfoSpace.com, Inc.	47%
		Mail.com, Inc.	29%
		Multex.com, Inc.	64%
		Onvia.com	92%
		Priceline.com Inc.	80%
		Snowball.com	42%
		Mean	**57%**
7379	Computer Related Services, Not Elsewhere Classified	Bamboo.com, Inc.	70%
		GoTo.com, Inc.	54%
		MiningCo.com, Inc.	78%
		Partsbase.com	81%
		Quespasa.com, Inc.	42%
		Mean	**65%**
7389	Business Services, Not Elsewhere Classified	PurchasePro.com, Inc.	71%
7549	Automotive Services, Except Repair and Car Washes	Autoweb.com, Inc.	83%

Note: See Exhibit 7.10D for footnotes.
Source: Emory Business Valuation, LLC *Dot-Com Pre-IPO Study* (2000):C-1–C-2, D-1.

results in the median and mean results of the other eight studies, because the dot-com study used different selection criteria.)

In spite of the consistency of the averages, the dispersion of observations within each study is quite wide. With the convenience of having all of the data here in one place (and also online at BVLibrary.com), the analyst can examine the individual transactions to select those most relevant to the subject valuation.

Exhibit 7.10C Supplementary Schedule, Pre-IPO Dot-Com Discount Study

Company	Transaction Price	IPO Price	Discount from IPO Price[1]	IPO Date Close Price	IPO Date Close Discount	90 Days After IPO Price	90 Days After IPO Discount	180 Days After IPO Price	180 Days After IPO Discount
Amazon.com, Inc.	$6.67	$18.00	63%	$23.50	72%	$26.38	75%	$50.50	87%
Ashford.com, Inc.	4.21	13.00	68%	13.00	68%	14.63	71%	7.06	40%
Autobytel.com, Inc.	13.20	23.00	43%	40.25	67%	19.69	33%	14.44	9%
Autoweb.com, Inc.	2.37	14.00	83%	40.00	94%	12.75	81%	9.00	74%
Bamboo.com, Inc. [a]	2.07	7.00	70%	17.56	88%	15.63	87%	31.00	93%
Biznessonline.com	5.71	10.00	43%	11.88	52%	7.50	24%	6.00	5%
Buy.com	9.07	13.00	30%	25.13	64%	NA	NA	NA	NA
COMPS.COM, Inc. [b]	3.68	15.00	75%	14.25	74%	7.75	53%	7.31	50%
Deltathree.com	7.98	15.00	47%	29.00	72%	42.75	81%	NA	NA
Drkoop.com, Inc.	4.78	9.00	47%	16.44	71%	17.31	72%	17.06	72%
drugstore.com, Inc.	7.83	18.00	57%	50.25	84%	37.00	79%	35.00	78%
Exactis.com	6.50	14.00	54%	24.00	73%	22.50	71%	NA	NA
Fashionmall.com	4.44	13.00	66%	13.00	66%	6.63	33%	6.16	28%
Garden.com, Inc.	7.15	12.00	40%	19.06	62%	12.63	43%	7.00	−2%
GoTo.com, Inc.	6.89	15.00	54%	22.38	69%	38.13	82%	80.94	91%
Healthcentral.com	5.20	11.00	53%	9.88	47%	6.81	24%	NA	NA
Homegrocer.com	5.80	12.00	52%	14.13	59%	NA	NA	NA	NA
HomeStore.com, Inc.	6.50	20.00	68%	22.75	71%	46.13	86%	97.56	93%
HotJobs.com, Ltd.	4.12	8.00	49%	7.63	46%	30.13	86%	30.94	87%
ImageX.com	4.20	7.00	40%	13.94	70%	23.50	82%	23.00	82%
InfoSpace.com, Inc.	8.00	15.00	47%	20.00	60%	77.50	90%	78.38	90%
Iprint.com	3.36	10.00	66%	15.75	79%	NA	NA	NA	NA
Lifeminders.com	6.74	14.00	52%	22.38	70%	35.56	81%	NA	NA

Loislaw.com, Inc.	2.91	14.00	79%	14.50	80%	39.00	93%	23.75	88%
Mail.com, Inc.	5.00	7.00	29%	11.88	58%	16.25	69%	20.75	76%
MiningCo.com, Inc.(c)	5.48	25.00	78%	47.50	88%	47.50	88%	35.00	84%
Mortgage.com, Inc.	8.00	8.00	0%	7.16	-12%	8.63	7%	5.38	-49%
MP3.com, Inc.	1.33	28.00	95%	63.31	98%	37.94	96%	31.00	96%
Multex.com, Inc.	5.00	14.00	64%	33.63	85%	26.88	81%	18.25	73%
Musicmaker.com, Inc.	5.71	14.00	59%	23.94	76%	10.50	46%	5.94	4%
MyPoints.com, Inc.	5.00	8.00	38%	11.00	55%	15.50	68%	48.00	90%
Neoforma.com	5.68	13.00	56%	52.38	89%	7.75	27%	NA	NA
Onvia.com	1.72	21.00	92%	61.50	97%	NA	NA	NA	NA
Partsbase.com	2.50	13.00	81%	11.38	78%	NA	NA	NA	NA
Pets.com	9.44	11.00	14%	11.00	14%	NA	NA	NA	NA
Phone.com, Inc.	7.24	16.00	55%	40.13	82%	168.38	96%	309.25	98%
PlanetRx.com, Inc.	8.68	16.00	46%	26.00	67%	13.00	33%	6.25	-39%
Priceline.com Inc.	3.20	16.00	80%	69.00	95%	105.50	97%	61.72	95%
PurchasePro.com, Inc.	3.50	12.00	71%	26.13	87%	188.00	98%	177.75	98%
Quespasa.com, Inc.	7.00	12.00	42%	17.13	59%	9.97	30%	15.00	53%
Sciquest.com	7.46	16.00	53%	30.00	75%	80.50	91%	NA	NA
ShopNow.com, Inc.	7.00	12.00	42%	12.69	45%	20.00	65%	15.44	55%
Shopping.com	3.00	9.00	67%	9.50	68%	22.44	87%	19.50	85%
SmarterKids.com	4.18	14.00	70%	14.00	70%	5.75	27%	NA	NA
Snowball.com	6.33	11.00	42%	15.31	59%	NA	NA	NA	NA
Software.com, Inc.	6.15	15.00	59%	18.06	66%	46.13	87%	88.25	93%
Stamps.com, Inc.	5.49	11.00	50%	13.69	60%	40.00	86%	63.06	91%
TheStreet.com, Inc.	12.00	19.00	37%	60.00	80%	17.75	32%	14.50	17%
Varsitybooks.com	6.72	10.00	33%	9.88	32%	NA	NA	NA	NA
VitaminShoppe.com, Inc.	9.15	11.00	17%	9.75	6%	8.75	-5%	3.96	-131%

continued

Exhibit 7.10C Supplementary Schedule, Pre-IPO Dot-Com Discount Study—*continued*

Company	Transaction Price	IPO Price	Discount from IPO Price[1]	IPO Date Close		90 Days After IPO		180 Days After IPO	
				Price	Discount	Price	Discount	Price	Discount
Webstakes.com, Inc.[d]	6.00	14.00	57%	11.50	48%	28.50	79%	13.00	NA
Xoom.com, Inc.[e]	10.80	14.00	23%	34.44	69%	58.00	81%	43.13	75%
Yesmail.com, Inc.[f]	1.75	11.00	84%	13.06	87%	33.25	95%	NA	NA
Mean			54%		67%		66%		56%
Median			54%		70%		79%		77%
Count			53		53		45		36

Note: See Exhibit 7.10D for footnotes.

Source of pricing information: CommScan, New York, NY. Prices are non split-adjusted.

Source: © Emory Business Valuation, LLC *Dot-Com Pre-IPO Study* (2000):B-1–B2, D-1.

150

Exhibit 7.10D Footnote Summary, Pre-IPO Dot-Com Discount Study

"C" Common Stock
"P" Convertible Preferred Stock
NA Not Available

(1) 1 minus (transaction price divided by offering price).
(2) Excludes redeemable preferred stock.
(3) Latest fiscal year, latest 12 months or interim sales annualized for meaningfulness.

The following footnotes highlight additional sale transactions within 5 months prior to the company's IPO.

(4) Autobytel.com, Inc. also had sales at $13.20 on November 10, 1998 and at $13.20 on December 21 and 24, 1998.
(5) Buy.com also had a sale at $9.07 in October, 1999.
(6) Drkoop.com, Inc. also had sales at $7.43 on March 3, 5, and 31, 1999.
(7) drugstore.com, Inc. also had sales at $19.86 in May, 1999 and at $17.65 in June, 1999.
(8) HomeStore.com, Inc. also had sales at $9.97 in June, 1999.
(9) Mail.com, Inc. also had sales at $5.00 in April, 1999.
(10) MiningCo.com, Inc. also had a sale at $5.48 in December, 1998.
(11) MP3.com, Inc. also had sales at $4.93 in May, 1999 and at $7.17 in June, 1999.
(12) Onvia.com also had a sale at $6.86 in December, 1999.
(13) Pets.com also had a sale at $9.97 in January, 2000.
(14) Phone.com, Inc. also had a sale at $12.00 in April, 1999.
(15) Quepasa.com, Inc. also had a sale at $6.50 in June, 1999.
(16) ShopNow.com, Inc. also had sales at $9.00 in May, June, and July 1999.
(17) Snowball.com also had a sale at $10.00 in January, 2000.
(18) Xoom.com, Inc. also had a sale at $10.80 in July, 1998.

(a) Bamboo.com, Inc. merged with Interactive Pictures in January, 2000 to form Internet Pictures Corp. (IPIX).
(b) COMPS.COM, Inc. was acquired by CoStar Group Inc. in January, 2000.
(c) MiningCo.com, Inc. changed its name to About.com in May, 1999.
(d) Webstakes.com, Inc. changed its name to Promotions.com in February, 2000.
(e) Xoom.com, Inc. acquired by NBC Inc. in May, 1999.
(f) Yesmail.com, Inc. acquired by CMGI Inc. in December, 1999.

Source: © Emory Business Valuation, LLC, *Dot-Com Pre-IPO Study* (2000): D-1.

Notes

1. John D. Emory, "The Value of Marketability as Illustrated in Initial Public Offerings of Common Stock—January 1980 through June 1981," *ASA Valuation* (June 1986): 66.
2. John D. Emory, "The Value of Marketability as Illustrated in Initial Public Offerings of Common Stock—February 1992 through July 1993," *Business Valuation Review* (March 1994): 3.
3. © Emory Business Valuation, LLC, *Dot-Com Pre-IPO Study* (2000).

Chapter 8

Factors Affecting Discounts for Lack of Marketability for Minority Interests

Barry Sziklay

      Management Planning Study
      FMV Opinions Study
      Johnson Study
Summary
Notes

This chapter draws on the material presented in Chapters 5, 6, and 7, organizing the findings in terms of the relevant factors impacting the magnitude of the discount for lack of marketability for minority interests. It also draws on material in Chapters 18 and 19, in which net asset value is the base to which the discount is applied.

While the classification in this chapter is somewhat arbitrary, and there is indeed some overlap among factors, the empirical data suggest that the primary drivers of the size of the discount for lack of marketability are as follows:

- Size of distributions (dividends, withdrawals)
- Prospects for liquidity (probable length of holding period)
- Pool of potential buyers (also affecting prospects for liquidity)
- Risk factors (affecting the investors' required rate of return during the holding period, i.e., the discount rate)
- Growth prospects (affecting the eventual potential sale price, i.e., terminal value)

SIZE OF DISTRIBUTIONS

Privately placed bonds and preferred stocks sell at little or no discount compared with publicly traded bonds and preferred stocks. Why is this so? It is because investors are receiving their returns as they go along in the form of interest and dividends, and these payments are in fixed amounts, so the investors know when and how much they expect to receive.

Distributions on common equity investments (e.g., common stocks and partnership interests) generally are not fixed, unlike the interest on bonds or the dividends on preferred stock. Nevertheless, the higher (and the more certain) the distribution, the lower the discount, whether the base from which the discount is taken is a publicly traded guideline group of securities or net asset value.

Unfortunately, neither the extensive restricted stock studies nor the pre-IPO studies shed light on the impact of the size of distributions. The reason is that virtually all of the stocks in both categories of studies are nondividend paying. One thing those studies *do* reveal is that discounts for lack of marketability when there are *no* distributions are quite high, with a median of around 45% in the pre-IPO studies.

For guidance on the size of discounts relative to various levels of distributions, the analyst must turn to other studies, such as *The Partnership Spectrum*. Most of these studies relate to discounts from net asset value.

The Partnership Spectrum Studies

A limited partnership interest in a public real estate limited partnership is an investment in an entity that itself has an interest in an operating real estate project (e.g., office buildings, industrial/warehouse facilities, research and development facilities, business parks, apartments and retirement centers, shopping centers, outlet malls and other retail-use space, manufactured housing communities, mobile home parks, hotels and other lodging facilities, restaurants, and mini-warehouses/self-storage facilities). For valuation purposes, appraisers use public market information related to secondary market transactions (see description below) in limited partner units that are similar to, but not the same as, the subject interest. They then take into consideration the unique characteristics of the subject interest and the fact that no public market exists for it. In deriving price-to-value discounts, appraisers frequently utilize a study conducted by Partnership Profiles, Inc., and reported in its annual May/June issue of *The Partnership Spectrum*.[1]

That issue reports on an annual study conducted by Partnership Profiles, Inc., featuring partnerships owning real estate assets. All of the partnerships included in this price-to-value discount study are publicly registered with the Securities and Exchange Commission (SEC), although none of the partnerships is publicly traded on any recognized securities exchange. Instead, units of the partnerships are bought and sold in the so-called limited partnership secondary market. This market is comprised of 10 to 12 independent securities brokerage firms that act primarily as intermediaries in matching buyers and sellers of units in unlisted partnerships of all types.

In a typical price-to-value discount study, the most recent unit net asset values reported by the sample group of partnerships are compared with the weighted average prices at which investors purchase units in these partnerships in the partnership secondary market during the two-month period of April and May of each year.

Partnership unit values used in the study are reported by the partnerships and represent either valuations prepared internally by general partners, independent valuations prepared by third-party appraisers retained on behalf of the partnerships, or some combination of the two. Each unit value generally represents an estimate of the total amount of the cash that would be distributed to limited partners on a per-unit basis, based on a hypothetical sale of the partnership's real estate assets and the liquidation of the partnership.

The results of price-to-value discount studies are consistent over the years reported by Partnership Profiles in that the two most important factors considered by secondary market buyers in pricing units of real estate partnerships are: (1) whether the partnership is consistently paying periodic cash distributions and (2) the degree of debt financing utilized by the partnership. This is evidenced by the relatively low price-to-value

Exhibit 8.1 *The Partnership Spectrum* Results

Partnership Category	No. of Partnerships	Average Discount	Average Yield
Insured Mortgages	9	21%	12.5%
Triple-Net-Lease	24	21%	10.5%
Equity—Distributing (low or no debt)	24	24%	9.2%
Equity—Distributing (moderate to high debt)	18	26%	7.7%
Equity—Nondistributing	9	35%	0%
Undeveloped Land	3	40%	0%

Source: The Partnership Spectrum (May/June 2000): 3.

discounts of debt-free insured mortgage and triple-net-lease programs, which consistently deliver high cash-distribution yields to buyers. At the other end of the discount spectrum are debt-laden partnerships, which are unable to pay cash distributions on a current basis and have no real prospects of doing so in the foreseeable future.

The results shown in Exhibit 8.1 are from the May/June 2000 issue of *The Partnership Spectrum,* from the highest distributions down through the lowest.

As can be seen, the average discounts range from 21% for the highest-distributing group up to 35 to 40% for those with no distributions.

Spencer Jefferies, editor and publisher of *The Partnership Spectrum,* discussed the results as follows:

> The question most often posed by business valuation professionals, real estate appraisers, and CPAs when using this discount study to determine discounts for minority interests involving real estate is how much of the price-to-value discounts applicable to secondary market trading in publicly-registered (but non-publicly traded) partnerships reflect lack of marketability versus lack of control/minority interest considerations.
>
> Although it is not possible to precisely quantify the amount of discount attributable to marketability versus minority interest considerations, it is the opinion of *The Partnership Spectrum*—as well as many appraisers—that most of this discount is due to minority interest considerations. Although the partnership secondary market is not a recognized securities exchange, it is nonetheless a market where there are usually multiple bidders who stand ready to make offers to purchase the units of virtually any publicly-registered partnership that has value. . . .
>
> Today, any qualified bidder can simply log on to the American Partnership Board Website and engage in e-Bay-like bidding for the units of hundreds of publicly-registered partnerships. While the partnership secondary market doesn't offer the liquidity of the New York Stock Exchange, the investments that change hands in this market are certainly more marketable than interests such as Family Limited Partnerships.
>
> The bottom line is that, with respect to the marketability of the partnerships included in the Re-Sale Discount Studies published annually . . . it is usually not a matter of *whether* a buyer can be found for the units of a particular partnership, but

how long it takes to locate a buyer, process the transaction, and get the seller paid. According to an internal study by American Partnership Board, the leading secondary market firm in terms of trading volume, the average amount of time required to find a buyer for the units of a publicly-registered partnership and send the net proceeds to the seller was approximately 60 days from the time the seller's paperwork was approved. . . .

For the reasons stated above, it does seem that most of the price-to-value discount applicable to secondary market trading in the units of public partnerships is due to minority interest considerations. But whether the breakdown of the minority interest versus the marketability component of the total discount is, say, 70/30 or 80/20 is impossible to quantify.

It is common practice for appraisers using the discount data presented in this study when valuing a minority interest in a Family Limited Partnership or some other highly illiquid investment involving real estate to adjust these discounts to account for the fact that the subject of their valuation is clearly less marketable than the partnership interests covered by this study.[2]

The analyst should also consider whether there is any indication of offers to acquire a limited partnership interest prior to the date of reported transactions. As often noted in the studies, price-to-value discounts typically shrink considerably when a partnership announces definitive, near-term liquidation plans. Accordingly, the study generally excludes any partnership that has announced definitive plans to liquidate within the next 12 months.

There does not appear to be any correlation between the size of the discount and the nature of the property. This conclusion is supported by the work of Christian L. Bendixen, ASA,[3] based on several multivariate regression analyses he performed on the 1997 Partnership Profiles, Inc. database of real estate limited partnerships. Bendixen concluded that, with respect to price-to-value discounts, there was little statistical significance due to the property variable. His findings corroborated the 1997 Partnership Profiles, Inc. findings regarding the yield and debt variables, which showed high statistical significance.

Comparison of the Subject Interest to Public Limited Partner Interests

In comparing subject interests to limited partner investments in publicly registered real estate partnerships, major differences include, but are not necessarily limited to, the following:

- Generally, no market currently exists for the subject interest since it generally is not registered with the SEC, and there are no plans to do so. The limited partnership interests of the public real estate partnerships trade in a secondary market, comprised of 10 to 12 independent brokerage firms, most of which operate as intermediaries in matching buyers and sellers of publicly registered limited partner interests. Subject interests are therefore less easily converted into cash than investments in publicly registered limited partnerships, thus impairing their marketability.

- As private companies not subject to SEC financial reporting requirements, subject companies' financial information normally is not disclosed, further impairing the marketability of such interests.

- Public limited partnerships often own a diversified portfolio of real estate investments in multiple states. The subject private interest may own only one building. This lack of diversification increases the risk associated with an investment in the subject interest as compared with an investment in the public limited partnerships. This impairs the marketability of the subject interest relative to a limited partner investment in a public real estate limited partnership.

PROSPECTS FOR LIQUIDITY

An extremely important factor driving the magnitude of the discount for lack of marketability is the prospect for liquidity within a known time frame, the shorter the better. In other words, the shorter the expected holding period, and the more certain the prospective transaction, the lower the discount. This factor is widely demonstrated in the empirical data. It is, of course, far more important for entities that do not make distributions, since the ultimate payoff is the only return that can be expected.

For the owner of a stock or partnership interest, liquidity can be achieved in several ways:

- Sale of all or part of the underlying asset(s) and payout of the proceeds
- Registration of the interest in an initial public offering, or lifting of restrictions on a block of restricted stock of a public company
- Sale of the entity and:
  - Receipt of cash proceeds
  - Receipt of stock that is more liquid than interests in the selling company

Restricted Stock Studies Pattern

The history of the restricted stock studies, as detailed in Chapter 6, certainly drives home the point that increased prospects for liquidity mean lower discounts for lack of marketability. From 1966 through the end of the 1980s, average discounts for restricted stock consistently ran about 33 to 35%. Then, when the rules changed in 1990, creating a more liquid market for restricted stocks, average discounts dropped to the low 20s. Finally, in 1997, when the required holding period was reduced from two years to one year, the only study done to date, the Columbia Financial Advisors study, found an average discount of only 13%.

Specific Restricted Stock and Pre–Initial Public Offering Study Findings

Securities and Exchange Commission Institutional Investor Study. The study found that discounts were related to the resale constraints applicable to the restricted securities. Essentially, any provisions that reduced the time or expense involved in reselling the stock tended to reduce the discount.

Standard Research Consultants Study. The Standard Research Consultants study reported that the longer the time needed to dispose of the restricted stock, the greater the discount.

Management Planning Study. The Management Planning, Inc. (MPI) study reported "some confirming tendency" to affirm the following expectations:

- **Number of Quarters to Dribble-Out.** The expectation was that longer calculated dribble-out periods would suggest higher discounts because of the longer period of time until liquidity could be achieved.
- **Number of Weeks Trading Volume to Sell.** The expectation was that longer calculated periods would suggest higher discounts because of the longer period of time until liquidity could be achieved.

Emory Pre–Initial Public Offering Studies. The John Emory pre-IPO studies covered transactions going back five months prior to completion of a public offering. As shown in Exhibit 7.10D, the discounts tended to drop as the transactions occurred closer to the IPO.

The Partnership Spectrum Findings

Over the last several years, more than 500 SEC-registered limited partnerships have liquidated, merged, or "rolled up" into a more marketable security. In anticipation of the possibilities of such liquidating events, average discounts from net asset value have shrunk sharply. When a partnership announces plans to liquidate, the discount immediately declines significantly. This is compelling evidence that the expected holding period has an important impact on the discount for lack of marketability.

POOL OF POTENTIAL BUYERS

Closely related to the prospects of liquidity for the entity is the pool of potential buyers for the block itself. As would be expected, the larger the pool of potential buyers, the lower the discount for lack of marketability, and vice versa.

Strength of Ultimate Trading Market

The more liquid the market in which the unrestricted stock traded, the lower the discount, and vice versa.

Securities and Exchange Commission Institutional Investor Study. The SEC study identified two factors that reflected the impact of the pool of potential buyers as reflected in the strength of the ultimate trading market:

> **The dollar amount of sales securities** (trading volume). Companies with the lowest dollar amount of sales of their securities during the test period accounted for most of the transactions with higher discounts, while they accounted for only a small portion of transactions involving lower discounts.
>
> **Trading market.** Discounts were greatest on restricted stocks with identical unrestricted securities traded over-the-counter, followed by those with unrestricted counterparts listed on the American Stock Exchange, and then by those with unrestricted counterparts listed on the New York Stock Exchange.[4]

Standard Research Consultants Study. The authors found that higher trading volume of the unrestricted stock was associated with lower discounts. They commented that the greater the company's trading volume, the greater the likelihood that, upon expiration of the resale restrictions, the restricted stock can be sold publicly without disrupting the market for the issuer's unrestricted stock.

Block Size

The larger the block, the smaller the pool of potential buyers.

Silber Study. The Silber study indicated some sensitivity to block size, with larger blocks tending to have higher discounts.

Management Planning Study. The MPI study found that block size divided by shares outstanding did not have an identifiable effect on the size of the discount. However, the study found that a higher block size divided by trading volume was associated with a higher discount.

Willamette Management Associates Pre–Initial Public Offering Studies. Although Willamette does not regularly report individual transaction data, they do from time to time study the effect of specific factors, often in conjunction with litigation.

In the case of *Howard v. Shay,*[5] an employee stock ownership plan (ESOP) owning just over 38% of the outstanding stock was terminated and the stock sold. In valuing the stock, the appraisers applied a 50% discount for lack of marketability. (Unlike most ESOPs, this one had no "put" option.)

Members of the ESOP brought a class action suit claiming undervaluation of the stock. Willamette searched its pre-IPO transaction database for all transactions that amounted to 25 to 49% of the outstanding stock for five years up to the ESOP's valuation date. The data showed average discounts of almost 50%, just a little higher than the average for transactions of all sizes. The court upheld the 50% discount.

FMV Opinions Study.   According to the FMV Opinions, Inc. (FMV) study, the discount was highest (20 to 30%) for blocks of stock valued at less than $10 million but decreased (10 to 20%) as the size of the block exceeded $10 million. For blocks of stock that exceeded 10% ownership, discounts were higher (20 to 30%) than for blocks representing less than 10% ownership.

RISK FACTORS

The studies confirm what one would expect in that higher levels of risk are associated with higher discounts for lack of marketability. This makes sense, since the potential negative impact of risk factors is exacerbated by inability to readily sell the investment. Risk is imbedded in the discount rate in the income approach and in the valuation multiples in the market approach when estimating the base value to which the discount for lack of marketability is applied. But high risk also makes it more difficult to sell the interest. Therefore, it is not "double dipping" to count the risk again as a factor exacerbating the discount for lack of marketability.

Level and Volatility of Issuer's Earnings

The studies show that high levels of earnings and stability of earnings are factors associated with lower discounts, while losses and/or high earnings volatility are associated with higher discounts.

Securities and Exchange Commission Institutional Investor Study.   The companies with the lowest dollar amount of earnings during the test period accounted for most of the transactions with higher discounts, while they accounted for only a small portion of transactions involving lower discounts. Issuers' earnings are far more related to size of discounts than are issuers' sales. For example, there were no transactions in restricted stocks of public companies with earnings deficits in the fiscal years preceding the dates of the transactions. The greater influence of earnings than of sales on the size of the discounts is probably due to the more proximate relationship of earnings than of sales to the riskiness of the investment.

Standard Research Consultants Study.   Approximately 60% of the transactions analyzed in the study were companies reporting net losses in the fiscal year prior to the placement date. Profitability in the fiscal year preceding the placement did not seem to influence the discount; the 11 companies showing a profit in the year pre-

Exhibit 8.2 Standard Research Consultants Study

Profitable Years of Latest Five	Median Discount
5	34%
2 to 4	39%
0 or 1	46%

ceding the year of the restricted sale had a median discount of 45% while the 17 that were unprofitable during the prior year had a median discount of 46%.

However, the *pattern* of earnings of the issuer did seem to matter. On average, companies that were profitable in each of the five years prior to the date of placement appeared to sell restricted stock at substantially smaller discounts than did those with two, three, or four unprofitable years during the five-year period. This correlation is best shown in Exhibit 8.2.

Management Planning Study. The expectation was that companies with lower earnings stability would lead to higher discounts and vice versa. This criteria yielded the clearest confirming correlation with the size of the discount of any factor. Exhibit 8.3 summarizes the updated study results concerning this criteria. (Transactions underlying these averages are shown in Exhibit 6.10.)

The first-quartile and fourth-quartile median and mean results using the earnings criteria were the lowest and highest discounts, respectively, of any of the 21 criteria analyzed by MPI.

The analysis also tended to clearly confirm the expectation that companies with higher earnings would have lower restricted stock discounts than companies with lower earnings, because substantial earning power tends to mitigate risk. Exhibit 8.4 summarizes the updated study correlation based on level of earnings. (Transactions underlying these averages are shown in Exhibit 6.9.)

Johnson Study. The Johnson data further supported the notion that the level of earnings impacts the discount, as seen in Exhibit 8.5.

Exhibit 8.3 Management Planning Study—Stability of Earnings

Discounts Relative to Stability of Earnings (Ranked Highest to Lowest)	Median	Mean
First Quartile	16.7%	19.3%
Second Quartile	30.4%	29.8%
Third Quartile	24.5%	24.9%
Fourth Quartile	37.8%	36%

Exhibit 8.4 Management Planning Study—Level of Earnings

Discounts Relative to Level of Earnings (Ranked Highest to Lowest)	Median	Mean
First Quartile	18.0%	21.1%
Second Quartile	29.3%	28.8%
Third Quartile	28.9%	28.6%
Fourth Quartile	31.4%	32.0%

Size of Issuer

Many studies have documented the fact that smaller size increases risk. The empirical data bears out the conclusion that higher risk associated with smaller size, as measured by either revenue or market capitalization is associated with higher discounts.

Securities and Exchange Commission Institutional Investor Study. The companies with the lowest dollar amount of sales during the test period accounted for most of the transactions with higher discounts, while they accounted for only a small portion of transactions involving lower discounts.

Standard Research Consultants Study. The authors indicated that the size of the issuer (in terms of revenues) had an inverse relationship to the size of the discount.

Management Planning Study. In general, the analysis indicated a clear tendency to confirm the expectation that companies with greater revenues would, on average, have lower restricted stock discounts than companies with lower revenues, because larger companies generally are viewed as less risky than smaller companies. Management Planning, Inc. noted, however, that several of the largest companies in terms of revenues had discounts well in excess of the discounts of several of the smallest companies.

FMV Opinions Study. The FMV study also corroborated the conclusion of the SEC study that the size of the discount is often a function of the size of the subject company's revenues.

Exhibit 8.5 Johnson Study—Net Income

	Average Discount
Sorted by Current Year Net Income	
Current Year Net Income	16%
Negative Net Income	23%
Sorted by Previous Year Net Income	
Positive Net Income	16%
Negative Net Income	23%

Exhibit 8.6 Johnson Study—Sales

	Average Discount
Sorted by Current Year Sales	
Greater than $12.7 million (median annual sales for companies examined)	18%
Less than $12.7 million	22%

FMV also reported that discounts appear to increase as the capitalization of a corporation decreases below $50 million (30 to 40%) compared with corporations having capitalizations in excess of $100 million (10 to 20%).

Johnson Study. As shown in Exhibit 8.6, the Johnson data also supports the tendency for smaller companies to sell at higher discounts.

SUMMARY

Factors affecting the magnitude of the discount for lack of marketability for minority interests especially include:

- Size of distributions during holding period
- Prospects for liquidity (length of likely holding period)
- Size of potential pool of buyers for the interest
- Risk factors affecting the issuing company during the holding period

Within each of the above are several subfactors.

Owners of blocks of minority stock with some limited degree of control may have the ability to influence the above factors and thus mitigate to some extent the discount for lack of marketability. Most analysts believe that prospects for growth in value mitigate the discount for lack of marketability, but none of the studies address this factor.

This chapter has summarized empirical studies, which have documented the reality of the foregoing factors. The dispersion of discounts in all the studies is very wide. To the greatest extent possible, the analyst should examine these factors for the subject company and judge discounts for lack of marketability accordingly, rather than just assuming that the broad averages of discount for lack of marketability studies automatically apply to any given company or interest in a company.

Notes

1. *The Partnership Spectrum,* Spencer Jeffries, ed. (May/June 2000).
2. Ibid., pp. 6–8.

3. The 1997 Partnership Profiles, Inc. database of real estate limited partnerships.
4. "Discounts Involved in Purchases of Common Stock (1966–1969)," *Institutional Investor Study Report of the Securities and Exchange Commission,* H.R. Doc. W. 64, part 5, 92nd Cong., 1st Session, 1971, 2444–2456.
5. *Howard v. Shay,* 1993 U.S. Dist. LEXIS 20153 (C.D. Cal. 1993), *rev'd* and *remanded by,* 100 F.3d 1484 (9th Cir. 1996), *cert. denied,* 520 U.S. 1237 (1997).

Chapter 9

Discounts for Lack of Marketability for Controlling Interests

It is often necessary to agree on the cash equivalent value today (or as of some date certain) for a controlling interest in a closely held business, whether or not the business will actually be sold. Examples of this cash equivalency analysis include federal estate taxes (in the case of death of controlling equity holder) or the value of a closely held business as marital property (in the case of a divorce).

In many reported decisions, the U.S. Tax Court has recognized that discounts for lack of marketability for controlling ownership interests in closely held companies are appropriate. The courts have used language such as the following:[1]

> Even controlling shares in a nonpublic corporation suffer from lack of marketability because of the absence of a ready private placement market and the fact that flotation costs would have to be incurred if the corporation were to publicly offer its stock.

The rationale for a marketability discount on controlling interests of closely held companies is that "[t]he controlling owner of a closely held business who wishes to liquidate his or her controlling ownership interest generally faces the following transactional considerations:"

- Uncertain time horizon to complete the offering or sale
- Cost to prepare for and execute the offering or sale
- Risk concerning eventual sale price
- Noncash and deferred transaction proceeds
- Inability to hypothecate (i.e., the inability to borrow against the estimated value of the stock)[2]

All of the above considerations make the sale of the controlling interest in a closely held business risky, difficult, and costly. For this reason, many valuators believe that such controlling interests suffer from some measure of lack of marketability that needs to be represented via a discount adjustment to value.

Discounts for lack of marketability (DLOMs) for controlling interests are an entirely different story from discounts for lack of marketability for minority interests. For one thing, unlike in minority interest transactions, there is no empirical transaction database from which to draw guidance for quantifying discounts for lack of marketability for controlling interests.

Second, while there is some overlap, the list of factors that affect the size of the DLOM for controlling interests is considerably different from the factors affecting minority interest DLOMs.

Addressing marketability discounts for controlling interests, Chris Mercer concludes as follows:

- "The marketability discount applicable to minority interests is clearly different than any "illiquidity discount" or "marketability discount" applicable to controlling interests.

- The two discounts (if, in fact, the latter exists) are applicable to different valuation bases.
- By obvious inference, market evidence applicable to minority interests, which comes from publicly traded minority interests, would not be relevant in assessing the magnitude of any "illiquidity discount" or "marketability discount" applicable to controlling interest transactions, which occur in a different market entirely than the public securities markets."[3]

I agree.

Where DLOMs are appropriate for controlling interests, they typically are much smaller than those for minority interests. Discounts for lack of marketability for controlling interests allowed in the U.S. Tax Court range from 3 to 33%, compared with the more typical 30 to 45% for minority interests.

DISCOUNTS FOR LACK OF MARKETABILITY FOR CONTROLLING INTERESTS: A CONTROVERSIAL CONCEPT

The whole concept of DLOMs for controlling interests is still controversial in the minds of some. There are those who believe that there should *never* be a discount for lack of marketability for controlling interests. Others have espoused the notion that whether a DLOM is appropriate for a controlling interest depends on how the control value was derived. The lack of an empirical database to serve as a benchmark exacerbates the problem.

As we examine what sound like very diverse positions, however, we find that much of the disagreement turns out to be more semantic than real.

"CONTROL, MARKETABLE" IS AN OXYMORON

A few take the position that there is no DLOM for controlling interests.[4] Even these people recognize, however, that it is impossible to call your friendly broker and sell your company instantly and receive cash in three days. They call this problem a lack of *liquidity* rather than marketability. As discussed in Chapter 1, I treat this as a semantic distinction without any difference as a practical matter.

As discussed in earlier chapters, the benchmark for marketability is being able to call your broker, sell the stock instantly at a nearly exactly known price, and receive cash in three business days. Since this is not possible with a controlling interest, it seems to me that there is no such thing as "control, marketable." This observation applies whether the company is public or private.

It is only for minority interests that the levels-of-value chart (Exhibit 9.1) makes a distinction between "marketable" and "nonmarketable." I know of no company, public or private, that could meet the benchmark criteria for marketability, that is, a

Exhibit 9.1   Levels of Value in Terms of Characteristics of Ownership

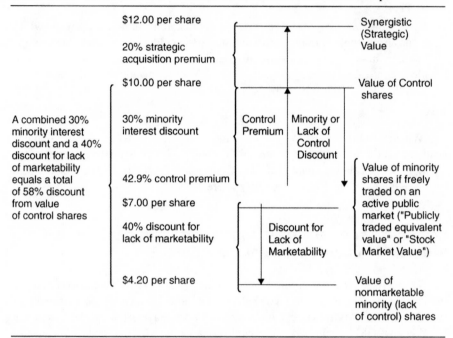

known sale price and cash in three days. Therefore, I submit that the expression "control, marketable" is an oxymoron.

In 2000 *The Business Broker* published the results of its fourth annual national survey of business brokers, which included responses to issues such as the lengths of time it took to sell businesses in the years 1999 and 2000. The survey revealed that the average time it took for a business to sell was approximately six months from listing to closing.[5] That ignores the time needed to prepare the business for listing, the average discount of the sale price from the listing price, and all the businesses that were listed but never sold.

Obviously, a controlling interest does not enjoy the same level of marketability that a publicly traded minority interest enjoys.

BASES FROM WHICH CONTROLLING INTEREST DISCOUNTS FOR LACK OF MARKETABILITY MAY BE DEDUCTED

As emphasized throughout this book, a discount is meaningless until the base to which it is applied is made clear. The three bases most often encountered from which a controlling interest discount for lack of marketability is deducted are:

1. Control buyout value (cash equivalent basis)[6]
2. Publicly traded stock value
3. Net asset value

Unfortunately, these bases and their implications may not always be as clear-cut as one might hope.

Buyout Price as Control Value Basis

The price that the control owner could expect to receive upon sale is a logical basis for a DLOM. This price could be estimated by the market approach, observing sales of similar companies. This value also could be estimated by the income approach, discounting or capitalizing estimated cash flows (or some other measure of income) that a control owner could expect to realize. Another possible way of estimating a buyout price is the excess earnings method.[7]

Public Offering Value of Stock as Control Value Basis

Unlike a minority stockholder, a controlling stockholder may register for a public offering of the stock. Thus, the estimated potential public trading price could be the basis for a control value.

When public markets are strong, especially for the industry in which the company operates, the potential public trading price could be as much as or more than the control owner could expect to receive for the sale of the company. Therefore, under such conditions, a control owner might maximize the price by going public. However, the owner is not likely to be able to sell (or even register) *all* the stock, so the balance retained should be discounted in value as restricted stock. Alternatively, if buyouts of public companies are rampant in the industry, one might estimate a control value by using the guideline public company method plus some premium for control.

Net Asset Value as Control Value Basis

Net asset value usually is construed to represent a control rather than a minority value. This is because the control owner has the option of liquidating, hypothecating, or otherwise utilizing the assets, an option not available to the minority owner. The assets usually are valued at their realizable value, either on a liquidation or going-concern premise of value, whichever is more appropriate for the given assignment.

The factors discussed in this chapter affecting the potential discount are also applicable when net asset value is the control value basis.

FACTORS AFFECTING CONTROLLING INTEREST DISCOUNTS FOR LACK OF MARKETABILITY

I noted earlier that two of the bases from which controlling interest DLOMs might be applied are:

1. A buyout price
2. A public offering price

In order to receive proceeds on any of the above bases, the company generally must accomplish several tasks:

-   Create accounting records satisfactory to buyers and/or regulatory authorities.
-   Incur legal expenses to document company attributes, often including representations and warranties regarding the state of various aspects of the company (e.g., contingent liabilities).
-   Utilize substantial management time to facilitate the above and cure negative factors that would be undesirable to the typical buyer (e.g., ease nonperforming relatives off the payroll).
-   Find a buyer or buyers (easier for some kinds of companies than for others).

The buyout price reflects accomplishment of the above tasks.

If a company is being valued as of a certain effective date (e.g., for taxes, a divorce, or a minority oppression suit) using any of the control valuation bases discussed earlier, rarely has it completed any of the above items as of the valuation date. The costs of accomplishing these tasks form part of the DLOM when comparing value at a given date to expected proceeds from any of the foregoing bases of value.

Furthermore, accomplishing these necessary steps takes time. Therefore, eventual expected proceeds need to be discounted to account for the time value of money. In some cases, the time value of money may be offset by expected positive cash flows during the holding period.

Very importantly, all the bases of value for the controlling interest are *estimates*. Risk-averse investors could not reasonably be expected to pay 100% of the estimated future proceeds, so the expected proceeds need to be discounted to reflect the uncertainty of the amount and timing of proceeds to be realized.

Finally, transaction costs usually are deducted from the price before arriving at net proceeds. Such costs may or may not be deducted in arriving at fair market value. Tax Court cases are mixed on this issue.

Remember that *fair market value* (FMV) means (1) cash equivalent (2) as of some specific effective valuation date. It is *not* what you might receive at some time in the future *after* you have spent thousands or millions of dollars "fixing" the company to make it more saleable. To arrive at FMV today, all such costs need to be deducted from proceeds ultimately expected and then adjusted to present value for the time necessary to complete them and also for risks (e.g., market changes in interim). Of course, such costs may have been deducted before arriving at the value of 100% of the company, in which case they should not be deducted again.

Flotation Costs

The costs of going public, called *flotation costs* (i.e., the costs of floating a public offering), often form the basis for the DLOM from an estimated public offering price. The major fixed costs required are audit fees, legal fees to register with the Securities and Exchange Commission (SEC), and printing costs for the preliminary and final offering circulars. These costs combined usually run well into six figures for smaller companies and seven figures or more for larger companies.

The major variable cost is underwriters' fees. These typically approach 15% of expected proceeds for smaller companies, scaling downward by a few percentage points for larger companies. The total cost of flotation for a smaller company—that is, the size of a few million dollars—can easily exceed 20% of expected proceeds.

Professional and Administrative Costs

At any given time, very few companies are ready for sale. Frequently, a company must incur some or all of the following costs to prepare for sale.

Accounting Costs.   Few small, privately owned companies routinely prepare financial statements that are both comprehensive and reliable enough to satisfy most buyers. Some additional accounting usually is required, often an audit, for multiple years.

Legal Costs.   Extensive legal documentation is required for a transfer of ownership. This expense varies greatly from one situation to another, but it is never low.

Appraisals.   If the company owns real estate, tangible personal property, or significant intangible assets, buyers often insist on independent appraisals. Such appraisals are performed not just to satisfy the buyers and possible financing sources, but often also to facilitate the allocation of purchase price, which has major tax consequences for both buyer and seller, who must agree on the allocation, at least in an asset sale. Many deals founder on this issue.

Management Time.   Working with outside professionals and potential buyers, as well as tending to all the internal details of preparing for a sale, can absorb much or even most of top management's time and attention during the process. This usually incurs a significant opportunity cost in terms of distracting management from other productive efforts for a period of many months.

Risk of Achieving Expectations

It is important to remember that each of the bases for control value involves estimates of what eventually can be realized. The control interest seller bears the risk of:

- Whether the sale or liquidation plan chosen can be accomplished
- If so, how long it will take
- How much the actual proceeds will be relative to the estimate

The degree of these uncertainties will vary greatly from one company to another and is a major factor in quantifying a DLOM. Investors shun risk. The discount rate to reach a present value from the expected proceeds must reflect both the time value of money and a substantial premium for the risk of not achieving expectations.

Lack of Ability to Hypothecate

A controlling interest in a private company does not necessarily, or even usually, make the stock acceptable collateral for a bank loan. When a control owner offers his or her stock as collateral, he or she should expect the friendly banker to accept it, as long as it is accompanied by a personal guarantee plus publicly traded stock worth 125% of the loan value.

Transaction Costs

In most cases there will be a commission due to an intermediary. If not, the company usually will have expended considerable funds in locating and negotiating with buyers. Depending on the situation, courts may or may not allow transaction costs as a factor in quantifying the DLOM. (For a case that did allow transaction costs, see *Estate of Borgatello v. Commissioner* in a subsequent section.)

PUBLIC VERSUS PRIVATE COMPANY ACQUISITION MULTIPLES

Some argue that controlling interests in private companies should have a DLOM because they almost always are acquired at lower valuation multiples than are otherwise comparable public companies. In support of this hypothesis, proponents cite *Mergerstat* statistics, as shown in Exhibit 9.2.

John Phillips and Neill Freeman challenged this conclusion in a 1995 article examining a relevant selection of the *Mergerstat* data and presented their own conclusion as follows:

> We confirmed that differences in size, industry, and profitability explain much of the difference between the P/E [price/earnings] multiples of different companies. Our

Exhibit 9.2   Median P/E Offered: Public versus Private, 1991–2000

Year	Acquisitions of Public Companies		Acquisitions of Private Companies	
1991	15.9	(93)	8.5	(23)
1992	18.1	(89)	17.6	(15)
1993	19.7	(113)	22.0	(14)
1994	19.8	(184)	22.0	(18)
1995	19.4	(239)	15.5	(16)
1996	21.7	(288)	17.7	(31)
1997	25.0	(389)	17.0	(83)
1998	24.0	(362)	16.0	(207)
1999	21.7	(434)	18.4	(174)
2000	18.0	(379)	16.0	(130)

Note: ( ) denotes number of transactions reporting P/E.
Source: Mergerstat Review 2001 (Los Angeles: Applied Financial Information, LP, 2001).

results suggest that the difference between median public and private P/E multiples reflects differences between these variables in the composition of the two samples, public and private. Therefore, once adjustments are made for differences in size, profitability and industry, no additional adjustment for marketability appears justified for controlling interests.[8]

The Phillips and Freeman research makes a worthwhile contribution to DLOM theory. However, it is neither comprehensive nor rigorous enough to answer once and for all the question as to the impact of the public versus private company factor. *Mergerstat* collects and analyzes data for transactions over $100 million, based entirely on data filed with the SEC. *Mergerstat/Shannon Pratt's Control Premium Study* compiles information on public companies of all sizes that have been acquired. Data are assembled at BVMarketData.com regarding sales of both private and public companies under $100 million, with data collected from business intermediaries as well as the SEC. We have initiated research on the public versus private impact for companies up to $500 million (face value of the transaction) and plan to report results in a future issue of *Shannon Pratt's Business Valuation Update.* We also plan to conduct additional research utilizing all three of the above databases.

COURT TREATMENT OF CONTROLLING INTEREST DISCOUNTS FOR LACK OF MARKETABILITY

The U.S. Tax Court clearly has recognized DLOMs for controlling interests. In fact, when DLOMs have been an issue in the U.S. Tax Court, they have been accepted far more often than they have been rejected. The Tax Court statement quoted most often on this issue is from the 1982 case, *Estate of Andrews v. Commissioner:* "Even controlling shares in a nonpublic corporation suffer from lack of marketability because of the absence of a ready private placement market and the fact that flotation costs would have to be incurred if the corporation were to publicly offer its stock."[9]

However, the Tax Court has been uneven in its application of DLOMs for controlling interests. I believe that this apparent inconsistency arises largely from three sources:

1. Differences in the facts and circumstances from one case to another, even though the differences may not be fully apparent from the summary of facts included in the written opinion
2. The quality of the expert testimony presented to the court, especially its direct relevance to the facts and circumstances of the case at hand
3. Which judge is deciding the case

As an aside, these three reasons should always be kept in mind when considering court cases. They lead inescapably to the conclusion that court decisions are often distorted by imperfections in information. This is one reason why appraisers, who should rely on market data, must avoid citing court cases as relevant evidence. In legal parlance, they are not probative for appraisers.

Examples of Cases Allowing Controlling Interest Discounts for Lack of Marketability

The following are examples of cases illustrating the wide range of discounts.

Estate of Hendrickson v. Commissioner, 30% Discount.[10]   The interest at issue was 49.97%, but the court deemed it a controlling interest because the balance of the stock was divided among 29 shareholders and the 49.97% block was deemed to constitute control "in substance."

Both discounted cash flow (DCF) and market approaches were presented, but the court ultimately based its decision on the market approach, using the guideline public company method. The IRS's expert testified to a 10% discount for lack of marketability because decedent's shares were effectively a controlling interest.

In accepting the taxpayer's expert's proposed 30% DLOM, the court cited the following factors regarding the marketability of the stock:

• The subject company, a bank, had few opportunities for growth.
• The bank's earnings were subject to significant interest rate risk.
• The bank had no employee stock option plan or history of repurchasing shares.
• There was no readily available public or private market for the bank's shares.

The court then went on to elaborate with the following:

> While we recognize that elements of control may enhance marketability, we do not think that the estate shares were rendered marketable by virtue of their effective con-

trol. . . . A buyer of the estate shares would either have to sell the block privately, cause [the bank] to make a public offering, or seek an acquiror. Any of these three options could take a number of months, and require significant transaction costs for the services of accountants, lawyers, and investment bankers.

Estate of Dunn v. Commissioner, **15% Discount.**[11]   The interest at issue was 62.96% of the outstanding stock. In arriving at its base value, the court allocated 65% weight to net asset value and 35% to capitalized net cash flow.

The parties conceded that a 15% discount for lack of marketability and a 7.5% discount for lack of supermajority control were appropriate, which the court applied additively in this case.

Estate of Jameson v. Commissioner, **3% Discount.**[12]   The interest at issue was 98% of a holding company with timberland as its primary asset. The court reached its base value by the net-asset-value method. It concluded a 3% DLOM because 97% of the assets of the corporation were highly marketable and only 3% of the assets were unmarketable. (As we go to press, this case is on appeal.)

Estate of Dougherty v. Commissioner, **25% Discount.**[13]   The court found a 25% DLOM applicable to a 100% interest in the stock of an investment company where the base value was the underlying net asset value.

Estate of Maggos v. Commissioner, **25% Discount.**[14]   The company was a Pepsi-Cola bottler. The court decided on a 25% DLOM, saying that "shares in the company could not be sold without the approval of Pepsi-Cola, Inc."

Estate of Borgatello v. Commissioner, **33% Discount.**[15]   On decedent's 82.76% interest in a real estate holding company, the Tax Court allowed a 33% DLOM, which it broke down as follows:

Potential tax on capital gains	25%
Restrictions on stock transfer	3%
Transaction and other costs	6%
Total DLOM	33% (rounded)

Case Denying Controlling Interest Discounts for Lack of Marketability

Estate of Cloutier v. Commissioner.[16] The interest at issue in this case was 100% of the stock of a company whose primary asset was a television station. The parties stipulated to the value apart from discounts and premiums, so the only issue was whether a DLOM applied and, if so, how much.

The stipulated value was based on "transactional and financial data," not on publicly traded guideline companies. Based largely on restricted stock and pre-IPO studies, the taxpayer's expert opined to a 25% DLOM.

The court rejected the discount entirely, because the discount to which the expert testified was based on publicly traded guideline companies, which were not used in arriving at the stipulated base value.

SUMMARY

Discounts for lack of marketability are very real for controlling interests. However, the reasons for them and, consequently, the analysis needed to quantify them are quite different from those for discounts for lack of marketability for minority interests. The lack of benchmark data exacerbates the measurement problem.

The base from which the discount is taken usually is an estimate of what could be realized in a sale of the controlling interest at some future time. Courts have widely accepted discounts for lack of marketability for controlling interests, but they expect relevant and adequate evidence and analysis to support the discount.

Notes

1. *Estate of Andrews v. Commissioner,* 79 T.C. 938 (1982).
2. Shannon P. Pratt, Robert F. Reilly, and Robert P. Schweihs, *Valuing a Business,* 4th ed. (New York, McGraw-Hill, 2000), pp. 412–413.
3. Z. Christopher Mercer, *Quantifying Marketability Discounts: Developing and Supporting Marketability Discounts in the Appraisal of Closely Held Business Interests* (Memphis: Peabody Publishing, LP, 1997), p. 344.
4. See Z. Christopher Mercer, "Should Marketability Discounts Be Applied to Controlling Interests of Private Companies?" *Business Valuation Review* (June 1994): 55–65.
5. *The Business Broker,* vol. 18, no. 9 (September 1999): 4.
6. If the standard of value is fair market value, it must be cash or cash equivalent. If part of consideration received was not in cash, the face value must be adjusted to a cash equivalent value before deducting a discount for lack of marketability.
7. For discussions of estimating control value by these various methods, see Fishman, Pratt, et al., *Guide to Business Valuations,* 11th ed. (Fort Worth: Practitioners Publishing Company, 2001), and Pratt, Reilly, and Schweihs, *Valuing a Business,* 4th ed. and *Valuing Small Businesses and Professional Practices,* 3rd ed. (New York: McGraw-Hill, 2000 and 1998 respectively).
8. John R. Phillips and Neill W. Freeman, "Do Privately-Held Controlling Interests Sell for Less?" *Business Valuation Review,* vol. 14, no. 3 (September 1995): 102.
9. *Estate of Andrews v. Commissioner,* 79 T.C. 938 (1982).
10. *Estate of Hendrickson v. Commissioner,* T.C. Memo 1999-278, 78 T.C.M. (CCH) 322 (1999).

11. *Estate of Dunn v. Commissioner,* T.C. Memo 2000-12, 79 T.C.M. (CCH) 1337 (2000).

12. *Estate of Jameson v. Commissioner,* T.C. Memo 1999-43, 77 T.C.M. (CCH) 1383 (1999).

13. *Estate of Dougherty v. Commissioner,* T.C. Memo 1990-274, 59 T.C.M. (CCH) 772 (1990).

14. *Estate of Maggos v. Commissioner,* T.C. Memo 2000-129, 79 T.C.M. (CCH) 1861 (2000).

15. *Estate of Borgatello v. Commissioner,* T.C. Memo 2000-264, 80 T.C.M. (CCH) 260 (2000).

16. *Estate of Cloutier v. Commissioner,* T.C. Memo 1996-49, 71 T.C.M. (CCH) 2001 (1996).

Chapter 10

Quantitative Marketability Discount Model

Z. Christopher Mercer

INTRODUCTION

In the context of the levels of value that appraisers discuss so frequently, the marketability discount is that conceptual valuation discount necessary to entice prospective investors in illiquid securities to purchase them rather than similar investments that are readily marketable.[1] It is the discount that converts an appraisal at the marketable minority (freely traded, freely tradable, as if freely traded) level of value into a nonmarketable minority interest conclusion, as indicated in the levels-of-value chart reproduced in Exhibit 10.1.

Approached more directly, the nonmarketable minority interest level of value can be developed by valuing cash flows expected to be available to the minority shareholder in the context of a marketable minority interest valuation.

This chapter summarizes the conceptual logic of one way to simulate the thinking of real or hypothetical investors to develop valuation indications at the nonmarketable minority interest level.[2] The Quantitative Marketability Discount Model (QMDM) was formally introduced in *Quantifying Marketability Discounts* in 1997.[3]

Unfortunately, many appraisers look at the typical results of the various restricted stock studies, which have had typical discounts in the general range of 30 to 35%, as an *absolute indication* of the magnitude of marketability discounts for

178

Exhibit 10.1   Levels of Value Chart

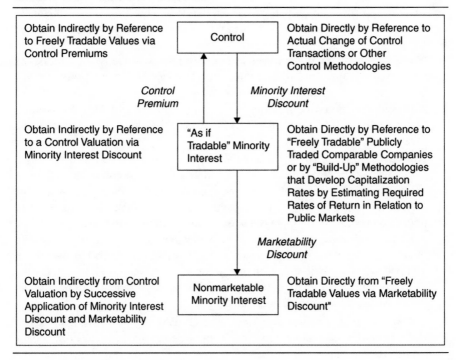

minority interests of private companies. *Quantifying Marketability Discounts* makes the point that the relevant economic information from the restricted studies is the implied required holding period returns (discount rates) for investments during the applicable period of illiquidity of the otherwise publicly tradable securities examined. This "relevant economic information" includes the expected holding period, the required returns of investors, and their expectations for growth in value and for interim cash flows. The QMDM enables appraisers to estimate the value of illiquid securities in relationship to their freely tradable value indications and to develop marketability discounts that are both reasoned and reasonable in the context of the facts and circumstances of individual appraisals.

WHAT IS THE QUANTITATIVE MARKETABILITY DISCOUNT MODEL?

The QMDM attempts to look at an investment in a closely held business interest much the way as real-life investors and the hypothetical willing investors of fair market value. There are five key inputs to the QMDM, and they correspond to the basic questions that I believe investors ask about illiquid investments.

The QMDM assumes that the hypothetical willing investor and the business appraiser consider the use of the model in the context of a fully developed business appraisal at the marketable minority interest level. In other words, the basis for comparison of the worth of an illiquid, minority interest in a business is investments in similar, publicly traded companies. It is in the context of such an appraisal that we develop the key assumptions of the QMDM.[4]

Given that we know the marketable minority interest value of a business, the basic questions that investors ask and the corresponding QMDM inputs are:

1. *How much can this business grow in value over time?* The QMDM input assumption is the *expected growth rate in value,* from the marketable minority value today.

2. *What can I expect to receive in distributions (i.e., spendable or investable cash) while I wait?* The QMDM assumes dividends on a C corporation-equivalent basis, expressed in terms of a yield on the marketable minority interest value derived in the appraisal. This corresponds to the comparable yields on publicly traded companies. When there is a reasonable expectation that dividends will be paid, the analyst must estimate the yield, relative to the marketable minority interest value indication, of the security. The QMDM then considers the impact of dividends or distributions on the value of the illiquid security over the expected holding period for the investment. For purposes of this brief discussion, we will assume there are no dividends.

3. *Will my distributions grow over time?* The QMDM allows for the appraiser to make an appropriate assumption about the expected growth rate in dividends over the expected holding period.

4. *How long will I have to wait until I can expect to achieve liquidity?* Since there is no active public market for the closely held company, investors desire to know how long before liquidity opportunities are available, whether from a stock repurchase program, an initial public offering, a sale of the business, or some other means.[5] The duration of the expected holding period is usually discussed in terms of an approximate range estimated by the appraiser based on the facts and circumstances of a particular company.

   Unfortunately, most of us do not know what will happen in the future until after it has happened. That is the plight of every investor and every appraiser, and is the essence of risk. Some appraisers have expressed far more discomfort with estimating a holding period that is essentially unknowable than in making other estimates or judgments regarding the future that are equally unknowable. However, investors must make decisions based on the facts and circumstances of each investment, and so must appraisers. For example, every forecast of earnings made in a discounted cash flow (DCF) valuation method requires the same kind of estimating in the face of uncertainty. Both kinds of estimates, DCF and expected holding periods using the QMDM, must be made in the context of the facts and circumstances of each investment. Rest assured, if an appraiser does not estimate the holding period specifically and nevertheless selects a marketability discount, he or she *has made an implicit assumption about the holding period that may or may not be consistent with the facts of a case.*

5. *What is my discount rate while I wait?* In the QMDM, we call the appropriate
    discount rate the *required holding period return.* The base for estimating the
    required holding period return is the equity discount rate in the appraisal at the
    marketable minority interest level. We then consider additional, specific risks
    that relate not to the value of the enterprise but specifically to investors in illiq-
    uid interests of the enterprise. It is generally accepted that the markets exact a
    price (i.e., a price reduction) for illiquidity. The specific risks relating to illiquid
    investments represent our attempt to begin to measure or quantify that price
    reduction. We usually express the required holding period return in terms of an
    approximate range.

While I have introduced these questions in the context of the QMDM, they have
broader application. In fact, they are the very same questions that rational investors
ask about virtually any type of investment. This is the beauty of the QMDM. It
requires the appraiser to ask, and answer, to the best of his or her ability, the essential questions that underlie rational investment decisions.

The important thing to remember about the QMDM is that it is an *expectational*
model. Its commonsense logic is geared to quantify the expectations of returns for
rational investors in illiquid, closely held securities. It is, therefore, grounded in
expectations for future growth in value and dividends over an expected holding
period. I believe that the model reflects how investment decisions actually get made
by rational, real-life investors.

The threshold question that investors must ask (and answer) is: *How much am I
willing to pay for (or accept) an illiquid investment with the characteristics of the subject illiquid interest in a closely held enterprise?*

This is the essential question addressed by the QMDM. In the process of answer-
ing it, we determine the implied marketability discount applicable to the subject interest from the base valuation at the marketable minority interest level of value.

QUANTITATIVE MARKETABILITY DISCOUNT MODEL: BASE CASE

Chapter 8 of *Quantifying Marketability Discounts* presents a base case for consideration. There was an error in the base case that had no impact on the theory or
results of the illustration. This chapter uses a corrected base case. Assume that a subject company earns $0.10 per share (after tax). This base case is summarized in
Exhibit 10.2, beginning with a simplified valuation at the marketable minority interest level of value.

Using this base example for illustration purposes, I will set out some assumptions for purposes of quantifying a marketability discount:

*   **Growth Rate of Value = 6%.** The buildup in the exhibit assumes an annual earn-
    ings growth of 6%. As no dividends or distributions to shareholders are implied
    by this assumption, we similarly assume a growth rate in value of 6%.

Exhibit 10.2   Summary of QMDM Base Case

Enterprise Level Valuation - 1
Single-Period Capitalization of Earnings

ACAPM Build-up of Cap Rate

Long-Term Treasury Yield	5.5%	Current Rate
+ Ibbotson Small Stock Premium	9.5%	Premium over Treasuries
+ Specific Company Risk Factors	1.0%	Specified by Analyst
= **Discount Rate (DR)**	**16.0%**	*Enterprise Level*
− **Anticipated Growth in Earnings**	**−6.0%**	
= **Capitalization Rate (CR)**	**10.0%**	*Enterprise Level*

Net Earnings Multiple (= 1/CR)	**10.0**	**P/E Multiple**
Assumed After-Tax Earning Power	**$0.10**	**Per Share**
Freely Tradable Value Per Share	**$1.00**	**Per Share**

How can this be? The enterprise level of value assumes that available earnings are distributed and, at least in theory, reinvested by the recipient at the discount rate. But in the present case, we know there will be no distributions. Perhaps the $0.10 per share of earnings reflects a significant adjustment to normalize management compensation. For valuation purposes at the marketable minority interest level, this may be appropriate. However, if the owner–manager is actually going to take bonus of those earnings at year-end, they will not be distributed to a minority shareholder. Nevertheless, earning power may well be growing at the stipulated rate of 6%. Other things being equal, if earning power grows, then the base value of the enterprise will also be growing.

The base case reflects the extreme case where *no earnings are reinvested.* Note that if we assume that *all earnings will be reinvested at the discount rate,* then the expected growth rate of value would be 16%. In specific valuation situations, the appraiser will have to estimate the expected growth rate in value based on the known facts and circumstances, including the subject company's history of and expectations for operations.

- **Interim Cash Flows (Yield) = 0%.** Later we will deal with the issue of interim returns in the quantification of marketability discounts. But in this first, more simplified example, assume that all earnings are paid out to management or otherwise made unavailable to minority shareholders.

- **Probable Holding Period = 10 years.** We will assume that the probable holding period is exactly 10 years and explain this in greater detail later in the chapter. Given the base value of $1.00, the expected growth rate of value of 6% per year, and the probable holding period of 10 years, the expected terminal cash flow is $1.79 per share, that is, $(1 + 6\%)$.

- **Required Holding Period (Rate of) Return = 20% per Year.** The required holding period rate of return is a *discount rate* applicable to the cash flows from the subject illiquid investment *from the perspective of the minority shareholder.* This required return represents a 4% premium, the underlying 16% discount rate applicable to the enterprise. The required holding period return reflects the investor's required rate of return or the opportunity cost of investing in the subject company versus another similar investment that has immediate market liquidity. The 4% holding-period premium accounts for the risks applicable to the interest that are not applicable to the enterprise. We will also look at this assumption in greater detail later in the chapter.

This analysis may seem simplistic; however, it reflects the kind of thinking that real-life investors apply in making investment decisions. The above assumptions are shown graphically in Exhibit 10.3.

Given these assumptions, we would value the subject interest at $0.29 per share. This represents the present value of the terminal cash flow of $1.79 per share (the result of $1.00 growing at 6% compounded for 10 years) to be received 10 years out, discounted to the present at the required holding period return of 20%, that is, $1.79/(1 + 20%).[10]

The implied marketability discount based on this analysis is 71% (the percentage difference between $1.00 per share enterprise value on a marketable minority interest basis and the indicated fair market value, or $0.29 per share, on a nonmarketable minority interest basis). Algebraically, the *calculated marketability discount, MD,* can be seen as shown in Exhibit 10.4.

Exhibit 10.3   Graphic Representation of Investor Assumptions

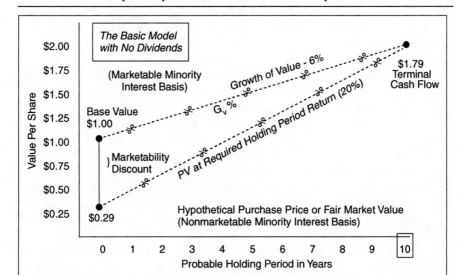

Exhibit 10.4   Calculated Marketability Discount

$$MD = \left[1 - \left(\frac{\text{Shareholders's Value}}{\text{Enterprise Value}} \right) \right]\%$$

or

$$\left[1 - \frac{\text{Value of Expected Cash Flows to Minority Shareholder}}{\text{Value of Expected Cash Flows in Context of Ongoing Business}} \right]\%$$

or, substituting numbers from the example

$$MD = \left(1 - \frac{\$\,0.29}{\$\,1.00} \right)$$
$$= (1 - 0.29)\%$$
$$= 71\%$$

In developing valuation indications at the marketable minority interest level, the QMDM assumes that normalizing adjustments, including those related to nonrecurring items and discretionary owner compensation or expenditures, have been made to the earnings stream that is capitalized.

A number of appraisers have suggested that the QMDM may be capturing elements of the *minority interest discount* as well as the marketability discount. There has been a recent exchange on this issue in *Shannon Pratt's Business Valuation Update* in vol. 7, no. 3 (March 2001) pp. 7–10 and vol. 7, no. 5 (May 2001) pp. 9–10. Assuming, as I do, that it is appropriate for appraisers to make normalizing adjustments in the development of marketable minority valuation indications, the QMDM captures the appropriate marketability discount. The rationale for my position on normalizing adjustments is outlined in Dr. Pratt's book, *Cost of Capital—Estimation and Applications,* in Appendix D which he asked me to write relating to the use of ValuSource PRO Software.[6]

Some appraisers assume that such normalizing adjustments for discretionary owner compensation and expenses are inappropriate in minority interest appraisals because they reflect elements of control not available to minority shareholders. They further assume that the diminution of value resulting from the "leakage" of discretionary cash flows reflects elements of a *minority interest discount.* Under these assumptions, which I do not believe to be correct, the QMDM captures elements of the minority interest discount. In a future publication, I will show how the earnings of an enterprise with discretionary owner expenses can be analyzed to segregate that portion of the marketability discount applicable to these expenses, and that portion applicable to risk factors not present in the enterprise. In the meantime, I think it should be clear that the QMDM is capturing the marketability discount that it is supposed to be capturing, given the assumptions under which the model is employed.

Accepting the assumptions in Exhibit 10.4, the calculated marketability discount is 71%. There can be little question about the theoretical or practical correctness of the calculation. Given the assumptions, the value of a minority interest is a straight-

Exhibit 10.5   QMDM Base Case Quantified

EXAMPLE PRIVATE COMPANY
QUANTITATIVE MARKETABILITY DISCOUNT MODEL
Calculations Assume Dividends Received Midyear

KEY ASSUMPTIONS OF THE MODEL

Base Value (Marketable Minority Interest)	$1.00
Expected Growth Rate of Value	6.00%
Expected Dividend Yield	0.00%
Expected Growth Rate of Dividend	0.00%
Lowest Value for Range of Required Holding Periods	12.0%
Range Increases in Increments of	2.0%

	Assumed Holding Periods in Years													
	1	2	3	4	5	6	7	8	9	10	15	20	25	30
	Implied Marketability Discounts													
12.0%	5%	10%	15%	20%	24%	28%	32%	36%	39%	42%	56%	67%	75%	81%
14.0%	7%	14%	20%	25%	30%	35%	40%	44%	48%	52%	66%	77%	84%	89%
16.0%	9%	16%	24%	30%	36%	42%	47%	51%	56%	59%	74%	84%	89%	93%
18.0%	10%	19%	28%	35%	42%	47%	53%	58%	62%	66%	80%	88%	93%	96%
20.0%	12%	22%	31%	39%	46%	52%	58%	63%	67%	71%	84%	92%	96%	98%
22.0%	13%	25%	34%	43%	50%	57%	63%	68%	72%	75%	88%	94%	97%	99%
24.0%	15%	27%	38%	47%	54%	61%	67%	71%	76%	79%	90%	96%	98%	99%
26.0%	16%	29%	40%	50%	58%	65%	70%	75%	79%	82%	93%	97%	99%	99%
28.0%	17%	31%	43%	53%	61%	68%	73%	78%	82%	85%	94%	98%	99%	100%
30.0%	18%	34%	46%	56%	64%	71%	76%	80%	84%	87%	95%	98%	99%	100%

Required Holding Period Return (Annual %)

PV = 100%

---

forward application of present-value concepts. The discount of 71% is the net impact of the factors that differentiate the postulated nonmarketable minority interest from a freely tradable interest, where the freely tradable value is $1.00 per share. A rational buyer (i.e., the hypothetical willing buyer) would pay no more than $0.29 per share for the stipulated investment. Likewise, a rational seller (i.e., the hypothetical willing seller) would realize these facts. A hypothetical transaction could occur at the derived price of $0.29 per share.

QUANTIFYING THE QUANTITATIVE MARKETABILITY DISCOUNT MODEL BASE CASE

I have "quantified" the calculations to estimate the appropriate marketability discount based on the base case assumptions in Exhibit 10.5.[7]

I need to illustrate several important points based on the calculations related to the QMDM base case.

- The base case conclusion of 71% is highlighted at the intersection of a required holding period return of 20% and an expected holding period of 10 years.
- The so-called rule-of-thumb range of 30 to 40%, plus or minus, for marketability discounts can be illustrated in the context of the base case. I have highlighted an expected holding period range of three to seven years and a range of required holding period returns from 18 to 22%. Focusing on the 20% level, at three years, the calculated discount is 31%, and at seven years, the resulting discount is 58%. Somewhat lower and higher returns are also shaded for reference and perspective. Even relatively short expected holding periods for investments in closely held companies can require significant marketability discounts.
- In any appraisal, of course, expectations regarding the holding period will be fact-specific. But the facts of a specific case can cause a significant swing around that rule-of-thumb range. The duration of the expected holding period clearly can impact the QMDM marketability discount significantly, as can be seen in Exhibit 10.5. And certainly the facts of individual cases will influence the required holding period return. Before we finish, I will show the general reasonableness of the expected holding period return assumption. Once again, however, the model highlights the importance of analyzing the facts in the process of developing a marketability discount.

In a recent Tax Court case, *Estate of Weinberg v. Commissioner,* the court believed that "small changes in QMDM assumptions lead to large changes in results."[8] It is unfortunate that the court actually made large changes in assumptions and got large changes in results. For example, the court increased the expected holding period by five years and the required holding period return by 3%. While the facts were different in *Weinberg,* the point remains the same: This change in assumptions, which I believe is a large change that alters the character of the subject investment, increases the calculated marketability discount from 71% to 89% (interpolating above). The same point can be made with similar, large changes at any point on Exhibit 10.5.[9]

MARKETABLE MINORITY VALUATION CONCEPTS

I have thus far outlined what the QMDM is and how it works in the context of a base case. It is now time to begin to briefly discuss how the QMDM fits in the context of prevailing financial theory. The Gordon Dividend Discount Model expresses the value of a business in terms of the discounted present value of expected dividends (or cash flows). We can generalize the model as follows:

Equation I. Value = Expected Cash Flow / (Discount Rate − Expected
Growth Rate of Cash Flow)

or, symbolically, as

Equation II. $V = CF_1 / (R - G)$

The present value of a publicly traded security, or the corresponding marketable minority (mm) interest value of a private company, can be expressed as follows:

Equation III. $V_{mm} = CF_{mm} / (R_{mm} - G_{mm})$

The model expressed in Equations I to III is actually a shorthand for a discounted cash flow model that assumes that the expected cash flow of the next period will grow into perpetuity at the constant rate of $G_{mm}\%$. The discount rate (R_{mm}) is an appropriate discount rate for the expected cash flow (Cf_{mm}). Appraisers routinely use variations of the Gordon Dividend Discount Model in appraisals to develop marketable minority interest value conclusions.

To put numbers to Equation III, assume that a company has expected earnings next year of $1.00 per share. Assume further that the appropriate equity discount rate, derived using a "buildup" method, is 17.5% (consisting of the long-term Treasury rate of 6.5%, plus a small-stock capitalization premium over Treasuries of 10.0%, plus 1.0% of company-specific risk attributed to the private company by the appraiser). The expected growth rate of earnings is in the range of 7 to 8%, and the appraiser assumes 7.5%. Value at the marketable minority interest level is, therefore, $10.00 per share, or $1.00 / (17.5% - 7.5%).

Implicit in the use of Equation III is that the cash flows are either reinvested in the company to yield a return equivalent to the discount rate, R_{mm}, or are distributed to the shareholders of the enterprise, who are able to reinvest the distributions at the discount rate.

Some critics of the QMDM raise a related issue at this point. If the discount rate is 17.5%, they suggest, then value should be growing at 17.5% if there are no dividends. This would be true if all earnings were successfully reinvested at the discount rate. However, many private companies pay out large bonuses to the major shareholders, thereby reducing the potential return available to minority shareholders who do not work for the company or who do not receive what may be disguised (and unequal) distributions. Other companies accumulate excess cash and assets because their reinvestment opportunities or inclinations are less than the level available in the marketplace. In the real world, the only ways that investors achieve the full 17.5% return is through the control, the distribution (for reinvestment elsewhere), or the public market capitalization of expected future cash flows. If choices are made that lower the effective returns or add risk to minority shareholders (relative to similar publicly traded shares), these choices should be reflected in the appraisal. They are reflected in the QMDM by focusing on cash flows expected to be received by minority shareholders.

The perspective provided by Equation III is the value of an *enterprise,* which is publicly traded. It should be apparent that it is the cash flows of the *enterprise* that give rise to enterprise value. In the context of a publicly traded security, a shareholder does not have access to the cash flows, except as distributed by the company. However, the shareholder has access to the *present value of all expected future cash flows* by selling his or her shares in the public securities markets.

The markets are continually capitalizing the expected earnings of public compa-nies based on consensus expectations with respect to cash flows, discount rates, and expected growth rates. Moreover, shareholders can achieve cash in their brokerage accounts in three days by calling their brokers or executing trades via the Internet. The important point is that *minority shareholders* in a publicly traded company derive the benefit of 100% of its cash flows through the mechanism of the public markets, even though they lack any aspect of control over the enterprise.

NONMARKETABLE MINORITY VALUATION CONCEPTS

The $10.00 per-share value derived using Equation III provides a value indica-tion for a public company. The same equation can be used to develop a value for a private company *as if there were an active public market for its shares.* But we know that no such market exists for the private company.

The situation faced by the shareholder in a private company with no market for its shares is different from that faced by a shareholder of a public company. Assume now that our example relates to a private company. That company has a *hypothetical value* at the marketable minority interest level of $10.00 per share. Appraisers rou-tinely develop *marketable minority interest* value indications for private companies in the process of determining the fair market value of minority interests in those com-panies at the *nonmarketable minority interest* level of value. The difference between the two levels of value is the so-called *marketability discount* (or, as some call it, the discount for lack of marketability).

In the context of the Gordon Dividend Discount Model, the simplified situation faced by minority shareholders in closely held companies looks like the following:

Equation IV. $V_{sh} = CF_{sh}$ (for all periods) $/ (R_{sh} - G_v)$
                  (discounted for each period)

In words, the value today for a shareholder (V_{sh}) of an illiquid interest is the pres-ent value of all expected cash flows *to the shareholder* (CF_{sh}), discounted to the pres-ent at the required holding period return (discount rate) applicable to those cash flows (or capitalized by the discount rate R_{sh}, less the expected growth rate in value (G_v).) In the case of a nondividend-paying investment, we would actually capitalize the cash flows expected by the *next buyer* at the point in time that the current hypothetical, or real investor can expect to sell the interest. That value is then discounted to the pres-ent at R_{sh}. The discounting process is simulated by the capitalization of the cash flows at the discount rate less the expected growth rate in the value of the interest.

In the QMDM, we speak of the expected growth rate of value rather than the expected growth rate in earnings. Since the terminal cash flow often will account for the majority of the present value of an investment in an illiquid security, it is appro-priate to focus on the expected growth in value. Earnings growth for the enterprise and growth in the marketable minority interest value can differ, particularly when a company employs extensive leverage or when there is a reasonable expectation for contraction or expansion in the multiple applied to earnings.

This analysis assumes that the subject private company pays no dividends to its shareholders. It can, of course, be expanded to include the payment of dividends. However, we can illustrate how the QMDM works with the no-dividend example.

The investor in the no-dividend example expects *a single cash flow* from his or her investment—the cash flow received upon an event of liquidity, at the point in time when the investment can be sold. Unlike in the marketable minority example above, *there are no interim cash flows to be capitalized from the perspective of the shareholder.* So for purposes of our illustration, assume that hypothetical (or real) investors can reasonably expect that the company will be sold in five years (i.e., a longer expected holding period than either the current one-year or the prior two-year minimum holding periods for restricted securities under SEC Rule 144).

For simplicity, assume that the company will be sold to a financial buyer who has no expectation of acquisition synergies and that the cash flows in developing the marketable minority value indication of $10.00 per share reflected all relevant normalizing adjustments. In this example, the expected sale price in the future would correspond to the marketable minority level of value. In other words, there would be no (or virtually no) *control premium* in this example.

Further, assume that there is no difference between the expected growth rates of earnings and value and that value is expected to grow at 7.5% per year, compounded.

Assume that prospective investors look at a base-level equity discount rate of 16.5%, which is identical to that derived in the marketable minority (enterprise) indication, less the 1.0% company-specific risk premium discussed above. But our prospective investors see additional risks that are applicable to the shareholder level. For example, the controlling shareholder could slow down growth by personally taking abnormally high bonuses (or by retaining large amounts of cash or investing in low-return nonoperating assets). The secondary shareholder could also decide not to sell the company in the indicated five-year time frame.

More personally, the prospective investor(s) might have an emergency need for liquidity. With no market for the shares, a loss could be sustained if the investment had to be sold prematurely. Assume that investors require a specific risk premium of 3.0% for these factors. Their *required holding period return* is therefore 19.5%, or the base-level equity discount rate of 16.5% plus the 3.0% of investment-specific risk.

We can now "value" this example company from the perspective of prospective minority shareholder(s). We know that the marketable minority interest value today is $10.00 per share and that value is expected to grow at 7.5% per year. Value in five years would be expected to be $14.36 per share ($10.00 $\times$ (1 + 7.5%)^5). So we know the expected terminal cash flow (future value) that will be received when the company is sold ($14.36 per share). Again, for simplicity, assume the sale will occur at the marketable minority interest level, or with a control premium of zero.

We also know the required holding period return of the prospective investors (19.5%) and the number of years to achieve the cash flow (five years). We can now determine the implied value to the shareholder today by calculating:

Future value	$14.36 per share
Holding period	5 years
Discount rate	19.5%
Present value	$5.89 per share (or, rounded, $6.00 per share)

The value of the subject minority interest to prospective shareholders of our example company is $6.00 per share. In the context of traditional appraisal, we have indirectly developed the appropriate marketability discount. If the hypothetical, marketable minority interest value indication *of the enterprise* is $10.00 per share, and we estimate a value of expected cash flows *to minority shareholders* of $6.00 per share, the implied marketability discount is 40% (1 − $6.00 / $10.00).

In using the QMDM, I generally recommend that appraisers use reasonable ranges for the assumptions relating to the expected holding period and required holding period return. Ranges for assumptions relating to expected dividends and expected growth rate in value also can be used, of course, but in many cases these factors lend themselves to closer estimation based on management's expected dividend policy and earnings retention and growth policies.

The above example has described the essence of the Quantitative Marketability Discount Model. It is based on financial and valuation theory and it makes sense. And the QMDM can easily be expanded to incorporate the impact of interim distributions on value.

EXPECTED GROWTH AND EXPECTED RETURNS

In many real-life valuation situations, there is a discrepancy between the rate of return (discount rate) implied in the valuation *of an enterprise* and the expected returns attributable to minority investors in the enterprise. There can be many sources of these differentials, several of which were noted above. (See also Exhibit 10.7 on page 192.)

In most cases in which the QMDM is applied, there is a differential between the expected growth rate in value assumed and the required holding period return (discount rate) applied. For example, in the 10 appraisals summarized in Chapter 10 of *Quantifying Marketability Discounts*, the required holding period return (the average of the range considered) exceeded the expected growth rate in value assumed by about 13% on average. The range of this premium in required return over the expected growth rate in value was from 8.5 to 21.4%. In the example of this chapter of *Quantifying Marketability Discounts*, this differential is 12.0% (19.5% required holding period return less 7.5% expected growth in value).

We can rely on existing market evidence from restricted stock studies to support the need for a differential in the expected growth rate and the required holding period return (discount) rate. The Management Planning Study, "Analysis of Restricted Stocks of Public Companies (1980–1995)," was first published, with permission of Management Planning, Inc. (MPI), as Chapter 12 of *Quantifying Marketability Dis-*

Exhibit 10.6 Holding Period under Rule 144

Assumed Market Price of Public Entity		$1.00
Average Management Planning Discount (rounded)	30.0%	($0.30)
Assumed Purchase Price of Restricted Shares		$0.70
Holding Period Until Restricted Shares Are Freely Tradable (years)		2.5

counts. The median and average restricted stock discounts in the MPI study were 27.7 and 28.9%, respectively. For this analysis, we will round the average to 30% in Exhibit 10.6.

We further assume that the typical expected holding period before the restrictions of Rule 144 were lifted was 2.5 years.

Now, we can examine a variety of assumptions about the "average" restricted stock transaction in the MPI study. (This analysis is for purposes of illustration only.) Chapters 2 and 3 of *Quantifying Marketability Discounts* raise significant questions about reliance on averages of widely varying transaction indications for both the restricted stock studies and the pre-IPO studies. The average public price has been indexed to $1.00 per share. As a result, the average MPI transaction price, as indexed, is $.70 per share.

We can estimate the implied returns that were required by investors in restricted stocks based on a variety of assumptions about the expected growth rates in value (or the expected returns of the publicly traded stocks). For purposes of this analysis, we have assumed that the consensus expectations for the public stock returns were somewhere in the range of 0% (no expected appreciation) to 30%, compounded. The most relevant portion of this range likely begins at about 10%, since stocks expected to appreciate less than that probably were not attractive for investments in their restricted shares. (Appraisers typically rely on publications of Ibbotson Associates and many others as a basis for establishing expected returns.)

Note that the implied holding period returns for the restricted stock transactions, on average, ranged from about 27% per year compounded (with value growing at 10%) to 50% per year compounded (with expected growth of 30%). As noted in Chapter 8 of *Quantifying Marketability Discounts,* the implied returns are in the range of expected venture capital returns for initial ("new money") investments (not *average* venture capital returns, which include unsuccessful investments). Interestingly, the differential between the implied holding period returns above and the expected growth rate in values used are quite high, ranging from 15.3 to 20.0% (the right column of Exhibit 10.7).

This analysis is *ex post.* We do not know how the actual investment decisions were made in the transactions included in the MPI study or any of the restricted stock studies. But it is clear that the investors in the "average" restricted stock transactions were either:

Exhibit 10.7 Estimated Implied Returns

Assumed Expected Growth in Value (G)	Expected Future Value in 2.5 Years	Implied Return for Holding Period (R)	Annualized Incremental Return Attributable to Restricted Stock Discount (R − G)
0%	$1.00	15.3%	15.3%
5%	$1.13	21.1%	16.1%
10%	$1.27	26.9%	16.9%
15%	$1.42	32.7%	17.7%
20%	$1.58	38.5%	18.5%
25%	$1.75	44.3%	19.3%
30%	$1.93	50.0%	20.0%

- Placing very high discount rates on their restricted stock transactions (ranging from 15 to 20% in excess of the expected returns of the public companies they were investing in).
- Questioning the consensus expectations for returns.
- Some combination of the above.

We can make several observations about the seemingly high differentials between the restricted stock investors' required returns and the expected value growth of the typical entity:

- The average discounts appear to indicate defensive pricing.
- The discounts would likely assure at least a market return if the expected growth is not realized.
- Very high implied returns as expected growth increases suggests that high growth is viewed with skepticism.
- The implied premiums of R over expected G are substantial at any level, suggesting that the base "cost" of 2.5 years of illiquidity is quite expensive.

Given varying assumptions about holding periods longer than 2.5 years and allowing for entities that pay regular dividends, we would expect some variation from the premium range found in appraisals of private company interests.

By way of comparison, we can make the same calculations for the example applications of the QMDM from Chapter 10 of *Quantifying Marketability Discounts*.

As noted in Exhibit 10.8, the range of differences between the average required returns and the expected growth rates in value assumed in the 10 appraisals was from 8.5 to 21.4%, with an average of about 13%. Exhibit 10.8 also indicates the range of

Exhibit 10.8 Summary of Results of Applying the QMDM in 10 Example
Appraisals

Example	Holding Period	Average Required Holding Period Return (R)	Expected Growth in Value Assumed (G)	(R − G) Difference	Dividend Yield	Concluded Marketability Discount
1	5–8 years	20.0%	10.0%	10.0%	0.0%	45.0%
2	5–9 years	20.5%	4.0%	16.5%	8.8%	25.0%
3	7–15 years	18.5%	7.0%	11.5%	8.0%	15.0%
4	1.5–5 years	19.5%	7.5%	12.0%	0.0%	20.0%
5	5–10 years	20.5%	9.8%	10.7%	3.2%	40.0%
6	5–10 years	18.5%	10.0%	8.5%	2.1%	25.0%
7	5–15 years	19.5%	6.0%	13.5%	0.0%	60.0%
8	10–15 years	19.5%	5.0%	14.5%	10.0%	25.0%
9	10 years	26.4%	5.0%	21.4%	0.6%	80.0%
10	3–5 years	22.5%	6.0%	16.5%	0.0%	35.0%
Averages		20.5%	7.0%	13.5%	3.3%	37.0%
Medians		19.8%	6.5%	12.8%	1.4%	30.0%

other assumptions that yielded the concluded marketability discounts in the illustrations. I believe that these results, which came from actual appraisals, are generally consistent with the market evidence from the restricted stock studies. Indeed, the premium returns required by the restricted stock investors, on average, exceed those applied in the above examples, suggesting that the conclusions yielded conservative marketability discounts on average.

SUMMARY

The QMDM, which is used primarily in valuing private companies, develops concrete estimates of expected growth in value of the enterprise and reasonable estimates of additional risk premiums to account for risks faced by investors in nonmarketable minority interests of companies. In its fully developed form, it incorporates expectations regarding distributions of cash flows to assist appraisers in reaching logical, supportable, and reasonable conclusions regarding the appropriate levels of marketability discounts for specific valuations.

Marketable minority (and controlling interest) appraisals are developed based on the capitalized expected cash flows of businesses. Minority interests in those businesses must be valued based on consideration of the cash flows expected to be available to minority investors. The QMDM allows the business appraiser to bridge the gap between these two cash flow concepts, enterprise and shareholder, to develop reasoned and reasonable valuation conclusions at the nonmarketable minority interest level.

Notes

1. Keep in mind that actual purchasers of illiquid securities do not think in terms of "marketability discounts." They consider the economics of investments and make their investment decisions in light of their analyses and intuitions about the prospects for those investments. Appraisers develop marketability discounts in efforts to simulate the thinking of real-life or hypothetical investors.

2. This chapter summarizes concepts found in the text on the subject: Z. Christopher Mercer, *Quantifying Marketability Discounts: Developing and Supporting Marketability Discounts in the Appraisal of Closely Held Business Interests* (Memphis: Peabody Publishing, LP, 1997). Available from the publisher at 1-800-769-0976. The QMDM will also be featured and placed within the context of mainstream financial theory in a forthcoming book by Mercer, to be published by John Wiley & Sons.

3. Prior to the publication of *Quantifying Marketability Discounts,* the QMDM was presented to the appraisal community in a number of conferences of the American Society of Appraisers and other appraisal organizations on several occasions beginning in 1994.

4. These concepts are discussed in considerable depth in a three-hour tape set with accompanying documentation prepared by Z. Christopher Mercer. See "Theoretical Determinants of Value in the Context of 'Levels of Value,'" available from Peabody Publishing, LP at 1-800-767-0967.

5. Note that with restricted stock of publicly traded securities, investors know the relevant period of restriction for their investments. Prior to April 1997, the Securities and Exchange Commission required a two-year holding period for restricted securities under Rule 144 before investors could begin to achieve liquidity. Subsequent to April 1997, the holding period was reduced to one year. All but one of the restricted stock studies to date have considered transactions prior to April 1997, or when the holding period was at least two years. A recent study prepared by Columbia Financial Advisors, Inc., considers transactions between April 1997 and 1998. (See Kathryn Aschwald, "Restricted Stock Discounts Decline as Result of 1-Year Holding Period," *Shannon Pratt's Business Valuation Update* (May 2000): 1. While Aschwald finds, as expected, that the *absolute value* of restricted stock discounts declined after the shortening of the Rule 144 holding period, the *implied required returns of investors* in those restricted stocks remains substantially in line with the returns discussed later in this chapter. For a discussion of the Aschwald/Columbia Financial Advisors restricted stock study, see Chapters 6 and 8.

6. Pratt, Shannon P. *Cost of Capital: Estimation and Applications* (NY: John Wiley & Sons, 1998), Appendix D.

7. A companion diskette to *Quantifying Marketability Discounts* is available from Peabody Publishing, LP (1-800-769-0967). The diskette provides a variety of calculation modes utilizing present value formulae and presenting the results of the QMDM in a variety of ways. This diskette will be republished by John Wiley & Sons in anticipation of my next book dealing with the QMDM and an integrated theory of business valuation.

8. *Estate of Weinberg v. Commissioner,* T.C. Memo 2000-51, 79 T.CM. (CCH) 1507 (2000). This message was repeated in *Janda v. Commissioner,* T.C. Memo 2001-24 (2001).

9. For a more detailed discussion of issues raised by *Weinberg* and *Janda,* see also: *E-Law Business Valuation Perspectives* 00-03 & 00-04: *Weinberg, et al. v. Commissioner* (www.bizval.com/Elaw/elaw0003.htm), March 13, 2000. *E-Law Business Valuation Perspectives* 01-01: *Janda v. Commissioner* (www.bizval.com/Elaw/elaw0101.htm), February 2001.

Marketability Discounts in the Courts

      Cases Allowing Discount for Lack of Marketability
         In re the Marriage of Tofte
         Michael v. Michael
         Crismon v. Crismon
         Ferguson v. Ferguson
         Rattee v. Rattee
Summary
Notes

This chapter deals with discounts for lack of marketability (DLOMs) in court cases involving valuation of noncontrolling interests. The cases selected are representative of the wide diversity of court decisions on the topic, especially from one legal context to another, but also within a given legal arena. In many cases, the diversity of opinions is explained by the relative strength of the evidence and expert testimony presented to the court. Court cases involving DLOMs for controlling interests were addressed in Chapter 9.

As with Chapter 4, this chapter is organized by type of case in varying courts because of differing rules of law:

- Gift and estate tax
- Employee stock ownership plan (ESOP)
- Dissenting shareholder
- Shareholder oppression
- Marital dissolution

Most business appraisers and courts treat discounts for lack of control and discounts for lack of marketability as separate items. Nevertheless, appraisers and courts sometimes lump the two factors into a single discount.

This chapter does not purport to be an exhaustive treatise of the many court cases involving DLOMs for noncontrolling interests.[1] That would be far too great a task for the scope of this book. What I have tried to do is select a representative sample that will show the diversity of opinions in each of the several areas of litigation listed above. Although only marketability issues are discussed in this chapter, most of the cases also involved other valuation issues and frequently another discount or premium issue.*

---

*The full texts of all court decisions discussed in this chapter and many more are available at BVLibrary.com and are key word searchable. In addition, the case summaries on BVLibrary.com contain the names of the testifying experts in most cases, even if the written opinion does not.

GIFT AND ESTATE TAX CASES

The U.S. Tax Court has a long history of allowing discounts for lack of marketability for noncontrolling interests in closely held companies. We have separated stock cases from partnership cases because, in many instances, the minority value of the partnership interest (to which the DLOM normally is applied) is often based on transactions in the secondary market for limited partnership interests that are registered with the Securities and Exchange Commission (SEC). This market is less liquid than the public stock markets, implying that the transaction prices might already reflect some portion of a discount for lack of marketability. See Chapter 18 for additional case references.

Cases Involving Corporate Stock

Estate of Rodriguez v. Commissioner.[2]   The Tax Court allowed a 10% DLOM rather than the 35% sought by taxpayers. The court wrote that the IRS, which had argued that the control premium offset the lack of marketability, had confused discount for lack of marketability with discount for minority interest. The case provided no discussion of how the taxpayer supported the 35% claimed, but the court stated: "[Taxpayers] . . . have not met their burden of proof that the appropriate discount is 35%." This suggests a case of insufficient evidence.

Estate of Gallo v. Commissioner.[3]   Decided in 1985, this was the first case in which the Willamette pre–initial public offering studies were introduced as evidence. Both parties based their appraisals on the guideline public company method, resulting in a minority, marketable level of value. The IRS's expert opined to a 10% discount for lack of marketability, and the estate's expert opined to 36%. The court's decision was 36%, which was the highest discount purely for lack of marketability decided by the Tax Court up to that time.

Mandelbaum v. Commissioner.[4]   This is probably the most famous case on discounts for lack of marketability. The parties stipulated to a freely traded (marketable) minority value, so the only issue was the discount for lack of marketability.

The expert for the taxpayer cited seven restricted stock studies and the John Emory (Baird & Co.) and Willamette Management pre-IPO studies. (These studies were discussed in Chapters 5, 6, and 7.) The court used the studies cited as a starting point (35% average discount for restricted stock studies and 45% average discount for private transactions prior to IPOs). He listed nine factors that might cause the marketability discount for a given instance to be higher or lower than the benchmark averages, concluding that, on balance, the facts and circumstances in the particular case led to a lower discount for lack of marketability than the benchmark averages. He decided on a 30% discount.

The factors cited in the case were:

- Financial statement analysis
- Dividend policy
- Nature of the company, its history, its position in the industry, and its economic outlook
- Management
- Amount of control in the transferred shares
- Restrictions on transferability
- Holding period for the stock
- Company's redemption policy
- Costs associated with a public offering

The above factors have often been referred to since as the "*Mandelbaum* factors." Many in the appraisal community believe that some of them, such as financial statement analysis, nature of the company, and management, constitute "double counting" because they would be reflected in the freely traded value. The court recognized this issue but felt that the factors also impacted the discount for lack of marketability.

Barnes v. Commissioner.[5] In this case of gifts of stock of two South Carolina telephone companies, the court agreed with taxpayer's expert and applied a 40% DLOM to the Home Telephone voting stock and a 45% DLOM for the Rock Hill Telephone Company nonvoting stock. The court agreed because:

- The Barnes family had controlled Rock Hill for 80 years and the Helmly and Barnes families had controlled Home for 50 years.
- Both families intended to keep control of the companies.
- The families had taken steps to bring in younger family members and had taken measures to avoid having to sell the shares to pay death taxes.
- Home and Rock Hill paid much lower dividends than the guideline companies.
- There had been so few sales of Rock Hill stock and only limited family and insider sales of Home stock at about book value.
- The Home and Rock Hill stocks were not registered or traded on any exchange or over the counter.
- The Home and Rock Hill stocks in question represented very small minority interests that had no ability to direct the affairs of either company or cause the sale of its assets.

The Tax Court was critical of the lack of preparation by the IRS's expert, who did not visit either company or talk with management, nor was his cash flow method for valuation available at trial for taxpayers to cross-examine. The Tax Court denied the IRS's posttrial motion to reopen the record to supplement the expert's report.

Case Involving Partnership Interest

Estate of Jones v. Commissioner.[6]   In two complex limited partnerships involving several large ranches, one an 83.08% interest and the other a 16.915% interest, the Tax Court applied an 8% discount for lack of marketability to each. This case involved the formation of trusts by Jones II to continue family ownership of ranches that had been in the family for several generations.[6] Two partnerships were formed with his children. The issue of interest here was the DLOM. The taxpayer's expert argued for a 20% discount. His valuation was based in part on values of syndicated limited partnerships where he acknowledged that a large DLOM is already built into the secondary market discount. Although taxpayer's expert adjusted his analysis of the data found in the restricted stock and pre-IPO studies to take into consideration the lack of marketability discount already allowed, the court found his adjustment inadequate. The court allowed an 8% lack of marketability discount from net asset value (NAV) on the 83.08% interest and an 8% discount after a 40% minority discount on the 16.915% interest.

EMPLOYEE STOCK OWNERSHIP PLAN CASE

Howard v. Shay.[7]   This case involved the termination of an employee stock ownership plan (ESOP) that owned approximately 38% of the stock of Pacific Architects and Engineers (PA&E). The stock was sold to a trust controlled by the stockholder who owned the other approximately 62% of PA&E stock. Other discounts were discussed in Chapter 4.

The final adjustment to value made by the ESOP financial advisor who valued the stock was a 50% DLOM. The employees brought a class action suit claiming that the stock was undervalued; the size of the DLOM was a major issue.

Unlike most ESOPs today, this ESOP stock had no "put" right, because it was established before ESOP laws were changed to require such rights. Consequently, its marketability (or lack of it) was no better than that of any other closely held minority interest.

The Willamette Management Associates pre–IPO database on discounts for lack of marketability was entered into evidence in defense of the discount. The evidence presented was all transactions in the database for the five years preceding the valuation date where the sale involved 25 to 49.9% of the outstanding stock. These data showed average discounts of very close to the 50% that was used in the original stock appraisal. The 50% discount was upheld at the trial level and again on remand from the Ninth Circuit for further valuation proceedings.

The case is a very important one for DLOMs, because, in spite of significant empirical evidence, the U.S. Tax Court has yet to allow a DLOM in excess of 45%.

DISSENTING SHAREHOLDER CASES

The courts have been mixed on treatment of the lack of marketability issue in dissenting shareholder cases. However, Delaware, the leading state in dissenting shareholder litigation, denies both marketability and minority discounts.

Cases Denying Discount for Lack of Marketability

Cavalier Oil Corp. v. Harnett.[8]   For example, in this often cited case, the Delaware Supreme Court stated: "In rejecting a minority or marketability discount, the Vice Chancellor concluded that the objective of [an] appraisal is 'to value the corporation itself, as distinguished from a specific fraction of its shares as they may exist in the hands of a particular shareholder.' We believe this to be a valid distinction . . . . [T]he Court of Chancery is not required to apply further . . . factors at the shareholder level, such as discounts to minority shares for asserted lack of marketability."

Lawson Mardon Wheaton, Inc. v. Smith.[9]   The New Jersey Supreme Court, in a dissenters' appraisal rights case, ruled against a marketability discount in determining the fair value of the dissenters' shares in a restructuring and later a merger. Both the trial court and the New Jersey Superior Court, Appellate Division upheld the marketability discount. The lower courts relied on the "extraordinary circumstances" exception to the American Law Institute's Principles of Corporate Governance section 7.22 (1992). The trial court concluded that the circumstances of this case dictated application of the exception to the general rule. The supreme court held that the application of the "extraordinary circumstances" rule was not supported by the record and ordered the case to be reopened to admit new evidence.

Sieg Co. v. Kelly.[10]   An Iowa corporate reorganization led to a decision by the trial court to allow a marketability discount. Although the supreme court found the overall valuation approach that supported the marketability discount "convincing," it found the marketability discount more problematic. Iowa law was clear at the time the valuation was made that a marketability discount was not permitted.

Blitch v. Peoples Bank.[11]   The Georgia Court of Appeals reversed a trial court in this case with facts similar to those above. In this case the trial court accepted the expert appraisal testimony of the bank. The appraiser applied both minority and marketability discounts in his calculations. The dissenting shareholder maintained a value based on the proportionate share of the corporation as a whole. The appeals court noted that the Georgia dissenting shareholder statute was clear and persuasive on the issue and ruled the marketability discount not applicable in Georgia *fair value* determination.

Swope v. Siegel-Robert, Inc.[12]   The U.S. District Court for the Eastern District of Missouri reached a decision consistent with the Missouri Court of Appeals in *King v. F.T.J., Inc.*[13] That case said that the question of whether minority and marketability discounts are applicable in Missouri dissenting stockholder cases is to be determined on the facts and circumstances, on a case-by-case basis. In the *Swope* case the court found that the shares should be valued on a minority basis, but that there should be no discount for lack of marketability.

   On appeal, the Eighth Circuit Court of Appeals upheld the denial of the discount for lack of marketability, although it held that this issue is a matter of law, not a discretionary matter. However, the expert for the plaintiffs had applied a 35% control premium, which the trial court rejected. The Eighth Circuit remanded the case for revaluation because the district court price per share "presumably reflected a discount for minority status."[14]

Applicability of Discount for Lack of Marketability to Be Determined on Case-by-Case Basis

***WCM Industries, Inc. v. Wilson.*[15]**   The Colorado Court of Appeals case upheld the trial court's determination that a DLOM was not appropriate. The case is similar to those above in that the disagreement is the result of a merger where the dissident shareholders have argued against a discount for lack of marketability. The appeals court ruled that "a marketability discount is not required as a matter of law, but, rather, may be employed by a fact finder, depending upon the particular facts and circumstances."

***M Life Insur. Co. v. Sapers & Wallack.*[16]**   In a subsequent case, the Colorado Court of Appeals, citing *WCM Industries,* found that the trial court erred in disallowing a discount for lack of marketability as a matter of law. The appellate court remanded the case back to the trial court to make findings of fact on this issue and, if necessary, revalue the shares to include the discount for lack of marketability.

Discounts for Lack of Marketability Not Addressed

***HMO-W, Inc. v. SSM Health Care System.*[17]**   Many states have not addressed the issue of discounts for lack of marketability, but the Supreme Court of Wisconsin specifically stated that it has not. In this case, the Wisconsin Supreme Court upheld the lower court's denial of a minority discount, but made a point of saying that it was not addressing the issue of a discount for lack of marketability.

MINORITY OPPRESSION CASES

In most states that have statutes regarding minority oppression, the statutory standard of value is *fair value.* However, even in states where fair value is defined the same way in the oppression statute as in the dissenting shareholder statute, court interpretations are not always the same in oppression cases as in dissenting shareholder cases.

Marketability Discount Depends on "Extraordinary Circumstances"

***Advanced Communication Design, Inc. v. Follett.*[18]**   Decided in November of 1999, the Minnesota Court of Appeals ruled that a marketability discount should not be applied to determine the fair value of Brian Follett's 33% interest in Advanced

Communication Design, Inc. (ACD). The corporation and its only voting shareholder, Marco Scibora, appealed to the Minnesota Supreme Court.

At trial of this matter, the parties agreed to an appraisal procedure in which each party appointed one appraiser and the court appointed a third appraiser. The court-appointed appraiser and the appraiser appointed by Follett agreed upon a "majority report," and the appraiser appointed by ACD and Scibora presented a "minority report." The trial court accepted the majority report with respect to the enterprise value but declined to apply a marketability discount. The court of appeals affirmed the trial court ruling.

On appeal, the Minnesota Supreme Court reviewed the Minnesota Business Corporation Act definition of fair value, as well as case law from other jurisdictions on the issue. The court found that, as a starting point, fair value in a court-ordered buyout "means the pro rata share of the value of the corporation as a going concern." The court rejected a "bright-line rule" rejecting the application of a marketability discount in all cases. The court then turned to the American Law Institute (ALI) Principles of Corporate Governance for guidance. The ALI principles suggest that a marketability discount should be applied in a case where "extraordinary circumstances" exist, such as the possibility of an unfair wealth transfer.

The Minnesota Supreme Court found that extraordinary circumstances existed in this case that warranted the application of a marketability discount. The court pointed out that the "fair value" of Follett's shared determination by the trial court was five times ACD's net worth, seven times its average operating cash flow, and eight times its average net income. The court noted that such payment would also interfere with ACD's historical practice of reinvesting cash flows to promote growth of the company, leaving the corporation and the remaining shareholders with an "extremely doubtful potential for growth."

The case was remanded to the trial court for a determination of the appropriate marketability discount, but directed that the discount should be somewhere between 35 and 55%, based on the marketability discounts recommended in the minority and majority reports, respectively. On remand, the district court applied a 35% discount, which was upheld on appeal.

Application of Marketability Discount Hinges on Conduct

***Balsamides v. Protameen Chemicals, Inc.*[19]** The New Jersey Supreme Court decided the *Wheaton* case and the *Balsamides* case on the same day. Unlike in *Wheaton,* the *Balsamides* court supported the application of a marketability discount. The oppressed shareholder was to buy out the oppressor (Perle). The court wrote that the "equities of the case must be considered when ascertaining 'fair value' in appraisal and oppressed shareholder actions. . . ." Requiring Balsamides to pay an undiscounted price for Perle's stock penalizes Balsamides and rewards Perle. The distinction in case law often hinges on the conduct of the parties.

MARITAL DISSOLUTION CASES

Cases Denying Discount for Lack of Marketability

Mexic v. Mexic.[20]   The Louisiana Court of Appeals held in this case that a 15% DLOM was not appropriate. In the case, the court ruled that the discount would be applicable if the property in question were sold to a third party. Since the property in question was not to be sold, no discount was allowed.

Ferraro v. Ferraro.[21]   The court in this Virginia decision where the husband owned a 34% interest, denied discounts for both minority and marketability because the husband did not need to sell his ownership to pay the wife's distribution, and there was no majority interest in the stores.

In re the Marriage of Connor.[22]   An Indiana appellate court in this case rejected a discount for lack of marketability, not as a matter of principle, but for lack of evidence. In its recalculation of the value of Associated Imaging, the court reduced the value by "applying a standard 20% lack of marketability discount." Neither expert had applied such a discount, nor was there any other evidence in the record to support it. The court of appeals stated that:

> Although there are ample examples in the body of law concerning application of a marketability discount, a search of recent opinions yielded no case in which a court had applied a discount without some testimony concerning the amount or validity of such a discount. Further, we cannot definitely state that application of a 20% marketability discount for the value of a health care business is a generally known fact.

In re the Marriage of Havrilak.[23]   Similarly, the Minnesota Court of Appeals remanded the valuation portion of the district court's decision in this marital dissolution case. The court recognized that the lower court is not bound by expert testimony regarding valuation, but it also stated that the district court cannot reject a seemingly valid valuation without a definite basis.

The district court based much of its decision regarding the valuation of the company on solid evidence. However, it applied an additional $30,000 marketability discount without a stated basis. Since this discount was not supported by the evidence, the court remanded for further proceedings.

Cases Allowing Discount for Lack of Marketability

In re the Marriage of Tofte.[24]   The Court of Appeals of Oregon allowed a DLOM in this case when no sale was contemplated. Experts for both parties used the capitalization of earnings approach but differed on whether it was appropriate to apply a marketability discount. The husband's expert applied a 35% discount to the fair market value of the shares "to reflect the minority shareholder interest to reflect lack of marketability." The court's statement shows the confusion in distinguishing between a minority interest discount and a marketability discount. "A marketability discount addresses the degree of liquidity of the interest. Such discounts compensate for the lack of a recognized market for a particular stock, lack of ready marketability, or restrictive provisions affecting ownership rights or limiting sale."

The wife argued that the marketability discount was inappropriate in this case because there was no evidence that the husband was contemplating a sale of his interest. The court argued, "[W]e have previously applied marketability and minority discount without consideration of or speculation about the owners' intention to sell shares."

Michael v. Michael.[25]   In another case, the court also allowed a discount for lack of marketability based on two factors. The first was that the business was highly dependent on the coal mining industry and was very risky. The second issue involved the holding of stock in a bank. The value of the stock was greater than the value of the operating assets of the business, but the cost basis was very low relative to the market value. If the business were sold to a third-party buyer, the liquidation of the stock would result in a material capital gains tax. The court applied a 25% discount because the evidence showed that the husband no longer worked closely with the business.

Crismon v. Crismon.[26]   In an Arkansas case, both experts testified to a discount for lack of marketability for a 50% partnership interest in a partnership owning two convenience stores and some commercial property. Wife appealed the trial court's application of a marketability discount. The appellate court affirmed the trial court's decision.

Ferguson v. Ferguson.[27]   The issue in this Connecticut marriage dissolution case was whether a marketability discount should be applied in determining the valuation of the common stock of the family business. The husband owned all of the common and preferred stock of Mohawk Manufacturing Company, Inc. of Middletown, Connecticut.

The wife's expert declined to use a marketability discount because the husband had articulated his strong position against a sale of the business. The husband's expert used a 35% marketability discount, claiming that it was the exception rather than the rule not to use a marketability discount in a closely held business. He also pointed to a negative business climate, and a "thin" management structure, with stagnant revenues, in support of his marketability discount rate.

The parties acknowledged that under the case law whether a marketability discount should be applied is a fact-laden, case-specific question. "The plaintiff [wife] claims that when a marketability discount is applied to a one hundred (100%) percent interest valuation, there is customarily a fact articulated which inhibits marketability in addition to the closely-held nature of ownership."

The court found that a marketability discount applied in this case solely due to the lack of a ready market for the business. The other negatives used by husband's expert simply did not comport with the observations from the financial statements of the parties and their testimony.

The court found that the rationale of approving a marketability discount was appropriate under the facts of this case, but that a 35% discount was excessive. "[H]igher marketability discounts [are] reserved for cases which describe . . . more than one facet of discount criteria." The court held that a fair marketability discount in this case was 15%.

Rattee v. Rattee.[28]   In this New Hampshire case the trial court adjusted the value of a 49.6% interest in a business by 28.5% to reach the fair market value because of the closely held nature of the company and the fact that the husband's interest was a minority interest. The trial court derived the amount of this combined minority and marketability discount from the testimony of the wife's expert.

On appeal, the wife argued that reducing the value of the husband's minority interest was improper and an abuse of discretion because he "controlled" the company, and neither he nor his mother planned to sell the business. The appellate court refused to consider whether "contemplation" of actual sale or the husband's management participation negated the application of minority and marketability discounts because the standard of value in a marital dissolution is fair market value, which is the willing seller/willing buyer standard.

SUMMARY

The U.S. Tax Court normally allows discounts for lack of marketability for noncontrolling interests in closely held companies. However, the size of the discounts varies greatly from one case to another. Apart from substantive factors affecting the magnitude of the discount, the quality of the expert evidence and testimony presented in the Tax Court makes a big difference in the outcome. The Tax Court expects good empirical evidence, relevant to the subject at hand, to support the amount of the discount. So far, however, in spite of studies showing much higher discounts in hundreds of arm's-length transactions, the highest discount that the Tax Court has allowed purely for lack of marketability is 45%, and most discounts have been considerably less.

The ESOP discounts for lack of marketability usually are relatively low (or sometimes nonexistent) because most ESOP stock has a "put" right to sell the stock back to the sponsoring company. However, in the case of one ESOP that lacked a "put" right (established before puts were required for ESOPs), the court upheld a 50% DLOM.

Dissenting shareholder and shareholder oppression cases are quite mixed on the matter of discounts for lack of marketability. It is necessary to carefully study the recent case law in the relevant jurisdiction. Some states' case law flatly rejects DLOMs as a matter of law. A fewer number of states routinely accept DLOMs as a matter of law. Many state decisions have said that it depends on the facts and circumstances and thus will be decided on a case-by-case basis. Many states do not have precedential case law on the issue.

There is little case law on DLOMs in divorce cases, and what exists is also quite mixed.

Cases discussing discounts for lack of marketability in family limited partnerships are addressed in Chapter 18, and Chapter 19 includes case law on DLOMs in undivided interests.

Notes

1. For an exhaustive treatise on court decisions on discounts for lack of marketability in the past decade, *see* Janet Hamilton, Duncan Kretovich, and Jill Johnson, *Discounts for Lack of Marketability in the Courts, 1991–2000* (Portland, OR: Business Valuation Resources, LLC, 2001).
2. *Estate of Rodriguez v. Commissioner,* T.C. Memo 1989-13, 56 T.C.M. (CCH) 1033 (1989).
3. *Estate of Gallo v. Commissioner,* T.C. Memo 1985-363, 50 T.C.M. (CCH) 470 (1985).
4. *Mandelbaum v. Commissioner,* T.C. Memo 1995-255, 69 T.C.M. (CCH) 2852 (1995), *aff'd*, 91 F.3d 124 (3rd Cir. 1996).
5. *Barnes v. Commissioner,* T.C. Memo 1998-413, 76 T.C.M. (CCH) 881 (1998).
6. *Estate of Jones v. Commissioner,* 2001 U.S. Tax Ct. LEXIS 11, 116 T.C. No. 11 (2001).
7. *Howard v. Shay,* 1993 U.S. Dist. LEXIS 20153 (C.D. Cal. 1993), *rev'd* and *remanded by,* 100 F.3d 1484 (9th Cir. 1996), *cert. denied,* 520 U.S. 1237 (1997).
8. *Cavalier Oil Corp. v. Harnett,* 564 A.2d 1137 (Del. 1989).
9. *Lawson Mardon Wheaton, Inc. v. Smith,* 160 N.J. 383, 734 A.2d 738 (N.J. 1999).
10. *Sieg Co. v. Kelly,* 568 N.W.2d 794 (Iowa 1997).
11. *Blitch v. Peoples Bank,* 246 Ga. App. 453, 540 S.E.2d 667 (Ga. Ct. App. 2000).
12. *Swope v. Siegel-Robert, Inc.,* 74 F. Supp.2d 876 (E.D. Mo. 1999), *aff'd in part, reversed in part by* 243 F.3d 486 (8th Cir. 2001).
13. *King v. F.T.J., Inc.* 765 S.W.2d 301 (Mo. Ct. App. 1988).
14. *Swope v. Siegel-Robert, Inc.,* 2001 U.S. App. LEXIS 2760 (2001).
15. *WCM Indus., Inc. v. Wilson,* 948 P.2d 36 (Colo. Ct. App. 1997).
16. *M Life Insur. Co. v. Sapers & Wallack,* 2001 Colo. App. LEXIS 166 (Colo. Ct. App. 2001).
17. *HMO-W, Inc. v. SSM Health Care System,* 234 Wis.2d 707, 611 N.W.2d 250 (Wis., 2000), *aff'g* 228 Wis.2d 815, 598 N.W.2d 577 (Wis. Ct. App. 1999).
18. *Advanced Communication Design, Inc. v. Follett,* 2000 Minn. LEXIS 546 (Minn., 2000), *aff'd on remand* 2001 Minn. App. LEXIS 589 (2001).
19. *Balsamides v. Protameen Chem., Inc.,* 160 N.J. 352, 734 A.2d 721 (N.J. 1999).
20. *Mexic v. Mexic,* 577 So.2d 1046 (La. Ct. App. 1991).
21. *Ferraro v. Ferraro,* 2000 Va. App. LEXIS 164 (Va. Ct. App. 2000).
22. *In re the Marriage of Connor,* 713 N.E.2d 883 (Ind. Ct. App. 1999).
23. *In re the Marriage of Havrilak,* 1999 Minn. App. LEXIS 479 (Minn. Ct. App. 1999).
24. *In re the Marriage of Tofte,* 134 Or. App. 449, 895 P.2d 1387 (Or. Ct. App. 1995).
25. *Michael v. Michael,* 196 W. Va. 155, 469 S.E.2d 14 (W. Va. 1996).
26. *Crismon v. Crismon,* 72 Ark. App. 116, 34 S.W.2d 763 (Ark. Ct. App. 2000).
27. *Ferguson v. Ferguson,* 1998 Conn. Super. LEXIS 3340 (Conn. Super. Ct. 1998).
28. *Rattee v. Rattee,* 767 A.2d 415 (N.H. 2001).

Voting versus Nonvoting Stock

If a company has both voting and nonvoting classes of stock, there may be a price difference between the two, usually in favor of the voting stock. In order to analyze the facts and estimate the difference for any specific situation, it is helpful to classify the basic set of facts into one of two groups:

1. Situations in which there is a large number of both voting and nonvoting shares (although in most such situations the number of voting shares considerably outnumbers the number of nonvoting shares)
2. Situations in which a very small number of voting shares controls, with the nonvoting shares vastly outnumbering the voting shares

VOTING versus NONVOTING STOCK SCENARIOS

Significant Number of Holders of Both Classes

When there are many owners of both voting and nonvoting classes, the price differential tends to be small, often in the range of 0 to 5%. If the block in question is just a small minority, the vote is not likely to carry much influence, if any.

The distribution of the voting stock also makes a difference. If one stockholder has the required majority control and the corporate governance documents do not provide for cumulative voting, the question of whether the minority shares are voting or nonvoting is academic, unless a split of the control block is foreseeable.

Another factor in favor of nonvoting stock price in some states is that certain corporate actions, such as liquidation of the company, require a majority vote by class. Thus, as Yale Kramer points out, a majority block of nonvoting stock could in effect veto such corporate actions.[1]

Restrictive agreements also can have a bearing. Some voting stocks are subject to an agreement that converts them to nonvoting stock in the event of transfer. This is common in public companies. Such a provision can render voting rights virtually powerless for valuation purposes.

Where Small Block Holds Voting Control

There appears to be an increasing number of situations, especially in private companies, in which a relatively small block of voting stock controls the entire company. If a control owner sells a control block, usually there is no obligation to make an offer to noncontrol shareholders at the same price. In fact, the control owner usually is not obligated to make any offer at all to noncontrol shareholders. I am aware of a significant number of cases where a voting control block received a substantial premium per share over nonvoting stock, as shown in a subsequent section.

EMPIRICAL STUDIES SHOW LITTLE DIFFERENTIAL FOR SMALL MINORITY INTERESTS

Empirical studies of the price differentials between voting and nonvoting publicly traded stocks indicate that, for small minority interests, the market generally accords very little or no value to voting rights. Where differentials in favor of voting stock exist, they generally have been under 5%, and no study of U.S. markets has indicated a differential of over 10%.

Lease, McConnell, and Mikkelson Study

Ronald Lease, John McConnell, and Wayne Mikkelson studied corporations having two classes of stock outstanding over the period from 1940 through 1978. They found 26 firms that had voting and nonvoting or limited voting common stock outstanding with equivalent dividend rights and liquidity preferences, and did not have voting preferred stock. On the basis of this study, they concluded: "For the 26 firms that have had two classes of common stock outstanding, but have had no voting preferred stock outstanding, the class of common stock with superior voting rights generally has traded at a premium relative to the other class of common stock. This relationship has persisted through time and across firms. The average of the mean price premiums for the stocks in this group of firms was 5.44 percent."[2]

Robinson, Rumsey, and White Study

Chris Robinson, John Rumsey, and Alan White studied firms having voting and nonvoting classes of stock listed on the Toronto Stock Exchange (TSE) from 1981 through 1990. A valuable quality of the data is the large number of dual class shares traded on the TSE. The total number of different firms in the sample was 93. The number of firms in the sample varied from a low of 47 in 1981 to a high of 77 in 1986. About half the sample had "coattail" protection for the nonvoting stock, which the authors explain as follows:

> An unusual characteristic of the data makes this estimation procedure more reveal-
> ing. About half of the companies in our sample have takeover protection for the B
> shareholders, spelled out in the Articles of Incorporation. This protection, called a
> "coattail," has not been reported for any country other than Canada. It is triggered
> by a takeover offer to the A shareholders which is not made identically to the B share-
> holders. The two basic mechanisms used are: (1) the B shares acquire the same vot-
> ing rights as the A shares; or (2) the B shares become convertible into the A shares
> for the purpose of tendering to the bid. Since the B shares outnumber the A shares in
> almost all cases, the B shareholders can defeat any takeover proposal, or make its
> acceptance very unlikely. Since August 1987 in Canada all new issues of dual class
> equity must include a coattail agreement for the B Shares, so that the proportion of
> firms with two classes of shares without coattails is diminishing.

The authors conclude:

> A takeover model became a significant explanatory variable for firms that had no
> coattail. A voting power model was a significant explanatory variable for firms that
> had a coattail provision.
>   The empirical results suggest that if the observed premium is a result of an
> expected windfall takeover (a relatively rare event in which substantial gains may be
> reaped by the buyer), the expected gain to the A [voting] shareholders in the event of

the takeover is between 8% and 18% of the total equity value. Under an alternative steady-state takeover model the premium merely reflects the value that anyone can capture by buying control. In this case the empirical results suggest that about 3.5–4.5% of the total equity value can be attributed to voting control.[3]

O'Shea and Siwicki Study

Two academic authors Kevin O'Shea and Robert M. Siwicki, compared prices of "supervoting" versus "limited voting" pairs of stock in the same companies in the United States, selected from the Standard & Poor's 1990 Year-End Stock Guide. They found a 3.5% average price differential in favor of the stocks having the greater vote. (These were not "supervoting" in the sense that a very small block had voting control.)[4]

Houlihan Lokey Howard & Zukin Study

Paul Much and Timothy Fagan of Houlihan Lokey Howard & Zukin completed an analysis of price differentials between voting and nonvoting publicly traded stocks, using 60-day to 260-day moving averages of the respective prices for the period ending December 31, 1994. After eliminations for differences in rights between classes, insufficient float and/or volume, and one company in bankruptcy, 18 pairs remained for comparative analysis.

They found overall positive average and median premiums of 2.05% and 1.46%, respectively. The 260-day moving average showed the highest average and median premiums of 3.20% and 2.73%, respectively. The results are shown in Exhibit 12.1. The authors conclude: "Taking these particular examples into consideration along with other information developed in the study leads us to conclude that the value of voting rights (absent a takeover situation) is probably somewhat less than [the] 5.4% premium derived by Lease, McConnell, and Mikkelson."[5]

TRANSACTIONS INVOLVING PREMIUMS FOR CONTROL BLOCKS

Gilbert E. Matthews of Sutter Securities, Incorporated compiled a table of transactions where both the high-vote and low-vote (or nonvoting) shares were acquired in takeovers or where the high-vote shares were eliminated in restructurings. As shown in Exhibit 12.2A, some significant differences existed between the prices per share paid for the voting control blocks and the prices paid for the noncontrol share blocks.

Exhibit 12.2B is an analysis of the premiums paid. The premium paid is in relation to the economic value of the high-vote shares. For example, in Bergen Brunswig, the high-vote shares accounted for 2.11% of the shares but received 17.07% of the consideration. Matthews called the difference (14.95%) the premium over economic interest. This is *not* the same concept as the 0 to 5% market premium discussed above.

Exhibit 12.1   Houlihan Lokey Howard & Zukin Study of Premiums Paid for Voting Rights

Ticker	Issue Name			Price 12/31/94
AZE.B	American Maize Prods Co	CLB	1 vote; remaining BOD	25.00
AZE.A	American Maize Prods Co	CLA	limited voting 30% of BOD	25.50
				−1.96%
BF.A	Brown Forman Corp	CLA	voting	31.00
BF.B	Brown Forman Corp	CLB	nonvoting	30.50
				1.64%
CMCSA	Comcast Corp	CLA	voting	15.38
CMCSK	Comcast Corp	CLASPL	nonvoting	15.69
				−1.99%
CALA	Continental Airls Inc	CLA	10 votes	9.38
CALB	Continental Airls Inc	CLB	1 vote	9.25
				1.35%
CNP.A	Crown Cent Pete Corp	CLA	1 vote	12.75
CNP.B	Crown Cent Pete Corp	CLB	1/10 vote	12.00
				6.25%
EXX.B	Exx Inc	CIB	elects 2/3 of BOD	16.25
EXX.A	Exx Inc	CIA	elects 1/3 of BOD	16.00
				1.56%
HUB.A	Hubbell Inc	CLA	20 votes	51.25
HUB.B	Hubbell Inc	CLB	1 vote	50.71
				1.06%
MARSA	Marsh Supermarkets Inc	CLA	voting	10.50
MARSB	Marsh Supermarkets Inc	CLB	nonvoting	9.50
				10.53%
MOLX	Molex Inc	COM	voting	34.50
MOLXA	Molex Inc	CLA	nonvoting	31.00
				11.29%
ODETB	Odetics Inc	CLB	1 vote	6.75
ODETA	Odetics Inc	CLA	1/10 vote	6.50
				3.85%
PHSYA	Pacificare Health Sys Inc	CLA	voting	65.13
PHSYB	Pacificare Health Sys Inc	CLB	nonvoting	66.00
				−1.33%
PDL.A	Presidential Rlty Corp New	CLA	elects 2/3 of BOD	8.50
PDL.B	Presidential Rlty Corp New	CLB	elects 1/3 of BOD	8.63

Volume 12/31/94	% Owned Shares Outstanding	by Largest Holder	Moving Average as of 12/31/94			
			60 Day	120 Day	180 Day	260 Day
2,400	1,742,000	54.5%	23.43	22.28	21.42	20.83
17,700	8,565,000	32.3%	23.55	22.37	21.52	20.96
			−0.48%	−0.38%	−0.45%	−0.61%
20,000	28,988,000	68.9%	29.55	28.91	28.84	28.76
20,500	40,008,000		29.55	28.83	28.13	28.81
			−0.01%	0.26%	2.54%	−0.15%
478,200	39,020,000	6.9%	16.21	16.19	16.58	18.54
901,200	200,580,000		16.20	16.22	16.53	17.48
			0.05%	−0.16%	0.27%	6.03%
34,600	6,301,000	45.6%	14.24	16.76	16.53	18.84
109,600	20,354,000	17.1%	13.81	16.10	15.63	17.47
			3.17%	4.09%	5.77%	7.89%
21,100	4,818,000	51.3%	15.45	16.81	17.57	18.05
15,100	4,985,000	12.3%	14.19	15.53	16.20	16.64
			8.85%	8.27%	8.42%	8.48%
21,600	677,000	46.4%	22.33	22.33	22.33	22.33
115,400	2,031,000		22.74	22.74	22.74	22.74
			−1.80%	−1.80%	−1.80%	−1.80%
7,500	6,187,000	39.0%	51.70	51.90	52.44	53.13
15,855	26,753,000		52.83	52.95	53.12	53.90
			−2.13%	−1.97%	−1.28%	−1.43%
2,700	4,487,000	24.8%	10.87	11.09	10.84	10.86
11,100	3,881,000	25.0%	10.03	10.18	9.96	10.04
			8.39%	8.94%	8.85%	8.19%
53,400	40,068,000	46.0%	33.69	33.42	32.20	31.05
115,800	39,546,000		31.36	31.13	30.22	29.34
			7.42%	7.38%	6.55%	5.83%
1,800	1,167,000	22.1%	6.48	7.29	7.67	8.49
71,100	4,769,000		6.65	7.49	7.87	8.62
			−2.58%	−2.67%	−2.53%	−1.49%
22,100	12,279,000	48.5%	68.89	67.27	62.97	58.76
35,900	18,384,000		67.38	65.60	61.82	57.86
			2.24%	2.55%	1.87%	1.55%
1,500	479,000	9.3%	8.15	8.03	7.85	7.53
19,500	3,022,000		7.91	7.85	7.71	7.43

continued

Ticker	Issue Name			Price 12/31/94
				−1.45%
PVB	Provident Life & Acc Ins Co	CLB	1 vote	21.75
PVA	Provident Life & Acc Ins Co	CLA	1/20 vote	20.75
				4.82%
RDB	Readers Digest Assn Inc	CLB	voting	44.75
RDA	Readers Digest Assn Inc	CLA	nonvoting	49.13
				−8.91%
TECUB	Tecumseh Prods Co	CLB	voting	45.50
TECUA	Tecumseh Prods Co	CLA	nonvoting	45.00
				1.11%
TCOMB	Tele Communications Inc	CLB	10 votes	23.25
TCOMA	Tele Communications Inc	CLA	1 vote	21.75
				6.90%
TBS.A	Turner Broadcasting Sys Inc	CLA	1 vote	16.38
TBS.B	Turner Broadcasting Sys Inc	CLB	1/5 vote	16.38
				0.00%
VIA	Viacom Inc	CLA	voting	41.63
VIA.B	Viacom Inc	CLB	nonvoting	40.75
				2.15%

Avg premium	2.05%
Median premium	1.46%
High	11.29%
Low	−8.91%
# of Companies used	18

NA - Not Available

Source: Paul Much and Timothy Fagan, *Financial Valuation: Businesses and Business Interests,* 1996 Update (Warren Gorham & Lamont, 1996), pp. U9B-4 and U9B-5. ©1996 Warren, Gorham + Lamont of RIA, 395 Hudson Street, New York, NY 10014, reprinted with permission.

Volume 12/31/94	% Owned Shares Outstanding	by Largest Holder	Moving Average as of 12/31/94			
			60 Day	120 Day	180 Day	260 Day
			3.00%	2.31%	1.89%	1.25%
55,400	36,766,000	49.0%	23.64	25.76	25.88	26.84
7,700	8,581,000		22.94	24.29	24.16	24.68
			3.02%	6.03%	7.14%	8.73%
15,100	21,515,000	36.0%	43.08	41.29	40.53	40.47
61,500	90,450,000		45.44	43.88	43.20	42.99
			−5.20%	−5.91%	−6.17%	−5.86%
23,400	5,470,000	25.0%	44.61	46.75	48.78	50.14
14,100	16,411,000		45.55	47.90	47.91	48.26
			−2.07%	2.40%	1.81%	3.91%
74,400	47,981,000	13.7%	23.20	23.33	23.06	24.40
1,288,200	584,663,000		22.49	22.48	21.81	22.56
			3.13%	3.80%	5.72%	8.17%
40,500	68,331,000	80.8%	17.02	17.75	17.93	19.55
79,600	137,347,000		17.13	17.84	18.03	19.62
			−0.65%	−0.51%	−0.57%	−0.36%
85,000	74,416,000	85.0%	40.29	39.70	36.96	36.20
679,600	282,916,000		39.08	37.05	34.39	33.16
			3.08%	7.15%	7.46%	9.19%

			60 Day	120 Day	180 Day	260 Day
			1.52%	1.94%	2.53%	3.20%
			1.15%	1.29%	1.88%	2.73%
			8.85%	8.94%	8.85%	9.19%
			−5.20%	−5.91%	−6.17	−5.86%
			18	18	18	18

Exhibit 12.2A Transactions in Which Premiums Were Paid for High-Vote Shares

Company	Year	Type of Transaction	Name of Class		Voting Rights		Consideration per Share	
			High-Vote	Low-Vote	High-Vote	Low-Vote	High-Vote	Low-Vote
Aberdeen Petroleum	1975	Acquisition by Adobe Oil & Gas	Class B	Class A	(a)	(a)	$8.25	$4.50
AEL Industries	1996	Acquisition by Tracor	Class B	Class A	1 vote	No votes	$52.39 (d)	$24.25
Bergen Brunswig	1989	Recapitalization	Class A	Class B	(a)	(a)	9.5285 Class A shares	1 share
Box Energy	1997	Purchase of 57.2% of A shares by Simplot	Class A	Class B	1 vote	No votes	$11.85	1 share (e)
Fischer & Porter	1993	Recapitalization	Class B	Common	10 votes	1 vote	1 sh. common + 2 warrants (f)	1 share
Forest Oil	1993	Recapitalization	Class B	Class A	10 votes	1 vote	1.1 shares of common	1 share
Home Shopping Network	1996	Merger with Silver King Communications	Class B	Common	10 votes	1 vote	0.54 shs.	0.45 shs.
Jones Intercable	1994	Investment by Bell Canada	Common	Class B	1 vote	0.1 votes	$19 for option (g)	26.125
National Old Line Insurance	1981	Acquisition by Ennia N.V.	Class AA	Class BB	1 vote	No votes	$67.80 (h)	$28.23 (h)
Pepsi-Cola Puerto Rico Bottling	1998	Acquisition of control by Pohlad Companies	Class A	Class B	6 votes	1 vote	$5.75	$3.63
Republic Pictures	1993	Recapitalization	Class B	Class A	10 votes	1 vote	1.2 shares of common	1 share
Resorts International	1987	Two-step acquisition by D. Trump & M. Griffin	Class B	Class A	1 vote	0.01 votes	$135.00	$36.00 (i)
Ritter Financial	1969	Recapitalization	Class A	Class B	(b)	(b)	2 shares	1 share
SFX Communications	1997	Acquisition by SBI Holdings	Class B	Class A	10 votes	1 vote (c)	$97.50	$75.00
Sikes Corporation	1990	Merger with Premark International	Class B	Class A	(a)	(a)	$26.78	$16.40

Smart & Final Iris	1984	Two-step acquisition by Casino U.S.A.	Class B	Class A	(a)	(a)	$541	$123.50
Stanhome	1986	Recapitalization	Voting	Nonvoting	1 vote	No votes	$46.50 cash	1 share (j)
United States Foil	1961	Merger with Reynolds Metals	Class B	Class A	1 vote	No votes	2.55 shares	0.85 shares

(a) High-vote shares elect majority of directors; 1 vote on other matters.

(b) High-votes share elect 5 of 7 directors; 1 vote on other matters.

(c) Class A elects 3 directors and votes with Class B for others.

(d) Premium paid for 59.6% of high-vote shares. Calculations herein treat the remaining 40.4% as noncontrol shares.

(e) $7 prior to announcement.

(f) Warrants @ $8.625 (market), valued at $1.20 at date of issuance.

(g) Bell Canada bought Class B shares at $26.125 (approximately double market) and an option to buy 56.3% of Common at $89.13 in eight years. Data herein calculated as if exercise price were $26.125 plus option price. Premium paid for 56.3% of high-vote shares. Calculations herein treat the remaining 43.7% as noncontrol shares.

(h) Changed from $80.00 for AA and $26.75 for BB in settlement of class action.

(i) Changed from $22.00 in settlement of class action.

(j) $39.75 prior to announcement.

Source: Gilbert E. Matthews, CFA, Sutter Securities Incorporated.

Exhibit 12.2B Analysis of Premiums Paid for High-Vote Shares

Company	As % of Total Shares	% Owned by Principal Shareholder	Premium per Share
Aberdeen Petroleum	17.7%	100%	83.3%
AEL Industries	5.5%	55%	116.0%
Bergen Brunswig	2.1%	90%	852.9%
Box Energy	8.9%	57%	69.3%
Fischer & Porter	10.8%	53%	27.8%
Forest Oil	24.0%	84%	10.0%
Home Shopping Network	21.7%	100%	20.0%
Jones Intercable	16.4%	56%	72.7%
National Old Line Insurance	8.8%	75%	140.2%
Pepsi-Cola Puerto Rico Bottling	23.3%	100%	58.4%
Republic Pictures	16.2%	41%	20.0%
Resorts International	11.7%	72%	275.0%
Ritter Financial	2.5%	100%	100.0%
SFX Communications	8.0%	98%	30.0%
Sikes Corporation	9.6%	95%	63.3%
Smart & Final Iris	9.2%	87%	338.1%
Stanhome	16.9%	78%	17.0%
United States Foil	5.9%	100.0%	200.0%

(a) Elects majority of directors.
(b) Elects 5 of 7 directors.
(c) Excludes value of low-vote shares' preferences; 13.05% if preferences of $1.00 annual dividend and $10.00 liquidation are valued at $0.50 per share; 15.97% if preferences are valued at $1.00 per share.
(d) For 59.6% of high-vote shares.
(e) For 57.2% of high-vote shares.
(f) 13.82% before changed terms resulting from settlement of class action.
(g) 33.14% before changed terms resulting from settlement of class action.
Source: Gilbert E. Matthews, CFA, Sutter Securities Incorporated.

COURT CASES INVOLVING VOTING VERSUS NONVOTING STOCK

Dissenting Stockholder Case

Manacher v. Reynolds is a very interesting case demonstrating the value of rights of voting control.[6] United States Foil Company (Foil) had outstanding a small number of "A" voting shares and a large class of "B" nonvoting shares. The only significant asset of Foil (through direct and indirect ownership) was a 50.09% inter-

Voting Interest	Economic Interest	% of Consideration	Premium over Economic Interest
(a)	17.75%	28.34%	10.60% (c)
100%	5.96% (c)	12.05% (c)	6.08% (d)
(a)	2.11%	17.07%	14.95%
100%	8.86% (e)	14.13% (e)	5.27% (e)
54.8%	10.81%	13.41%	2.60%
75.9%	23.97%	25.75%	1.78%
73.5%	21.74%	25.00%	3.26%
66.2%	9.20%	14.90%	5.70%
100%	8.80%	18.81%	10.01% (f)
64.5%	23.26%	32.43%	9.18%
65.9%	16.22%	18.85%	2.63%
93.0%	11.69%	33.18%	21.49% (g)
(b)	2.47%	4.82%	2.35%
46.6%	8.03%	10.19%	2.16%
(a)	9.62%	14.80%	5.19%
(a)	9.16%	30.63%	21.48%
100%	16.94%	19.26%	2.32%
100%	5.91%	13.81%	7.90%

Median	5.27%
Mean: All	7.60%
Excluding 3 highest	5.10%

est in Reynolds Metals Company (Metals), which traded on the New York Stock Exchange (NYSE).

Foils' Class A (voting) stock had no public market. Foils' Class B (nonvoting) stock had unlisted trading privileges on the American Stock Exchange (ASE). The Foils Class B stock generally traded at about a 33% discount from the value of the equity interest that it represented in the Reynolds shares.

For years the Foils Class B (nonvoting) shareholders had made proposals to try to narrow or close this gap, but to no avail. Finally, after much negotiation, representatives of the Class A and Class B shares came to a settlement agreement. They would convert all shares of both classes to a new class of common stock, with the Class A stock getting three shares for one and the Class B stock getting one share for one. Then the new common stock would be converted into shares of Reynolds Metals Company. This worked out to be about a $40,000,000 premium that the Class A stockholders would receive (at the expense of the Class B stockholders) compared with simply converting all the shares on a one-for-one basis.

Some of the minority Class B (nonvoting) stockholders objected to the settlement agreement as being unfair. Thus, it came to the Court of Chancery of Delaware to rule on the fairness of the settlement agreement.

Following are relevant quotes from the opinion of the Delaware Court of Chancery:

> The court is met at the outset with the Objectors' contention that the officials of Foil, being members of the Reynolds' Group, violated a fiduciary duty which they owed the B shareholders. It consisted of their exacting the 3 for 1 premium as their price for letting "their" board act on a merger which they could not prevent by their votes as stockholders. Was the Reynolds' Group prohibited from asking for the premium as a condition to their agreeing to vote in favor of the merger? . . .
>
> The B stockholders were fully advised and, of real importance, had to give their approval as a condition precedent to court approval. They were not controlled by the Reynolds Group. Under such circumstances I do not believe the officials of Foil or its A stockholders breached any fiduciary duty owed the B. . . .
>
> I next consider the terms of the settlement. The Objectors contend that they constitute nothing but a gift of a large portion of B's equity in Metals to A. . . . Under the plan each B share will receive $5.16 less than it would receive were the conversion after reclassification on a 1 for 1 basis. The Objectors say that under the plan the A is exacting from the B a 4% premium amounting to about $40,000,000 without any recognizable benefit passing to the B. . . .
>
> By relinquishing absolute control of Foil the A will give up a valuable right which they now possess. Such relinquishment will benefit the B shares. The principal benefit will come from the elimination of the discount. The objectors appear to argue that the "discount" is not something of value passing from the A to the B. . . . [T]he hard fact of life is that the proposed action by the A is an indispensable prerequisite to the realization of any benefit by the B from the elimination of the discount.
>
> . . . [T]he A shareholders hold the key with which to unlock the "discount" treasure chest for the B. No other factor being present, they may demand a reasonable premium for the use of their key.
>
> I return to the central question: What was the A fairly entitled to exact from the B for the rights relinquished and the consequent benefits to the B? . . .
>
> I conclude that when overwhelming stockholder approval is added to the facts, it justifies a business-judgment approval of the settlement. . . . I conclude that their terms are fair in this setting.

U.S. Tax Court Cases

In *Barnes v. Commissioner,* one expert discounted the nonvoting stock by 3.66% and the other expert by 5%.[7] The court concluded:

Prospective buyers will pay a premium for shares with voting power or obtain a discount for nonvoting shares. Wallace v. United States, 566 F. Supp. 904, 917 (D. Mass. 1981) (voting shares appraised 5 percent higher than nonvoting shares); Kosman v. Commissioner, T.C.Memo 1996-112 (nonvoting shares discounted by 4 percent); Estate of Winkler v. Commissioner, T.C.Memo 1989-231.

[One expert] applied a discount of 3.66 percent for lack of voting power to the value ($337.87) of the Rock Hill stock. [He] based this discount on a study of 43 public companies with voting and nonvoting shares. The study found that the average discount for nonvoting stock was 3.66 percent. [The other expert] discounted the nonvoting stock of Rock Hill by an additional 5 percent. We find that use of a 3.66-percent discount for nonvoting stock was reasonable.

In *Kosman v. Commissioner,* the taxpayer's expert testified to a 10% nonvoting stock discount, and the IRS's expert opined to 4%.[8] The court accepted the 4%, explaining that the taxpayer's expert did not explain why he chose a 10% discount for nonvoting shares, whereas the IRS expert based his 4% nonvoting discount on the Lease, McConnell, and Mikkelson study published in the *Journal of Financial Economics* in April 1983.

In *Estate of Winkler v. Commissioner,* the estate held 10% of the 80,000 shares of voting stock, and there were also 720,000 shares of nonvoting stock outstanding.[9] The expert for the IRS opined to a 10% premium in the per-share value of the voting stock over the nonvoting stock. The court accepted this differential, explaining:

Another point at which respondent's appraisal report diverged from that of petitioner's experts was [the IRS expert's] determination that the voting stock was worth more than the non-voting stock in Rock Island. There were only 80,000 shares of voting stock compared to 720,000 shares of non-voting stock. In this case the difference between the voting and non-voting stock in Rock Island is the ability to vote for a board of directors and any "swing vote characteristics" of a 10 percent block of voting stock. In being able to vote for a board of directors, a shareholder has a voice, albeit perhaps a small voice in certain instances, in deciding corporate policy, directing the payment of dividends, and compelling a liquidation. Thus, the owner of a 10 percent voting interest in a corporation retains the possibility of control, even if it must be exercised in conjunction with other shareholders, over the closely held corporation. On the other hand, the owner of a non-voting share of stock has no likelihood of influencing corporate policy, other than by selling his shares of stock in disapproval over what the board of directors has done. We think petitioner's experts could not reasonably treat the voting and non-voting stock as having the same value. Thus, we find that the value of the Class A voting, common stock was higher than the Class B non-voting, common stock.

Estate of Bosca v. Commissioner involved a recapitalization, in which the father exchanged his 50% block of voting stock for a 50% block of nonvoting stock.[10] The corporation then canceled the voting stock it received, thus giving 100% voting rights to his two sons. The taxpayer initially took the position that no value was transferred to the sons, because the father's interest in the company was undiminished, except for loss of voting rights.

By the time of the trial, the taxpayer had conceded that some value was transferred. The biggest issue for the court was whether the transfers should be valued as one 50% block or two 25% blocks. For reasons that unfortunately were not explained, the parties had agreed beforehand that, if the court decided the stock should be valued as a single 50% block, the premium would be 25.62% over the nonvoting stock value, for a tax liability of $970,830. If the stock were valued as two separate 25% blocks, however, the premium would be 2.72%, for a tax liability of $103,040.

With respect to the question of whether there was a gift, the Tax Court said: "In short, a transfer that involves relinquishing property with a bundle of rights and receiving back the same property with the bundle of rights reduced is a direct gift with the value of the rights transferred determined under I.R.C. section 2512(a). Where a transfer involves relinquishing property with a bundle of rights and receiving some of those rights back, plus others, or totally different rights, the issue or 'money's worth' comes up and the valuation is under I.R.C. section 2512(b)."

In essence, therefore, there were indirect gifts of the value of the voting rights to each of the two sons. Since this constituted two gifts, and each gift must be valued separately, the court ruled in favor of two 25% blocks rather than one 50% block.

The most controversial case ever on the subject of voting versus nonvoting stock value was *Estate of Simplot v. Commissioner.*[11] Rounding the numbers slightly, decedent and two of his brothers each owned 18 shares and another brother owned 22 shares of the 76 shares of voting stock outstanding in J.R. Simplot Company. There were also outstanding 141,289 shares of nonvoting stock, of which the decedent owned 3,942 shares. The Tax Court found that the nonvoting stock was worth $3,417 per share and that the 18 shares of voting stock were worth $215,539 per share!

On May 14, 2001, the Ninth Circuit Court of Appeals reversed *Simplot* and remanded for entry in favor of the taxpayer.[12] The Ninth Circuit said that the Tax Court valued something that was not at issue—namely, the entire block of voting stock—in the process of reaching its decision. The appellate court also commented that a control premium should be applied only if economic advantage could be shown, and that the Commissioner had failed to do so.

SUMMARY

If a company has both voting and nonvoting stock, there may be a price differential between the two in favor of the voting stock. For small minority interests, this differential is usually small, but it could be more substantial for a voting control block.

In the United States, most state laws and company articles of incorporation do not guarantee nonvoting (or other minority) shareholders the same per-share price (or any offer at all) if a controlling block is sold. There have been many instances where control blocks have sold at substantial premiums over offers to other stockholders.

Empirical research on both the U.S. and Canadian markets show that differentials between voting and nonvoting share prices are small, averaging under 5%, absent a takeover scenario. But courts have upheld substantial premiums paid for voting blocks compared to nonvoting blocks.

The U.S. Tax Court recognizes the differential between voting and nonvoting stock values. It has made a variety of findings as to the amount of the difference, depending on the varied facts and circumstances of each case.

Notes

1. Yale Kramer, "Majority Block of Nonvoting Stock May Have Slightly Greater Value than Minority Interest," *Shannon Pratt's Business Valuation Update* (July 1997): 15.
2. Ronald C. Lease, John J. McConnell, and Wayne H. Mikkelson, "The Market Value of Control in Publicly-Traded Corporations," *Journal of Financial Economics* (1983): 439–471, at 469. Reprinted with permission from Elsevier Science.
3. Chris Robinson, John Rumsey, and Alan White, "The Value of a Vote in the Market for Corporate Control," paper published by York University Faculty of Administrative Studies, February 1996. Used with permission from authors, Alan White (Peter L. Mitchelson / Sit Investment Associates Foundation Professor of Investment Strategy, Joseph L. Rotman School of Management, University of Toronto), John Rumsey and Dr. Chris Robinson, whose work will appear in *Convergence and Diversity of Corporate Governance Regimes and Capital Markets,* ed. J. McCahery, P. Moerland, T. Raaijmakers and L. Renneboog, Oxford University Press, 2001 (forthcoming).
4. Kevin C. O'Shea and Robert M. Siwicki, "Stock Price Premiums for Voting Rights Attributable to Minority Interests," *Business Valuation Review* (December 1991): 165–171.
5. Paul J. Much and Timothy J. Fagan, "The Value of Voting Rights," in *Financial Valuation: Business and Business Interests,* 1996 Update, James H. Zukin, ed. (New York: Warren Gorham & Lamont, 1996).
6. *Manacher v. Reynolds,* 39 Del. Ch. 401, 165 A.2d 741 (Del. Ch. 1960).
7. *Barnes v. Commissioner,* T.C. Memo 1998-413, 76 T.C.M. (CCH) 881 (1998).
8. *Kosman v. Commissioner,* T.C. Memo 1996-112, 71 T.C.M. (CCH) 2356 (1996).
9. *Estate of Winkler v. Commissioner,* T.C. Memo 1989-231, 57 T.C.M. (CCH) 373 (1989).
10. *Estate of Bosca v. Commissioner,* T.C. Memo 1998-251, 76 T.C.M. (CCH) 62 (1998).
11. *Estate of Simplot v. Commissioner,* 112 T.C. 130 (1999).
12. *Estate of Simplot v. Commissioner,* 2001 U.S. App. LEXIS 9220 (9th Cir., 2001).

Chapter 13

Key Person Discounts

Many private companies are highly dependent on a single key person or a few key people. The actual death or potential loss of such a person, whether by death, disability, or resignation, entails risk of adverse consequences. Such consequences can include a variety of losses, as suggested by that key person's unique attributes. In smaller, technology-oriented companies, for example, the reliance on a key person is often magnified because of the necessity for the organization to be nimble and proactive to market opportunities that require swift, high-quality decisions and cutting-edge technical competence.

Some of the key person attributes that may be lost include:

- Relationships with suppliers
- Relationships with customers
- Employee loyalty to key person
- Unique marketing vision, insight, and ability
- Unique technological or product innovation capability
- Extraordinary management and leadership skill
- Financial strength (ability to obtain debt or equity capital, personal guarantees)

Sometimes the impact or potential impact of the loss of the key person may be reflected in an adjustment to a discount or capitalization rate in the income approach or to valuation multiples in the market approach. Alternatively, the key person discount may be quantified as a separate discount, sometimes as a dollar amount but more often as a percentage. It is generally considered to be an enterprise-level discount (taken before shareholder-level adjustments), because it impacts the entire company. All else being equal, a company with a *realized* key person loss is worth less than a company with a *potential* key person loss.

EMPIRICAL EVIDENCE SUPPORTS KEY PERSON DISCOUNT

Steven Bolten and Yan Wang prepared an interesting study on market reaction to management changes in public companies, especially small ones. They concluded that the market evidence supports the key person discount. The following is a summary of their findings:

The Data

We examined the "Who's News" columns of the *Wall Street Journal* from August 1, 1996 through November 28, 1996 for announcements of senior management changes above the rank of vice-president. We selected all that had distinct changes in senior persons with clear indications of policy power. We eliminated many internal promotions where little changed in personnel. For example, we excluded announcements where existing management did not change or an additional new position was created with or without a new person added to the senior management team.

We selected 101 observations within our criteria. When the announcement was made after the markets closed we used the opening price of the next trading day.

Methodology

We observed both increases and decreases in stock prices associated with the announcement of change in senior management. . . . We had to split the increase and decrease responses to avoid the arithmetic distortion of their offsetting effects on the averages. The risk of management disruption is our concern in the smaller, closely held firms, so it is the average decrease we are most interested herein.

We stratified the sample by size based on capitalization below and above $280 million and, more importantly, on the number of senior management as listed in the Compact Disclosure data base. The latter was stratified as fewer than six; six to ten; eleven to fifteen; and more than fifteen.

Results

The results clearly supported the intuitive belief that the departure for whatever reason of a significant key person negatively impacts the firm's valuation. . . . On average, the departure of a key management person caused the stock of the smaller, public firms (less than $280 million capitalization) to fall 8.65%. An average negative 4.83% impact was observed for the larger capitalization firms with presumably greater management depth. Of course, we observed increases in the valuation when a perceived favorable change occurred in senior management, as we would logically anticipate.

The smaller firms, where the impact is potentially greater, had the larger observed average percentage change. Since the private firms typically are structured such that the departure of the key person would be negative, the average decrease is typically more significant for the valuation of closely held firms, except in those rare instances where it can be documented that the departure of the key person (usually a family member) may be advantageous. We might add that this is hard to document even in the rare case where it may be true.

The impact of the departure of the key person is increasingly greater as the number of persons on the management team decreases. This observed inverse relationship is, of course, what we would anticipate. With fewer than six persons on the management team, as reported in Compact Disclosure, the average decrease in stock value for the public firms was 9.43%. This result was the highest among the smaller public firms, progressively and consistently rising from −2.65% for firms with more than 16 persons on the management team. We could easily conclude from extrapolation that the negative impact would be even higher for firms with still fewer persons on the management team, such as typically observed in closely held firms. We could not specifically measure the extrapolation because there are no data on those size firms. . . .

We also stratified the sample by the market in which the stock was traded as a proxy for liquidity, but the results were about the same regardless of the exchange or market where the stock was traded. The exception was the few foreign traded stocks that showed much larger reactions to the change in key persons.

We also stratified the sample by reasons for leaving, such as health, including death. The results showed no clear pattern that any particular reason caused a greater or lesser impact on the valuation, except for the few, very sudden departures such as unexpected deaths, which caused an over 10% decrease in the valuation.

Conclusion

We believe the observed results definitively support the generally accepted assumption that the lack of management depth and the potential loss of a key person(s) negatively impacts valuation. This is particularly true in small, closely held firms where the number of persons on the management team may be as few as one. The degree of negative impact increases as the number on the team decreases. We observed it as high as negative 9.43% for public firms with fewer than six persons on the management team before the lack of data made it impossible to extrapolate any further. However, the negative impact of the discount should obviously be higher as the number of persons on the team decreases.[1]

Of course, adding a premium to the discount rate in the income approach to reflect the "size effect" can capture some of the above differential discussed by these authors.

FACTORS TO CONSIDER IN ANALYZING THE KEY PERSON DISCOUNT

Some of the factors to consider in estimating the magnitude of a key person discount, in addition to special characteristics of the person listed above, include:

- Services rendered by the key person and degree of dependence on that person
- Likelihood of loss of the key person (if still active)
- Depth and quality of other company management
- Availability and adequacy of potential replacement
- Compensation paid to key person and probable compensation for replacement

- Value of irreplaceable factors lost, such as vital customer and supplier relationships, insight and recognition, and personal management styles to ensure company-wide harmony among employees
- Risks associated with disruption and operation under new management
- Lost debt capacity

There are three potential offsets to the loss of a key person:

1. Life or disability insurance proceeds payable to the company and not earmarked for other purposes, such as repurchase of a decedent's stock
2. Compensation saved (after any continuing obligations) if the compensation to the key person was greater than the cost of replacement
3. Employment and/or noncompete agreements

QUANTIFYING THE MAGNITUDE OF THE KEY PERSON DISCOUNT

Ideally, the magnitude of the key person discount should be the estimated difference in the present value of net cash flows with and without the involvement of the key person. If the key person were still involved, the projected cash flows for each year would be multiplied by the mean of the probability distribution of that person's remaining alive and active during that year.

A significant factor in the quantification of the key person discount is the presence or absence of employment and/or noncompete agreements. In the absence of such agreements, the stock may be worth only its tangible asset value. Valuation of such agreements is addressed in "Human Capital Intangible Assets," Chapter 21 in *Valuing Intangible Assets* by Robert Reilly and Robert Schweihs.[2]

Jerome Osteryoung and Derek Newman propose a fairly rigorous analytical approach to quantifying the key person discount. In the summary to their article, they write:

> This paper suggests that the key person impact on the valuation of a business is important. The smaller the business the more important the key person becomes.
>
> The key person impact cannot be thought of as applying a certain percentage to normal valuation of the business. This is not appropriate for two reasons. First, there is no viable research or theory that substantiates this point. Second, the key person loss will be different with each type of business.
>
> In order to evaluate the loss of a key person on the value of a business, each component in the future income and cash-flow stream must be evaluated for the exiting key person. Only by undertaking such a rigorous approach can any losses resulting form [*sic*] the departure of the key person be quantified.[3]

Notwithstanding the above, the fact is that most practitioners and most courts do express their estimate of the key person discount as a percentage of the otherwise undiscounted enterprise value.

In any case, the analyst should investigate the key person's actual duties and areas of active involvement. A key person may contribute value to a company both in day-to-day management duties and in strategic judgment responsibilities based on long-standing contacts and reputation within an industry.[4] The more detail presented about the impact of the key person the better.

INTERNAL REVENUE SERVICE RECOGNIZES KEY PERSON DISCOUNT

The IRS recognizes the key person discount factor in Revenue Ruling 59-60:

Rev. Rul. 59-60
Section 4.02

    * * * * * * *

. . . The loss of the manager of a so-called "one-man" business may have a depressing effect upon the value of the stock of such business, particularly if there is a lack of trained personnel capable of succeeding to the management of the enterprise. In valuing the stock of this type of business, therefore, the effect of the loss of the manager on the future expectancy of the business, and the absence of management-succession potentialities are pertinent factors to be taken into consideration. On the other hand, there may be factors, which offset, in whole or in part, the loss of the manager's services. For instance, the nature of the business and of its assets may be such that they will not be impaired by the loss of the manager. Furthermore, the loss may be adequately covered by life insurance, or competent management might be employed on the basis of the consideration paid for the former manager's services. These, or other offsetting factors, if found to exist, should be carefully weighed against the loss of the manager's services in valuing the stock of the enterprise.

Moreover, the IRS discusses the key person discount in its *IRS Valuation Training for Appeals Officers Coursebook:*

Key Person

A key person is an individual whose contribution to a business is so significant that there is certainty that future earning levels will be adversely affected by the loss of the individual. . . .

Rev. Rul. 59-60 recognizes the fact that in many types of businesses, the loss of a key person may have a depressing effect upon value. . . .

Some courts have accounted for this depressing effect on value by applying a key person discount. In determining whether to apply a key person discount certain factors should be considered:

1. Whether the claimed individual was actually responsible for the company's profit levels.
2. If there is a key person, whether the individual can be adequately replaced.

Though an individual may be the founder and controlling officer of a corporation, it does not necessarily follow that he or she is a key person. Earnings may be attributable to intangibles such as patents and copyrights or long-term contracts. Evidence of special expertise and current significant management decisions should be presented. Finally, subsequent years' financial statements should be reviewed to see if earnings actually declined. In many situations, the loss of a so-called key person may actually result in increased profits.

The size of the company, in terms of number of employees, is also significant. The greater the number of employees, the greater the burden of showing that the contributions of one person were responsible for the firm's earnings history.

Even where there is a key person, the possibility exists that the individual can be adequately replaced. Consideration should be given to whether other long-term employees can assume management positions. On occasion, a company may own key person life insurance. The proceeds from this type of policy may enable the company to survive a period of decreased earnings and to attract competent replacements.

There is no set percentage or format for reflecting a key person discount. It is essentially based on the facts and circumstances of each case.[5]

U.S. TAX COURT CASES INVOLVING KEY PERSON DISCOUNTS

Cases Involving Decedent's Estate

In *Estate of Mitchell v. Commissioner,* the court commented that the moment-of-death concept of valuation for estate tax purposes is important, because it requires focus on the *property transferred.*[6] This meant that, at the moment of death, the company was without the services of Paul Mitchell. Because (1) the court considered him a very key person, (2) alleged earlier offers to acquire the entire company were contingent upon his continuing service, and (3) there was a marked lack of depth of management, the court determined a 10% discount from the company's enterprise stock value.

The court's discussion of the key person factor is instructive:

We next consider the impact of Mr. Mitchell's death on [John Paul Mitchell Systems.] Mr. Mitchell embodied JPMS to distributors, hair stylists, and salon owners. He was vitally important to its product development, marketing, and training. Moreover, he possessed a unique vision that enabled him to foresee fashion trends in the hair styling industry. It is clear that the loss of Mr. Mitchell, along with the structural inadequacies of JPMS, created uncertainties as to the future of JPMS at the moment of death.

Accordingly, after determining an enterprise value of $150,000,000 for John Paul Mitchell Systems stock, the court deducted $15,000,000 to arrive at $135,000,000 before calculation of the estate's proportionate value and then applying discounts for minority interest, lack of marketability, and litigation risk.

The estate, however, appealed the Tax Court's conclusion on other grounds. On May 2, 2001, the Ninth Circuit Court of Appeals reversed and remanded *Mitchell.* The Ninth Circuit decision held that the Tax Court was internally inconsistent in its ruling on minority and marketability issues and failed to adequately explain its conclusion.[7]

In *Estate of Feldmar v. Commissioner,* the court gave a lengthy explanation before ultimately arriving at a 25% key person discount:[8]

Management. [United Equitable Corporation] was founded by decedent in 1972. From its inception until the date of decedent's death, UEC has been a company highly dependent upon specialized marketing techniques which are employed in selected markets to encourage the sale of UEC's non-traditional insurance products and services. Throughout the company's history, decedent had been heavily involved in the daily operation of UEC. Decedent was the creative driving force behind both UEC's innovative marketing techniques, and UEC's creation of, or acquisition and exploitation of, new products and services.

In 1981, decedent was paid a salary of $270,000 by UEC and of $98,466 by [American Warranty Corporation] for his services. Such salary was, as compared to the salaries of the executives in positions and companies comparable to decedent's, approximately $100,000 higher than the norm. However, decedent never received any payments from UEC in the form of dividends. Despite the higher salary decedent received, UEC recognized that the prospects for finding someone to replace decedent as the head of UEC's management team were not hopeful. In recognition of UEC's probable inability to acquire the services of a competent leader to replace decedent, UEC attempted to partially ameliorate that eventuality by obtaining an insurance policy on decedent's life under which UEC was the beneficiary. Such insurance policy provided for proceeds of $2,000,000 upon decedent's death. . . .

We further recognize, however, that where a corporation is substantially dependent upon the services of one person, and where that person is no longer able to perform services for the corporation by reason of death or incapacitation, an investor would expect some form of discount below fair market value when purchasing stock in the corporation to compensate for the loss of that key employee (key employee discount). See Estate of Huntsman v. Commissioner, 66 T.C. 861 (1976); Edwards v. Commissioner, a Memorandum Opinion of this Court dated January 23, 1945. We find that Milton Feldmar was an innovative driving force upon which UEC was substantially dependent for the implementation of new marketing strategies and acquisition policies. Therefore, we find that a key employee discount is appropriate.

Respondent asserts that no key man discount should be applied because, respondent argues, any detriment UEC suffered from the loss of decedent's services is more than compensated for by the life insurance policy upon decedent's life. We do not find merit in such a position. The life insurance proceeds UEC was to receive upon decedent's death are more appropriately considered as a non-operating asset of UEC. See Estate of Huntsman v. Commissioner, supra. We did this when we determined a value of UEC's stock by using the market-to-book valuation method.

Respondent also argues that the key employee discount should not be applied because, respondent asserts, UEC could rely upon the services of the management structure already controlling UEC, or UEC could obtain the services of a new manager, comparable to the decedent, by using the salary decedent had received at the time of his demise. With respect to the existing management, [taxpayer's expert] conducted interviews of such managers and found them to be inexperienced and incapable of filling the void created by decedent's absence. By contrast, neither of respondent's experts offered an opinion on such management's ability to replace decedent. From the evidence represented, we conclude that UEC could not compensate for the loss of decedent by drawing upon its management reserves as such existed on the valuation date.

Taking into account the control premium and key employee discount, we find that an investor would be willing to pay a 15% premium for a controlling block of shares in UEC, but the same investor would expect a 35% discount for the loss of a key employee. A control premium of 15% is proper in the case at hand because, although an investor would be acquiring a corporation over which he could exercise dominion, that investor would also be acquiring a corporation which was already facing declining profitability and serious concerns regarding the adequacy of its claims reservs [*sic*]. A key man discount of 35% is appropriate in this case because UEC suffered a serious loss when decedent took to his grave his considerable expertise in finding and exploiting innovative insurance products and services. Such 35% discount should be reduced, however, to account for UEC's potential for finding a new leader, from outside of its existing management, to replace decedent. Although we find it to be a very remote possibility that UEC might find a new helmsman with knowledge, experience, innovative skills, and resources comparable to those of the decedent, we shall reduce the key employee discount to be applied form [*sic*] 35% to 25% to account for such potentiality.

Combining the control premium of 15% and the key employee discount of 25%, the result is an overall downward adjustment of 10% to the per share weighted average fair market value of $14.41.

In *Estate of Rodriguez v. Commissioner*, the company subject to valuation was Los Amigos Tortilla Manufacturing, a corn and flour tortilla manufacturing business providing shells used by Mexican restaurants for tacos, burritos, and so forth.[9]

Respective experts for the IRS and the taxpayer presented diverging testimony on the key person issue. The taxpayer's expert adjusted pretax income to account for the loss of the decedent. The expert for the IRS said that he normally would adjust the capitalization rate to account for the loss of a key person, but did not in this case because of the $250,000 corporate-owned life insurance policy on the decedent. He also testified that decedent's salary would pay for a replacement.

The court decided the issue in favor of the taxpayer:

> [W]e do not agree with respondent's expert that no adjustment for the loss of a key man is necessary in this case. Respondent argues that an adjustment is inappropriate because Los Amigos maintained $250,000 of insurance on decedent's life. Also, respondent's expert witness testified that he did not make any allowance for the value of decedent as a key man because his replacement cost was equal to his salary. These arguments understate the importance of decedent to Los Amigos and the adverse effect his death had on business. We agree with petitioners that an adjustment is necessary to account for the loss of decedent.
>
> The evidence shows that decedent was the dominant force behind Los Amigos. He worked long hours supervising every aspect of the business. At the time of his death, Los Amigos' customers and suppliers were genuinely and understandably concerned about the future of the business without decedent. In fact, Los Amigos soon lost one of its largest accounts due to an inability to maintain quality. The failure was due to decedent's absence from operations. Profits fell dramatically without decedent to run the business. No one was trained to take decedent's place.

Capitalizing earnings is a sound valuation method requiring no adjustment only in a case where the earning power of the business can reasonably be projected to continue as in the past. Where, as in this case, a traumatic event shakes the business so that its earning power is demonstrably diminished, earnings should properly be adjusted. See Central Trust Co. v. United States, 305 F.2d at 403. An adjustment to earnings before capitalizing them to determine the company's value rather than a discount at the end of the computation is appropriate to reflect the diminished earnings capacity of the business. We adopt petitioners' expert's adjustment to earnings for the loss of the key man.

In *Estate of Huntsman v. Commissioner,* the Tax Court applied a key person discount as the final adjustment to value with little discussion:[10]

Using our best judgment, we find that the value of the stock in Steel and Supply, on the date of the decedent's death, based upon both their earnings and net asset values, giving consideration to the insurance proceeds received by each, was $33 and $11 per share, respectively.

One final adjustment is necessary to determine the actual price a willing buyer would pay for the stock of these two companies. The decedent was the dominant force in both businesses, and his untimely death obviously reduced the value of the stock in the two corporations. However, both corporations had competent officers who were able to assume successfully the decedent's duties. Both experts agreed that some discount must be made to reflect the loss of the decedent. Using our best judgment, we find that after discounting the value of the stock to reflect the loss of the decedent, the fair market value of the Steel and Supply stock at the date of the decedent's death was $29 and $10 per share, respectively.

In *Estate of Yeager v. Commissioner,* decedent was the controlling stockholder of a complicated holding company with several subsidiaries.[11] The court decided on a 10% discount for the loss of the key person. In its opinion, the court commented:

Until his death, the decedent was president, chief executive officer, and a director of Cascade Olympic, Capital Cascade, and Capitol Center. He was the only officer and director of these corporations who was involved in their day-to-day affairs. The decedent was also president of Center Offices until 1979. The presence of the decedent was critical to the operation of both Cascade Olympic and the affiliated corporations.

Case Where Key Person Is Still Active

In *Furman v. Commissioner,* the issue was valuation of minority interests in a 27-store Burger King chain.[12] The U.S. Tax Court rejected in toto the IRS's expert's valuation. Besides rejecting his methodology, the court noted that he had represented that he possessed certain qualifications and credentials to perform business valuations, which he did not in fact have.

The taxpayer's expert's appraisal used a multiple of earnings before interest, taxes, depreciation, and amortization (EBITDA) and applied discounts of 30% for minority interest, 35% for lack of marketability, and a 10% key person discount for a total discount of 59.05%. The court adjusted the EBITDA multiple upward, decided on a combined 40% minority and marketability discount, and agreed with the application of a 10% key person discount, for a total discount of 46%.

It is instructive to read the court's discussion supporting the key person discount:

Robert Furman a Key Person

At the times of the 1980 Gifts and the Recapitalization, Robert actively managed [Furman's, Inc.], and no succession plan was in effect. FIC employed no individual who was qualified to succeed Robert in the management of FIC. Robert's active participation, experience, business contacts, and reputation as a Burger King franchisee contributed to value of FIC. Specifically, it was Robert whose contacts had made possible the 1976 Purchase, and whose expertise in selecting sites for new restaurants and supervising their construction and startup were of critical importance in enabling FIC to avail itself of the expansion opportunities created by the Territorial Agreement. The possibility of Robert's untimely death, disability, or resignation contributed to uncertainty in the value of FIC's operations and future cash-flows. Although a professional manager could have been hired to replace Robert, the following risks would still have been present: (i) Lack of management until a replacement was hired; (ii) the risk that a professional manager would require higher compensation than Robert had received; and (iii) the risk that a professional manager would not perform as well as Robert.

Robert was a key person in the management of FIC. His potential absence or inability were risks that had a negative impact on the fair market value of FIC. On February 2, 1980, the fair market value of each decedent's gratuitous transfer of 6 shares of FIC's common stock was subject to a key-person discount of 10 percent. On August 24, 1981, the fair market value of the 24 shares of FIC's common stock transferred by each decedent in the Recapitalization was subject to a key-person discount of 10 percent.

KEY PERSON DISCOUNTS IN MARITAL DISSOLUTIONS

A key person discount crops up occasionally in the context of a marital dissolution. A trilogy of Minnesota cases is representative of family law courts' recognition of this issue.

In *Rogers v. Rogers,* the husband was 85% owner of a firm providing engineering services.[13] The Supreme Court of Minnesota found great flaws in the valuation opinion of the expert that was accepted by the trial court:

The third major defect in [wife's expert's] methodology is his apparent failure to take into account appellant's importance to [Rogers, Freels & Associates]. [Wife's expert] applied a purely arbitrary risk factor in his calculations and there is no indication that factor bore any relationship to the importance of appellant to the continuing success of RFA. While the testimony did not establish that RFA would be worthless without appellant, it is clear that appellant is a key man—if not the key man—in RFA, and the profitability of the corporation could be substantially reduced if he were to leave. However, the valuation of appellant's share of RFA should not be based upon the assumption that appellant will remain. Such an assumption would compel appellant to continue with RFA, perhaps against his wishes, simply in order to earn enough money to pay for the award to respondent. The property acquired during marriage should be limited to that portion of the value of RFA that is not dependent upon appellant's continued services. To capitalize the earnings of RFA on the assumption that appellant will continue to contribute his talents and services is, essentially, to capitalize appellant. An award made on this basis would, in effect, give respondent a forced share of appellant's future work. If appellant were to become disabled and RFA lost its earning capacity, appellant's interests would be worth substantially less than [wife's expert's] valuations, but because the award to respondent was a "property" award, the court could not subsequently change the award to reflect the changed circumstances. . . . Reversed and remanded with instructions.

In re the Marriage of Nelson, the company in question tested and optimized designs of large heating and ventilating systems for commercial, industrial, and government buildings.[14] Although the company had four other employees, the husband, who had highly specialized training, was solely responsible for generating all business and for all analysis and supervision of projects.

The trial court applied a 30% combined discount for key person and lack of marketability, without specifying the percentage for each. The court of appeals found that the discount was far too low. The opinion stated:

Respondent is entitled to property acquired during the marriage, but she is not entitled to a lien on appellant himself. . .

As in Rogers, the trial court's discount in this case simply does not accurately reflect appellant's importance to the corporation. Here, the trial court was presented with evidence that: (a) Mechanical Data would cease operation if appellant left the business; (b) appellant is the sole fee generating professional employed by the corporation; (c) appellant is specially certified as a test balance engineer (one of only 95 in the country and the only one so certified in Minnesota, North and South Dakota); and (d) the corporation derives the majority, if not all, of its business through appellant's personal contacts with mechanical contractors in the area. This evidence, particularly in the absence of expert testimony establishing 30% as a reasonable key man/marketability discount, compels the conclusion that the trial court's discount was arbitrarily low. We so hold. The trial court did not err in valuing the corporation under the capitalization of income approach. The trial court's key man/marketability discount is reversed and the matter remanded for findings consistent with this opinion, including the taking of additional testimony, if necessary.

Unfortunately, we do not know the ultimate dispositions of the above two cases.

In one more Minnesota case, *In re the Marriage of Buchanan,* the court of appeals accepted the trial court's finding:[15]

The trial court's valuation reflects a 25% discount for appellant's influence and importance to the business and for the inherent risk and limitations on marketability associated with the business. The trial court did not abuse its discretion in applying this discount rather than the higher "key-man" discount urged by appellant, where the evidence shows J.L. Buchanan, Inc. would not cease operation if appellant left the business, appellant is not the corporation's sole fee generating person and expert testimony established 25% as a reasonable discount.

While the above three cases all refer to a key person discount, the unmentioned but real issue at stake was the exclusion of personal goodwill from the marital estate. Some states consider personal goodwill a marital asset, some do not, and the case law in other states is unclear. In states that do not include personal goodwill in the marital estate, my preference is to value the company assuming the absence of the owner/operator, thereby accounting for the impact of the owner/operator's contribution.

SUMMARY

Many private companies (and some small public ones) are highly dependent on a key individual. This creates a significant risk factor to the company while that key person is active and an actual loss results upon death, disability, or resignation. Evidence of adverse market reaction to the loss of a key person in small public companies supports the economic reality of the key person discount. This chapter has discussed the many factors involved in analyzing and quantifying the key person discount.

One way to quantify the key person discount is by calculating the difference between the present value of expected cash flows with and without the key person, as opposed to taking a percentage discount from enterprise value. If the key person is alive and active in the business, the cash flow differential for each year would be multiplied by the probability of the person's remaining alive and active during that year.

The IRS has recognized the key person discount factor in Revenue Ruling 59-60 and has discussed it in its *Valuation Training for Appeals Officers Coursebook*. The Tax Court recognizes the key person discount factor, when appropriate, both in estate valuations and also while the key person is still active. On occasion, the key person discount also has been recognized in marital dissolution cases.

Notes

1. Steven E. Bolten and Yan Wang, "The Impact of Management Depth on Valuation," *Business Valuation Review* (September 1997): 143–146, at 143–144.
2. Robert F. Reilly and Robert P. Schweihs, "Human Capital Intangible Assets," Chapter 21 in *Valuing Intangible Assets* (New York: McGraw-Hill, 1999), pp. 399–409.
3. Jerome S. Osteryoung and Derek Newman, "Key Person Valuation Issues for Private Businesses," *Business Valuation Review* (September 1994): 115–119, at 118.

4. Shannon P. Pratt, Robert F. Reilly, and Robert P. Schweihs, "Loss of Key Person," *Valuing a Business,* 4th ed. (New York: McGraw-Hill, 2000), pp. 601–602.

5. Internal Revenue Service, *IRS Valuation Training for Appeals Officers Coursebook* (Chicago: Commerce Clearing House, 1998), pp. 9–11 to 9–13. Published and copyrighted by CCH Incorporated, 1998, 2700 Lake Cook Road, Riverwoods, IL 60015, reprinted with permission.

6. *Estate of Mitchell v. Commissioner,* T.C. Memo 1997-461, 74 T.C.M. (CCH) 872 (1997).

7. *Estate of Mitchell v. Commissioner,* 2001 U.S. App. LEXIS 7990 (9th Cir, 2001).

8. *Estate of Feldmar v. Commissioner,* T.C. Memo 1988-429, 56 T.C.M. (CCH) 118 (1988).

9. *Estate of Rodriguez v. Commissioner,* T.C. Memo 1989-13, 56 T.C.M. (CCH) 1033 (1989).

10. *Estate of Huntsman v. Commissioner,* 66 T.C. 861 (1976).

11. *Estate of Yeager v. Commissioner,* T.C. Memo 1986-448, 52 T.C.M. (CCH) 524 (1986).

12. *Furman v. Commissioner,* T.C. Memo 1998-157, 75 T.C.M. (CCH) 2206 (1998).

13. *Rogers v. Rogers,* 296 N.W.2d 849, 1980 Minn. LEXIS 1565 (Minn. 1980).

14. *In re the Marriage of Nelson,* 411 N.W.2d 868, 1987 Minn. App. LEXIS 4759 (Minn. Ct. App. 1987).

15. *In re the Marriage of Buchanan,* 1989 Minn. App. LEXIS 642 (Minn. Ct. App. 1989).

Discounts for Trapped-In Capital Gains Taxes

The concept of trapped-in capital gains is that a company holding an appreciated asset would have to pay a capital gains tax on the sale of the asset. If ownership of the company were to change, the liability for the tax on the sale of the appreciated asset would not disappear.

To review fundamentals, the embedded capital gains tax liability is relative to the company's appreciated asset. This liability would be incurred if the *asset* were sold. Transactions in the company's *stock* might also incur capital gains, but these would be based on the cost and selling price of the stock, not the asset. The capital gains tax would be a corporate expense, not a personal expense, and it would influence what a buyer would pay. In this chapter, I speak only of embedded capital gains in the *asset*.

RATIONALE FOR TRAPPED-IN CAPITAL GAINS TAX DISCOUNT

An ongoing issue in gift and estate tax valuation is whether, or the extent to which, the liability for unrealized capital gains on appreciated assets should be reflected in valuation of the stock or partnership interest that owns the assets.

237

In most (if not all) cases, I believe that the liability for trapped-in capital gains taxes *should* be reflected in the value of the stock or partnership that owns the assets. However, until 1998 the Internal Revenue Service and the U.S. Tax Court steadfastly held that the trapped-in capital gains tax was *not* a basis for a discount. That all changed with the *Davis* case in 1998 (discussed later in the chapter).

Assuming that the standard of value is fair market value, the premise seems very simple. Suppose that a privately held corporation owns a single asset (e.g., a piece of land) with a fair market value of $1 million and a cost basis of $100,000. Would the buyer pay $1 million for the stock knowing the underlying asset is subject to a corporate tax on a $900,000 gain, when he or she could buy the asset (or a comparable asset) directly for $1 million? Of course not.

And would the hypothetical, willing seller of the private corporation discount his or her stock below $1 million to receive cash not subject to the corporate capital gains tax? Of course.

The most common reason cited in court decisions for denying a discount for trapped-in capital gains is lack of intent to sell. If the reason for rejecting the discount for trapped-in capital gains tax is that liquidation is not contemplated, then this same logic should also lead to the conclusion that the asset approach is irrelevant, and the interest should be valued only by the income approach and/or possibly the market approach.

There have been dramatic developments in U.S. Tax Court decisions, starting in 1998, with explicit recognition of liability for capital gains taxes on significantly appreciated property. This recognition has trailed in the wake, albeit somewhat belatedly, of the 1986 elimination of the "*General Utilities* Doctrine." We can only hope that the family law courts will take note and follow suit.

This issue is typical of many in business valuation, in which sound theory dictates a certain conclusion, but the courts, the law, and legal practitioners are, to put it simply, "behind the curve." It is the job of appraisers to educate others as to these economic realities. Note the 12-year time lag between the 1986 repeal of the *General Utilities* Doctrine and the 1998 and subsequent court cases discussed in this chapter. This education process requires years. The law is slow to change, despite economic reality.

"*GENERAL UTILITIES* DOCTRINE"

Prior to 1986, a rule of law known as the "*General Utilities* Doctrine" (named after a U.S. Supreme Court case, *General Utilities & Operating Co. v. Commissioner,* was in effect.[1] This law allowed corporations to elect to liquidate, sell all their assets, and distribute the proceeds to shareholders without paying corporate capital gains taxes. The Tax Reform Act of 1986 eliminated this option, thus leaving no reasonable method of avoiding the corporate capital gains tax liability on the sale of appreciated assets.

With no way to eliminate the capital gains tax on the sale of an asset, it is impossible to believe that an asset subject to the tax (e.g., buying stock of a company owning a highly appreciated piece of real estate) could be worth as much as an asset not subject to the tax (e.g., direct investment in the same piece of real estate). Even with no intent to sell the entity or the appreciated asset in the foreseeable future, it seems that any rational buyer or seller would see a value difference.

TAX COURT RECOGNIZES TRAPPED-IN CAPITAL GAINS

The U.S. Tax Court first recognized the rational buyer/seller viewpoint in 1998 in *Estate of Davis v. Commissioner.*[2] The primary asset of the corporation whose stock was being valued was a large block of highly appreciated stock of Winn Dixie, a publicly traded company. The IRS held tenaciously to its historical position that, as a matter of law, a discount to recognize the trapped-in capital gain was inappropriate. In recognizing a discount to reflect the built-in capital gains factor, the court held:

> [E]ven though no liquidation of [the company] or sale of its assets was planned or contemplated on the valuation date, a hypothetical willing seller and a hypothetical willing buyer would not have agreed on that date on a price . . . that took no account of [the company's] built-in capital gains tax. We are also persuaded . . . that such a willing seller and such a willing buyer . . . would have agreed on a price . . . that was less than the price that they would have agreed upon if there had been no . . . built-in capital gains tax. . . .

The amount of the discount allowed in *Davis* was between one-third and one-half of the trapped-in capital gains tax liability.

Carsten Hoffmann, a business appraiser, wrote this summary of the *Davis* case result:

> Davis Estate has been a startling, but logical, victory for the taxpayer. Through in-depth analysis of all relevant circumstances and expert testimony of several well-respected experts, the Tax Court decided that in a post–General Utilities environment the tax liability resulting from built-in capital gains can be considered when there is no intent to liquidate the assets of the corporation. Logic and the Tax Court agree, however, that a dollar-for-dollar subtraction of the tax liability is not the correct valuation approach when there is no intent to liquidate. As a result, it is up to the valuation community to gather the appropriate data and establish the most accurate methodology to quantify the diminution in value resulting from built-in capital gains tax liabilities.[3]

As we will see shortly, many appraisers *do* believe that the discount should be the full amount of the impounded tax.

At the time of the *Davis* decision, *Eisenberg v. Commissioner* was on appeal in the Second Circuit Court of Appeals.[4] The Tax Court had denied the trapped-in gains discount, relying on Tax Court decisions prior to the 1986 repeal of the *General Utilities* Doctrine. The Second Circuit opinion noted that, because of the change in the law, those decisions were no longer controlling. The Second Circuit, commenting favorably on the *Davis* decision, vacated the Tax Court decision denying the discount and held:

> Fair market value is based on a hypothetical transaction between a willing buyer and a willing seller, and in applying this willing buyer–willing seller rule, "the potential transaction is to be analyzed from the viewpoint of a hypothetical buyer whose only goal is to maximize his advantage. . . ." Our concern in this case is not whether or when the donees will sell, distribute or liquidate the property at issue, but what a hypothetical buyer would take into account in computing [the] fair market value of the stock. We believe it is common business practice and not mere speculation to conclude a hypothetical willing buyer, having reasonable knowledge of the relevant facts, would take some account of the tax consequences of contingent built-in capital gains. . . . The issue is not what a hypothetical willing buyer plans to do with the property, but what considerations affect the fair market value. . . . We believe that an adjustment for potential capital gains tax liabilities should be taken into account in valuing the stock at issue in the closely held C corporation even though no liquidation or sale of the Corporation or its asset was planned. . . .

The Second Circuit remanded the case back to the Tax Court for revaluation recognizing the trapped-in capital gains factor. There is no written decision on the valuation on remand, but I understand that the discount agreed to in settlement was consistent with that concluded in *Davis*.

In *Estate of Simplot v. Commissioner*, the company being valued owned a large block of highly appreciated stock in a publicly traded company, Micron Technology.[5] Experts for both the taxpayer and the IRS deducted 100% of the trapped-in capital gains tax in valuing this nonoperating asset held by the operating company, and the Tax Court accepted this conclusion. (This aspect of *Simplot* is distinct from the control premium issue on which the decision was reversed. Treatment of trapped-in capital gains was not at issue on appeal.)

Many members of the professional business valuation community applauded this result of deducting the full amount of the tax liability. For example, Chris Mercer commented: "The Court's finding is consistent with the position I have long advocated. This is an exciting result. Good economic evidence is the basis for sound decisions by the courts."[6]

Another example of this school of thought has been offered by John Gilbert. In an article in the *CPA Expert*, he analyzes alternate scenarios and concludes that "the proper amount of the discount is the full amount of the tax liability."[7]

Notwithstanding these opinions, some business appraisers believe that in some cases only a portion of the capital gains tax should be deducted, depending on the facts and circumstances of each case. This remains a controversial issue, with some appraisers taking the position that the discount should always be 100% of the tax liability, and others saying that it is economically incorrect to do so in some (or even most) situations.

Another 1999 case, *Estate of Jameson v. Commissioner*, also clearly recognized the trapped-in capital gains tax discount, in this case involving a timber company.[8]

The court found that where a timber company must recognize built-in capital gains under Internal Revenue Code section 1231 (because of its IRC section 631(a) election), each time it cuts and sells timber, valuation of the company must take the built-in capital gains into account.

INTERNAL REVENUE SERVICE ACQUIESCES TO TRAPPED-IN CAPITAL GAINS DISCOUNT

The IRS finally posted a notice on its Website, www.irs.gov, acquiescing that there is no legal prohibition against a discount for trapped-in capital gains.

Referring to the *Eisenberg* case, the notice stated:

> The Second Circuit reversed the Tax Court and held that, in valuing closely-held stock, a discount for the built in capital gains tax liabilities could apply depending on the facts presented. The court noted that the Tax Court itself had recently reached a similar conclusion in *Estate of Davis v. Commissioner* 110 T.C. 530 (1998).
>
> We acquiesce in this opinion to the extent that it holds that there is no legal prohibition against such a discount. The applicability of such a discount, as well as its amount, will hereafter be treated as factual matters to be determined by competent expert testimony based upon the circumstances of each case and generally applicable valuation principles. Recommendation: Acquiescence.

The notice indicated that it was approved by Stuart L. Brown, Chief Counsel, and Judith C. Dunn, Associate Chief Counsel. Of course, it contained the standard caveat: "This document is not to be relied upon or otherwise cited as precedent by taxpayers."[9]

SUBSEQUENT TAX CASES REGULARLY RECOGNIZE TRAPPED-IN CAPITAL GAINS TAX DISCOUNT

Through the time of this writing, there have been several additional cases decided in the U.S. Tax Court involving discounts for trapped-in capital gains, and all, except a partnership case, have recognized the discount, with the amounts varying considerably.

In *Estate of Dunn v. Commissioner,* the subject company was an operating equipment leasing company, and the appreciated assets in question were the equipment available for lease.[10] Because it viewed liquidation as unlikely, the Tax Court allowed only a 5% discount for trapped-in capital gains. However, at this writing, the case is on appeal on this issue.

In *Estate of Welch v. Commissioner,* the Tax Court denied the capital gains tax deduction because the appreciated property was real estate subject to condemnation, which made the company eligible for an IRC section 1033 election to roll over the sale proceeds and defer the capital gains tax, an option it exercised.[11] On appeal the Sixth Circuit Court of Appeals reversed.

The Sixth Circuit specifically addressed the issue of the corporation's potential IRC section 1033 election, stating that the availability of the election does not automatically foreclose the application of a capital gains discount. The Tax Court must consider it as a factor in determining fair market value, just as a hypothetical willing buyer would.

The point to be gleaned from this case is that while a section 1033 election may be available, the value of that election and its effect on the value of the stock still depend on all of the circumstances a hypothetical buyer of the stock would consider. In the present case, the corporation's exercise of the section 1033 election after the valuation date was therefore irrelevant.

In *Estate of Borgatello v. Commissioner,* the estate held an 82.76% interest in a real estate holding company.[12] Both experts applied a discount for trapped-in capital gains, but by using very different methods.

The expert for the taxpayer assumed immediate sale. On that basis, the combined federal and California state tax warranted a 32.3% discount.

The expert for the IRS assumed a 10-year holding period and a 2% growth rate in asset value. On the basis of those assumptions, he calculated the amount of the combined federal and California tax and discounted that amount back to a present value at a discount rate of 8.3%. On that basis the discount worked out to be 20.5%.

The court held that the taxpayer's expert's methodology was unrealistic, because it did not account for any holding period by a potential purchaser. The court also found that the IRS's expert's 10-year holding period was too long. Therefore, the court looked at the range of discounts opined by the experts and tried to find a middle ground between the immediate sale and the 10-year holding period. The court concluded that a 24% discount attributable to the trapped-in capital gains was reasonable.

The only case since *Davis* in which the capital gains tax discount was denied was *Estate of Jones v. Commissioner,* where the estate owned an 83.08% partnership interest.[13] In denying the discount, the Tax Court elaborated at length to distinguish the circumstances from *Davis*:

> The parties and the experts agree that tax on the built-in gains could be avoided by a section 754 election in effect at the time of sale of partnership assets. If such an election is in effect, and the property is sold, the basis of the partnership's assets (the inside basis) is raised to match the cost basis of the transferee in the transferred partnership interest (the outside basis) for the benefit of the transferee. See sec. 743(b). Otherwise, a hypothetical buyer who forces a liquidation could be subject to capital gains tax on the buyer's pro rata share of the amount realized on the sale of the underlying assets of the partnership over the buyer's pro rata share of the partnership's adjusted basis in the underlying assets. See sec. 1001. Because the [limited partnership] agreement does not give the limited partners the ability to effect a section 754 election, in this case the election would have to be made by the general partner.
>
> [Taxpayer's expert] opined that a hypothetical buyer would demand a discount for built-in gains. He acknowledged in his report a 75- to 80-percent chance that an election would be made and that the election would not create any adverse consequences or burdens on the partnership. His opinion that the election was not certain to be made was based solely on the position of [decedent's son], asserted in his trial

testimony, that, as general partner, he might refuse to cooperate with an unrelated buyer of the 83.08-percent limited partnership interest (i.e., the interest he received as a gift from his father). We view [decedent's son's] testimony as an attempt to boot-strap the facts to justify a discount that is not reasonable under the circumstances.

[The IRS's expert,] on the other hand, opined, and respondent contends, that a hypothetical willing seller of the 83.08-percent interest would not accept a price based on a reduction for built-in capital gains. The owner of that interest has effec-tive control, as discussed above, and would influence the general partner to make a section 754 election, eliminating any gains for the purchaser and getting the highest price for the seller. Such an election would have no material or adverse impact on the preexisting partners. We agree with [the IRS's expert]. . . .

In the cases in which the discount was allowed, there was no readily available means by which the tax on built-in gains would be avoided. By contrast, disregard-ing the bootstrapping testimony of [decedent's son] in this case, the only situation identified in the record where a section 754 election would not be made by a part-nership is an example by [taxpayer's expert] of a publicly syndicated partnership with "lots of partners . . . and a lot of assets" where the administrative burden would be great if an election were made. We do not believe that this scenario has applica-tion to the facts regarding the partnerships in issue in this case. We are persuaded that, in this case, the buyer and seller of the partnership interest would negotiate with the understanding that an election would be made and the price agreed upon would not reflect a discount for built-in gains.

TRAPPED-IN CAPITAL GAINS IN DISSENTING STOCKHOLDER ACTIONS

Courts have been mixed in their treatment of trapped-in capital gains tax liabil-ity in dissenting stockholder actions. The issue does not often arise in this context, because liquidation value is not often the premise of value. Most corporations (except holding companies) are valued on a going concern basis.

A case that denied a trapped-in capital gains liability deduction was *In re 75,629 Shares of Common Stock of Trapp Family Lodge, Inc.* (Vermont).[14] The Supreme Court of Vermont said, "[W]e conclude that the trial court correctly determined that no tax consequences of a sale should be considered where no such sale is contemplated." The court characterized the base value from which it denied the discount as going concern value, although a net asset value approach was incorporated in reaching the value.

TRAPPED-IN CAPITAL GAINS IN BANKRUPTCY COURT

Trapped-in capital gains tax liability was an issue in *In re Frezzo.*[15] An appraiser presented the trustee with an appraisal that utilized both an income approach and an asset approach. The asset approach value was net of 35% hypothetical capital gains tax on a sale of the company's assets. The trustee accepted the appraised value and the court approved it. The court stated, "A reduction for potential taxes is certainly appropriate."

TRAPPED-IN CAPITAL GAINS TAXES IN MARITAL DISSOLUTIONS[16]

In many cases the marital estate owns property that is worth more than its cost basis. In such a situation, if the marital estate or one of the spouses were to sell the property, the seller would be subject to federal capital gains taxes.

Whether to consider tax liabilities that would be triggered by the sale of assets is one of the most common issues in marital property divisions. For the most part, family law courts have been unwilling to make any allowance for trapped-in capital gains on appreciated property unless a sale of the property is imminent. Since family law courts often take Tax Court positions into consideration, perhaps the Tax Court's sharp change of direction on this issue in 1998, instructing that valuations reflect trapped-in capital gains taxes, will lead family law courts to give renewed consideration to this issue.

It seems economically inequitable to give one spouse cash or an asset that is free and clear of tax liability while the other spouse receives property of equal market value but subject to tax liability if the spouse desires or needs to liquidate it. Yet that is exactly what the preponderance of family law courts do. The principal factor cited in denying a discount for capital gains tax liability is lack of intent to sell. As stated in an earlier section, if lack of intent to sell is the basis for denying consideration of the built-in capital gains tax liability, then the value to the marital estate should be determined solely on an income approach basis because the asset's market value is rendered irrelevant.

This section presents a representative selection of cases. For more case references, readers are referred to the 139-page paper by Tracy Bateman, "Divorce and Separation: Consideration of Tax Consequences in Distribution of Marital Property" published in 2000.[17]

Marital Cases Denying Trapped-In Capital Gains Discounts

A Washington case, *In re the Marriage of Hay,*[18] is typical. The trial court adjusted the gross value of the parties' interest in a real estate partnership from $119,049 to $101,000 to reflect the capital gains tax that would be paid if it were sold. The court of appeals reversed. The appellate court noted, "There is no Washington case specifically addressing whether capital gains tax consequences should be a factor in determining the value of marital assets." Thus, the court looked to other states for precedent, citing cases in seven other states. The court then concluded:

> Courts have generally found that consideration of tax consequences is either required or at least appropriate where the consequences are immediate and specific and/or arise directly from the court's decree, but find they are not an appropriate consideration where speculation as to a party's future dealings with property awarded to him or her would be required. We agree with the rule adopted by most jurisdictions. . . . Mr. Hay testified at trial that he had no plans to sell his partnership interest. . . . [We]

remand to enable the trial court to consider the property division without regard to the capital gains tax consequences of a hypothetical sale of H&L Investments.

The practice of reviewing decisions from other states is very common in the family law arena. A typical example of the result of such practice is *Kaiser v. Kaiser* (North Dakota).[19] This opinion stated that a court should consider potential tax consequences in valuing marital assets only if:

- The recognition of a tax liability is required by dissolution or will occur within a short time;
- The party's future dealings with the assets are definite enough that the court need not speculate; and
- The future consequences are definite enough that the court need not speculate, and the tax liability can be reasonably predicted.

The courts usually factor in the tax consequences when it is clear that they will be triggered as part of the divorce action. However, in the Indiana case of *Granger v. Granger,* a trial court ordered the husband to pay a mortgage, a car loan, and a cash judgment to the wife from the sale of at least one of two laundromats that he owned.[20] The trial court reduced the marital estate by $53,200 tax liability to be incurred on the sale of the laundromats. The trial court explained that although it did not specifically order the sale of the laundromats, this sale was the only way that the husband could comply with the orders of the court. Nevertheless, the appellate court found that the sale of both laundromats was not an immediate or necessary consequence of the property disposition and that the trial court erred in reducing the marital estate by the amount of the tax liability.

The Kansas case of *Bohl v. Bohl* is an example of extreme denial of consideration of tax consequences.[21] The property division mandated by the trial court in effect required the husband to liquidate his closely held business and turn the proceeds over to the wife to satisfy a cash award. Nevertheless, the court rejected the husband's argument that the stock should have been valued at its liquidation value rather than its going-concern value because of the tax consequences, reasoning that to follow this argument would universally prevent a court from valuing property at more than cost because of tax consequences.

In *Knotts v. Knotts* (Indiana), the husband held an option to buy Eli Lilly stock.[22] The market price at the time of dissolution was well above the strike price, so the option clearly had intrinsic value, but the husband would have had to pay capital gains tax if he exercised it. The trial court valued the option at its intrinsic value less the capital gains tax that would have to be paid to realize that intrinsic value.

The court of appeals reversed, stating "That a trial court must consider tax consequences related to the disposition of marital property. However, the "statute requires the trial court to consider only the direct or inherent and necessarily incurred tax consequences 'of the property disposition.' "

"In the present case, the trial court improperly considered tax consequences incident to the future disposition of the Lilly stock option. As a result, we reverse the property distribution and order the trial court, upon remand, to award [the wife] an additional $2,394.50."

Isn't this the height of inequity? First, the husband has to pay his wife half the amount of tax that he will have to pay to the government when he exercises the option. Then, when he exercises it, he will have to pay the government the full amount of the tax! If the stock price falls so that the amount realized is less or nothing, the wife has collected half of the amount of the tax that the husband would have had to pay on exercise if the stock had maintained its market value!

Marital Cases Allowing Trapped-In Capital Gains Discounts

There are, however, cases where the potential tax consequences on sale have been deducted in valuing the marital estate, even when no immediate sale was contemplated. For example, in *Liddle v. Liddle* (Washington), the court concluded that it was proper to deduct the amount of capital gains tax that the husband would have to pay on the anticipated sale of limited partnership interests.[23] The wife objected to reducing the value by the impounded taxes, claiming that they were "hypothetical, speculative, imaginary, unfair, and arbitrary." Evidence was introduced to show that the partnership was a tax shelter that would lose its desirability in five to seven years and would probably be sold. The court concluded that the date of sale was neither imaginary nor hypothetical.

The court then offered an interesting broader statement that *"partnerships ought to be reduced by future capital gains taxes"* where the partnerships were investments that *"were only valuable as long as other investments were not more desirable,"* and the husband *"was more likely to sell his interest in the partnerships than die owning them,"* and would, therefore, incur a capital gains tax from the sale of the partnerships. (Emphasis added.) From the viewpoint of a financial analyst, it is reasonable to think that this reasoning should apply to *any* investment asset.

Another interesting decision upholding subtraction of capital gains tax involved a commercial building. In *Hogan v. Hogan* (Missouri), the appellate court held that the trial court did not abuse its discretion in subtracting the capital gains tax that would be incurred on sale, even though there was no evidence that the property was going to be sold.[24] The court found that experts for both parties attested to the property's fair market value and that the concept of fair market value assumes the sale of the property to an interested buyer. Thus, the court was reluctant to find any error by the trial court in presuming a sale of the real estate with its attendant tax consequences in order to value that marital asset.

In *Zoldan v. Zoldan* (Ohio), the trial court accepted the valuation of the husband's expert, which was net of tax consequences (and also net of both minority and marketability discounts).[25] The trial court stated that it found the husband's expert more credible. The wife's expert "did not consider all the facts and procedures the court considered applicable." The court of appeals upheld, stating that "there was sufficient credible evidence considering the totality of the circumstances, from which the trial court could have accepted the valuations given by [wife's] expert witness."

TREATMENT OF CAPITAL GAINS TAX LIABILITY IN S CORPORATIONS

The question of how to treat trapped-in capital gains tax liability when valuing stock in an S corporation is a complicated one. James Reto concludes, in a lengthy article on the subject, that there are circumstances in which the appraiser should reduce the value of S corporation stock to account for embedded capital gains, particularly when using an asset-based valuation approach:

> The actual calculation will require assumptions concerning the utilization of the loss carryover and an appropriate discount rate, or it may be as simple as increasing the discount from net asset value or the discount for lack of marketability.[26]

William Raby and Burgess Raby posit several scenarios, most of which the authors believe should trigger some amount of deduction for the trapped-in gains:

> For some potential buyers, those who are eligible S corporation shareholders and are buying a controlling interest, there may be no tax detriment. Assume, however, that the valuation situation is the more common one of a minority interest. With eligible shareholders, the corporation can remain an S corporation. Any disposition of assets by the continuing S corporation will trigger recognition of the built-in gain. While it will not be taxed to the corporation, it will be taxed to the shareholders. . . . Where the block of stock to be valued is an interest too small to force a liquidation, the incoming shareholder will find that for all income determination purposes he or she is acquiring the tax consequences of the corporation's tax basis and the price that a prospective shareholder will be willing to pay will reflect this gap between basis to the corporation and basis to the shareholder. . . .
>
> In the world we live in, corporations, partnerships (including LLCs), or even nonresident aliens constitute major parts of the pool of potential buyers for many businesses, especially the larger ones. Not one of these is a qualified S corporation shareholder (with the exception of the S corporation that acquires 100 percent of the stock and converts the target into a qualified subchapter S subsidiary, or QSSS). Assume a $10 million purchase by a C corporation of 100 percent of the stock of an S corporation (target) whose net assets have a $2 million tax basis. Immediately upon its acquisition, the target ceases to be an S corporation. The assets can get stepped-up to the purchase price only through a *section 338* election. That generates tax on $8 million to the target corporation. Otherwise, while a liquidation of the target is tax-free, any tax benefit from the $8 million excess paid over the tax basis is forever given up.
>
> If the situation involves valuing a minority interest in an S corporation, and we hypothesize, as we must, a hypothetical willing buyer, what will we see? There will not be any potential buyers who can ignore the tax liability they will be assuming as compared to buying the underlying assets directly. (We ignore the nonprofits who can now be S corporation shareholders because these will, with the exception of ESOPs, have unrelated business income and will thus be in the same tax boat as other potential shareholders.) What, though, are the likely tax consequences of this tax liability? In Eisenberg and Davis, the liability was a tax at C corporation rates. With the S corporation, the liability is that income will be generated at the corporate level but, aside from *section 1374* when it applies, the tax will be at the shareholder level. That makes the tax no less

real, but it does make more difficult the job of the appraiser who must come up with a dollar amount of discount. We suggest that a distinction should get drawn between depreciable and amortizable assets, on the one hand, and investment assets like corporate stock, on the other. The present value of the future tax deductions forgone, at the top individual ordinary income rate, could be the basis for valuing the tax detriment in the first category; and the amount of the capital gains tax that will be incurred at some point in the future, because even in death there is no way to step up the underlying asset basis, should be the starting point for the second. Then comes the question of what discount to use, and we think that the assumption for that will depend on the nature of the asset, the corporation's history in dealing with similar assets, and the likely timing of disposition of this asset. Thus, if the S corporation holds a controlling interest in the family corporation, and all of the stock except for the block to be valued is owned by people currently employed by that corporation, the answer may be that no disposition of the stock is likely. While this will result in a rather low discount, the situation is likely to be one where the marketability and minority interest discounts will be substantial.

It may not be crucial to the final outcome whether, as in Davis, the tax discount is factored into the marketability discount; or, as in Eisenberg, is shown as a separate discount; or, as we might suggest in many S corporation situations, is viewed as part of a minority discount. What is important is that practitioners now have two well-reasoned cases saying that the hypothetical willing buyer should not be assumed to be willing to pay the same for two assets when there are tax detriments attached to one and not to the other. While this may seem like common sense, it is only with these two cases that tax practitioners have a clear rejection of the IRS contention that tax discounts were simply not allowable as a matter of law regardless of the facts. Since business appraisers are not necessarily tax experts, tax practitioners should make sure that the appraisers with whom they work have a clear understanding of the tax detriments that a hypothetical willing buyer would be apt to see in the asset that is being valued. This advance understanding may be especially important when that asset is S corporation stock since casual readers of either Davis or Eisenberg are apt to get a confusing notion of how the reasoning of those decisions will apply in an S corporation situation.[27]

SUMMARY

From the repeal of the *General Utilities* Doctrine in 1986, it took the U.S. Tax Court until the *Davis* case in 1998 to recognize the reality of trapped-in capital gains tax liability as a discount in determining fair market value. Since then the Tax Court has consistently recognized the capital gains tax factor, applying varying discounts up to 100% of the trapped-in capital gain.

Courts in dissenting stockholder cases have produced mixed decisions on the issue. In bankruptcy court, where the sale of assets usually is an option, the trapped-in capital gain discount tends to be recognized.

Some marital dissolution cases recognize a discount for trapped-in capital gains on appreciated property for marital property distribution. However, the majority have not, unless there was an immediate prospect of a sale. This disinclination has caused what appear to be some serious inequities in property distribution. Family law courts often refer to Tax Court decisions. Possibly the compelling reality of the recent stance of the U.S. Tax Court will spill over into family law courts.

The treatment of trapped-in capital gains tax liability for S corporations is complicated, and so far there is no definitive case law. Experts are exploring the subject and surely will continue to do so for some time.

Notes

1. *General Util. & Operating Co. v. Commisioner,* 296 U.S. 200 (1935).
2. *Estate of Davis v. Commissioner,* 110 T.C. 530 (1998).
3. Carsten Hoffmann, "Life After Davis Estate: Valuation Discounts for Built-in Capital Gains Tax Liabilities" *77 Taxes—The Tax Magazine* 36 (August 1999): 42. Published and copyrighted by CCH Incorporated, 2700 Lake Cook Road, Riverwoods, IL 60015, reproduced with permission.
4. *Eisenberg v. Commissioner,* 155 F.3d 50 (2d Cir. 1998).
5. *Estate of Simplot v. Commissioner,* 112 T.C. 130 (1999), *rev'd,* 2001 U.S. App. LEXIS 9220 (9th Cir. 2001).
6. Z. Christopher Mercer, "Tax Court Accords Superpremium to Small Voting Block; Allows Deduction of 100% of Trapped in Capital Gains Tax," *Judges & Lawyers Business Valuation Update* (April 1999): 1, 6–7.
7. John R. Gilbert, "Built-in Gain Valuation Adjustment: No Longer 'If'—But 'How' and 'How Much,'" *CPA Expert* (Winter 1999): 7–10.
8. *Estate of Jameson v. Commissioner,* T.C. Memo 1999-43, 77 T.C.M. (CCH) 1383 (1999).
9. IRS Acquiesces Regarding Trapped-in Gains Discount," *Judges & Lawyers Business Valuation Update* (August 1999): 15. Quoted from Internal Revenue Bulletin 1999-4 (Jan. 25, 1999).
10. *Estate of Dunn v. Commissioner,* T.C. Memo 2000-12, 79 T.C.M. (CCH) 1337 (2000).
11. *Estate of Welch v. Commissioner,* 2000 U.S. App. LEXIS 3315 (6th Cir. 2000).
12. *Estate of Borgatello v. Commisioner,* T.C. Memo 2000-264, 80 T.C.M. (CCH) 260 (2000).
13. *Estate of Jones v. Commissioner,* 2001 U.S. Tax Ct. LEXIS 11, 116 T.C. No. 11 (2001).
14. *In re 75,629 Shares of Common Stock of Trapp Family Lodge, Inc.,* 169 Vt. 82, 725 A.2d 927 (Vt. 1999).
15. *In re Frezzo,* 217 B.R. 985 (Bankr. E.D. Pa. 1998).
16. Portions of this section are adapted from Shannon P. Pratt, "Marital Dissolution Valuations," Chapter 19 in *The Lawyers Business Valuation Handbook* (Chicago: American Bar Association, 2000).
17. Tracy A. Bateman, "Divorce and Separation: Consideration of Tax Consequences in Distribution of Marital Property," 9 A.L.R.5th 568, 2000 Lawyers Cooperative Publishing Co.
18. *In re the Marriage of Hay,* 80 Wash. App. 202, 907 P.2d 334 (Wash. Ct. App. 1995).
19. *Kaiser v. Kaiser,* 555 N.W.2d 585 (N.D. 1996).
20. *Granger v. Granger,* 579 N.E.2d 1319 (Ind. Ct. App. 1991).
21. *Bohl v. Bohl,* 232 Kan. 557, 657 P.2d 1106 (Kan. 1983).
22. *Knotts v. Knotts,* 693 N.E.2d 962 (Ind. Ct. App. 1998).
23. *Liddle v. Liddle,* 140 Wis.2d 132, 410 N.W.2d 196 (Wis. Ct. App. 1987)
24. *Hogan v. Hogan,* 796 S.W.2d 400 (Mo. Ct. App. 1990).
25. *Zoldan v. Zoldan,* 1999 Ohio App. LEXIS 2644 (Ohio Ct. App. 1999).
26. James J. Reto, "Are S Corporations Entitled to Valuation Discounts for Embedded Capital Gains?" *Valuation Strategies* (January/February 2000): 48. ©2000, RIA, 395 Hudson Street, New York, NY 10014, reprinted with permission.
27. William L. Raby and Burgess J. W. Raby, "Stock Valuations, as a Matter of Law, Require Tax Discount," *98 Tax Notes Today,* (August 27, 1998): 166–57. Copyright 1998 Tax Analysts, reprinted with permission. To contact Tax Analysts, see their Website at www.tax.org.

Blockage Discounts

The concept of *blockage* applies primarily to a holding of publicly traded stock, when the block is so large relative to normal trading volume that either an instant sale probably would be at a discounted price compared to the prevailing market or else it would take a long time to sell. (See Exhibit 15.1 for definitions.) The concept also applies to real estate, when the quantity being appraised could only be sold at a discounted price compared to the prevailing market for small parcels or else it would take the market a long time to absorb it. The principle also applies to property such as collections of art and antiques.

Exhibit 15.1   Definitions of Blockage and Blockage Discount

Blockage Discount   An amount or percentage deducted from the current market price of a publicly traded security to reflect the decrease in the per share value of a block of those securities that is of a size that could not be sold in a reasonable period of time given normal trading volume.[a]

Blockage   Recognition in the field of taxation of fact that in some instances a large block of stock cannot be marketed and turned into cash as readily as a few shares. *Citizens Fidelity Bank & Trust Co. v. Reeves*, Ky., 259 S.W.2d 432, 433. The discount at which a large block of stock sells below the price of a smaller block is blockage. It is generally a phenomenon of shares which do not represent the controlling interest in a corporation. *See* Blockage Rule.[b]

Blockage Rule   Process of determining value of large blocks of corporate stock for gift and estate tax purposes, based on the postulate that a large block of stock cannot be marketed as readily and as advantageously in price as can a few shares. *Montclair Trust Co. v. Zink. Prerog.*, 141 N.J.Eq. 401, 57 A.2d 372, 376, 380. Application of this rule generally justifies a discount in the fair market value since the disposition of a large amount of stock at any one time may well depress the value of such shares in the market place.[b]

---

[a]*Source: International Glossary of Business Valuation Terms.*
[b]*Source: Black's Law Dictionary,* 6th ed.

Disputes as to whether a discount for blockage is applicable and, if so, the magnitude of the discount arise most commonly in the determination of fair market value for gift and estate tax purposes, but they could apply in divorce, insolvency, and other contexts as well.

BLOCKAGE IS DISTINCT FROM RESTRICTED STOCK

Like minority and marketability, the concepts of blockage and restricted stock are separate concepts, although they can be related. Blockage refers to difficulty in selling because of the size of the block relative to the market. Restricted stock refers to difficulty in selling because of regulatory or contractual restraints on selling. While restricted stock discounts may easily be over 30%, discounts for blockage usually are considerably less, typically under 15%, although they have been as high as 25%.

In some cases the detrimental effects of blockage and restricted stock are lumped together and reported only as a single discount. In other cases both restricted stock and blockage discounts have been allowed and quantified separately.[1]

FACTORS TO ANALYZE IN QUANTIFYING BLOCKAGE DISCOUNT

This section lists factors to consider in estimating the size of the blockage discount. To the extent that they are relevant, they should be presented in detail in the valuation report. Some excellent illustrative tables are contained in Joseph Estabrook's chapter on blockage discounts in *Handbook of Advanced Business Valuation.*[2]

Size of Block Relative to Trading Volume

The most important single factor is how many shares the block constitutes relative to normal daily, weekly, monthly, or annual trading volume. Tabular support can include a record of prices and volume for some relevant period.

Other factors relating to size of the block could also be relevant.

Number of Shares as a Percentage of Outstanding Shares.   The larger the number relative to the total, the greater the likely necessary discount.

Size of the Block Relative to the Float.   The *float* is the amount of stock available for market trading, generally considered to be stock not held by insiders or control owners. Generally speaking, the larger the float, the better the potential liquidity.

Number of Individual and Institutional Shareholders.   A large number of shareholders and, particularly, a significant number of institutional shareholders could contribute to liquidity for a large block.

Characteristics of the Stock Itself

Certain characteristics of the stock itself could be important. For example, does it pay dividends? A block of stock with no dividend yield probably would be harder to place than one with a good dividend yield. The analyst should note any special features, such as whether there is more than one class of stock, as well as consider the implications of those features.

Market Factors

Several aspects of the market for the stock may impact the potential discount.

Trading Market.   Is it traded on the New York Stock Exchange (NYSE), American Stock Exchange (ASE), a regional exchange, NASDAQ, or over-the-counter (OTC) market? Active markets like the NYSE and NASDAQ could ease the problem compared to less active markets (unless, of course, the desire to unload was known to traders and others who might short the stock in anticipation of market weakness).

Price Volatility.   Risk and expected return go hand in hand. High price volatility is often a negative factor that exacerbates the blockage discount. A high beta also would be a negative factor.

Other Block Trades.   Is there any history of other large block trades or secondary offerings?

Market Exposure.   How many analysts follow the stock, and what reports have been issued? Have there been any recent changes in their recommendations?

Price Trends.   Has the stock been on an upward or downward price trend? This factor seems to arise in every discussion of blockage discounts. It appears that a downward price trend is considered a negative factor (higher discount) and an upward price trend a positive factor (lower discount). If one believes that stock market prices are a random walk, recent trends should not make any difference. However, in *Estate of Davis v. Commissioner,* Judge Carolyn Chiechi recognized that it would take a long time to sell the block of stock in question, yet she denied a blockage discount. The only clue to the denial of the discount in the written opinion is that the stock had been on an upward price trend, a fact emphasized by the expert for the IRS.[3]

Current Outlook

As with any valuation report, there should be some discussion of the outlook, at least for company fundamentals, and also for the industry and the economy. While one would expect these factors already to be reflected in the market price of the stock, they could impinge still further on the blockage discount.

Market Impact of the Block

Ultimately the question is: What would be the impact on the market of the sale of this block of stock? If marketed as a block, what price concession would be necessary? If dribbled out, how much additional volume could the market absorb, if any, without affecting the price, and how long would it take to sell the block in the normal course of open market transactions?

The analyst may be able to gain some insight by interviewing brokers and/or market makers. This seems like a reasonable step to consider in the overall process of estimating a blockage discount. As George Hawkins explains it:

> The market maker in the shares of the public company is normally the best place to start. Market makers are specialists who actually serve as the intermediaries who match purchase and sell orders for the stock, maintaining an inventory on hand of the shares to match the needs of buyers and sellers and create an orderly market. Since they are in daily contact with the liquidity and supply and demand forces of the stock, they are normally the best equipped to estimate the price impacts of dumping a larger block of the shares on the market.[4]

Institutional Ownership

A higher blockage discount is much more likely in a smaller company with little or no institutional ownership than in a larger company with more institutional ownership. The reason is because, for the latter types of companies, the large-block trading desks of most of the big investment banks will buy the block at, often, just a 1 to 7% discount, because they know they can find a ready institutional buyer without much delay. However, these desks tend to shy away from blocks of companies for which they cannot readily find a block buyer. For those companies with low institutional holdings, then, the owner of the block is often left with no alternative but to sell the shares gradually into the market.

MUST CONSIDER WAYS OF SELLING STOCK

In the valuation report, the analyst should consider the various mechanisms for selling the stock, suggesting which method or methods would be likely to have the least depressing effect on value.

The two most common methods of selling a large block would be a private placement or dribbling the stock out onto the open market in small lots that would not be likely to affect the price significantly. In the case of a private placement, one would estimate the percentage discount that would be required to induce a buyer to purchase the entire block outright. In the case of a dribble-out, one would estimate the present value of the expected proceeds at a discount rate that reflected the time value of money and the risk of depression in the stock price over the selling period.

Other possible mechanisms for selling include:

* The sale to an underwriting syndicate for resale to the public—secondary distribution
* A special offering by which a broker may buy the entire block and resell it or offer it
* Exchange distributions, in which one member acting as a principal or agent sells a block to other members of the exchange who have solicited purchases.[5]

"PRICE PRESSURE" AND "MARKET EXPOSURE"

Will Frazier has suggested two components of cost that should be measured in estimating a blockage discount: price pressure and market exposure.

"Price pressure" is the impact on the stock price when a large block depresses the market. Frazier suggests measuring this by analyzing the factors outlined above, using various assumed numbers of days to sell the stock.

What Frazier means by "market exposure" is the risk of encountering a lower stock price during the holding period necessary to complete the liquidation of the shares, again using various holding period scenarios. He suggests measuring this by estimating the cost of a "put" option.[6]

BLOCK BUYER COULD AMELIORATE BLOCKAGE DISCOUNT

Brian Becker and Gary Gutzler comment on the basic principle that markets are a function of supply and demand. They note that traditional blockage literature focuses on the willing seller, generally assuming no willing buyers at the time for a block of the subject's size. They point out that it is difficult to buy as well as difficult to sell large blocks. If someone were looking for a large block of the subject company at the same time that the block became available, the increased demand would offset the increased supply, and the depressing effect on the market price would be neutralized.[7] While this hypothesis makes sense, its occurrence in real-world markets would be purely coincidental.

BLOCKAGE DISCOUNTS RECOGNIZED IN ESTATE AND GIFT TAX REGULATIONS

The concept of a discount for blockage is specifically recognized in the estate and gift tax regulations:

> In certain exceptional cases, the size of the block of stock to be valued in relation to the number of shares changing hands in sales may be relevant in determining whether selling prices reflect the fair market value of the block of stock to be valued. If the executor can show that the block of stock to be valued is so large in relation to the actual sales on the existing market that it could not be liquidated in a reasonable time without depressing the market, the price at which the block could be sold as such outside the usual market, as through an underwriter, may be a more accurate indication of value than market quotations. Complete data in support of any allowance claimed due to the size of the block of stock shall be submitted with the return (Form 706 Estate Tax Return or Form 709 Gift Tax Return). On the other hand, if the block of stock to be valued represents a controlling interest, either actual or effective, in a going business, the price at which other lots change hands may have little relation to its true value.[8]

BLOCKAGE DISCOUNTS IN U.S. TAX COURT

The concept of a discount for blockage for tax purposes goes all the way back to 1937. In a landmark decision that is still frequently quoted, *Safe Deposit and Trust Co. v. Commissioner,* the Tax Court said: "Blockage is not a law of economics, a principle of law or a rule of evidence. If the value of a given number of shares is influenced by the size of the block, this is a matter of evidence and not of doctrinaire assumption."[9] In other words, it is based on the facts and circumstances of each case.

Exhibit 15.2 is a summary of tax cases dealing with blockage. While the exhibit is self-explanatory, I will comment on a few of the principles demonstrated in the cases.

One of the largest discounts for blockage was found in a 1999 case, *Estate of Mellinger v. Commissioner.* The stock in question was a very large block of a very thinly traded public stock, Frederick's of Hollywood. Both the taxpayer and the Internal Revenue Service presented expert testimony, and Chief Judge Mary Ann Cohen concluded a blockage discount of 25%.[10]

Multiple Gifts Must Be Valued Separately

The important principle that each gift must be valued separately may work against the taxpayer for the purpose of estimating blockage discounts applicable to gifts. A block of stock in an estate is valued as a whole, regardless of how it may be split up among multiple heirs. This is an important legal concept that many appraisers misunderstand. In estate taxes, what is valued is what the estate owns, regardless of the decedent's will, trusts, or other dispositive arrangements. By contrast, in gift taxes, multiple gifts to various donees, even if made on the same day, must be valued separately. This principle was affirmed with respect to blockage discounts in *Rushton v. Commissioner.*[11]

Each Case Depends on Unique Facts and Circumstances

As with other aspects of valuation, the facts and circumstances of each case must stand on their own. A quantification of blockage discounts cannot be determined by reference to past blockage court cases.

In *Estate of Christie v. Commissioner,* the taxpayer suggested using an average of discounts allowed in past court cases. The court opinion stated, "The suggestion is too simplistic to require detailed comment."[12]

In *Estate of Foote v. Commissioner,* taxpayer's expert opined to a 22.5% blockage discount based on reported Tax Court cases that involved a blockage discount and were factually similar to the subject. The expert for the IRS considered at least 16 factors in arriving at a discount of 3.3%, including:

- Decedent's shares were only 2.2% of the total shares outstanding.
- Decedent's block was equal to the number of the subject company's shares traded during a 29-day period.
- The trading "float" of the stock.
- Dividend-paying record of the company.
- Current outlook for the company.
- The percentage of institutional ownership of stock.
- Effect of trading more than 50,000 shares of stock in eight separate trading days.[13]

The court adopted the IRS expert's opinion in toto, noting that he properly considered all the relevant factors.

Exhibit 15.2   Summary of Selected Tax Cases Involving Blockage Discounts

Year	Case Citation	Blockage Discount	Comments
2000	*Estate of Brocato v. Commissioner,* T.C. Memo 1999-424	11% (on 7 of 8 real properties)	Petitioner asserted a 12.5% blockage discount for all eight real properties while the IRS argued that a discount of 1.92% should be applied to only seven properties.
1999	*Estate of Mellinger v. Commissioner,* 112 T.C. 26	25%	Both parties presented expert testimony for a blockage discount ranging from 15% to 35%; the court made adjustments to petitioner's methods.
1999	*Estate of Foote v. Commissioner,* T.C. Memo 1999-37	3.3%	Court accepted IRS expert opinion of a 3.3% blockage discount based on 16 factors; rejected taxpayer's expert's reliance on past cases and a 22.5% blockage discount.
1998	*Estate of Davis v. Commissioner,* 110 T.C. 530	Zero	Court disallowed a blockage discount because Estate failed to carry burden of establishing that a blockage or SEC Rule 144 discount should apply.
1998	*Estate of McClatchy v. Commissioner,* 147 F.3d 1089 (9th Cir.)	15%	IRS conceded a 15% blockage discount opined by petitioner. Issue on appeal related to federal securities law restrictions.
1997	*Estate of Wright v. Commissioner,* T.C. Memo 1997-53	10%	Starting with the over-the-counter price of $50 per share, taxpayer's experts applied a 24% discount for blockage and other factors; IRS expert applied a control premium but no blockage discount.
1987	*Adair v. Commissioner,* T.C. Memo 1987-494	5%	For valuation of petitioner Adair's stock, a blockage discount was inappropriate. For valuation of petitioner Borgeson's stock, IRS expert opined to no blockage discount and petitioner's expert opined to a 15% blockage discount.
1985	*Robinson v. Commissioner,* T.C. Memo 1985-275	18%	Respondent opined to a 6% blockage discount; petitioner Robinson opined to a 40% combined discount for federal securities restrictions and blockage; petitioner Centronics to opined to no blockage discount.
1983	*Steinberg v. Commissioner,* T.C. Memo 1983-534	27.5%	Petitioner argued for a 30% a blockage discount; IRS argued for a 12.5% blockage discount.
1974	*Rushton v. Commissioner,* 498 F.2d 88 (5th Cir.)	Zero	Commissioner disallowed a blockage discount for sale of 4 blocks of stock.

Estate of Branson v. Commissioner was unique in that there was no organized market for the stock, but the company (a bank) maintained a list of interested buyers. Decedent's block size equaled several years' worth of historical transactions, but the court also considered transactions of about a tenth to a quarter of decedent's block size shortly before death and within a year after death in deciding that the blockage discount should be 10%.[14] The opinion also cites and quotes several earlier blockage discount cases.

SUMMARY

A *blockage discount* is a discount related to the size of a block, recognizing that selling it all at once would likely flood the market and depress the price. This discount can apply to publicly traded stock, real estate, or collections of personal property. Blockage discounts usually are applied in the context of estate and gift taxes, and are specifically recognized in estate and gift tax regulations.

Blockage is different from illiquidity due to transfer restrictions. There are no hard and fast rules for quantifying blockage discounts, but, as with other aspects of valuation, each case must be analyzed on its specific facts and circumstances. This chapter discussed the factors to be analyzed in quantifying the blockage discount and summarized selected U.S. Tax Court decisions in blockage discount cases.

Notes

1. See, for example, *Adair v. Commissioner,* T.C. Memo 1987-494, 54 T.C.M. (CCH) 705 (1987), in which the court allowed a discount for lack of marketability and also allowed a 5% additional discount for blockage.
2. Joseph S. Estabrook, "Blockage Discounts," Chapter 7 in *Handbook of Advanced Business Valuation,* Robert F. Reilly and Robert P. Schweihs, eds. (New York: McGraw-Hill, 2000), pp. 139–153.
3. *Estate of Davis v. Commissioner,* 110 T.C. 530 (1998).
4. George B. Hawkins, "Selling Out to a Public Company Buyer—Blockage, Restricted Shares, and Value. The State Price Versus Reality," *Fair Value* (Spring/Summer 1997). © Banister Financial, Inc. All rights reserved, (704) 334–4932.
5. See note 2, above.
6. William H. Frazier, "The Use of Capital Gains Tax Liability When Employing an Asset-Based Approach to the Valuation of C Corporation and 'Pure' Blockage," unpublished paper, available on BVLibrary.com.
7. Brian Becker and Gary Gutzler, "Should a Blockage Discount Apply? Perspectives of Both a Hypothetical Willing Buyer and Hypothetical Willing Seller," *Business Valuation Review* (March 2000): 3–9.
8. Estate Tax. Reg. Sec. 2031-2(b)(1). Gift Tax Reg. Sec. 25.2512-2(e) contains the same language.

9. *Safe Deposit and Trust Co. v. Commissioner,* 35 B.T.A. 259 (1937).

10. *Estate of Mellinger v. Commissioner,* 112 T.C. 26 (1999).

11. *Rushton v. Commissioner,* 498 F.2d 88 (5th Cir. 1974).

12. *Estate of Christie v. Commissioner,* T.C. Memo 1974-95, 33 T.C.M. (CCH) 476 (1974).

13. *Estate of Foote v. Commissioner,* T.C. Memo 1999-37, 77 T.C.M. (CCH) 1356 (1999).

14. *Estate of Branson v. Commissioner,* T.C. Memo 1999-231, 78 T.C.M. 78 (1999).

Chapter 16

Nonhomogeneous Assets ("Portfolio") Discounts

A "portfolio discount" is applied, usually at the entity level, to a company or interest in a company that holds disparate operations or assets. This chapter explains the principle, discusses empirical evidence of its existence and magnitude, and offers some suggestions for applying it in practice. Finally, we note that it has been accepted by the U.S. Tax Court.

PORTFOLIO DISCOUNT PRINCIPLE

Investors generally prefer to buy "pure plays" rather than packages of dissimilar operations and/or assets. Therefore, companies or interests in companies that hold a nonhomogeneous group of operations and/or assets frequently sell at a discount from the aggregate amount those operations and/or assets would sell for individually. The latter is often referred to as the breakup value. This disinclination to buy a miscellaneous assortment of operations and/or assets and the resulting discount from breakup value is often called the portfolio effect.

It is quite common for family-owned companies, especially multigenerational ones, to accumulate an unusual (and often unrelated) group of operations and/or assets over the years. This often happens when different decision makers acquire holdings that particularly interest them at different points in time. For example, a large privately owned company might own a life insurance company, a cable television operation, and a hospitality division.

The following have been suggested as some of the reasons for the portfolio discount:

- The diversity of investments held within the corporate umbrella
- The difficulty of managing the diverse set of investments
- The expected time needed to sell undesired assets
- Costs expected to be incurred upon sale of the investments
- The risk associated with disposal of undesired investments[1]

The portfolio discount effect is especially important when valuing minority interests, because minority stockholders have no ability to redeploy underperforming or nonperforming assets, nor can they cause a liquidation of the asset portfolio and/or a dissolution of the company. Minority stockholders give little or no weight to non-earning or low-earning assets in pricing stocks in a free and open, well-informed public market. Thus, the portfolio discount might be greater for a minority position, because the minority stockholder has no power to implement changes that might improve the value of the operations and/or assets, even if the stockholder desires to.

EMPIRICAL EVIDENCE SUPPORTING PORTFOLIO DISCOUNTS

Empirical evidence supporting the existence and quantification of the portfolio discount for minority interests is abundant in the public markets. This evidence falls into three distinct categories:

1. Increases in aggregate market value when a conglomerate company announces and/or completes a breakup or a tax-free spinoff
2. Analysts' estimates of breakup values of conglomerates compared to the conglomerate stocks' public trading prices
3. Differences in discounts from net asset value for real estate holding companies with homogeneous versus nonhomogeneous real estate holdings

Evidence from Actual Breakups

Unquestionably, the breakup of conglomerates has created value for their stockholders in almost every instance. Quantifying this value increase (which would

Exhibit 16.1   Portfolio Discounts Implied by AT&T and ITT Breakups

Company	Low Before	Date of Breakup	Price Before	High After	Percent Increase	Implied Portfolio Discount*	10/23/95 Price
		Announcement					
AT&T	$47.25	9/20/95	$57.575	$66.375	15.3%	13.3%	$61.25
ITT	$77.00	6/13/95	$109.25	$128.50	15.0%	13.0%	$123.625

* $(1 - 1/(1 + \text{percent increase}))$

As illustrated in the AT&T example: $1 - \dfrac{1}{1 + .153} \approx .153$

Source: Jamie Mikami, "AT&T Breakup Is Empirical Evidence of 'Portfolio Discount' Theory," *Shannon Pratt's Business Valuation Update* (November 1995): 8.

represent the portfolio discount from the post-breakup values) presents a measurement problem that defies precision. One might start with the conglomerate value the day before the announcement and compare it to the value the day after the announcement, or to the aggregate trading prices of the components when the breakup is effective, or to the aggregate trading values of the components at some time after the market has "seasoned" them.

None of the above procedures, however, reflects the extent of the value increase already reflected in the preannouncement price as a result of rumors of the breakup. For example, on February 14, 2001, Canadian Pacific announced plans to divide itself into five separate publicly traded companies. The *New York Times* reported, "Rumors over the last month about such a plan had lifted the stock price 25 percent."[2]

Two of the most widely publicized breakups were AT&T on September 20, 1995, and ITT on June 13, 1995. Exhibit 16.1 shows the implied portfolio discount based on the price immediately before the announcement and the aggregate prices of the components shortly after the breakups. This does not reflect any run-up in the stock prices prior to the announcements.

Another example is the announcement by Anheuser Busch that it would sell off its money-losing Eagle Snacks operation and its baseball subsidiary, consisting of the St. Louis National Baseball Club (the St. Louis Cardinals), Busch Memorial Stadium, and several nearby parking garages. The stock immediately experienced a favorable price reaction.[3]

A 1997 book titled *Breakup!: When Large Companies Are Worth More Dead than Alive* posits that "the successful demerging of the most obvious corporate candidates in the United States alone would unlock $1 trillion of value"[4] otherwise trapped by the very nature of what the book calls multibusiness companies. The result in each case would be several single businesses, or what the authors call focused-business companies. Although the book focuses on large public companies, the principle is equally applicable to companies of all sizes, public or private.

Online searches yield dozens of examples of positive stock market price reactions to the announcement or completion of breakups of public conglomerates.

Exhibit 16.2 Companies Classified as Conglomerates by *Yahoo!*

• ALLETE	• Ogden Corp.
• American Int'l Indus.	• Olin Corp.
• Bass Pub. Ltd. Co.	• Pacific Dunlop Ltd.
• Canadian Pac. Ltd.	• Pentair, Inc.
• City Dev. Ltd.	• Raytheon Co.
• Covanta Energy Corp.	• Sequa Corp.
• Dover Corp.	• St. Joc Co.
• Emerson	• Standex Int'l Corp.
• Federal Signal Corp.	• Stone & Webster, Inc.
• GenCorp Inc.	• TRW, Inc.
• General Elec. Co.	• Temple-Inland, Inc.
• Hallwood Group Inc.	• Textron, Inc.
• Hanson PLC	• Tomkins PLC ADR
• Honeywell Int'l	• Tyco Int'l Ltd. (NEW)
• ITT Indust., Inc.	• U.S. Indus., Inc.
• Johnson Controls, Inc.	• United Tech.
• Koninklijke Philips Elec.	• Valhi Inc.
• MAXXAM Inc.	• Vivendi Universal
• Minnesota Mining & Mfg.	• Wesco Fin. Corp.
• National Serv. Indust.	

Source: Yahoo! Finance Market Guide, April 16, 2001.

Conglomerate Discounts from Estimated Breakup Value

At the time of this writing, *Yahoo! Finance Market Guide* listed almost 40 public companies that are regarded in the financial industry as conglomerates. These are listed in Exhibit 16.2. From time to time, brokerage house analysts issue reports on these companies comparing their breakup values with their public trading prices.

Exhibit 16.3 summarizes a sampling of analysts' reports comparing stock price to estimated breakup value, showing the dates at which reports were issued.

Evidence from Real Estate Holding Companies

An article on real estate holding companies made the point that the negative effect of a disparate portfolio applies to real estate holding companies, such as real estate investment trusts (REITs), as well as to operating companies: "REITs that enjoy geographic concentrations of their properties and specialize in specific types of properties, e.g., outlet malls, commercial office buildings, apartment complexes, shopping centers, golf courses . . . etc., are the most favored by investors. This is similar to investor preferences for the focused 'pure play' company in other industries."[5]

Exhibit 16.3 Estimated Breakup Values of Existing Conglomerates

Date of Analyst Report	Conglomerate Name[1]	Stock Price at Date of Report	Analyst's Breakup Value[2]	Portfolio Discount[3]
10/31/99	Monsanto Co.	$38.50	$55	30%
1/25/00	B&H	$27	$37	27%
1/28/00	Pac. Dunlop	$1.98	$3.48	43%
10/25/00	IBM	$112	$150	25%
10/30/00	British Telecomm.	$117 ADR[4]	$165 ADR[4]	29%
11/6/00	AT&T	$21.94	$36.25	65%
11/24/00	Optus	$4.37	$4.55	39%
2/13/01	Canadian Pac. Ltd.	$36.52	$43	15%
			Mean	26.5%
			Median	28%

[1] At the time of the analyst's report, all conglomerates still existed.
[2] The estimated breakup value is based on several analysts' reports and is as of the date of the analysts' reports. This represents estimated minority value in the public market if traded separately.
[3] Portfolio Discount = (Breakup Value − Stock Price) / Breakup Value.
[4] ADR–American Depository Receipt.
Source: Compiled in March 2001 by Paul Heidt, Business Valuation Resources.™

HOW TO VALUE COMPANIES WITH DISPARATE PORTFOLIOS

There are several workable procedures for valuing companies with multiple lines of operation and/or diverse assets. The most common are:

- Conduct separate valuations of each operating line and/or asset, followed by a portfolio discount
- Blend multiples in the market approach and discount or capitalization rates in the income approach (each derived from market data for the respective industry), followed by a portfolio discount
- Compare directly with selected guideline conglomerates[6]

Separate Valuations Followed by a Discount

A common procedure is to value each operating unit and/or asset separately, sum the values, and apply an appropriate portfolio discount. An advantage of this procedure is that each piece can be valued using whatever valuation approaches and/or methods are most appropriate for the particular operation and/or asset.

Blended Multiples or Discount Rates Followed by a Discount

Another procedure is to develop blended market value multiples and/or a discount or capitalization rate for each part of the company, based on the proportion of the company that each part represents. The weightings usually are based on either revenues or gross margin dollars. Using asset values for weighting usually is not advisable (except for holding companies), because asset values may be difficult to determine and are not the primary value drivers.

Direct Use of Conglomerates

Another possible procedure is to use value measures from publicly traded guideline conglomerates, in which case no further portfolio discount would be necessary, because the discount already would be reflected in the value measures. The practical difficulty with this procedure is finding guideline conglomerates that are reasonably similar to the subject.

QUANTIFYING THE PORTFOLIO DISCOUNT

Quantifying the portfolio discount for any individual company remains as much a matter of judgment as of science. This is because any given portfolio's divergence usually will not match up very closely with any particular company or companies observed in the market. The best procedure would be to base the discount on a group of guideline companies having similar characteristics. More often than not, this will not be possible, and the analyst will have to list the factors that drive the discount (see factors listed earlier in chapter, and add any others that are specific to the subject company) and estimate the total impact on value.

PORTFOLIO DISCOUNTS IN THE U.S. TAX COURT

The U.S. Tax Court has recognized the concept of a portfolio discount. It must be supported, however, by convincing expert testimony.

Portfolio Discount Accepted

In *Estate of Maxcy v. Commissioner,* the company in question owned citrus groves, cattle and horses, a ranch, mortgages, acreage and undeveloped lots, and over 6,000 acres of pastureland.[7] The expert for the taxpayer opined that it would require a 15% discount from underlying asset value to induce a single purchaser to buy this assortment of assets. The expert for the Internal Revenue Service opposed this discount, saying that a control owner could liquidate the corporation and sell the assets at fair market value. (This case was decided before repeal of the *General Utilities* Doctrine, discussed in Chapter 14).

The Tax Court agreed with the taxpayer's expert:

> Without deciding the validity of respondent's contention, we fail to see how this power to liquidate inherent in a majority interest requires a higher value than [taxpayer's expert's] testimony indicates. Whether or not a purchaser of a controlling interest in Maxcy Securities could liquidate the corporation and sell its assets is immaterial, as there must still be found a purchaser of the stock who would be willing to undertake such a procedure. [Taxpayer's expert's] opinion was that this type purchaser is relatively scarce and not easily found at a sales price more than 85 percent of the assets' fair market value.
>
> Section 20.2031-1(b), Estate Tax Regs., provides that: "The fair market value [of property] is the price at which the property would change hands between a willing buyer and a willing seller, neither being under any compulsion to buy or sell and both having reasonable knowledge of relevant facts." In the instant case, we are attempting to determine the price a willing seller of Maxcy Securities shares could get from a willing buyer, not what the buyer may eventually realize.
>
> [Taxpayer's expert's] testimony impresses us as a rational analysis of the value of the stock in issue, and in the absence of contrary evidence, we find and hold on the facts here present that a majority interest in such stock was worth 85 percent of the underlying assets' fair market value on the respective valuation dates.

Since *Maxcy,* the only other U.S. Tax Court case applying the portfolio discount is *Estate of Piper v. Commissioner.*[8] At issue was the valuation of a gift of stock in two investment companies, Piper Investment and Castanea Realty. The companies each owned various real estate holdings, as well as stock in Piper Aircraft, which manufactured light aircraft.

The parties agreed that, because of the investment companies' nondiversified portfolios, the value of their stock was less than their net asset values. The size of the discount, however, was still in dispute. The IRS argued that the discount should be 10%, a value in between the values proposed by its two expert witnesses. The estate contended that the discount should exceed 17%, the higher of the two values suggested by the IRS's experts. Curiously, neither the estate nor its expert witnesses suggested a specific value for the portfolio discount.

The IRS's valuation experts took similar approaches to the problem of determining the portfolio discount. The IRS's first expert proposed a discount of 7.7% below NAV based on the average discount from NAV of the prices of 14 nondiversified investment companies. The IRS's second expert, on the other hand, found that the relation of market price to NAV of 24 publicly traded closed-end investment companies ranged from a discount of 16.7% to a premium of 82.4%. He concluded that because of Piper Investment's and Castanea Realty's relatively unattractive portfolios, the highest discount, approximately 17%, should be applied.

The court discussed both experts' methods in turn:

While we consider [the IRS's first expert's] approach somewhat superior to that of [the IRS's second expert] because [the first] limited his analysis to nondiversified investment companies, we believe that he erred in selecting the average discount of the nondiversified investment companies he considered. The weight of the evidence indicates that the portfolios of Piper Investment and Castanea were less attractive than that of the average nondiversified investment company. We reject [the IRS's] attempt to bolster [the first expert's] position by reference to the premiums above net asset value at which certain investment companies, either diversified or specialized in industries other than light aircraft, were selling. Those companies simply are not comparable to Piper Investment and Castanea, nondiversified investment companies owning only realty and [Piper Aircraft] stock.

The court rejected the estate's contention that the discount should exceed 17% and chose 17% as the appropriate discount:

[The estate] has also failed to introduce specific data to support its assertion that Piper Investment and Castanea were substantially inferior to the worst of the companies considered by [the IRS's second expert]. [The estate] made no attempt to elicit evidence as to the portfolios of the companies considered by [the second expert], and its expert witness commented only on [the first expert's], and not on [the second expert's], report. . . . On the basis of the record before us, we conclude that the discount selected by [the first expert] was too low, but that there is insufficient evidence to support [the estate's] position that the discount should be higher than that proposed by [the second expert]. Therefore, we find that 17 percent is an appropriate discount from net asset value to reflect the relatively unattractive nature of the investment portfolios of Piper Investment and Castanea.

Portfolio Discount Denied

In *Knight v. Commissioner,* the entity in question was a family limited partnership that held real estate and marketable securities.[9] Citing the section in *Valuing a Business* on discounts for conglomerates, the expert for the taxpayer claimed a 10% "portfolio discount." In denying the discount, the court said, "the Knight family partnership is not a conglomerate public company . . . [Taxpayer's expert] gave no convincing reason why the partnership's mix of assets would be unattractive to a buyer. We apply no portfolio discount."

SUMMARY

Investors prefer to buy companies with clearly focused operations or groups of assets rather than companies with disparate operations and/or assets. As a result, companies having disparate operations and/or assets, especially minority interests in such companies, tend to sell at a discount compared to the sum of the values of their component parts.

The reality of the portfolio discount is amply evidenced in the public stock markets. One line of evidence is the success of conglomerates that have broken up, with the aggregate values of the resulting companies being greater than the preannouncement values of the stocks before breakup. Another line of evidence is the wealth of published analyst estimates showing how much conglomerate companies' stock prices are discounted from their estimated breakup values. Evidence also shows that real estate holding companies focusing on a single type of property sell at less of a discount from their underlying asset value than real estate holding companies with diverse portfolios.

Stocks of conglomerate corporations (or partnerships) can be valued by estimating the value of each piece separately and taking a portfolio discount from the total, by using a blended multiple or discount rate reflecting the proportionate share of each component, or by direct comparison to guideline conglomerate stocks.

Although there is a great deal of empirical evidence, the portfolio discount is hard to quantify because of the uniqueness of each company.

The U.S. Tax Court has recognized the portfolio discount as a separately quantified discrete discount.

Notes

1. Wayne Jankowske, "Second-Stage Adjustments to Value," presented at American Society of Appraisers International Appraisal Conference, Toronto, June 16–19, 1996. Available online at www.BVLibrary.com with the author's permission.
2. Timothy Pritchard, "A Canadian Rail Pioneer Plans Split-Up," *New York Times* (February 14, 2001): C7.
3. Mozette Jefferson, "Liquidation of Underperforming Assets Gets Positive Minority Stock Reaction," *Shannon Pratt's Business Valuation Update* (December 1995): 11.
4. David Sadtler, Andrew Campbell, and Richard Koch, *Breakup!: When Large Companies Are Worth More Dead Than Alive* (UK: Capstone Publishing, 1997).
5. Phillip S. Scherrer, "Why REITs Face a Merger-Driven Consolidation Wave," *Mergers & Acquisitions, The Dealmaker's Journal* (July/August 1995): 42.
6. Shannon P. Pratt, Robert F. Reilly, and Robert P. Schweihs, *Valuing a Business,* 4th ed. (New York: McGraw-Hill, 2000), pp. 251–252.
7. *Estate of Maxcy v. Commissioner,* T.C. Memo 1969-158, 28 T.C.M. (CCH) 783 (1969).
8. *Estate of Piper v. Commissioner,* 72 T.C. 1062 (1979).
9. *Knight v. Commissioner,* 2000 U.S. Tax Ct. LEXIS 88, 115 T.C. No. 36 (2000).

Chapter 17

Discounts for Environmental, Litigation, and Other Contingent Liabilities

Concept of the Contingent Liability Discount
Financial Accounting Standard #5 May Provide Guidance in Quantifying
    Contingent Liabilities
Treatment of Contingencies in the U.S. Tax Court
Summary
Notes

Contingent assets and liabilities are among the most difficult to value simply because of their nature. The challenge lies in estimating just how much may be collected or will have to be paid out, and thus in quantifying the valuation adjustments.

CONCEPT OF THE CONTINGENT LIABILITY DISCOUNT

In purchases and sales of businesses and business interests in the real world, such items often are handled through a contingency account. For example, suppose a company with an environmental problem were being sold, and estimates had placed the cost to cure the environmental problem at $10 million to $20 million. The seller would place $20 million in an escrow account to pay for the cleanup, and once the problem was cured, any money remaining would be released back to the seller.

In gift and estate and some other situations, however, a point estimate of value is required as of the valuation date without the luxury of waiting for the actual result. In such cases some estimate of the cost of recovery must be made. It can be expressed as a percent of value or as a dollar-denominated amount.

I once conducted an estate tax valuation with a high probability of the subject company's going completely out of business because of known contamination in its waterfront location. The problem had been known and studied for 10 years, and the company was still in business. I proposed a 50% discount from the going-concern value, and the parties accepted it.

I was retained in another case in which the subject company did not carry product liability insurance, although claims in the industry were common and most companies carried insurance. I handled the issue (in both the income and market approaches) by deducting from income (before capitalizing or applying market multiples) the cost of product liability insurance. The chief executive officer protested, "But we've never been sued!" I replied, "But it's still a contingent liability with your type of products, and others in your industry have been sued. Sometimes the greatest risks we face are ones that we haven't experienced yet."

These anecdotes summarize the two means available to reflect contingency discounts: apply a percentage discount to value or adjust the balance sheet and the benefit stream.

A third way to value a contingent liability might be to consider its effect on marketability. Most people would probably agree that, at the instant a liability is detected and verified, but before the feasibility and cost to cure are determined, the equity of a private company with an environmental liability would be very difficult to sell. Thus, there would be a substantially increased discount for lack of marketability.

A fourth way to value a contingent liability has just emerged as the book goes to press. Certain property and casualty insurers have begun to offer after-the-fact coverages tailored to specific contingencies. The insured pays a premium and in exchange the insurer takes on a specified amount (or perhaps all) of the liability. This, in effect, takes some or all of the liability off the financial statements and simplifies the valuation analyst's task.

FINANCIAL ACCOUNTING STANDARD #5 MAY PROVIDE GUIDANCE IN QUANTIFYING CONTINGENT LIABILITIES

Financial Accounting Standard (FAS) #5 deals with contingent liabilities for purposes of financial statement reporting. In valuing a company with a full disclosure financial statement (compilation, review, or audit), FAS #5 would require consideration of any contingent liabilities and they would be covered in the legal letters (lawyers are required to respond to accountants' inquiries in an audit regarding the probability of contingent liabilities and their potential impact). This information could be of significant value to the appraiser in determining a discount or reduction in value related to contingent liabilities.

TREATMENT OF CONTINGENCIES IN THE U.S. TAX COURT

The U.S. Tax Court recognizes discounts for contingent liabilities where appropriate.

In *Estate of Klauss v. Commissioner,* both the taxpayer's and the IRS's experts applied substantial discounts for product liability and environmental claims.[1] The taxpayer's expert enumerated specific items and applied a discount of $921,000. The IRS's expert applied a 10% discount, which amounted to $1,130,000. The court agreed with taxpayer's expert's method because "[i]t more accurately accounted for the effects."

In *Payne v. Commissioner,* the IRS contended that the value of the stock, $500,000 received and claimed by Payne on his tax returns, was significantly understated.[2] Payne argued that there should be a discount on the value due to pending litigation over the company's business license. The IRS's expert valued the stock at $1,140,000 as a going concern and at $230,000 if the company did not receive the business license. The Tax Court allowed a 50% discount on the going concern value due to the pending litigation and found the stock to be worth $570,000.

In *Estate of Mitchell v. Commissioner,* after applying a 10% key person deduction at the enterprise level (as discussed in Chapter 13), the Tax Court then applied a $1.5 million discount for a pending compensation lawsuit, but only *after* computing the estate's 40% pro rata interest in the enterprise value and *after* deduction of a 35% combined lack of control/lack of marketability discount.[3] (The court did not explain why this discount, which logically should be an entity-level discount, was applied at the shareholder level.)

However, in May of 2001, the Ninth Circuit reversed and remanded, saying that the starting point was acquisition value, and that the Tax Court misstated the range of combined minority/marketability discounts as 30 to 45%, when the record showed a range of 46.2 to 61.5% for the combined discounts. The appellate court also held that the Tax Court provided an inadequate explanation of the way it reached its conclusion.[4]

The court's treatment of the contingent liability is quite interesting in *Estate of Desmond v. Commissioner.*[5] Before giving equal weight to the income and guideline public company methods in valuing a paint company's stock, the court applied a 20% discount for marketability to account for the result of the market approach and a 30% discount for marketability to account for the result of the income approach. The extra 10% reflected the environmental liability associated with the paint operation.

The reason for not applying the extra discount to the market approach was the assumption that the public market multiples of the two guideline paint companies used already reflected similar contingent liabilities. The IRS's expert argued that the companies had higher than average betas, and thus the volatility reflected in the betas in the income approach were because of the contingencies. The court said that no evidence was presented to support this argument and rejected it.

SUMMARY

Contingent assets and liabilities can arise from a number of sources, such as lawsuits, environmental liability, and product liability. When a value has to be determined at a point in time before actual cost of the liability has been determined, the dollar amount of the impact must be estimated so that it can be reflected in the value. Courts are open to reasonable estimation, realizing that the potential impact cannot be measured with precision. However, if possible, the estimated impact should be determined by a qualified, independent expert, in writing, who understands that the business appraiser will be relying on the expert's opinion.

Notes

1. *Estate of Klauss v. Commissioner,* T.C. Memo 2000-191, 79 T.C.M. (CCH) 2177 (2000).
2. *Payne v. Commissioner,* T.C. Memo 1998-227, 75 T.C.M. 2548 (CCH) (1998).
3. *Estate of Mitchell v. Commissioner,* T.C. Memo 1997-461, 74 T.C.M. (CCH) 872 (1997).
4. *Estate of Mitchell v. Commissioner,* 2001 U.S. App. LEXIS 7990 (9th Cir., 2001).
5. *Estate of Desmond v. Commissioner,* T.C. Memo 1999-76, 77 T.C.M. 1529 (CCH) (1999).

Discount Adjustments for Limited Partnership Interests and Other Asset Management Entities

Curtis R. Kimball

Combining assets into a portfolio managed within a limited partnership (LP) or a limited liability company (LLC) has received increasing emphasis over the past two decades as a wealth management and estate planning tool. This chapter discusses the framework for the primary valuation discount adjustments to consider in appraising limited partnership and limited liability company or similar interests (collectively called "entities").

The first area of due diligence in valuing entities revolves around the rights and features of the subject interest. This requires a closer interface with the legal and tax counsel for the entity and its owners than many appraisers may be accustomed but this contact at the beginning of the project is very beneficial. State law has a substantial influence over how interests are viewed for appraisal. Federal income tax and estate and gift tax laws and regulations are also important for analyzing and understanding influences and constraints on value.

The second area of analysis for valuation of these entities is the asset and liability structure of the entity. The appraiser must analyze the values and business risks contributed to or subtracted from the entity by each asset and liability and arrive at a conclusion of how the assets and liabilities interact with each other in a final conclusion of the overall risks and returns of the portfolio.

The third area of analysis relates the net asset value of the portfolio of the entity to the value of individual noncontrolling interests. Depending on the influential issues analyzed in the first and second steps above for the subject interest, a value adjustment for relative lack of control and relative lack of marketability may be justified. Research into the magnitude of such value adjustments comes from guideline public companies and other securities of a similar type in the same or similar lines of business.

One of the advantages of an entity is that individual noncontrolling interests are minority interests for appraisal purposes, even though the entire entity may be owned by a group of related people. Therefore, a timely series of gifts or sales of noncontrolling interests under a fair market value standard for gift planning purposes can reduce the overall value that is taxed in a generational shift of ownership within a family.

The range of discounts applicable in such transactions depends on the analysis and application of these factors. Studies of partnership interests and securities of firms in the same or similar lines of business show that these factors produce discounts as small as 10% and as large as 85%.

INTRODUCTION

Limited partnerships have existed for quite a while; thus, the notion of a limited partnership as an investment vehicle is not new. Many real estate investments in the 1970s and 1980s used a limited partnership format to syndicate investment ventures. Limited liability companies are a relatively newer form of organization that has achieved popularity ever since the Internal Revenue Service provided for more certainty of treatment with check-the-box pass-through income tax status.

Beginning in 1986, with the passage of the Tax Reform Act and the adoption of the new rules repealing the *General Utilities* Doctrine, it became very difficult for C corporations to avoid double taxation of capital gains at the entity and shareholder levels. Limited partnerships are a more flexible organization type to manage wealth. As a result, many financial planning practitioners utilized limited partnerships and, later, limited liability companies as holding and management vehicles for their clients' assets. Individual minority interests of such entities usually are subject to discounts from their underlying net asset values for the valuation transfers.

The flexibility of entities is further evidenced by the potential to reduce management cost for a portfolio of assets that might otherwise be held in multiple accounts, for multiple family members, with multiple investment managers. Entity interests are less difficult to divide into partial interests and to transfer than are fractional interests in many other types of property, such as real estate. Out-of-state probate proceedings, which are required if property is owned directly by the client, often can be avoided for real property located in another state but held by an entity.

PARTNERSHIP FEATURES

The first area of due diligence necessary in valuing a minority entity interest is an analysis of the features of the existing or proposed entity.

Every entity is formed under the laws of its home state. State laws regarding partnerships have benefited greatly from the suggested statutes in the Uniform Limited Partnership Act (ULPA) of 1976 and the Revisions of 1985, which have promoted consistency among the states. However, the appraiser must work closely with the attorney for the client at this stage of the appraisal to ensure that the entity interests combine the rights and privileges that reflect the needs of the client, consistent with state requirements. This involves the state's requirements for formation of the entity and the appropriate documents to be executed. Typically, a limited partnership agreement will spell out the details of formation and operation. As further discussed below, these features form the basis for the economic rights and constraints that result in discounts from the adjusted net asset value of the underlying assets of the entity.

The following features are key in determining the fair market value of an interest:

- The length of time the entity will operate until dissolution or termination
- Which interests will manage the day-to-day affairs of the entity
- How the election of new managing partners, members, or agents is accomplished
- Which interests have voting rights to liquidate the entity
- Withdrawal rights of various ownership interests
- Which interests control distributions to the other entity interests
- What preferences exist among the classes of entity interests
- What restrictions, terms, and conditions apply to transfers of entity interests

OTHER STATE LAW AND REGULATORY ISSUES

An understanding of state laws also is required to comply with (or avoid) state transfer and excise taxes that may be triggered by the transfer of the contributed assets into the entity. State income tax issues also may be affected by placement of operating or investment assets into an entity, and some states may deem the transfer into an entity as the equivalent of a change in ownership for property tax assessment purposes.

Zoning and land use issues also may be affected by a transfer, as some states require reapplication for protected status for some forms of farming or special use zoning. Creditor notification rules also may be triggered if the property contributed to an entity is encumbered by debt.

COMPLIANCE WITH FEDERAL INCOME TAX REGULATIONS

The comparison of an entity's features relative to state laws also comes into play in the formation of an entity for a range of federal income and estate and gift tax issues.

Internal Revenue Code (IRC) section 754 may create concerns among potential buyers that their purchase of an interest in the entity may not allow them to step up their cost basis in the assets of the entity to their cost basis of the interest (i.e., their purchase price). Therefore, a buyer may have built-in gains on a partial interest in an entity if an asset within the portfolio, or the entire portfolio, of the entity is later sold.

IRC section 704 requires allocation of income factors among the partners based on the economic substance of each interest, and not just as a method to transfer income to partners with lower marginal tax brackets. Other provisions of Section 704 require real business purposes in the formation and operation of limited partnerships.

IRC section 721 also applies to the formation and the contribution of appreciated securities into an entity. If partners achieve additional diversification beyond de minimis (approximately 1%) changes to the portfolio of securities held before the formation of the entity, then income taxes on the securities' gains may become due upon the formation of the entity.

IRC section 752 is also a potential trap for the unwary in triggering income taxes on the portion of debts on an encumbered property contributed to an entity and assigned to the other partners. The regulations view such an assumption as an extinguishment of the debt from the original holder's personal tax capacity, even though the partner may remain liable for the debt.

COMPLIANCE WITH FEDERAL TRANSFER TAX REGULATIONS

Estate and gift tax regulations are perhaps the biggest federal tax hurdle faced in the successful planning and valuation of entity interests.

The basic standard of value in estate and gift tax transfers is fair market value (FMV). The FMV standard assumes that a hypothetical willing buyer and willing seller have no special relationship to each other and are dealing at arm's length. Revenue Ruling 93-12 reversed the IRS's earlier position that joint family member control of an asset meant that no discounts for minority interest lack of control could be taken for a fractional interest. Revenue Ruling 93-12 opened the floodgates for entity planning since a limited partnership interest could be accorded minority interest status.

However, the IRS in all probability would not have issued as sweeping a concession as Revenue Ruling 93-12 without the assurance of a backstop to control behavior regarded as abusive under other regulations. This was done with the addition of chapter 14 (sections 2701–2704) to the estate and gift tax laws for all transactions entered into or in some cases substantially modified after October 8, 1990.

Section 2701 of chapter 14 calls for special valuation procedures when preferred partnership interests have certain preferences designed to enhance value. However, under current entity planning, most LP and LLC structures avoid section 2701 by giving interest holders proportionate rights to income and in liquidation.

Section 2703 covers buy–sell agreements. Generally, the buy–sell provisions included in an entity agreement closely follow those between arm's-length investors. Because of the long-term nature of most entity ventures, the investors often need assurances that the owner group, or anyone subsequently acquiring an interest in the entity, is willing to stay the full term of the entity.

Section 2704 addresses restrictions on liquidation and lapsing restrictions on such items as voting rights, when the family owns control of an entity. Generally, legal counsel will need to coordinate the entity agreement with the basic "default" provisions in state laws regarding the extent to which investors can withdraw or otherwise liquidate their interests. Typically, by making the entity operate for a fixed term of years and by the addition of nonfamily-member interest holders with unanimous agreement required for liquidation, the entity will comply with the requirements of this section of chapter 14.

ANALYSIS OF OWNERSHIP AND CLASSES OF INTERESTS

Equally important to the valuation is the analysis of the existing or proposed ownership group of the entity and the classes of entity interest that will be created. Usually, but not always, only general and limited partnership classes are created for entities. Usually, but not always, family members are the primary owners of the entity. The analyst must consider these factors because of the potential for triggering the special valuation rules discussed above that may result in the valuation being determined without regard to certain restrictions contained in the entity agreement. Family members' ownership interests are aggregated for determining whether control over liquidation exists. Such family members are defined as: the individual transferor and spouse; any ancestor or lineal descendant of the individual or spouse; any siblings of the individual or spouse; and any spouse of any such ancestor, lineal descendant, or sibling.

ANALYSIS OF UNDERLYING ADJUSTED NET ASSET VALUE

The first reference point of entity valuation is usually the adjusted net asset value of the underlying assets and liabilities of the entity. When starting with the adjusted net asset value of the underlying assets of the entity, discounts typically are applied to the underlying asset for the relative lack of control and relative lack of marketability of the subject entity interest. The basis for the discounts is discussed below.

Cash, publicly traded securities, and other easily valued assets typically do not require formal appraisals. Real estate often requires a documented value analysis (such as a formal written appraisal) as of the date of transfer of any interest. Other factors, such as the ability of the typical market to absorb the volume of the entity asset held (particularly for large real estate interests clustered in a single market or large blocks of publicly traded stock), may require an adjustment of the appraised values of the assets before further analysis of the value of partial entity interests.

Significant privately held investments, such as closely held business interests and other limited partnership investments, usually will require separate valuations. As an alternative approach to establishing the discount, these assets may be valued instead without any applicable discounts for minority interest and limited marketability. Thus, such discounts are recognized only at the entity interest level under this methodology, on the theory that the buyer of such an interest is acquiring an overall interest in the entity's portfolio of net assets and such discounts can only be determined with reference to the interest being transferred.

An analysis of the portfolio of assets in the entity is also important to determine:

- The combined riskiness of the portfolio of assets, as opposed to the risk of each asset and liability. Entity interest owners are exposed to the combined risk of all net assets.
- The interaction among assets in the entity portfolio. The combination of different types of assets may render an entity interest unattractive to some potential buyers that might otherwise be interested in investing in some of the entity's operations. As an example, many multifamily real estate investors may be uncomfortable also investing in agricultural properties.

ANALYSIS OF INCOME CAPACITY VALUE

A second reference point in the valuation of entity interests is the determination of an income-based value. This analysis typically requires the consideration of current income capacity and possible projection of the magnitude and timing of future income from operations. The income stream measured is most often the cash flow from operations of each asset owned by the entity, net of all related operating expenses of the asset and the entity, but before consideration of any income tax issues for the interest holders. Such an analysis is conducted on the assumption that the investor has control over operations of the entity and that any expenses fall into the range of reasonableness and typicality for the assets under management.

Because the proceeds of asset sales and capital gains typically are reinvested within the entity structure and not distributed until the end of the term of the partnership, these types of capital asset cash flows usually are not considered in calculating the sustainable cash flows from operations under this approach.

Income analysis is critical to the valuation of entities and entity interests, as there may be dramatic differences among the ways hypothetical buyers look at the subject investment, depending on their primary motives for investment. Investors seeking income returns from the investment will focus on sustainable operating income and distribution yields. Investors seeking returns through appreciation of the underlying assets of the entity will be influenced more strongly by the prospect of asset appreciation and the timing of any returns on the investment.

The stability of income is a significant factor in determining the business risk of the entity and its interests. There may be interactions among cash flows from different assets and liabilities that will create refinancing risks or temporary (or even permanent) negative cash flows that will require additional capital contributions from the investors.

A comparison of potential growth rates of income of the assets within the entity and comparison of the entity to other investments in the same or similar lines of business (see Revenue Ruling 59-60) is essential in establishing the required capitalization rate on the income capacity of the interest or the discount rate on projected cash flows.

One method of establishing an income-based value is to capitalize the current indicated cash flows from entity operations to the subject interest. Most often the capacity of the entity to make distributions to the subject interest is capitalized in the same manner as a dividend yield calculation. These typically are calculated on a control basis, under the initial assumption that any remaining available income will be distributed in the manner of the comparable publicly traded securities, such as closed-end mutual funds.

Sources of data for distribution yields on entities come from investments with similar characteristics. These include publicly traded limited partnerships (PLPs), real estate investment trusts (REITs), closed-end mutual fund units (CEFs), and publicly registered limited partnerships traded in the secondary market (RLPs).

VALUATION OF NONCONTROLLING ENTITY INTERESTS

Valuing partial interests in entities is based on the application of standard valuation techniques. In fact, Revenue Ruling 68-609 extended the same elements of value utilized in Revenue Ruling 59-60 for corporate stock to the valuation of partnership interests. The most common methods are based on establishing a relationship between the adjusted net asset value and the cash flow income from operations of the underlying assets of the entity to the subject partial interest.

Applicable discounts are:

- The relative lack of control of the subject interest over the management of the assets and income
- The relative lack of marketability of the entity interest, when compared to otherwise similar securities that have the benefit of a public market

These discounts are taken in sequence. The first taken is typically the adjustment for relative lack of control. The adjustment for the entity's relative lack of marketability usually is taken after the lack-of-control discount.

Qualitative factors also come into play in the analysis of appropriate discount adjustments. One critical area that requires close scrutiny is the quality of management of the entity. Many of the similar public investments are run by experienced investment managers with deeply staffed groups of support personnel that have an extensive history of solid industry performance. In contrast, many entities have rudimentary management organizations attempting to follow a wide array of operations and investments.

General Partnership Interests

These are usually controlling interests in the entity, and state laws may give general partners withdrawal rights prior to the end of the term of the partnership. As a result, the value of a general partnership interest is more closely aligned to the underlying net asset value of the entity as a whole. However, for entities that may not terminate for many years, the fair market value to a withdrawing general partner may be reduced by any damages to the other partners caused by a breach of the agreement due to early withdrawal. Both the adjusted net asset and income-based reference points are important in arriving at fair market value. Similar issues typically may apply to a managing member of an LLC.

Partial general partnership interests that are, in effect, minority voting interests, due to required majority voting rights among general partners, often are valued more in the manner of limited partnership interests as discussed below.

The withdrawal by a general partner from a real estate–oriented entity may result in the investor receiving an undivided interest in real property that itself is subject to discounts for shared control and relative lack of marketability.

Limited Partnership Interests

Most commonly, limited partnership interests are the securities transferred by investors for financial planning purposes. Limited partnership interests are, by definition, permanent minority interests, except for those cases in which the limited partners as a class possess certain rights under state law or the partnership agreement to block actions by the entity (such as dissolution). Both adjusted net asset and income-based reference points cited above are appropriate starting points for arriving at fair market value.

Assignee Interests

An assignee interest may not be allowed to succeed to a partnership interest, but instead it may have the right merely to obtain a charging order to receive distributions, if any, from the entity. Additional relative lack-of-control and lack-of-marketability discounts typically are necessary to reflect any incremental additional problems associated with assignee status.

Valuation discounts for assignee interests are typically greater than those seen for similar limited partnership interests and can be comparable to those seen on distressed securities, as the issues of timing and certainty of collection of cash flows can be comparable. Other problems that tend to increase the discount can include the lack of access to data and the obligation to pay income taxes on earnings without the receipt of cash distributions to pay such obligations.

DISCOUNTS FOR LACK OF CONTROL AND MARKETABILITY

Sources of data for discounts on entities come from investments with similar characteristics. These include:

- Publicly traded limited partnerships (PLPs)
- Real estate investment trusts (REITs)
- Closed-end mutual fund units (CEFs)
- Publicly registered limited partnerships traded in the secondary market (RLPs)

Studies of the magnitude of such discounts are discussed in Chapter 19 and sources are detailed in Appendix B.

In the case of data on discounts of trading prices relative to adjusted net asset values, it may be difficult to separate the portion of the total discount that arises from relative lack of control from the portion that is due to the relative lack of marketability of the subject entity interest. This is particularly true for registered limited partnership interests trading in the secondary market. In fact, the discounts seen in transactions in RLP interests may not fully capture the illiquidity of private entity interests if there have never been any trades in the subject private interest.

Other marketability evidence for minority interests is found in the Willamette Management Associates pre-IPO studies discussed in Chapter 5 and the studies of restricted securities of firms that are already publicly traded. In addition, Exhibit 18.1 lists settlements between taxpayers and the IRS in which Willamette Management Associates was involved or is aware of.

Exhibit 18.1 Case Settlements with the IRS

No.	Source	Date	Type	Interest	State Law	Assets	Other Factors	Discount
1	WMA[1]	1993	Estate, plus 6 prior gifts (1987–92)	Family Limited Partnership	Ga.	Real estate and a closely held business conducted on the real estate (bed and breakfast)	The real estate was environmentally sensitive	75%
2	WMA[1]	1997	Gift (1995)	Family Limited Partnership	Ala.	Real estate (60%), municipal bonds, and a closely held business (real estate management company)	Gift made under a power of attorney; IRS hired outside appraiser after this case was docketed for Tax Court	35.6%
3	WMA[1]	1996	Gift (1995)	Family Limited Partnership	Ariz.	Real estate—shopping center interests	Significant leverage	55%
4	Attorney	1997	Gift (1992)	Family Limited Partnership	Nev.	Predominantly real estate (no debt) and some publicly traded securities	83-year-old donor	30%
5	Attorney	1997	Estate and gifts (1986–91)	General Partnership (preferred interest)	Calif.	Real estate, promissory note, vehicles, and equipment	Real estate management activities	35%
6	Attorney	1998	Gift	Family Limited Partnership	Wash.	Publicly traded stock	Other problems with prior family gifts made attorney willing to settle quickly	35%

#	Preparer	Year	Gift/Estate	Entity	State	Assets	Reason	Percentage
7	Attorney	1997	Gift	Family Limited Partnership	Del.	Publicly traded stock	Client instructed attorney to avoid Tax Court at all costs	25%
8	Attorney	1997	Estate (1994)	Family Limited Partnership	Texas	Publicly traded stocks and municipal bonds (93%) and real estate and oil and gas (7%)	Settlement after taxpayer's attorney filed motion for partial summary judgment	56%
9	Attorney	1997	Estate (1993)	Family Limited Partnership	Texas	Publicly traded stocks (39%), real estate (13%), cash (12%), municipal bonds (10%), other assets including mineral interests	Settlement after taxpayer's attorney filed motion for partial summary judgment	55%
10	Attorney	1998	Gift (1992)	Family Limited Partnership	Calif.	Real estate (unimproved)	Small size of FLP and gift made it uneconomical to litigate	15%
11	Attorney	1998	Gift (1992)	Family Limited Partnership	Calif.	Real estate (improved)	None	33.33%
12	Attorney	1998	Gift (1993)	Family Limited Partnership	Calif.	Real estate	None	40%
13	WMA[1]	1997	Gift (1995)	Family Limited Partnership	Ga.	Cash (to be invested in venture capital interests over a multiyear period)	None	42%
14	Attorney	1998	Gift (1993)	Family Limited Partnership	Texas	Cash (67%) and marketable securities (33%)	No appraisal report filed initially, per decision of clients' CPA	15%

continued

Exhibit 18.1 Case Settlements with the IRS—*continued*

No.	Source	Date	Type	Interest	State Law	Assets	Other Factors	Discount
15	Attorney	1998	Gift (1992)	Family Limited Partnership	Texas	Real estate	None	40%
16	Attorney	1998	Gift (1992)	Family Limited Partnership	Md.	Real estate	Senior-generation donor died within two months after gift (no prior history of health problems)	41%
17	WMA[1]	1997	Estate (1995)	S Corporation Stock (control block)	Ga.	Publicly traded common stock (97%), real estate (3%)	S election made just prior to date of death; substantial built-in gains on stock	30%
18	WMA[1] & MPI[2]	1998	Gift (1994)	S Corporation Stock (minority)	Pa.	Municipal bonds (80%), publicly traded stocks (15%), real estate (5%)	Review by IRS National Office	43%
19	Attorney	1999	Estate (1993)	General Partnership	Fla.	Real estate (timberland)	A 2032A special use valuation deduction was also allowed	30%
20	Attorney	1999	Estate	General Partnership	Ore.	Real estate (unimproved), cash, equipment	Fractional interest in the real estate; partnership alleged to have dissolved upon death of partner; IRS faced trial date without having retained an expert witness on valuation	35%

#									%
21	HVA[3]	1999	Gift	Limited Partnership	Colo.	Municipal bonds, real estate (ranch land)	Municipal bonds represented most of the assets; an additional discount was allowed to account for call and bidding inconsistencies which made the value of the bonds less certain		36%
22	WMA[1]	1996	Gift	Limited Partnership	N.C.	One block of publicly traded stock (not large enough to require a blockage discount)	Transferor was in a coma		33%
23	WMA[1]	1996	Gift	Limited Partnership	N.C.	One block of publicly traded stock (50%), undeveloped real estate (20%), money market and bond funds (30%)	Donor terminally ill at transfer date, died just over one year later		35%
24	Appraiser	12–1995	Gift	Limited Partnership	Texas	Municipal bonds and bond funds (85%), common stock, and undeveloped real estate	No independent appraisal made of the gift until it was audited; attorney "estimated" a discount for the original filing		39%

continued

285

Exhibit 18.1 Case Settlements with the IRS—*continued*

No.	Source	Date	Type	Interest	State Law	Assets	Other Factors	Discount
25	Attorney	12–1997	Estate	Limited Partnership	S.C.	Publicly traded stock and money market funds	Death occurred within one year of formation and transfer, but there was no evidence of illness at the time of formation and transfer	23%
26	Attorney	10–1995	Estate	Limited Partnership	S.C.	Publicly traded stocks (50%) and undeveloped real estate (50%)	Decedent was terminally ill at formation and died within 10 months	37.5%
27	Attorney	1997	Estate	Limited Partnership	Calif.	Apartment buildings	None	39%
28	WMA[1]	9–1995	Gift	Limited Partnership	Ga.	Mutual funds of publicly traded stocks (86%) and undeveloped real estate (14%)	No independent appraisal made of the gift until it was audited, at which time Willamette was retained; attorney "estimated" a discount for the original filing	40%

[1]Willamette Management Associates.
[2]Management Planning, Inc.
[3]Houlihan Valuation Advisors.
Source: Curtis Kimball, Willamette Management Associates.

The factors that appear to affect the magnitude of the discount are:

- The disparity between income-based and adjusted net asset-based values. A poor earnings outlook increases the discount. Large amounts of debt service relative to cash flow also may be a cause of poor earnings for equity holders.
- Low levels of income distributions. Low current income increases the discount.
- Time to dissolution or liquidation. The longer an interest holder has to wait for an exit via a dissolution or liquidation of the entity, the greater the discount.
- Elements of voting issues and restrictions placed on general partner actions. More protection for the limited partners decreases the discount.
- Differences between the subject entity and the guideline interest. For example, some closed-end funds use a number of techniques to reduce the discount between their trading prices and their net asset values that are not used by the subject private entity.

Generalized Discount Adjustment Model

Discounts Drawn from Publicly Registered Limited Partnership Transactions

1. Calculate the adjusted net asset value of the entity (control basis).
2. Based on discounts of trading prices to net asset value from PLP data, determine the discount adjustment from net asset value for the subject entity.
3. Determine if any further relative marketability discounts are necessary, if the subject entity has greater exposure than PLPs to other risk factors:
   - Restrictions on transfer
   - Built-in gains exposure due to a lack of an IRC section 754 election
   - Concentration of assets in a single investment (lack of diversification)

Data Source Example: *The Partnership Spectrum* Study 2000

This study was updated in a periodic survey of combined lack-of-control and lack-of-marketability discounts for registered LP interests actively trading in the secondary market. The partnerships studied totaled 87, and partnership discounts showed some additional decline as investors anticipated partnership liquidations and buyouts. Exhibit 18.2 shows the study published in the May/June 2000 issue of *The Partnership Spectrum*, which indicated the listed discounts for limited partnership interests, all real estate investment related.

Generalized Discount Adjustment Model

Discounts Drawn from Closed-End Mutual Fund Transactions

1. Calculate the adjusted net asset value of the entity (control basis).
2. Calculate the income-based value of the entity (control basis).

Exhibit 18.2 Discounts Indicated in *The Partnership Spectrum* Study 2000

Category	Number of LPs	Average Discount (%)	Average Yield (%)
Equity—Distributing (Low/No Debt)	24	24	9.2
Equity—Distributing (Larger Debt)	18	26	7.7
Equity—Nondistributing	9	35	0.0
Undeveloped Land	3	40	0.0
Triple Net Lease	24	21	10.5
Mortgages—Insured	9	21	12.5

Source: The Partnership Spectrum, (May/June 2000).

3. Reconcile the indicated control values.
4. Based on discounts from net asset value and yields on closed-end funds, determine a discount for the relative lack of control.
5. Based on the empirical studies and theoretical models (see other chapters), determine a discount for the relative lack of marketability of the entity interest.

Limited Liability Companies

The limited liability company (LLC) is a relatively recent organizational form that is being used as a substitute for limited partnerships in financial planning. Although organized more similarly to a partnership, and taxed as such, an LLC provides its owners with protection from unlimited liability similar to a corporation. Usually liability is limited to the owner's investment in the LLC.

Utilizing LLCs for wealth planning in the same manner as an LP is potentially feasible but depends in part on the state law under which the subject LLC operates. The major issue for LLCs is the degree to which state LLC laws protect liquidation, withdrawal, and marketability restrictions that may be contained in the LLC membership agreement from being deemed applicable restrictions under IRC section 2704. As noted above, if these restrictions on LLC interests are more restrictive than the basic state law provisions, they must be ignored for gift valuation purposes under Chapter 14 of the Internal Revenue Code. Many state laws treat LLC memberships as interests subject to withdrawal in a manner similar to general partnership interests. See comments above regarding minority general partnership interests.

Other legal entities such as limited liability limited partnerships are also being used in a manner similar to LLCs.

Closely Held Interests Inside Entities

One issue that occasionally arises in valuing entity interests is the extent to which closely held securities, which are already illiquid securities, are further discounted if held inside an entity. My research indicates that additional discounting typically is warranted but that such discounts are usually incremental in nature. Incremental discounts can be similar in magnitude to typical marketability discounts when the features of the entity interest further restrict or otherwise provide much lesser marketability than the closely held securities held by the entity.

COURT CASES REGARDING LIMITED PARTNERSHIP VALUES

Although not very useful for direct use by the appraiser, U.S. Tax Court and other rulings on the values and discounts associated with limited partnership interests can be helpful in understanding what factors the courts find significant and under what circumstances.

***Harwood v. Commissioner.*[1]** A 50% discount from the underlying adjusted net asset value was determined by the court for a small limited partnership interest subject to transfer restrictions that probably would be required to be ignored under current special valuation rules in IRC section 2703 of chapter 14.

***Knott v. Commissioner.*[2]** A 50% limited partnership interest in an LP owning apartments was given a 30% discount by the court from adjusted net asset value.

***Moore v. Commissioner.*[3]** The court allowed a 35% discount from the underlying adjusted net asset value for a minority general partnership interest with certain restrictions on selling, withdrawing, or assigning the partnership interest.

***LeFrak v. Commissioner.*[4]** Although the judge decided that the structure of the transaction consisted of the transfer of minority undivided interest in real estate rather than limited partnerships as the taxpayer had maintained, the analysis was similar to LP valuation. The court allowed discounts from adjusted net asset values totaling 30%.

***Estate of McCormick v. Commissioner.*[5]** A series of gifts of minority (North Dakota) general partnership interests were valued by the Tax Court utilizing a combined minority interest and marketability discount to underlying asset value between 34.4 to 47.0%. The two partnerships owned real estate held for development and land contract receivables.

***Estate of Barudin v. Commissioner.*[6]** The issue concerned the valuation of one general partnership unit of a total of 95 units outstanding. This New York partnership owned commercial office buildings. An unrelated party owned a majority of the partnership units, and the partnership agreement required a majority vote on such significant issues as the sale or transfer of these general partnership units. The legal right under state law of any general partner to dissolve the partnership was given little weight by the court, and the court assessed a total discount for lack of control and lack of marketability of 45%.

Estate of Schauerhamer v. Commissioner.[7]   The commingling of cash flows from assets supposedly conveyed to an LP with the personal accounts of the senior-generation founder invalidated the basis for any discounts in this case. The court decided that the LP's assets should be included directly in the estate without recognizing any impact of the LP.

Estate of Lehman v. Commissioner.[8]   The general and limited partnership interests in this case owned real estate leased for a hotel in the District of Columbia. The court allowed a total discount of 39%.

Estate of Nowell v. Commissioner.[9]   In this case the Tax Court decided that the two Arizona LP interests should be valued as assignee interests rather than as limited partnership interests. The terms of the partnership agreement and state law had a direct effect on the outcome in this case.

Kerr v. Commissioner.[10]   In this case, an LP held a limited partnership interest in another LP. The LP interest held was allowed a discount of 25% (combined adjustment for lack of control and lack of marketability), and the LP interest subject to gift tax was allowed discounts of 17.5% (lack of control) and 35% (lack of marketability), taken consecutively.

Church v. United States.[11]   This LP owned ranchlands and publicly traded securities. The court allowed a combined discount of 57.6% from the underlying net asset value of the partnership.

Shepherd v. Commissioner.[12]   The court in this case ruled that real estate contributed to the subject LP resulted, in effect, in a gift of undivided interests in the real estate to the other partners. Thus, no discounts were allowed for the effect of the LP ownership, but rather a combined 15% discount was allowed for relative lack of control and lack of marketability represented by the fractional interest nature of the real estate interests.

Knight v. Commissioner.[13]   The court in this case concluded that the taxpayer's valuation report lacked credibility in part and therefore allowed a combined discount of 15% for lack of control and lack of marketability for the subject LP interests.

Estate of Strangi v. Commissioner.[14]   There were two securities at issue in this case. A large minority interest in the stock of the corporation owning the general partner, received discounts of 5% (lack of control) and 15% (lack of marketability), or a combined discount of 19% overall. An LP interest was allowed discounts of 8% (lack of control) and 25% (lack of marketability), or a combined discount of 31% overall. The substantial influence that the stock interest could exert over the LP and the fact that the estate could have sold both as a unit, influenced the court's decision in this case. Approximately 75% of the assets of the LP were publicly traded securities, and the remainder were real estate and other assets.

Estate of Jones v. Commissioner.[15]   In this case, interests in two LPs were valued. In the first issue, the size of the LP was large enough to allow the LP interest holder to exercise influence over the general partner under the provisions of the partnership agreement. Therefore the court determined that no discount for lack of control was allowable and an 8% discount for lack of marketability was appropriate. In the second issue, the size of the blocks of LP interests transferred were not sufficient to provide them with any significant influence. The court allowed a discount of 40% from net asset value based on publicly registered limited partnership transaction data and an 8% additional discount for lack of marketability, based on restrictions on transfer within the LP agreement—particularly an opinion forcing the exiting LP holder to receive payment over 10 years at a minimum allowable interest rate.

Other Courts.   It is reasonable to assume that bankruptcy courts and divorce courts will have to address issues relating to the valuation of limited partnerships and other entities increasingly in the future as owners of these types of interests become enmeshed in insolvency and marital division proceedings.

SUMMARY

The development of discount adjustments for LP and LLC interests for financial planning purposes is an exercise subject to professional appraisal standards and methods. Analysts developing valuation techniques for entity interests need to be aware of the empirical evidence and may want to maintain or purchase proprietary databases applicable to such entities. The appraiser practicing in this area needs to work closely with legal and tax counsel to adhere to IRS regulations applicable to entity valuations.

Notes

1. *Harwood v. Commissioner,* 82 T.C. 239 (1984).
2. *Knott v. Commissioner,* 55 T.C.M. (CCH) 424 (1988).
3. *Moore v. Commissioner,* 62 T.C.M. (CCH) 1128 (1991).
4. *LeFrak v. Commissioner,* 66 T.C.M. (CCH) 1297 (1993).
5. *Estate of McCormick v. Commissioner,* T.C. Memo 1995-371 (1995).
6. *Estate of Barudin v. Commissioner,* T.C. Memo 1996-395, 72 T.C.M. (CCH) 488 (1996).
7. *Estate of Schauerhamer v. Commissioner,* T.C. Memo 1997-242 (1997).
8. *Estate of Lehman v. Commissioner,* T.C. Memo 1997-392 (1997).
9. *Estate of Nowell v. Commissioner,* T.C. Memo 1999-15 (1999).
10. *Kerr v. Commissioner,* 113 T.C. No. 30, 1999 U.S. Tax Ct. LEXIS 58 (1999).
11. *Church v. United States,* 2000 U.S. Dist. LEXIS 714 (W.D. Tex 2000).
12. *Shepherd v. Commissioner,* 115 T.C. No. 30, 2000 U.S. Tax Ct. LEXIS 77 (2000).
13. *Knight v. Commissioner,* 115 T.C. No. 36, 2000 U.S. Tax Ct. LEXIS 88 (2000).
14. *Estate of Strangi v. Commissioner,* 115 T.C. No. 35, 2000 U.S. Tax Ct. LEXIS 89 (2000).
15. *Estate of Jones v. Commissioner,* 116 T.C. No. 11, 2001 U.S. Tax Ct. LEXIS 11 (2001).

Premium and Discount Issues in Undivided Interest Valuations

Daniel R. Van Vleet

When an analyst is asked to estimate the value of an undivided interest in real or personal property, the quantification and application of valuation adjustments applicable to the appraisal value of the property in fee-simple interest is often controversial. The controversy typically surrounds one or more of the following issues:

- Scarcity of empirical studies on market transactions involving undivided interests
- Economic characteristics of the subject property
- Applicability of empirical studies of fractional ownership interests to undivided interests
- Applicability and assumptions used in a partition analysis
- Applicability and assumptions used in the appraisals of assets in fee-simple interest

It is important to point out that an undivided interest is a fractional equity ownership interest and not a pro rata share of property. An undivided interest has much more in common with a minority equity position in a closely held business than with a proportional ownership interest in a real property. Consequently, asset appraisal techniques do not adequately address the economic issues of an undivided interest.

This chapter examines the relevant economic characteristics of an undivided interest and potential methods to quantify appropriate valuation adjustments to the appraised value of the underlying assets in fee-simple interest. Also provided are certain examples of court case opinions involving valuation discounts attributable to undivided interests.

DESCRIPTION AND CHARACTERISTICS OF UNDIVIDED INTERESTS

An undivided interest is a form of co-ownership in which each tenant has an equal right to use and enjoy the underlying asset. Typically, undivided interests are formed as either a joint tenancy or tenancy in common. Relevant definitions are shown in Exhibit 19.1.

Exhibit 19.1 Definitions Related to Undivided Ownership Interests

Concurrent Ownership Persons who share ownership rights simultaneously in particular property are said to be concurrent owners. The principal types of concurrent owners are twofold: (1) joint tenancy and (2) tenancy in common.

Fee Simple A fee-simple estate is one in which the owner is entitled to the entire property, with unconditional power of disposition during life, and which descends to the heirs and legal representatives upon the owner's death intestate. A fee-simple estate is unlimited as to duration, disposition, and descendibility.

Highest and Best Use The reasonably probable and legal use of vacant land or an improved property, which is physically possible, appropriately supported, financially feasible, and that results in the highest value. The four criteria of highest and best use are legal permissibility, physical possibility, financial feasibility, and maximum profitability.

Joint Tenancy A form of concurrent ownership in which each of two or more persons owns an equal and undivided interest in the whole (property), attached to which is the right of survivorship.

Partition The division of property, held by joint tenants or tenants in common, into distinct portions, so that the tenants may hold the ownership of these portions individually. Partitioning may by compulsory (judicial) or voluntary.

Right of Survivorship The right of a survivor of a deceased person to the property of said deceased. A distinguishing characteristic of a joint tenancy relationship.

Tenancy in Common A form of concurrent ownership in which each of two or more persons owns an undivided portion of the property. It is an ownership interest in which there is unity of possession but separate and distinct titles.

Unity of Interest In the case of joint tenancy, no single tenant can have a greater interest in the property than any of the others. In the case of tenancy in common, one tenant may have a larger share than any of the other tenants.

Unity of Possession The requirement that concurrent owners must hold the same undivided possession of the whole and enjoy same rights until the death of one of the tenants.

Sources: Adapted from *West's Business Law*, 6th ed., *Black's Law Dictionary*, 6th ed., and *The Dictionary of Real Estate Appraisal*, 3d ed.

Joint Tenancy

A joint tenancy is a form of concurrent ownership in which two or more people own equal and undivided interests in the whole (property). A joint tenancy has the right of survivorship. In other words, the property interest of a deceased tenant will transfer to the remaining tenant(s) and not to the heirs of the deceased. Joint tenancy can be terminated at any time prior to a tenant's death either by gift or by sale of the ownership interest.

If a joint tenancy is terminated, the new owner(s) become tenants in common unless some other arrangements have been made. A joint tenancy also can be transferred by partition; that is, the tenants can physically divide the property into equal parts when that option is legally permissible and physically possible. A joint tenant's interest can be conveyed without the approval of other tenants.

Tenancy in Common

A tenancy in common is a form of concurrent ownership in which two or more people own an undivided portion of a property. Unity of possession (i.e., all tenants are entitled to equal use and possession of the property) and separate and distinct ownership titles are necessary components of a tenancy in common.

There are two primary differences between a joint tenancy and tenancy in common:

1. A tenant in common may own a greater percentage of the property than another tenant.
2. The interest of a tenant in common does not terminate upon death (i.e., there is no right of survivorship).

Tenants in common are entitled to a pro rata share of the revenues of the property and bear the responsibility for an equivalent share of the expenses. Similar to joint tenancy, an interest in a tenancy in common can be transferred by partition and conveyed without the approval of other tenants.

General Ownership Characteristics of an Undivided Interest

An undivided interest in a property is subject to greater risk—and consequently may be a less desirable investment—than a fee-simple interest in an identical property. This additional risk is primarily attributable to the relative lack of control and lack of marketability (or liquidity) of an undivided interest when compared with a fee-simple interest.

Lack of Control.   A fee-simple owner has the following unilateral rights, among others, to:

- Use the property and maintain exclusive occupancy.
- Lease the property.
- Liquidate the property.
- Improve or maintain the property.
- Leverage the property.

These "control rights" are assumed in an appraisal of a fee-simple interest. An undivided interest does not have the unilateral ability to engage in any of these activities.

By contrast, an undivided interest only has the right to occupy the property without permission from the other cotenants. Most decisions related to the management and liquidation of the property require unanimous consent among the cotenants.

Lack of Marketability.   In addition to lack of control, an undivided interest also is characterized by a lack of marketability compared with a fee-simple interest. This lack of marketability is primarily attributable to the following:

- The market for undivided interests is limited.
- Obtaining financing for a fractional ownership interest is usually more difficult than for a fee-simple interest.
- Cotenants may be jointly and severally liable for the debt obligations of the property.
- There are expenses, risks, delays, and negative tax consequences attendant to the alternative of suing for partition of the property.
- Creditors of individual cotenants may be able to force the sale of the property.

Partition Rights.   A partition is the division of property—held by joint tenants or tenants in common—into distinct portions, so that the tenants may hold ownership of these portions individually. A partition of the property may by compulsory (i.e., judicial) or voluntary. The right to partition provides a cotenant with a theoretical liquidation option. However, partition actions may be costly and require significant delays prior to actual liquidation. The time and expense required for a partition action may substantially reduce the desirability of an undivided interest to a potential investor. Typically, investors are wary of purchasing an asset that may require litigation to obtain liquidity.

Summary of Undivided Ownership Characteristics

An undivided interest suffers from a lack of control and lack of marketability when compared with a fee-simple interest. Consequently, the market for undivided interests is limited and typically subject to discounts from the pro rata share of the appraised value in fee-simple interest. However, in *Estate of Young v. Commissioner,* the U.S. Tax Court found that a joint tenancy arrangement was not subject to valuation adjustments for undivided interests.[1] Consequently, it is important for the analyst to determine whether the subject ownership interest is a joint tenancy or tenancy in common and, thus, whether valuation adjustments are appropriate. For the purpose of this chapter, references to undivided interests will refer to tenancy in common arrangements.

APPRAISAL OF ASSETS IN FEE-SIMPLE INTEREST

Typically, the first step in determining the value of an undivided interest is to have the underlying assets appraised in fee-simple interest. This is often accomplished by an independent appraisal of the subject assets by a qualified appraiser. Appraisals of assets in fee-simple interest inherently assume that the ownership interest being appraised has all of the rights and prerogatives of control associated with a fee-simple interest. The asset appraisal may include adjustments and assumptions that only a controlling interest owner could contemplate. Consequently, the components of an appraisal in fee-simple interest may not be relevant to the valuation of an undivided interest. Therefore, the analyst should review and analyze the assumptions and approaches used to appraise the value of the property in fee-simple interest.

Asset Appraisal Approaches

Asset appraisal approaches generally are categorized as follows:

- Income approach
- Sales comparison approach
- Cost approach

Income Approach. Income approach methods are based on the premise that the value of the asset is the present value of the future income to be derived by the owners of the asset. Income approach methods typically fall into one of the following two categories:

1. Yield capitalization method
2. Direct capitalization method

The yield capitalization method is similar to the discounted cash flow method used by business appraisers. Under this method, a projection of economic returns is prepared for multiple periods over a discrete period of time. A present value discount rate is then applied to these economic returns to estimate the present value of the property in fee-simple interest. The direct capitalization method is similar except that a single period of economic returns is capitalized to conclude value.

The income approach assumptions used in an asset appraisal may affect the determination and selection of appropriate valuation adjustments for an undivided interest. For example, the appraisal may be based on a highest-and-best-use assumption that is inconsistent with the current use of the property. If so, the property may require significant modifications to achieve its highest and best use. Modifications of this type typically require significant time and the unanimous consent of all cotenants. If the other tenants are not favorably disposed to the proposed modifications, the probability of the highest-and-best-use realization may be low. Consequently, it may be necessary to consider the partition of the property and how the resulting division of ownership would affect the highest-and-best-use assumption.

In addition to highest-and-best-use issues, income approach methods involve the quantification of capitalization rates. These capitalization rates typically are based on an assumed level of interest-bearing debt. The assumed level of debt may not be appropriate for the following reasons:

- Lenders may be reluctant or unwilling to provide debt capital to a property owned by several undivided interests.
- Other cotenants may not be favorably disposed to increasing the leverage on the property.

Therefore, the assumed level of debt used in an asset appraisal may not be appropriate for the valuation of an undivided interest.

Sales Comparison Approach.   The sales comparison approach typically is based on an analysis of sales of comparable properties in fee-simple interest. Within this approach, an appraiser will make adjustments for differences between the subject property and the comparable property. These adjustments may include differences related to:

- Age of the transaction
- Physical condition of the property
- Location of the property
- Age of the property

As with the income approach, the assumptions used in the sales comparison approach may not be consistent with the appraisal of an undivided interest. For instance, if a theoretical partition of the property is used to value the undivided interest, the analyst should recognize that the fundamental characteristics of the property might change upon partition. If so, the appraised value of the property quantified using the sales comparison approach may be misleading when estimating the value of an undivided interest.

Cost Approach.   The cost approach is based on the assumption that an asset is worth no more than the costs necessary to reproduce an identical asset or an asset of equal utility. The cost approach assumes that the subject asset is fungible and that assets of similar utility may be obtained by purchase or by construction. If the asset is unique, it may not be appropriate to use the cost approach.

The cost approach often is used to appraise the value of buildings and improvements. Within this approach, assumptions are made regarding the current cost of replacing the actual buildings or improvements. These cost estimates are then adjusted for various types of depreciation, including:

- Physical deterioration
- Functional obsolescence
- Economic obsolescence

As with the sales comparison approach, the assumptions used in the cost approach may not be consistent with the appraisal of an undivided interest. For instance, it may not be possible to partition buildings or improvements. Consequently, a judge may order the sale of the property in a partition action. In that case, the cost approach may be less relevant than other asset appraisal approaches.

Asset Appraisal Information

The Financial Institution Reform, Recovery, and Enforcement Act (FIRREA) requires that appraisers comply with the Uniform Standards of Professional Appraisal Practice (USPAP) for all federally related real estate transactions. Although not mandated by law, USPAP has been adopted and endorsed by major appraisal organizations, including the Appraisal Institute and the American Society of Appraisers.

The USPAP standards state that written real property appraisal reports must be prepared in one of the following three formats:

1. Self-contained appraisal report
2. Summary appraisal report
3. Restricted use appraisal report

The essential difference between these three options is the level of disclosure. The self-contained appraisal report provides the greatest level of disclosure, and the restricted use appraisal report provides the least.

Asset appraisal information can come in other forms, including the following:

- Written or verbal estimation of sale price by a broker or auctioneer
- Property tax assessment values
- Opinions of value provided by the owner

Obviously, the best indication of asset value is provided by a contemporaneous cash transaction involving the subject property to an arm's-length buyer. Most often this type of information is not available. Consequently, a self-contained appraisal report prepared by a qualified asset appraiser is typically the best indication of value.

Summary of Asset Appraisal Factors to Consider

Analysts should be familiar with the approaches and assumptions used in the asset appraisal when valuing an undivided interest. Aggressive and unsupportable asset appraisals will cause difficulty and unnecessary complexity in supporting opinions of value for an undivided interest. Also, the assumptions used in an appraisal of assets in a fee-simple interest may not be relevant to the appraisal of an undivided interest.

FACTORS AFFECTING THE VALUE OF AN UNDIVIDED INTEREST

In most states, cotenancy rights require unanimous consent of the undivided interest owners to manage or liquidate the property. Therefore, an undivided interest suffers from a significant lack of control when compared with a fee-simple interest. Also, the market for undivided interests is very limited compared with the market for fee-simple interests. Consequently, an undivided interest has some of the same economic characteristics as a minority equity position in a closely held company. The lack of control and lack of marketability of an undivided interest are mitigated by the fact that, in most states, an investor can file suit to have the property partitioned by the court. If the court decides that the property cannot be partitioned equitably, then it can order a forced sale of the property and a division of the net proceeds after costs.

Despite the ability to achieve liquidity through a partition action, an undivided interest lacks elements of control and marketability when compared with a fee-simple interest. Consequently, it is often necessary to adjust the indication of value provided by a property appraisal to value an undivided interest properly. Assuming the analysis contained in the appraisal is reasonable and properly supported, the analyst should then consider the following relevant factors:

- Partition of the property
- Operational business enterprise
- Financial performance of the property
- Debt obligations
- Prior transactions in the undivided interests
- Number of owners

Partition of the Property

One of the most consistent themes in various court cases dealing with undivided interests is an analysis of the expense and time necessary to conduct a judicial partition of the subject property. When conducting a partition analysis, the analyst should obtain answers to the following questions:

- Is a partition legally permissible and physically possible?
- Would a partition action result in the sale of the entire property or merely a division of ownership?
- Would a division of ownership change the assumptions used in the appraisal of assets in fee-simple interest?
- Are the assumed future proceeds based on a highest-and-best-use analysis that is inconsistent with the current use of the subject property?

- What are the out-of-pocket expenses associated with the partitioning action?
- How much time is necessary to conduct the partition action and liquidate the property?
- Will the property generate income and/or necessitate expenses during the assumed time period necessary to conduct a partition action?
- What is the appropriate present value discount rate applicable to the future proceeds derived from a partition action?

Operational Business Enterprise

The empirical studies of valuation adjustments for lack of control or lack of marketability are based most often on transactions of securities of operational business enterprises. In general, these studies fall into one of the following categories:

- Private transactions in the common stock of companies prior to an initial public offering
- Price to net asset value of registered limited partnership interests
- Price to net asset value of closed-end mutual funds
- Private transactions of restricted stocks (i.e., letter stock) of publicly traded companies
- Acquisition premiums paid by acquirers of publicly traded companies

Occasionally the courts have been critical of the naïve application of these empirical studies when the underlying assets of an undivided interest did not involve an operational business enterprise. For instance, certain courts have criticized the application of discounts for lack of control to the appraised value of nonoperational assets such as vacant land.

Financial Performance of the Property

Undivided interests are entitled to a pro rata share of the revenues and expenses attributable to the property. Consequently, a property with a history of income or expenses may be a more or less desirable investment, depending on the historical and projected financial performance. Obviously, properties that are expected to provide substantial cash distributions are more desirable than otherwise identical properties with little or no anticipated cash distributions. Also, the projected income and expenses associated with a property during the time period necessary to conduct a partition action will likely be a consideration in the valuation of an undivided interest.

Debt Obligations

Typically, debt obligations attributable to a property are subtracted from the appraised value in the process of valuing an undivided interest. In addition to this calculation, the analyst should ask the following questions:

- Are the cotenants jointly and severally liable for the debt obligations of the property?
- Would the partition and sale of the property result in the call of the debt obligation?
- Are the debt obligations assumable by the purchaser of an undivided interest?

Depending on the answers to these questions, the analyst may elect to increase or decrease the valuation adjustment applicable to the appraised value of the property in fee-simple interest.

Prior Transactions in the Undivided Interest

Almost without exception, the analyst should consider arm's-length transactions in the subject undivided interest during the three- to five-year period prior to the valuation date. In most cases, historical transactions involving the subject interest do not exist. If transactions are present, often they were not on an arm's-length basis. Consequently, a review of the factors and motivations behind any historical transaction should be conducted.

Number of Cotenants

Another factor to consider is the total number of cotenants. The complexity of managing any asset increases with the number of cotenants. Consequently, the relative lack of control increases as the number of cotenants increases. However, even if the property has only two cotenants, valuation adjustments for lack of control and lack of marketability typically are justified.

VALUATION ADJUSTMENTS FOR UNDIVIDED INTERESTS

If the starting point for an appraisal of an undivided interest is the appraised value of the underlying property in fee-simple interest, valuation adjustments for lack of control and lack of marketability should be considered. Ideally, these discounts should be derived from empirical studies of market transactions involving undivided interests. Unfortunately, transactions in undivided interests typically are conducted between private parties, and the pertinent data are difficult or impossible to obtain. Thus, the analyst should consider whether to use proxies for valuation adjustments derived from market evidence and/or empirical studies of other types of ownership interests. This section provides a brief summary of these studies and market evidence as well as a discussion of valuation adjustments based on a theoretical partition of the subject property.

Lack of Control

Empirical studies and/or market evidence on lack of control valuation adjustments generally fall into one of the following categories: acquisition premiums paid by acquirers of publicly traded companies or publicly traded real estate investment trusts (REITs).

Acquisition Premium Evidence. Acquisition premiums paid for publicly traded companies often are used to quantify the discount for lack of control. The notion that acquisition premiums paid for publicly traded companies are attributable solely to issues surrounding control is subject to debate as of this writing, as discussed in Chapters 2 and 3. However, these empirical studies indicate that investors are generally willing to pay more for the acquisition of an entire business enterprise than for a minority interest position on a pro rata basis. If control premiums are used in the analysis of an undivided interest, the analyst should attempt to locate financial acquisitions of acquired companies with similar risk profiles as the subject property.

Publicly Traded Real Estate Investment Trusts (REITs). Publicly traded REITs may provide additional market evidence regarding the discount for lack of control. A comparison of the public price of REIT units to the underlying net asset value of the properties owned by the REIT may provide insight into the valuation adjustment that investors consider appropriate for a minority interest position in a publicly traded REIT.

Lack of Marketability

Empirical studies on the lack of marketability generally fall into one of the following categories: private transactions of restricted stocks (i.e., letter stock) of publicly traded companies or private transactions in the common stock of companies prior to an initial public offering. These studies were described in Chapter 5.

The restricted stock studies quantify the price discount for securities that are restricted from trading for a specified period of time. Upon the removal of these restrictions, the securities will possess all the benefits of an unrestricted publicly traded stock, including a liquid market. Conversely, the prospect for liquidity of undivided interests may be dependent on a partition of the subject property. A partition action may require costly litigation and several years to complete. Consequently, the empirical evidence provided by restricted stock studies may understate the appropriate valuation adjustment when used to value an undivided interest.

In general, the empirical studies on the lack-of-marketability discounts are based on transactions of securities of operational business enterprises. If the risk profile of the property owned by the undivided interests is different from the risk profile of the securities included in the empirical studies, the appropriate discount for lack of marketability may be different. For instance, the historical price volatility and risk profile of real estate tends to be less than that of publicly traded equity securities. Thus, there is less risk associated with a mandatory holding period for real estate than for corporate equity securities. Based solely on this factor, the discount for lack of marketability would be less for an undivided interest than for publicly traded equity securities.

Combined Lack of Control and Lack of Marketability

Publicly syndicated limited partnership interests trade in a limited and somewhat illiquid secondary market. Also, limited partnership interests have no vote in the operations of a partnership. These ownership interests therefore suffer from a lack of control and lack of ready marketability. Consequently, transactions involving these partnership interests can be studied and used to quantify combined discounts for lack of control and lack of marketability.

Limited Partnership Interest Studies.   *The Partnership Spectrum* is a research publication published by Partnership Profiles, Inc. that tracks the secondary market in publicly registered limited partnership interests. This publication provides the market trading prices of the limited partnership interests as well as distribution yields and the estimated net asset value of the partnerships. The partnerships studied in *The Partnership Spectrum* contain a variety of assets, including undeveloped land, triple-net lease programs, cable and television systems, conventional real estate, and oil and gas properties.

The Partnership Spectrum conducts an annual survey that compares the market price of limited partnership interests with the pro rata net asset value of the partnership. The results of these surveys for the 1993 through 2000 period are presented in Exhibit 19.2.

As indicated by the studies highlighted in the exhibit, there is a general trend of slightly declining price-to-net-asset-value discounts in recent years, especially for partnerships that consistently pay significant distributions or carry low levels of debt. This may be attributable to an increase in the number of partnership liquidations in recent years. Even with this slight decline, the price-to-net-asset-value discounts remain significant.

Similarly to undivided interests, registered limited partnership interests suffer from lack of control and a relative lack of marketability compared with fee-simple interests. However, these partnership interests are generally more liquid than undivided interests. Typically, it takes approximately two to three months to effectively liquidate a registered limited partnership interest. Theoretically, it may take years to liquidate an undivided interest, especially if a partition action is required.

These limited partnership interests trade at significant price discounts to the net asset value of the underlying assets. As a result, one would expect that undivided interests—which are less liquid than limited partnership interests—would be subject

Exhibit 19.2 *The Partnership Spectrum* Annual Survey Results, 1993–2000

1993 Study

	Number of LPs	Average Discount (%)
Equity	65	51
Triple Net Lease	21	20
Equity/Mortgage Hybrids	9	60
Mortgages—Uninsured	12	59
Mortgages—Insured	7	13
Mortgages—Zero Coupon	3	78

1994 Study

	Number of LPs	Average Discount (%)
Equity—Distributing	71	49
Equity—Nondistributing	17	76
Triple-Net Lease	22	19
Equity/Mortgage Hybrids	23	54
Mortgages—Uninsured	6	53
Mortgages—Insured	4	28

1995 Study

	Number of LPs	Average Discount (%)
Equity—Distributing	87	41
Equity—Nondistributing	32	64
Triple-Net Lease	26	20
Equity/Mortgage Hybrids	24	42
Mortgages—Uninsured	6	44
Mortgages—Insured	14	19

1996 Study

	Number of LPs	Average Discount (%)
Equity—Distributing	77	37
Equity—Nondistributing	33	56
Triple-Net Lease	27	22
Equity/Mortgage Hybrids	15	37
Mortgages—Uninsured	3	66
Mortgages—Insured	12	25

1997 Study

	Number of LPs	Average Discount (%)
Equity—Distributing (No Debt)	48	28
Equity—Distributing	24	37
Equity—Nondistributing	27	42
Triple-Net Lease	19	16
Mortgages—Insured	12	20

continued

305

Exhibit 19.2   *The Partnership Spectrum* Annual Survey Results, 1993–2000
                   —continued

1998 Study

	Number of LPs	Average Discount (%)	Average Yield (%)
Equity—Distributing (Low Debt)	34	27	8.0
Equity—Distributing	29	36	6.7
Equity—Nondistributing	21	43	0.0
Triple-Net Lease	19	17	9.7
Mortgages—Insured	10	12	9.8

1999 Study

	Number of LPs	Average Discount (%)	Average Yield (%)
Equity—Distributing (Low/No Debt)	27	25	8.8
Equity—Distributing (Larger Debt)	17	35	6.9
Equity—Nondistributing	15	46	0.0
Undeveloped Land	4	46	0.0
Triple-Net Lease	22	14	9.5
Mortgages—Insured	10	14	11.8

2000 Study

	Number of LPs	Average Discount (%)	Average Yield (%)
Equity—Distributing (Low/No Debt)	24	24	9.2
Equity—Distributing (Higher Debt)	18	26	7.7
Equity—Nondistributing	9	35	0.0
Undeveloped Land	3	40	0.0
Triple-Net Lease	24	21	10.5
Mortgages—Insured	9	21	12.5

Source: The Partnership Spectrum (May/June 1993–2000).

to even greater valuation discounts. When using this information to value an undivided interest, it is appropriate to evaluate the distribution yields and level of debt associated with the subject property.

Partition Analysis

A theoretical partition of the property often is used to quantify a valuation adjustment to apply to the appraised value in fee-simple interest. This analysis estimates the value of an undivided interest by subtracting the costs attributable to a partition action from the appraised value of the property. The Internal Revenue Service generally favors this approach and often assumes that the total economic cost to partition is limited to out-of-pocket attorney fees and that these expenses are borne equally by all cotenants. Neither of these assumptions is necessarily correct.

When conducting a partition analysis, the analyst should consider whether a partition action would result in the sale of the entire property or merely a division of ownership. If the property can be partitioned, it may be necessary to consider whether the division of ownership would change the underlying assumptions used in the appraisal of the interest. For instance, the shape or configuration of land may be an important characteristic of the appraisal value. If the property is theoretically partitioned, the assumptions used in the appraisal may no longer be relevant.

A partition analysis is primarily based on the following three factors:

1. Quantification of the proceeds and expenses
2. Amount of time necessary to conduct a partition action
3. Present value discount rate used to estimate the present value of the proceeds and expenses

Proceeds and Expenses of a Partition Action.   The future value of the net proceeds available from the hypothetical sale of the property should be considered in the analysis. The future value of the property should be based on the projected price appreciation of the property, if any, during the partition period. Also, the expenses necessary to liquidate the property should be considered in the determination of the future net proceeds. These expenses may include sales commissions, legal fees, survey fees, taxes, and so forth. The present value of these future net proceeds can then be estimated using a present value discount rate appropriate for undivided interests. If the property is expected to produce income or incur expenses during the partition period, the present value of these projected revenues and expenses should be recognized and included in the analysis.

The expenses associated with a partition action should also be estimated and included. These expenses may include the following, among others:

- Attorney fees
- Court costs
- Survey expenses
- Expenses related to governmental licensing and zoning changes
- Costs associated with the replacement of shared infrastructure

The present value of these expenses should be calculated using an appropriate present value discount rate.

Partition Period.   The amount of time necessary to conduct a partition varies by jurisdiction and by the characteristics of the subject property. Generally, the courts have considered two to four years to be reasonable. Under certain circumstances, the partition period may be longer. If the appraised value in fee-simple interest is estimated based on a highest-and-best-use assumption that is inconsistent with the current use of the subject property, the assumed length of time associated with conversion and subsequent partition may be significantly greater than two to four years.

Present Value Discount Rate.   The calculation of a present value discount rate to use in a partition analysis should consider the following ownership characteristics of an undivided interest:

- Lack of control over the management and operations of the property
- A likely holding period of two to four years
- The prospect of negative economic consequences resulting from actions by other cotenants
- The expenses and headaches associated with litigation in order to achieve liquidity

Often the courts will use capitalization rates derived from appraisals of fee-simple interests to estimate the value of the economic returns associated with a partition action. These rates of return are derived from transactions involving the sales of entire properties in fee-simple interest. Thus, the capitalization rates assume a controlling interest owner with the ability to liquidate the assets at will. Obviously, these assumptions are not valid for an undivided interest. A capitalization rate derived from the sales of properties in fee-simple interest is likely understated when used to estimate the present value of proceeds attributable to an undivided interest. Therefore, other proxy present value discount rates should be considered.

Depending on the characteristics of the underlying property, it may be possible to identify proxy rates of return from publicly available market evidence. Since an undivided interest is an equity interest in the subject property, the following sources of equity rates of return should be considered:

- *Cost of Capital Quarterly,* Ibbotson Associates a source of equity rates of returns on publicly traded companies in a wide variety of industries. Data is sorted by standard industrial classification (SIC) code.
- *Stocks, Bonds, Bills and Inflation, Valuation Edition,* Ibbotson Associates a source of equity risk premiums of publicly traded companies. This data typically is used in the capital asset pricing model (CAPM) to quantify equity rates of return specific to certain industries.
- *Appraiser News,* Appraisal Institute—a source of equity yield rates for real property investments. These rates of return typically are based on transactions involving fee-simple interests.
- *Korpacz Real Estate Investor Survey,* PriceWaterhouseCoopers—a source of equity yield rates for real property investments. These rates of return typically are based on transactions involving fee-simple interests.
- *Real Estate Report,* Real Estate Research Corporation—a source of equity yield rates for real property investments. These rates of return typically are based on transactions involving fee-simple interests.

The equity rates of returns provided by these publications may assist in quantifying appropriate present value discount rates for undivided interests. The Ibbotson

Associates equity rates assume the ownership interest is readily marketable and lacks control. The Appraisal Institute and PriceWaterhouseCoopers studies assume the equity ownership is in fee-simple interest. Consequently, it may be necessary to adjust the indications of value provided by these rates of return for lack of control and/or lack of marketability.

Summary of Valuation Adjustments Discussion

Although no universally accepted rule to assist in the selection of valuation adjustments has been developed, the following factors should be considered in the analysis:

- Historical and projected cash distributions to the undivided interest
- Historical and projected income and expenses of the subject property
- Total number of undivided interest owners
- Length of time and expenses necessary to conduct a partition action
- Whether the subject property can be subdivided
- Arm's-length transactions involving comparable undivided interests
- Length of time necessary to sell the subject property at the conclusion of a partition action if physical partition is impossible or impractical
- The assumptions and analysis used in the appraisal of the subject property in fee-simple interest
- The debt obligations of the subject property

COURT DECISIONS RELATED TO UNDIVIDED INTEREST DISCOUNTS

The courts consider a variety of quantitative and qualitative factors when determining the value of an undivided interest. Obviously, each decision is based on various facts and circumstances. In general, no valuation methodologies for undivided interests are universally accepted by the courts. As a result, analysts should be familiar with the factors that influence courts' thinking regarding the valuation of undivided interests.

The courts have been somewhat fickle in their selection and application of valuation adjustments. Certain courts have allowed valuation adjustments of nearly 45%. Other courts have selected valuation adjustments closer to 5 to 10%. Some courts have cited the relative lack of control and lack of marketability of an undivided interest when compared with a fee-simple interest. Other courts have solely focused on the out-of-pocket expenses associated with a partition action. Obviously, the facts and circumstances of each court case differ. Also, the quality and nature of the fee-simple interest appraisal report can have a substantial impact on the disposition of the court towards valuation adjustments.

Estate of Forbes v. Commissioner. [2] One of the primary issues in this case was the fair market value of undivided interests in two parcels of real property held in a qualified terminable interest property (QTIP) trust. The undivided interests at issue included a 42% undivided interest in 3,321 acres and a 42.9% undivided interest in 2,033 acres. The value of the undivided interest reported on the decedent's federal estate tax return included a 30% fractional interest discount.

The taxpayer and the IRS stipulated that the fair market value of the entire 5,354 acres of the subject property in fee-simple interest was $1,746,795. The taxpayer then adjusted this value downward using a 30% discount. At trial, the expert for the taxpayer testified that a valuation discount was appropriate because the undivided interests lacked control and also ready marketability. The expert did not locate comparable sales but testified that local real estate brokers had applied fractional interest discounts of 10 to 30% in liquidating partnerships. In calculating the valuation adjustment, the expert also took into consideration the following:

- Specific characteristics of the subject property
- Limited pool of potential buyers
- The difficulty of securing financing
- The costs of partitioning the two separate parcels
- Possible intrafamily conflicts
- Other factors adversely affecting the marketability of the undivided interests

He concluded that a valuation discount of 30% was appropriate.

The expert for the IRS identified and selected "comparable" transactions that the court did not consider credible or relevant. Incredibly, this expert's own comparable transactions indicated valuation discounts in the range of 25 to 64%. With little explanation, this expert then selected 18% as the appropriate valuation adjustment. Consequently, the court disregarded the testimony from the IRS expert.

In general, the court expressed dissatisfaction with the analysis provided by all experts. The court conceded that this lack of support might have been attributable to the lack of available empirical data related to undivided interests. Since the taxpayer and the IRS agreed that some valuation discount was warranted, the court accepted the taxpayer's expert's recommendation for a 30% valuation discount.

Estate of Busch v. Commissioner. [3] At the date of death, the decedent owned a 50% undivided interest in 90.74 acres of real property. In its decision, the court calculated the value of the property in its highest and best use as a residential development in fee-simple interest. Since the property was not a residential development at the date of death, the court determined the value of the property based on the future proceeds derived from the hypothetical sale of the property as a residential development.

The court concluded the initial value of the property at $13.6 million based on appraisals of the property in fee-simple interest provided by experts for the taxpayer and the IRS. The court then assumed it would require three to six years to convert the property to its highest and best use as a residential development. The future value of the property three to six years into the future was assumed to be the appraised value in fee-simple interest as of the date of death. These future proceeds were then discounted back to the present value at a 9% discount rate to conclude a value of $9.3 million. The 9% discount rate was derived from capitalization rates provided in the property appraisal reports. The court then subtracted from this amount the out-of-pocket costs associated with a judicial partitioning of the property. The out-of-pocket costs were estimated based on a factor of 10% of the appraised value of the undivided interest. Based on the court's calculations, the total discount from the appraised value in fee-simple interest appraisal was over 38%. A summary of the court's calculations is provided in Exhibit 19.3.

Estate of Williams v. Commissioner.[4]   At the date of death, the decedent owned a 50% undivided interest in Florida timberland. In this case, the court accepted the tax-payer's 44% total discount from the appraised value of the property in fee-simple interest. This decision ignored the position often taken by the IRS that any discount from the appraised value of the property in fee-simple interest should be limited to the estimated cost of a partition action. The 44% discount was based on a lack-of-control discount of 30% and a lack-of-marketability discount of 20%, with the two discounts applied multiplicatively. The court considered the potential $413,000 in partition costs and real estate commissions of 10% that would be incurred upon the partition and sale of the property in determining the discount for lack of control. The court viewed the lack of relevant market transactions in undivided interests as an indication of the lack of marketability of the subject interest.

The expert for the IRS argued that a business appraiser was not qualified to value the subject undivided interests. The court disagreed, stating that taxpayer's expert "was an experienced business appraiser who has given expert opinions in valuing fractional interests in partnerships, businesses and real property." The court went on to say that he "correctly considered various factors affecting the potential costs of partitioning the properties in issue," "the time and expense of selling real property in that market," and "gave a reasonable explanation" for his discounts.

Exhibit 19.3   Tax Court's Calculations in *Estate of Busch v. Commissioner*

Value of the Property in Fee-Simple Estate[a]	$13,611,000
Present Value of the Sales Proceeds[b]	$9,312,992
Multiplied by: Undivided Interest Percentage	50.0%
Equals: Value Attributable to the Subject Undivided Interest	$4,656,496
Less: Cost to Partition[c]	$466,000
Equals: Value of the Undivided Interest	$4,190,496
Total Discount from Fee-Simple Appraisal[d]	38.4%

[a]Proceeds available from the hypothetical sale in three to six years.
[b]Assumes a 9% present value discount rate.
[c]$4,656,496 × 10%.
[d]1 − [($4,190,496 × 2) / $13,611,000].

Exhibit 19.4   Tax Court's Calculations in *Estate of Williams v. Commissioner*

Value of the Property in Fee-Simple Estate	$3,093,250
Multiplied by: Undivided Interest Percentage	50.0%
Equals: Value Attributable to the Subject Undivided Interest	$1,546,625
Less: Lack of Control Discount @ 30%	$463,988
Equals: Marketable Minority Value	$1,082,637
Less: Lack of Marketability Discount @ 20%	$216,527
Equals: Nonmarketable Minority Value	$866,110
Total Discount from Fee-Simple Appraisal[a]	44.0%

[a] $1 - [(\$866,110 \times 2) / \$3,093,250]$.

A summary of the courts calculations are provided in Exhibit 19.4.

In the *Williams* decision, the court recognized real estate commissions associated with the partitioning and sale of the property. The court also acknowledged that an undivided interest suffers from both lack of control and lack of marketability and applied these discounts in succession. If further acknowledged that business valuation experts are qualified to value an undivided interest in real property.

Estate of Barge v. Commissioner.[5]   The taxpayer and the IRS stipulated that the fair market value of the Mississippi timberland in fee-simple interest was $40 million. The taxpayer requested that the court apply a discount of 50% to the appraised value of the property in order to calculate the value of the undivided interests. The record is unclear whether the taxpayer's experts—who were registered foresters—provided any empirical evidence that would establish discounts for lack of control or lack of marketability.

In its decision, the court used a partition analysis to calculate the value of the undivided interest. The partition analysis was based on the following assumptions:

- A 10% present value discount rate
- A partition period of four years
- A future income stream of $293,000 per year
- A $41 million property value at the end of four years
- Estimated partition costs of $1,325,000 allocated evenly to each 50% ownership interest over the four-year partition period

Exhibit 19.5 provides a summary of the court's calculations.

The court determined the fair market value of the 1987 gift to be $7,404,649, resulting in an effective undivided interest discount of 26% from the appraised value in fee-simple interest. The present value discount rate used by the court was derived from information contained in the asset appraisals. It appears that the court did not consider costs associated with marketing and selling the partitioned property at the

Exhibit 19.5   Tax Court's Calculations in *Estate of Barge v. Commissioner*

Year	Timber Income	Partition Costs	Partition Payment[a]	Total	Present Value[b]
1	$293,000	$165,625	$0	$127,375	$115,795
2	$293,000	$165,625	$0	$127,325	$105,268
3	$293,000	$165,625	$0	$127,325	$95,699
4	$293,000	$165,625	$10,250,000	$127,325	$7,087,887
Total					$7,404,649
Total Discount from Fee-Simple Appraisal					26.0%

[a]Assumes that the appraised fee-simple value of the property will increase from $40 million to $41 million during the four-year partition period.
[b]Based on a present value discount rate of 10%.

end of the four-year period. Also, the court did not address the propriety of using a capitalization rate derived from an appraisal of a fee-simple interest as the present value discount rate in determining the value of an undivided interest.

Shepherd v. Commissioner.[6]   The taxpayer provided an appraisal report that indicated that the value of property in fee-simple interest was $400,000. Experts for the IRS determined that the value of the property in fee-simple interest was $1,278,600. The taxpayer presented three real estate appraisers to support its valuation of the leased timberland. Each appraiser used slightly different approaches and assumptions. Two of the appraisers applied discounts for undivided interests of 27% and 15%, respectively. The IRS presented one appraiser who appraised the value of the land in fee-simple interest using an income approach at $1,547,000. The determination of value by the IRS's expert reflected no discounts for lack of control or lack of marketability.

The experts for the taxpayer and the IRS disagreed over the following issues:

- Valuation discounts for the undivided interest
- The discount rate to use in calculating the present value of the property lease payments
- Whether to use pretax or after-tax lease income in the discounting calculation

The IRS argued that the discount for an undivided interest should be limited to the cost to partition. The court rejected this argument, saying that this approach failed to give adequate consideration to factors such as lack of control in managing and disposing of the property.

Ultimately, the court determined that one of the taxpayer's experts had taken the lack of marketability into the calculation of the capitalization rate used in the appraisal of the fee-simple appraisal interest. This same expert then opined that an appropriate discount for the undivided interest was 27%. The court determined that this analysis amounted to double counting. Consequently, the court rejected the expert's opinion on undivided interest discounts. The taxpayer's other expert concluded an undivided interest discount of 15% based on the following:

- Lack of control
- Potential disposition of the property due to disagreements between co-owners
- The negative consequences of a partitioning action

Apparently, no empirical evidence was offered to establish any of these discounts. The court ultimately concluded that the appropriate discount for the undivided interest was 15%.

The IRS's expert concluded that the discount should be limited to the estimated cost to partition of $25,000. The court rejected this opinion as "failing to give adequate weight to other reasons for discounting a fractional interest in the leased land, such as lack of control in managing and disposing of the property."

SUMMARY

Undivided interests suffer from a variety of relatively unattractive economic and ownership characteristics. These characteristics contribute to the relative lack of marketability of these ownership interests when compared with fee-simple interests. The dearth of market-based data on undivided interests is indicative of the limited and inefficient market for these ownership interests. Also, the lack of control associated with an undivided interest leaves the unsatisfied investor with one of three options:

1. Sell the ownership interest to the other cotenants.
2. Attempt to locate another willing investor.
3. Conduct a potentially protracted and expensive partition lawsuit.

Whichever means is selected to obtain liquidity, it is likely that the resulting transaction price will be considerably less than the pro rata value of the property in fee-simple interest.

Empirical studies and market evidence related to valuation adjustments for lack of control and lack of marketability generally are available to the analyst. This information may provide guidance in selecting appropriate valuation adjustments for undivided interests. Market transaction evidence also may be available for undivided interests. The applicability of this evidence, however, generally is limited due to the differing characteristics that the subject undivided interests may have when compared with the undivided interests involved in the market transactions. These differences may include various transaction dates, geographic locations, and types of property, among others.

The analyst should attempt to locate transactions involving comparable undivided interests; however, the results of this exercise often are less than satisfactory. Consequently, the analyst should consider whether empirical studies and market evidence regarding other types of ownership interests are applicable to the subject undivided interest. To the extent that the general characteristics of the securities in the empirical studies differ from undivided interests, these differences should be pointed out in the valuation report and appropriate adjustments made.

Almost without exception, a theoretical partition of the property should be considered in the analysis. A partition analysis should be based on all of the costs and proceeds associated with a partition and subsequent sale of a property. Also, an appropriate present value discount rate—consistent with the risks and investment characteristics of an undivided interest—should be quantified and applied in the analysis. Remember that capitalization rates used in the appraisals of fee-simple interests are not necessarily relevant to the analysis of an undivided interest.

The valuation of an undivided interest requires knowledge and expertise from two appraisal disciplines: asset appraisal and business valuation appraisal. The court decisions seem to indicate that litigants often rely on asset appraisal experts to value both the underlying assets and the undivided interest. The courts continue to express frustration with the lack of reasonable evidence and supportable analysis when determining the value of an undivided interest.

It is important to point out that an undivided interest is a fractional equity ownership interest and not a pro rata share of property. An undivided interest has much more in common with a minority equity position in a closely held business than with a proportional ownership interest in a real property. Consequently, asset appraisal techniques do not adequately address the economic issues of an undivided interest. Therefore, it is inappropriate to automatically assume that an asset appraiser is qualified to appraise the value of an undivided interest.

Notes

1. *Estate of Young v. Commissioner,* 110 T.C. 297 (1998).
2. *Estate of Forbes v. Commissioner,* T.C. Memo 2001-72 (2001).
3. *Estate of Busch v. Commissioner,* T.C. Memo 2000-3, 79 T.C.M. (CCH) 1276 (2000).
4. *Estate of Williams v. Commissioner,* T.C. Memo 1998-59, 75 T.C.M. (CCH) 1758 (1998).
5. *Estate of Barge v. Commissioner,* T.C. Memo 1997-188, 73 T.C.M. (CCH) 2615 (1997).
6. *Shepherd v. Commissioner,* 2000 U.S. Tax Ct. LEXIS 77 115 T.C. 376 (2000).

Chapter 20

Common Errors in Applying Discounts and Premiums

This chapter discusses some of the most common errors in applying discounts and premiums that have been encountered repeatedly in actual practice. I hope that the chapter will provide a heads-up so that practitioners will not allow such errors to slip through in the future.

Perhaps more importantly I hope that this chapter will help the reviewer of an appraisal report—whether a supervisor, lawyer, judge, trustee, IRS agent or examiner, or other interested party—to identify any such errors for what they are and not allow them to be accepted by the decision maker without challenge.

USING SYNERGISTIC ACQUISITION PREMIUMS TO QUANTIFY PREMIUMS FOR CONTROL

In many cases, if not a majority, premiums paid in corporate takeover transactions include some part of the value of synergies to the buyer. If the object is to value the company on a stand-alone basis, as is the case in dissenting stockholder or corporate dissolution actions, data involving premiums for synergistic acquisitions should not form part of the basis for the control premium. Analysts can eliminate synergistic transactions by utilizing the transaction purpose codes in the *Control Premium Study* (online version at BVMarketdata.com) back from the beginning of 1998.

If fair market value is the applicable standard of value, then normally any value that reflects synergies would not be appropriate. The reason is because the synergies would be applicable to a *particular* buyer, thus resulting in *investment value,* while fair market value reflects value to a *hypothetical* buyer. The exception to this rule is in situations in which there is a *group* of prospective buyers having the same synergies with the subject, in which case they might collectively create a market, as with industries undergoing consolidation.

ASSUMING THAT THE DISCOUNTED CASH FLOW VALUATION METHOD ALWAYS PRODUCES A MINORITY VALUE

Some believe that the discounted cash flow (DCF) valuation method always results in a minority value. Thus, when seeking a control value and using a DCF valuation result as a starting point, such people would always apply a control premium. They are wrong.

The reasoning leading to the conclusion that DCF always results in a minority value is based on the fact that the discount rate used in the DCF method often is developed using Ibbotson Associates' data, which are based on minority interest public trading prices. While this is correct, it does *not* follow that DCF values necessarily are minority. As discussed in Chapter 2, the DCF can produce *either* a minority or a control value. *Whether the DCF result represents a minority or control value depends primarily on whether control or minority cash flows are projected in the analysis, not on the discount rate.* The discount rate varies little or not at all between minority and control DCF valuations. So when faced with a DCF base value, it is necessary to examine the underlying assumptions, especially the minority or control nature of the projected cash flows, to determine whether a control premium is warranted.

ASSUMING THAT THE GUIDELINE PUBLIC COMPANY METHOD ALWAYS PRODUCES A MINORITY VALUE

As detailed in Chapters 1 and 2, marketable minority interests in the public market can provide an indication of value for a private company that is below, at, or above what control buyers would be expected to pay, based on either a guideline merged and acquired company analysis, a DCF analysis, or a capitalization analysis. When the guideline public company market value is at or above control value, application of a control premium could significantly overvalue a firm. Likewise, failure to apply a discount for lack of control could overvalue a minority interest.

This is a new perspective on the meaning of public market data and where it fits as a level of value (see Exhibits 1.2, 1.3, 1.4, 2.3, 2.4, and 2.5). Although it is not without controversy, professionals should be aware of and understand this perspective. Appraisers can no longer blindly apply control premiums to public market value indicators to derive control value. Nor can they safely assume that discounts for lack of control must never be applied when using guideline public companies as the base.

VALUING UNDERLYING ASSETS RATHER THAN STOCK OR PARTNERSHIP INTERESTS

Sometimes reports determine the underlying net asset value and then simply assume that the stock or partnership interest is worth a proportionate share. That is almost never the case. An intervening entity between the owner and the assets almost always leads to a lower value for the minority stock or partnership interest than for a proportional share of the assets. This is because the owner of the stock or partnership assets has no control over those assets. The entity shareowner cannot redeploy, liquidate, or hypothecate the assets. It is for this reason that discounts from net asset value usually are greater for stock or partnership interests than for individual fractional direct ownership interests in assets.

USING MINORITY INTEREST MARKETABILITY DISCOUNT DATA TO QUANTIFY MARKETABILITY DISCOUNTS FOR CONTROLLING INTERESTS

Examiners who conduct the peer reviews of reports submitted for accreditation for both the American Society of Appraisers and the Institute of Business Appraisers say that a common failure is trying to support discounts for lack of marketability for controlling interests with empirical data from observed minority interest transactions.

Extensive empirical studies are available, as detailed in this book, to help quantify discounts for lack of marketability for minority interests. However, starting with such data and somehow moving from there to a controlling interest discount for lack of marketability is an unacceptable leap of faith, not grounded in a logical connection. The rationale for discounts for lack of marketability for controlling interests is different from the reasons for discounts for lack of marketability for minority interests. Chapter 9 explains this difference.

USING ONLY RESTRICTED STOCK STUDIES (AND NOT PRE-INITIAL PUBLIC OFFERING STUDIES) AS BENCHMARK FOR DISCOUNTS FOR LACK OF MARKETABILITY

Even though pre-IPO studies have been available and well publicized for over a decade, some analysts only reference restricted stock studies as a benchmark for discounts for lack of marketability. Judge Carolyn Chiechi commented on the shortcoming of this limited focus in *Estate of Davis v. Commissioner:*[1]

> We agree [with the estate] and find that [the IRS's expert] should have considered the pre-valuation date price data reflected in those IPO studies because they, together with the restricted stock studies, would have provided a more accurate base range and starting point for determining the appropriate lack-of-marketability discount than the base range that he determined.

INADEQUATE ANALYSIS OF RELEVANT FACTORS

For every type of premium or discount addressed in this book, the discussion has included the relevant factors that bear on the validity and the magnitude of the particular discount or premium. When dealing with any premium or discount issue, it is helpful to refer to the applicable chapter to develop a check list of relevant factors to investigate and discuss.

It is amazing how many "experts" throw out a number with little or no analysis. Courts tend to reject such unsupported conclusions.

INDISCRIMINATE USE OF AVERAGE DISCOUNTS OR PREMIUMS

As seen in the empirical data throughout this book, the dispersion observed in most categories of discounts and premiums is quite wide. Yet many appraisal reports simply apply a discount or premium based on the averages without analysis of why the discount or premium applicable to the subject should be at, above, or below the average.

When adequate data is available, the best methodology to quantify the discount or premium in the particular case is to select a subset from the data with characteristics most directly comparable to the subject and base the amount of the discount or premium on that group rather than on the broad average of the total data. When this procedure is not feasible, then the broad average may serve as a benchmark and a discussion of the factors affecting the subject relative to the typical factors in the broad average can support either an adjustment upward or downward from the average or else the conclusion that the average actually is applicable to the subject.

This error is especially acute in applying control premiums. If doing so using the *Control Premium Study,* the analyst should recompute the medians to include negative premiums and eliminate synergistic transactions. Even better, use average market multiples. The *Control Premium Study* gives five market value multiples for each transaction. The analyst can select the most comparable transactions and use the multiples to develop a guideline merged and acquired company method.

APPLYING (OR OMITTING) A PREMIUM OR DISCOUNT INAPPROPRIATELY FOR THE LEGAL CONTEXT

As noted in several places in the book, discounts or premiums that might be appropriate in one legal context might be disallowed in another. For example, a minority interest discount that might be clearly applicable in a valuation for tax purposes under the standard of *fair market value* might be either totally disallowed or questionable in a dissenter's appraisal rights action under some states' interpretation of the standard of *fair value*. It is important to study the legal context, especially the case law, to determine whether there is clear direction on the applicability of any particular discount or premium being considered.

APPLYING DISCOUNTS OR PREMIUMS TO THE ENTIRE CAPITAL STRUCTURE RATHER THAN ONLY TO EQUITY

Most, if not all, of the discounts and premiums, and the empirical data to quantify them, are based on the company's common equity, not on its entire capital structure. Occasionally, someone applies a percentage discount or premium to the entire capital structure when the basis for the percentage was equity observations. This inflates the dollar amount of the discount or premium and thus incorrectly determines the value of the subject interest.

QUANTIFYING DISCOUNTS OR PREMIUMS BASED ON PAST COURT CASES

Past court cases are *not* the basis on which to quantify any of the discounts or premiums discussed in this book. Courts will not accept expert testimony on magnitudes of discounts or premiums based on other court decisions. Courts take the position that the facts and circumstances of each case are unique. They demand empirical data and/or analysis as directly relevant as possible to the specific facts and circumstances of the subject being valued in that case.

This does not mean that the analyst should not *know* what has been accepted and rejected in other cases and what factors were considered in those decisions. If the proposed discount or premium is at the extreme or outside the range of discounts or premiums previously accepted, the analyst should be on notice that it will require unusually comprehensive and convincing data and analysis to persuade the court.

USING AN ASSET APPRAISER TO QUANTIFY DISCOUNTS OR PREMIUMS FOR STOCK OR PARTNERSHIP INTERESTS

Well-qualified asset appraisers (e.g., real estate, timber) are experts in the appraisal of assets, but that expertise normally does *not* extend to appraisal of stock or partnership interests in the entities that own those assets.

In several U.S. Tax Court decisions, I believe the taxpayer was shortchanged because the lawyer engaged an asset appraiser rather than a business appraiser to analyze and testify on the issue of the discounts applicable to the stock or partnership interest.

SUMMARY

This chapter has pointed out and discussed some of the errors repeatedly encountered in practice in applying discounts and premiums. Application of a premium or discount that may be acceptable for one appraisal purpose may be unacceptable or uncertain in a valuation for some other purpose, with the guidance often found in precedential case law.

Courts like specific empirical evidence. They tend to reject discounts or premiums that are not well supported. In this respect, broad averages of highly divergent empirical data should be used only if it can be concluded that the characteristics of the subject are comparable to the average companies from which the data are drawn. Otherwise, subsets of the broad data group should be selected on the basis of characteristics comparable to the subject, or analysis should be presented to consider a discount above or below the broad average.

It is now well recognized that many "control premiums" are actually "acquisition premiums" reflecting synergistic values that may not be part of fair market value (for tax purposes) or stand-alone value (for dissent and dissolution purposes). The updated online *Control Premium Study* provides transaction codes to help sort out synergistic from financial control premiums.

Asset appraisers usually are not qualified to deal with discounts or premiums applicable to stock or partnership interests rather than directly to assets. Business appraisers are trained to deal with these issues.

Note

1. *Estate of Davis v. Commissioner,* 110 T.C. 530 (1998).

Bibliography

Books
Articles
Periodicals

BOOKS

Alerding, R. James. *Valuation of a Closely Held Business.* New York: Research Institute of America, 1995.

Black, Henry Campbell. *Black's Law Dictionary: Definitions of the Terms and Phrases of American and English Jurisprudence, Ancient and Modern,* 7th ed. St. Paul: West Publishing Co., 1999.

Blackman, Irving L. *Valuing Your Privately Held Business: The Art & Science of Establishing Your Company's Worth.* Burr Ridge, IL: Irwin Professional Publishing, 1995.

Bogdanski, John A. *Federal Tax Valuation.* Boston: Warren, Gorham & Lamont, 1996.

———. *Federal Tax Valuation, 2000 Cumulative Supplement No. 2.* Boston: Warren, Gorham & Lamont, 2000.

Brown, Ronald L., ed. *Valuing Professional Practices and Licenses: A Guide for the Matrimonial Practitioner.* New York: Aspen Law & Business, 1998.

Copeland, Tom, Tim Koller, and Jack Murrin. *Valuation: Measuring and Managing the Value of Companies,* 3rd ed. New York: John Wiley & Sons, Inc., 2000.

Cornell, Bradford. *Corporate Valuation: Tools for Effective Appraisal and Decision Making.* Burr Ridge, IL: Irwin Professional Publishing, 1993.

Cottle, Sidney, Roger F. Murray, and Frank E. Block. *Graham and Dodd's Security Analysis,* 5th ed. New York: McGraw-Hill, 1988.

Damodaran, Aswath. *Damodaran on Valuation.* New York: John Wiley & Sons, Inc., 1996.

Elliott, W. Curtis, Jr., William R. Culp, Jr., et al. *Valuation Practice in Estate Planning and Litigation.* Deerfield, IL: Clark, Boardman, Callaghan, 1996.

Feder, Robert D., Ed. *Valuation Strategies in Divorce,* Volumes 1 and 2, 4th ed. New York: Aspen Law & Business, 1997, cumulative supplement 2001.

Feld, Daniel E. *Estate and Gift Tax Digest,* 3rd ed. Boston: Warren, Gorham & Lamont, 1993.

Fishman, Jay, Shannon P. Pratt, J. Clifford Griffith, and D. Keith Wilson. *Guide to Business Valuations,* 11th ed. Fort Worth, TX: Practitioners Publishing Company, Inc., 2001.

Hawkins, George B., and Michael A. Paschall. *CCH Business Valuation Guide.* Chicago: CCH Incorporated, 2001.

Howitt, Idelle A. *Federal Tax Valuation Digest: Business Enterprise and Business Interests (1999/2000 Cumulative Edition).* Boston: Warren, Gorham & Lamont, 1999 (annual editions are cumulative).

IRS Valuation Training for Appeals Officers Coursebook. Chicago: Commerce Clearing House Incorporated, 1998 (available online at www.BVLibrary.com).

IRS Valuation Guide for Income, Estate and Gift Taxes. Chicago: Commerce Clearing House Incorporated, 1994.

Johnson, Bruce A., and Spencer Jeffries. *Comprehensive Guide for the Valuation of Family Limited Partnerships.* Houston: Partnership Profiles, Inc., 2001.

Jones, Gary E., and Dirk Van Dyke. *The Business of Business Valuation.* New York: McGraw-Hill, 1998.

Kasper, Larry J. *Business Valuation: Advanced Topics.* Westport, CT: Greenwood Publishing, 1997.

Lori, James H., and Mary Hamilton. *The Stock Market, Theories & Evidence.* Burr Ridge, IL: Irwin Professional Publishing, 1973.

Marren, Joseph H. *Mergers & Acquisitions: A Valuation Handbook.* Burr Ridge, IL: Irwin Professional Publishing, 1993.

Mercer, Z. Christopher. *Quantifying Marketability Discounts: Developing and Supporting Marketability Discounts in the Appraisal of Closely Held Business Interests.* Memphis: Peabody Publishing, LP, 1997.

———. *Valuing Financial Institutions.* Burr Ridge, IL: Irwin Professional Publishing, 1992.

Miles, Raymond C. *Basic Business Appraisal.* New York: John Wiley & Sons, Inc., 1984.

O'Neal, F. Hodge, and Robert B. Thompson. *O'Neal's Oppression of Minority Shareholders: Protecting Minority Rights in Squeeze-Outs and Other Intracorporate Conflicts,* 2nd ed. St. Paul: West Group, 1999.

———. *O'Neal's Oppression of Minority Shareholders: Protecting Minority Rights in Squeeze-Outs and Other Intracorporate Conflicts, 2001 Cumulative Supplement,* St. Paul: West Group, 2001.

Pratt, Shannon P. *Business Valuation Body of Knowledge: Exam Review and Professional Reference.* New York: John Wiley & Sons, Inc., 1998.

———. *Cost of Capital: Estimation and Applications.* New York: John Wiley & Sons, Inc., 1998.

———. *The Lawyer's Business Valuation Handbook.* Chicago: American Bar Association, 2000.

————. *The Market Approach to Valuing Businesses.* New York: John Wiley & Sons, Inc., 2001.

Pratt, Shannon P., Robert F. Reilly, and Robert P. Schweihs. *Valuing a Business: The Analysis and Appraisal of Closely Held Companies,* 4th ed. New York: McGraw-Hill, 2000.

————. *Valuing Small Businesses and Professional Practices,* 3rd ed. New York: McGraw-Hill, 1998.

Pratt, Shannon P., Robert F. Reilly, Robert P. Schweihs, and Jay E. Fishman. *Business Valuation Videocourse* (Videotape and Course Handbook). Jersey City, NJ: American Institute of Certified Public Accountants, 1993.

Reeves, James F., and Linda A. Markwood, *Guide to Family Partnerships* (part of the Biebl-Ranweiler Portfolio Series) 3rd ed. Fort Worth, TX: Practitioners Publishing Company, 1999.

Reilly, Robert F., and Robert P. Schweihs. *Handbook of Advanced Business Valuation.* New York: McGraw-Hill, 2000.

————. *Valuing Accounting Practices.* New York: John Wiley & Sons, Inc., 1997.

————. *Valuing Intangible Assets.* New York: McGraw-Hill, 1999.

————. *Valuing Professional Practices: A Practitioner's Guide.* Chicago: Commerce Clearing House Incorporated, 1997.

Saltzman, Michael I. *IRS Practice and Procedure,* 2nd ed. New York: Research Institute of America, 1991.

Stephens, Richard B., Guy B. Maxfield, Stephen A. Lind, and Dennis A. Calfee. *Federal Estate and Gift Taxation,* 7th ed. Boston: Warren, Gorham & Lamont of the RIA Group, 1998.

Stocks, Bonds, Bills, and Inflation: Valuation Edition 2001 Yearbook. Chicago: Ibbotson Associates, 2001.

Tinsley, Reed. *Valuation of a Medical Practice.* New York: John Wiley & Sons, Inc., 1999.

Trugman, Gary R. *Conducting a Valuation of a Closely Held Business,* Practice Aid 93-3. New York: American Institute of Certified Public Accountants, Inc., 1993.

————. *Understanding Business Valuation: A Practical Guide to Valuing Small to Medium-Sized Businesses.* New York: American Institute of Certified Public Accountants, Inc., 1998.

Uniform Standards of Professional Appraisal Practice, 2001 Edition. Washington, D.C.: The Appraisal Foundation, 2001.

Valuing ESOP Shares, revised ed. Washington, D.C.: The ESOP Association, 1994.

West, Thomas L., and Jeffrey D. Jones. *Handbook of Business Valuation,* 2nd ed. New York: John Wiley & Sons, 1999.

West, Tom, ed. *The 2001 Business Reference Guide,* 11th ed. Concord, MA: Business Brokerage Press, 2001.

Woelfel, Charles. *Encyclopedia of Banking & Finance,* 10th ed. Seattle: Probus Publishing (now New York: McGraw-Hill), 1994.

Zukin, James H., ed.-in-chief. *Financial Valuation: Businesses and Business Interests.* Boston: Research Institute of America, 1990.

———. *Financial Valuation: Businesses and Business Interests: 1998 Update with Cumulative Index.* Boston: Warren, Gorman & Lamont of the RIA Group, 1998.

ARTICLES

Abrams, Jay B., "Discount for Lack of Marketability: A Theoretical Model." *Business Valuation Review* (September 1994): 132–139.

Annin, Michael. "Understanding and Quantifying Control Premiums: The Value of Control vs. Synergies or Strategic Advantages, Part I." *The Journal of Business Valuation* (Proceedings of the 4th Joint Business Valuation Conference of the Canadian Institute of Chartered Business Valuators and the American Society of Appraisers). Toronto: Canadian Institute of Chartered Business Valuators (1999): 31–35.

Aschwald, Kathryn F., "Restricted Stock Discounts Decline as Result of 1-Year Holding Period." *Shannon Pratt's Business Valuation Update* (May 2000): 1–5.

Aschwald, Kathryn F. and Donna J. Walker. "Valuing S Corporation ESOP Companies." *Journal of Employee Ownership Law and Finance* (Summer 1999): 27–34.

August, Jerald D. "Artificial Valuation of Closely Held Interest: Sec. 2704." *Estate Planning* (November/December 1995): 339–344.

Barron, Michael S. "Is a Discount for Locked-In Capital Gains Tax Justified after *General Utilities* Repeal?" *Journal of Taxation* (April 1992): 218–222.

———. "When Will the Tax Court Allow a Discount for Lack of Marketability?" *Journal of Taxation* (January 1997): 46–50.

Barron, Robert A. "Control and Restricted Securities—Some Comments on the Discount Valuation of Publicly Traded Stock for Federal Estate, Gift, and Income Tax Purposes (Part 1)." *Securities Regulation Law Journal,* Vol. 24 (1996): 82–90.

———. "Control and Restricted Securities—Some Comments on the Discount Valuation of Publicly Traded Stock for Federal Estate, Gift, and Income Tax Purposes (Part 2)." *Securities Regulation Law Journal,* Vol. 24 (1996): 199–207.

Barson, Kalman A. "Should Hypothetical Taxes Be Considered in the Property Distribution?" *Fair$hare: The Matrimonial Law Monthly,* Vol. 19, No. 12 (December 1999): 7–8.

Bateman, Tracy A. "Divorce and Separation: Consideration of Tax Consequences in Distribution of Marital Property." *9 A.L.R. 5th 568, Lawyers Cooperative Publishing Co.* (2000): 568–707.

Batten, Jonathan S. "No Estate Tax Fractional Interest or Lack of Marketability Discount Allowed for Jointly Owned Property Held by Married Couple: Estate of Young v. Commissioner." *The Tax Lawyer,* Vol. 52, No. 2 (Winter 1999): 391–397.

Becker, Brian B., and Gary Gutzler, "Should a Blockage Discount Apply? Perspectives of Both a Hypothetical Willing Buyer and a Hypothetical Willing Seller." *Business Valuation Review* (March 2000): 3–9.

Bishop, David M. "Trapped-in Capital Gains: Where Do We Go from Here?" *Business Valuation Review* (June 1999): 64–68.

Bishop, David M., and Steven F. Schroeder. "Business Valuation Standard of Value for Divorce Should Be Fair Market Value." *American Journal of Family Law* (Spring 1999): 48–52.

"Blockage and Restricted Stock," *Tax Management, Inc.* Washington: Bureau of National Affairs, Inc., Portfolio 831, 2d (1998).

Bogdanski, John A. "Dissecting the Discount for Lack of Marketability." *Estate Planning* (February 1996): 91–95.

————. "Further Adventures with the Lack-of-Marketability Discount." *Estate Planning* (June 1999): 235.

————. "For Tax Court Valuation Decisions, a String of Reversals." *Estate Planning,* Vol. 25, No. 10 (December 1998): 474.

Bolotsky, Michael J. "Adjustments for Differences in Ownership Rights, Liquidity, Information Access, and Information Reliability: An Assessment of 'Prevailing Wisdom' versus the 'Nath Hypothesis.' " *Business Valuation Review* (September 1991): 94–110.

————. "Is the 'Levels of Value' Concept Still Viable?" American Society of Appraisers International Appraisal Conference, Denver, CO. (June 1995): 21–34.

Brown, Karen W. "Payment of Control Premiums by ESOPs." *ESOP Report* (November/December 1993): 6–8.

Brown, William J., Mark I. Wolk, and Leo N. Hitt. "Family Limited Partnerships: The Roles of the Players with a Focus on Valuation Discounts." *Business Entities* (May/June 1999): 4–13.

Budyak, James T. "Estate Freeze Rules Affect Partnership Valuation Discounts." *Taxation for Accountants* (December 1996): 340–347.

Casey, Christopher. "Marketability Discounts for Controlling Interests Revisited." *Business Valuation Review* (March 2000): 10–15.

Cavanaugh, James C. "Valuation Discounts Are Available in an Estate Plan." *Taxation for Accountants* (July 1995): 31–37.

Chaffe, David B. H. III. "Option Pricing as a Proxy for Discount for Lack of Marketability in Private Company Valuations." *Business Valuation Review* (December 1993): 182–188.

Clay, Kimberly E. "The IRS and Family Limited Partnerships—Issues and Opinions." *BizVal.com,* Vol. 11, No. 3 (1999): 1–2.

Coolidge, H. Calvin. "Fixing Value of Minority Interest in Business: Actual Sales Suggest Discount as High as 70%." *Estate Planning* (Spring 1975): 141.

Crow, Matthew R. "Discounts and Family Limited Partnerships Holding Only Marketable Securities." *CPA Litigation Service Counselor* (May 1999): 9–12.

Curtiss, Rand M. "A Practical Methodology for Determining Premiums and Discounts." *Business Valuation Review* (December 1997): 172–179.

Dufendach, David C. "Valuation of Closely Held Corporations: 'C' v. 'S' Differentials." *Business Valuation Review* (December 1996): 176–179.

Eastland, S. Stacy (interview). "Family Limited Partnership Interests Enjoy 40 to 85% Discounts from NAV." *Shannon Pratt's Business Valuation Update* (January 1997): 1–3.

———. "The Art of Making Uncle Sam Your Assignee Instead of Your Senior Partner: The Use of Family Partnerships in Estate Planning." Available to subscribers on www.BVLibrary.com.

Eckstein, David. "Black-Scholes and Marketability: Another View." *Valuation Strategies* (January/February 1999): 41.

Ellis, Barnes. "Oregon Court of Appeals Finds no Minority Discount Applies in Buyout of Oppressed Shareholder." *Judges & Lawyers Business Valuation Update* (February 2000): 6.

Elliot, Charles. "An Outline of Valuation Considerations Related to Limited Partnerships." Presented to the 1998 AICPA National Business Valuation Conference, Palm Beach Gardens, Florida. (November 15, 1998). Available to subscribers on www.BVLibrary.com.

Emory, John D. "The Value of Marketability as Illustrated in Initial Public Offerings of Common Stock—January 1980 through June 1981, "*Business Valuation News* (September 1985): 21–24 (also in *ASA Valuation* [June 1986]: 62–66).

———. "The Value of Marketability as Illustrated in Initial Public Offerings of Common Stock, January 1985 through June 1986. *Business Valuation Review* (December 1986): 12–15.

———. "The Value of Marketability as Illustrated in Initial Public Offerings of Common Stock (August 1987–January 1989)." *Business Valuation Review* (June 1989): 55–57.

———. "The Value of Marketability as Illustrated in Initial Public Offerings of Common Stock, February 1989–July 1990." *Business Valuation Review* (December 1990): 114–116.

———. "The Value of Marketability as Illustrated in Initial Public Offerings of Common Stock, February 1992 through July 1993." *Business Valuation Review* (March 1994): 3–5.

———. "The Value of Marketability as Illustrated in Initial Public Offerings of Common Stock, January 1994 through June 1995." *Business Valuation Review* (December 1995): 155–160.

———. "The Value of Marketability as Illustrated in Initial Public Offerings of Common Stock, November 1995 through April 1997." *Business Valuation Review* (September 1997): 123–131.

Emory, John D., F. R. Dengel III, and John D. Emory, Jr. "The Value of Marketability as Illustrated in Dot.Com IPOs: May 1997–March 2000." *Shannon Pratt's Business Valuation Update* (July 2000): 1–2.

————. "The Value of Marketability as Illustrated in Initial Public Offerings of Dot-Com Companies May 1997 through March 2000." *Business Valuation Review* (September 2000): 111–121.

Emory, John D., Jr. "The Role of Discounts in Determining 'Fair Value' Under Wisconsin's Dissenters' Rights Statutes: The Case for Discounts." *Wisconsin Law Review* (March 1996): 1155–1175.

Finkel, Sidney R. "The Portfolio Discount for Closely Held Investment Holding Companies." *Valuation Strategies* (January/February 1999): 20–25, 46, 48.

Fiore, Owen G. "FLPs LLCs: Ideal Wealth Preservation Vehicles Part I" *Valuation Examiner* (February/March 1997): 18, 30–34. Available to subscribers on www. BVLibrary.com.

————. "FLPs LLCs: Ideal Wealth Preservation Vehicles Part II." *Valuation Examiner* (April/May 1997): 16, 28–29. Available to subscribers on www.BVLibrary.com.

————. "Greater Due Diligence Required of Tax Lawyers in Planning Entity-based Valuation Discount Cases." Available to subscribers on www.BVLibrary.com.

————. "How Should Trust & Estate Lawyers Respond to the IRS Attack on Certain FLP-based Transfer Tax Valuation Discounts?" ACTEC Chicago Summer Meeting, June 1997. Available to subscribers on www.BVLibrary.com.

————. "A Tax Lawyer's Attitude Toward the Estate and Gift Tax Business Valuation Appraisal Process." Available to subscribers on www.BVLibrary.com.

————. "Valuation Adjustment Planning: Solid Reality or Fleeting Fantasy?" Fiore Law Group, LLP (January 1998). Available to subscribers on www.BVLibrary.com.

Fisher, Charles H., Jr., and Martin B. Solomon. "Valuation Discounts for Family Limited Partnerships." *Valuation Strategies* (January/February 1999): 26–37.

Fishman, Jay E., Shannon P. Pratt, J. Clifford Griffith, and D. Keith Wilson. "Premiums and Discounts in Business Valuations—Part I." *Fair$hare: The Matrimonial Law Monthly* (May 1992): 11–17.

————. "Premiums and Discounts in Business Valuation—Part II." *Fair$hare: The Matrimonial Law Monthly* (June 1992): 14–16.

Fowler, Bradley A. "How Do You Handle It? Family Partnership Valuations." *Business Valuation Review* (March 1997): 41–44.

Frazier, William H. "The Use of Capital Gains Tax Liability When Employing an Asset-Based Approach to the Valuation of A C Corporation and 'Pure' Blockage." Unpublished paper. (April 1996): Available on BVLibrary.com.

Freeman, Ronald S. "Valuation of Family Limited Partnerships." AICPA National Business Valuation Conference (1999). Available to subscribers on www. BVLibrary.com.

Garber, Steven A. "A Proposed Methodology for Estimating the Lack of Marketability Discount Related to ESOP Repurchase Liability." *Business Valuation Review* (December 1993): 172–181.

Gasiorowski, John R., "Is a Discount for Built-In Capital Gains Tax Justified?" *Business Valuation Review* (June 1993): 76–79.

Gelman, Milton. "An Economist-Financial Analyst's Approach to Valuing Stock of a Closely-Held Company." *Journal of Taxation* (June 1972): 353–354.

Gilbert, John R. "Built-in Gain Valuation Adjustment: No Longer 'If'—But 'How' and 'How Much'." *CPA Expert* (Winter 1999): 7–10.

Goldberg, Leonard M., and Denice P. Gilchrist. "Income Tax and Transfer Tax Issues in the Use of Family Limited Partnerships and Family Limited Liability Companies," ABA Tax Section Midyear Meeting (1999). Available to subscribers on www. BVLibrary.com.

Hall, Lance S. "Corporate Structure Discount and Valuation of Asset-Holding C Corps." *Trusts & Estates* (September 1996): 45–48.

———. "The Lastest in Discounting Family Limited Partnerships." 18th Annual Business Valuation Conference of the American Society of Appraisers (1999). Available to subscribers on www.BVLibrary.com.

Hall, Lance S., and Timothy C. Polacek. "Strategies for Obtaining the Largest Valuation Discounts." *Estate Planning* (January–February 1994): 38–44.

Hamilton, Janet, Duncan Kretovich, and Jill Johnson. "Marketability Discounts in the Courts, 1991–2000" (special report). *Judges and Lawyers Business Valuation Update*. Business Valuation Resources, LLC (2001).

Hawkins, George B. "Selling Out to a Public Company Buyer: Blockage, Restricted Shares, and Value—The Stated Price Versus Reality." *Fair Value* (Spring/Summer 1997): 1–2.

Hayes, John W., and Scott D. Miller. "Marketability Issues in the Valuation of ESOPs." *CPA Expert* (Summer 1996): 7–11.

Hayward, Matthew L. A., and Donald C. Hambrick. "Explaining Premiums Paid for Large Acquisitions: Evidence of CEO Hubris." New York: Columbia University Graduate School of Business (June 1995).

Hempstead, John E. "Conduct of the Parties Now a Factor in New Jersey Fair Value Determinations." *Judges & Lawyers Business Valuation Update* (September 1999): 1–3.

Herber, William C., Patrick D. Schmidt, and Robert J. Strachota. "Fairness in Minority Interest Valuation: Adjusting Financial Statements and the Valuation of Minority Interests." *Business Valuation Review* (September 1992): 140–146.

Herpe, David A. "Climate for Valuation Discounts Remains Good Despite IRS Obstinacy." *Trusts & Estate* (January 1995): 66–76.

Hitchner, James R. "Large Discounts Allowed in Real Estate Partnership." *CPA Expert* (Spring 1997): 10–11.

Hitchner, James R., and Gary Roland. "Marketability and Control Govern Value of Family Businesses." *Taxation for Lawyers* (July/August 1993): 14–17.

———. "Tax Court Reviews Nine Factors for Selecting Marketability Discounts." *CPA Expert* (Winter 1996): 11–13.

Hitchner, James R., and Kevin J. Rudd. "The Use of Discounts in Estate and Gift Tax Valuations." *Trusts & Estates* (August 1992): 49–52, 60.

Hoffman, Carsten. "Life After Davis Estate: Valuation Discounts for Built-in Capital Gains Tax Liabilities." *Taxes—The Tax Magazine* (August 1999): 42.

Holmer, William E. " 'Control, Marketable' Is No Oxymoron." *Shannon Pratt's Business Valuation Update* (letter to editor) (January 2000): 15.

Houren, Jay R., "Family Limited Partnerships." ABA Tax Section Midyear Meeting (1999). Available to subscribers on www.BVLibrary.com.

Howitt, Idelle A. "Estate of Cameron W. Bommer." *Valuation Strategies* (September/October 1998): 38–39, 42.

———. "Estate of Joseph R. Cloutier." *Valuation Strategies* (November/December 1997): 40–41.

"IRS Acquiesces Regarding Trapped-in Gains Discount." *Judges & Lawyers Business Valuation Update* (August 1999): 15.

Jankowske, Wayne. "Is the 'Levels of Value' Concept Still Viable?" American Society of Appraisers, International Appraisal Conference, Denver, CO. (June 1995): 35–45.

———. "Second-Stage Adjustments to Value." American Society of Appraisers, International Appraisal Conference, Toronto, Ontario (June 1996): 1–71.

Jefferson, Mozette. "Liquidation of Underperforming Assets Gets Positive Minority Stock Reaction." *Shannon Pratt's Business Valuation Update* (December 1995): 11.

Johnson, Bruce. "Quantitative Support for Discounts for Lack of Marketability." *Business Valuation Review* (December 1999): 152–155.

———. "Restricted Stock Discounts, 1991–95." *Shannon Pratt's Business Valuation Update* (March 1999): 1–3.

Jordon, Jim. "Clearinghouse Debacle Illustrates Value of Marketability." *Shannon Pratt's Business Valuation Update* (April 1997): 9.

Kaplan, Steven. "Valuation Issues in Corporate Control Transactions." American Society of Appraisers Advanced Business Valuation Conference (1995).

Kasner, Jerry A. "Valuation of Family Partnership Interests." *Tax Analysts—Special Reports,* 97 TNT 50-47 (March 14, 1997).

Kimball, Curtis R. "Discounts Settlements on Recent Family Limited Partnership Cases." ASA International Appraisal Conference, August 1999. Available to subscribers on www.BVLibrary.com.

Kramer, Yale. "Majority Block of Nonvoting Stock May Have Slightly Greater Value Than Minority Interest." *Shannon Pratt's Business Valuation Update* (July 1997): 15.

Kubersky, Andrew S. "Marketability Discounts and ESOP Acquisitions of Minority Share Interests." *Journal of Employee Ownership Law & Finance,* Vol. 10, No. 4 (Fall 1998): 97–103.

————. "Marketability Discounting Issues for ESOP Acquisitions of Minority Shares." *Business Valuation Review* (September 1999): 100–103.

Laro, The Honorable David., U.S. Tax Court. "Judge Laro's View on Discounts & Valuation Reports." *Judges & Lawyers Business Valuation Update* (part 2 of 2) (June 1999): 1, 3–4.

————. "Judge Laro's Views on 'Fair Market Value.' " *Judges & Lawyers Business Valuation Update* (part 1 of 2) (May 1999): 1–3.

Larson, James A., and Jeffrey P. Wright. "Key Person Discount in Small Firms: An Update." *Business Valuation Review* (September 1998): 85–94.

Lease, Ronald C., John J. McConnell, and Wayne H. Mikkelson. "The Market Value of Control in Publicly-Traded Corporations." *Journal of Financial Economics* (1983): 439–471.

Levine, Lawrence M., Carl F. Luft, and John Howe. "Considerations in Valuing Stock Options." *Valuation Strategies* (May/June 1998): 15–21, 46, 48.

Maher, J. Michael. "Discounts for Lack of Marketability for Closely Held Business Interests." *Taxes—The Tax Magazine* (September 1976): 562–571.

Mason, Miriam E. "A Brief Review of Control Premiums and Minority Interest Discounts." *Journal of Business Valuation* (12th Biennial Business Valuation Conference of the Canadian Institute of Chartered Business Valuators). Toronto: Canadian Institute of Chartered Business Valuators (1997): 365–387.

————. "Understanding and Quantifying Control Premiums: The Value of Control vs. Synergies or Strategic Advantages, Part II." *Journal of Business Valuation* (4th Joint Business Valuation Conference of the Canadian Institute of Chartered Business Valuators and the American Society of Appraisers). Toronto: Canadian Institute of Chartered Business Valuators (1999): 36–54.

Matthews, Gil. "Matthews Critiques Mercer's Simplot Case Review." *Judges & Lawyers Business Valuation Update* (July 1999): 10.

May, Richard C., Robert L. McDonald, and Brad Van Horn. "Valuation Issues in Leveraged ESOPs." *Journal of Employee Ownership Law and Finance* (Summer 1994): 61–82.

McCarter, Mary. "The Application and Uses of Discounts and Premia in Business Valuation." AICPA National Business Valuation Conference (1999). Available to subscribers on www.BVLibrary.com.

Mercer, Z. Christopher. "Are Marketability Discounts Applicable to Controlling Interests in Private Companies?" *Valuation Strategies* (November/December 1997): 31–36.

————. "Are Qualifying Marketability Discounts New or Not?" *Trusts & Estates* (February 1998): 39–46.

———. "A Brief Review of Control Premiums and Minority Interest Discounts." *Journal of Business Valuation* (Proceedings of the 12th Biennial Business Valuation Conference of the Canadian Institute of Chartered Business Valuators). Toronto: Canadian Institute of Chartered Business Valuators (1997): 365–387.

———. "Is the 'Levels of Value' Concept Still Viable?" American Society of Appraisers, International Appraisal Conference, Denver, CO. (June 1995): 14–20.

———. "Should Marketability Discounts Be Applied to Controlling Interests of Private Companies?" *Business Valuation Review* (June 1994): 55–65.

———. "Tax Court Accords Superpremium to Small Voting Block; Allows Deduction of 100% of Trapped-in Capital Gains Tax." *Judges & Lawyers Business Valuation Update* (April 1999): 1, 6–7.

———. "Understanding and Quantifying Control Premiums: The Value of Control vs. Synergies or Strategic Advantages, Part II." *Journal of Business Valuation* (Proceedings of the 4th Joint Business Valuation Conference of the Canadian Institute of Chartered Business Valuators and the American Society of Appraisers). Toronto: Canadian Institute of Chartered Business Valuators (1999): 36–54.

Mercer, Z. Christopher, and Matthew R. Crow. "Black-Scholes Rather Than the Quantitative Marketability Discount Model?" *Valuation Strategies* (September/October 1998): 5–13, 44.

Moore, M. Read, and D. Alan Hungate. "Valuation Discounts for Private Debt in Estate Administration." *Estate Planning* (June 1998): 195–203.

Moore, Philip W. " 'Blockage' Redux: The Challenge Posed by Blockage." *Trusts & Estates* (February 1992): 35–44, 60.

Moroney, Robert E. "Most Courts Overvalue Closely Held Stocks." *Taxes—The Tax Magazine* (March 1973): 144–156.

———. "Why 25% Discount for Non-marketability in One Valuation, 100% in Another?" *Taxes—The Tax Magazine* (May 1977): 316–320.

Mulligan, Michael D., and Angela Fick Braly. "Family Limited Partnerships Can Create Discounts." *Estate Planning* (July/August 1994): 195–204.

Nath, Eric W. "Control Premiums and Minority Interest Discounts in Private Companies." *Business Valuation Review* (June 1990): 39–46.

———. "How Public Guideline Companies Represent 'Control' Value for a Private Company." *Business Valuation Review* (December 1997): 167–171.

———. "Is the 'Levels of Value' Concept Still Viable?" American Society of Appraisers, International Appraisal Conference, Denver, CO. (June 1995): 4–13.

———. "A Tale of Two Markets," *Business Valuation Review* (September 1994): 107–112.

O'Shea, Kevin C., and Robert M. Siwicki. "Stock Price Premiums for Voting Rights Attributable to Minority Interests." *Business Valuation Review* (December 1991): 165–171.

Osteryoung, Jerome S., and Derek Newman. "Key Person Valuation Issues for Private Businesses." *Business Valuation Review* (September 1994): 115–119.

Paulsen, Jon. "More Evidence on IPO Marketability Discounts." *Business Valuation Review* (March 1998): 10–12.

Pearson, Brian K. "1999 Marketability Discounts as Reflected in Initial Public Offerings." *CPA Expert* (Spring 2000): 1–5.

Peters, Jerry O. "Lack of Marketability Discounts for Controlling Interests: An Analysis of Public vs. Private Transactions." *Business Valuation Review* (June 1995): 59–61.

Phillips, John R., and Neill W. Freeman. "Do Privately-Held Controlling Interests Sell for Less?" *Business Valuation Review* (September 1995): 102–113.

———. "What Is the Marketability Discount for Controlling Interests?" *Business Valuation Review* (March 1999): 3–11.

Pittock, William F., and Charles H. Stryker. "Revenue Ruling 77-287 Revisited." *SRC Quarterly Reports,* Vol. 10, No. 1 (Spring 1983): 1–3.

Polacek, Timothy C., and Richard A. Lehn. "Tax Court Allows Sizeable Fractional Interest Discounts." *Trusts & Estates* (September 1994): 29–40.

Pratt, Shannon P. "Control Premiums? Maybe Not—34% of the 3rd Quarter Buyouts at Discounts." *Shannon Pratt's Business Valuation Update* (January 1999): 1–2.

———. "The Oxymoron of 'Control, Marketable.' " *Shannon Pratt's Business Valuation Update* (October 1999): 1, 4.

———. "Public Market Values Inflated in Comparison with Private Companies," *Shannon Pratt's Business Valuation Update* (November 1997): 1, 3.

Pritchard, Timothy. "A Canadian Rail Pioneer Plans Split-Up." *New York Times* (February 14, 2001): C7.

Rabe, James G., and David Ackerman. "*Howard v. Shay* Redux." *Willamette Management Associates Insights* (Spring 1999): 23–25.

Raby, William L., and Burgess J. W. Raby. "Stock Valuations, as a Matter of Law, Require Tax Discount." 98 *Tax Notes Today* 166–57 (August 27, 1998).

Reilly, Robert F. "The Identification and Quantification of Business Valuation Discounts and Premia." *Fair$hare: The Matrimonial Law Monthly* (July 1996): 2–5.

Ressegieu, Matthew. "Valuation Discounts: What Is Required?" *Taxation for Lawyers* (March/April 1995): 283–288.

Reto, James J. "Are S Corporations Entitled to Valuation Discounts for Embedded Capital Gains?" *Valuation Strategies* (January/February 2000): 48.

Reynolds, Bruce M. "IRS Modified Position and Allows Discounts on Intra-Family Stock Transfers." *Taxes* (June 1993): 381–387.

Roach, George P. "Control Premiums and Strategic Mergers." *Business Valuation Review* (June 1998): 42–49.

Robinson, Chris, John Rumsey, and Alan White. "The Value of a Vote in the Market for Corporate Counsel." York University Faculty of Administrative Studies (February 1996).

Robinson, Debra A., and Edward J. Rappaport. "Impact of Valuation Discounts on Estate and Income Tax Basis." *Estate Planning* (June 1997): 223–230.

Roll, Richard. "The Hubris Hypothesis of Corporate Takeovers." *Journal of Business* 59, no. 2 (1986): 212. (Reprinted with permission of the University of Chicago Press.)

Rothschild, Gideon. "IRS Turns Around on Discounts for Intra-Family Gifts of Businesses." *The Practical Accountant* (April 1993): 59–60.

Saliba, R. Gary, and Jason K. Chung. "When Linking Post IPO Return Data with Pre-IPO Marketability Discount Data, Should Initial Public Offering (IPO) Discounts Be Considered When Estimating Value at the Shareholder Level?" *Business Valuation Review* (December 1998): 128–135.

Scherrer, Phillip S. "Why REITs Face a Merger-Driven Consolidation Wave." *Mergers & Acquisitions, The Dealmaker's Journal* (July/August 1995): 42.

Shiffrin, Daniel. "Recent Developments in the Treatment of Built-in Gains: *Davis, Jameson, and Eisenberg.*" *CPA Litigation Service Counselor* (May 1999): 3–4.

———. "Tax Court: No Discount for Built-in Gain Tax." *CPA Litigation Service Counselor* (March 1998): 1–2.

———. "Tax Court Reduces Blockage Discount: *Estate of Foote.*" *CPA Litigation Service Counselor* (March 1999): 4.

———. "Value Adjusted to Reflect Built-in Gains." *CPA Litigation Service Counselor* (August 1998): 3–4.

Shishido, Zenichi. "The Fair Value of Minority Stock in Closely Held Corporations." *Fordham Law Review* (October 1993): 65–110.

Silber, William L. "Discounts on Restricted Stock: The Impact of Illiquidity on Stock Prices." *Financial Analysts Journal* (July/August 1991): 60–64.

Silverstein, Bruce. "1999 Delaware Appraisal Actions Set Precedents on Some Issues." *Judges & Lawyers Business Valuation Update* (January 2000): 1–3.

Simpson, David W. "Minority Interest and Marketability Discounts: A Perspective, Part I." *Business Valuation Review* (March 1991): 7–13.

———. "Minority Interest and Marketability Discounts: A Perspective, Part II." *Business Valuation Review* (June 1991): 47–50.

Sliwoski, Leonard J. "Built in Gains Tax, Discounts for Lack of Marketability, and *Eisenberg v. Commissioner.*" *Business Valuation Review* (March 1998): 3–6.

Soled, Jay A. "Gifts of Partnership Interests: An Income Tax Perspective." *Business Entities* (May/June 1999): 30–35.

Sonneman, Donald. "The Single Customer Business—Valuation of a Captive Business." *Business Valuation Review* (March 2000): 44–48.

"Stock Marketability Restrictions That Apply to Decedent, But Not Estate, Will Affect Its Valuation." *The Tax Adviser* (September 1998): 644, 646.

Sziklay, Barry. "Landmark Cases." *AICPA National Business Valuation Conference* (1998). Available to subscribers on www.BVLibrary.com.

Thompson, Mark S., and Eric S. Spunt. "The Widespread Overvaluation of Fractional Ownership Positions." *Trusts & Estates* (June 1993): 62–66.

Tiernan, Peter B. "How 50% Ownership Affects Estate Planning for Closely Held Stock." *Journal of Taxation* (October 1999): 232–240.

Trout, Robert R. "Estimation of the Discount Associated with the Transfer of Restricted Securities." *Taxes—The Tax Magazine* (June 1977): 381–385.

"Valuation Discount Allowed for Built-in Capital Gains Tax." *The Federal Tax Course Letter* (December 1998): 8–9.

Walker, James R. "Valuation Adjustments for Interests in Closely Held Businesses." Law Education Institute National CLE Conference (January 2000). Available to subscribers on www.BVLibrary.com.

Wallgren, Don. "Jointly Owned Property May Not Be Subject to Valuation Discounts." *The Tax Adviser* (April 1999): 218–220.

Warnken, Wayne L., and Pamela R. Champine. "Security the Minority Discount for Family Business Transfers." *Trusts & Estates* (April 1993): 49–50.

Willis, Robert T., Jr. "Preparing Valuation Reports to Withstand Judicial Challenge." *Estate Planning* (December 1998): 455–462.

Wise, Richard M. "Practice Standards, Tax Valuations and Valuation Methodologies— CICBV vs. ASA." *Journal of Business Valuation* (Proceedings of the 12th Biennial Conference of the Canadian Institute of Chartered Business Valuators) Toronto: Canadian Institute of Chartered Business Valuators (1997): 235–258.

PERIODICALS

American Business Law Journal, quarterly, Academy of Legal Studies in Business, c/o Daniel J. Herron, Dept. of Finance, 120 Upham Hall, Miami University, Oxford, OH 45056; ph: (513) 529-2945, fax: (513) 529-6992.

American Journal of Family Law, quarterly, Aspen Law and Business, 1185 Avenue of the Americas, New York, NY 10036; ph: (888) 859-8081.

ASA Valuation, semiannually, American Society of Appraisers, Box 17265, Washington, DC 20041-0265.

Business Appraisal Practice, published three times a year, The Institute of Business Appraisers, Inc., Box 17410, Plantation, FL 33318; ph: (954) 584-1144, fax: (954) 584-1184, e-mail: ibahq@go-iba.org.

Business Law Today, bimonthly (5 times a year), American Bar Association Section of Business Law, ABA Service Center, 541 N. Fairbanks Court, Chicago, IL 60611.

Business Valuation Litigation Reporter (formerly *Judges & Lawyers Business Valuation Update*), monthly, Business Valuation Resources, LLC, 7412 S.W. Beaverton-Hillsdale Highway, #106, Portland, OR 97225; ph: (503) 291-7963 or (888) 287-8258; fax: (503) 291-7955; www.BVLibrary.com.

Business Valuation Review, monthly, American Society of Appraisers, P.O. Box 17265, Washington, DC 20041; ph: (703) 478-2228, fax: (703) 472-8471.

Canadian Tax Highlights, monthly, Canadian Tax Foundation, 1200-595 Bay Street, Toronto, ON M5G 2N5, Canada; ph: (416) 599-0283, fax: (416) 599-9283.

CPA Expert, quarterly, American Institute of Certified Public Accountants, Harborside Financial Center, 201 Plaza Three, Jersey City, NJ 07311-3881; ph: (888) 777-7077 or (201) 938-3000.

CPA Litigation Service Counselor, monthly, Harcourt Brace Professional Publishing, Subscription Fulfillment, 6277 Sea Harbor Drive, Orlando, FL 32887; ph: (800) 831-7799.

Delaware Journal of Corporate Law, 3 times a year, Widener University, School of Law, Box 7286, Wilmington, DE 19803; ph: (302) 477-2145, fax: (302) 477-2042.

E-Law Business Valuation Perspective, 20 times a year, Mercer Capital Management, Inc., 5850 Ridgeway Center Parkway, Suite 410, Memphis, TN 38120; www.bizval.com.

The ESOP Report, monthly, ESOP Association, 1726 M Street, NW, Suite 501, Washington, DC 20036; ph: (202) 293-2971, fax: (202) 293-7568.

Estate Planning (New York), base vol. (plus semiannual updates), Warren, Gorham & Lamont of the RIA Group, 90 Fifth Avenue, New York, NY 10011; ph: (212) 645-4800, fax: (212) 337-4280.

Fair$hare: The Matrimonial Law Monthly, monthly, Aspen Law & Business, 1185 Avenue of the Americas, 37th Floor, New York, NY 10036; ph: (212) 597-0200 or (800) 638-8437, fax: (212) 597-0338.

Fair Value, quarterly, Banister Financial, Inc., 1914 Brunswick Avenue, Suite 1-B, Charlotte, NC 28207; ph: (704) 334-4932; www.businessvalue.com.

Family Advocate, quarterly, Section of Family Law, American Bar Association, 750 N. Lake Shore Drive, Chicago, IL 60611; ph: (312) 988-6113; www.abanet.org/family/advocate.

Family Law Quarterly, Section of Family Law, American Bar Association, 750 N. Lake Shore Drive, Chicago, IL 60611; ph: (312) 988-5000; www.abanet.org/family/advocate.

The Federal Tax Course Letter, monthly, Aspen Law & Business, 1185 Avenue of the Americas, New York, NY 10036; ph: (212) 597-0200 or (800) 638-8437, fax: (212) 597-0338.

Fordham Law Review, bimonthly, Fordham University, School of Law, Lincoln Center, 140 W. 62nd Street, New York, NY 10023; ph: (212) 636-6876, fax: (212) 636-6965.

Journal of the American Academy of Matrimonial Lawyers, annually, American Academy of Matrimonial Lawyers, University of Wisconsin-Madison Law School, 150 N. Michigan Avenue, #2040, Chicago, IL 60601; ph: (312) 263-6477.

Journal of Accountancy, monthly, American Institute of Certified Public Accountants, Harborside Financial Center, 201 Plaza Three, Jersey City, NJ 07311; ph: (201) 938-3796 or (888) 777-7077, fax: (201) 329-1112.

Journal of Business Valuation, annually, The Canadian Institute of Business Valuators, 277 Wellington Street West, 5th Floor, Toronto, Ontario M5V 3H2; ph: (416) 204-3397, fax: (416) 977-8585; e-mail: admin@cicbv.va, www.businessvaluators.com.

Journal of Employee Ownership Law and Finance, quarterly, National Center for Employee Ownership, Inc., 1201 Martin Luther King Jr. Way, Oakland, CA 94612; ph: (510) 272-9461, fax: (510) 272-9510.

Journal of Pension Planning and Compliance, Panel Publishers, c/o Aspen Law and Business, 1185 Avenue of the Americas, New York, NY 10036; ph: (212) 597-0200 or (800) 638-8437, fax: (212) 597-0338.

The Journal of Taxation, monthly, Warren, Gorham & Lamont of the RIA Group, 90 Fifth Avenue, New York, NY 10011; ph: (212) 645-4800, fax: (212) 337-4280.

Judges & Lawyers Business Valuation Update (as of October 2001, renamed the *Business Valuation Litigation Reporter,* monthly, Business Valuation Resources, LLC, 7412 S.W. Beaverton-Hillsdale Highway, Suite 106, Portland, OR 97225; ph: (503) 291-7963 or (888) 287-8258, fax: (503) 291-7955; www.BVLibrary.com.

Matrimonial Strategist, monthly, American Lawyer Media, Inc., d.b.a. Leader Publications, 345 Park Avenue, S., New York, NY 10010; ph: (212) 545-6170, fax: (212) 969-1848.

Mergers & Acquisitions, bimonthly, Securities Data Publishing, 40 W. 57th Street, 11th Fl., New York, NY 10019; ph: (212) 765-5311, fax: (212) 765-6123.

Mergerstat/Shannon Pratt's Control Premium Study, quarterly, Mergerstat, LP and Business Valuation Resources, LLC, 7412 S.W. Beaverton-Hillsdale Hwy., Suite 106, Portland, OR 97225; ph: (888) BUS-VALU [287-8258], fax: (503) 291-7955.

Mergerstat Review, annually, Mergerstat, LP, 1933 Ponitus Avenue, Los Angeles, CA 90025; ph: (310) 966-9492; www.mergerstat1.com.

Michigan Business Law Journal, State Bar of Michigan, 306 Townsend Street, Lansing, MI 48933; ph: (517) 372-9030.

Nation's Business, monthly, U.S. Chamber of Commerce, 1615 H Street, NW, Washington, DC 20062-2000.

National Law Journal, weekly, American Lawyer Media, Inc., d.b.a. Leader Publications, 345 Park Avenue, S., New York, NY 10010; ph: (212) 779-9200.

New York Law Journal, quarterly, American Lawyer Media, Inc., d.b.a. Leader Publications, 345 Park Avenue, S., New York, NY 10010; ph: (212) 779-9200, fax: (212) 969-1848.

The Partnership Spectrum, bimonthly, Partnership Profiles, P.O. Box 7938, Dallas, TX 75209; ph: (800) 634-4614.

The Review of Securities & Commodities Regulation, semimonthly (22 times a year), Standard & Poor's of McGraw-Hill Companies, 25 Broadway, New York, NY 10004; ph: (212) 208-8650, fax: (212) 412-0240.

Shannon Pratt's Business Valuation Update, monthly, Business Valuation Resources, LLC, 7412 S.W. Beaverton-Hillsdale Highway, #106, Portland, OR 97225; ph: (503) 291-7963 or (888) 287-8258, fax: (503) 291-7955; www.BVLibrary.com.

The Tax Adviser, monthly, American Institute of Certified Public Accountants, Harborside Financial Center, 201 Plaza Three, Jersey City, NJ 07311-9808; ph: (201) 938-4796 or (800) 862-4272, fax: (201) 329-1112.

The Tax Executive, bimonthly, Tax Executives Institute, Inc., 1200 G Street, NW, No. 300, Washington, DC 20005-3814; ph: (202) 638-5601, fax: (202) 638-5607.

The Tax Lawyer, quarterly, Section of Taxation, American Bar Association, 750 N. Lake Shore Drive, Chicago, IL 60611; www.abanet.org/tax.

Tax Management Memorandum, biweekly, Tax Management, Inc., 1231 25th Street, NW, Washington, DC 20037; ph: (202) 785-7191 or (800) 223-7270, fax: (202) 785-7195.

Taxation for Accountants, monthly, Warren, Gorham & Lamont of the RIA Group, 90 Fifth Avenue, New York, NY 10011; ph: (212) 645-4800, fax: (212) 337-4280.

Taxation for Lawyers, bimonthly, Warren, Gorham & Lamont of the RIA Group, 90 Fifth Avenue, New York, NY 10011; ph: (212) 645-4800, fax: (212) 337-4280.

Taxes—The Tax Magazine, monthly, CCH, Inc., 2700 Lake Cook Road, Riverwood, IL 60015; ph: (847) 267-7000.

Trusts & Estates, 10 times a year, Monitor Press Ltd., Suffolk House, Church Field Road, Sudbury, Suffolk CO10 6YA, England; ph: 44-1787-378607, fax: 44-178-881147.

Valuation Strategies, bimonthly, RIA Group, 31 St. James Street, Boston, MA 02116; ph: (800) 431-9025.

Wisconsin Law Review, bimonthly, University of Wisconsin at Madison, Law School, 975 Bascom Mall, Madison, WI 53706-1399; ph: (608) 262-5815, fax: (608) 262-5485.

Data Resources

Control Premiums/Minority Discounts
Discount for Lack of Marketability
Discounts from Net Asset Value for Limited Partnership Interests
Discounts from Net Asset Value for REITs and REOCs
Discounts from Net Asset Value for Closed-End Investment Funds
Discounts and Capitalization Rates

CONTROL PREMIUMS/MINORITY DISCOUNTS

Mergerstat/Shannon Pratt's Control Premium Study™. Business Valuation Resources, LLC. 7412 S.W. Beaverton-Hillsdale Hwy., Suite 106, Portland, OR 97225, (888) BUS-VALU [287-8258], www.bvresources.com. Updated quarterly, available in print and online at www.bvmarketdata.com™. The *Mergerstat/Shannon Pratt's Control Premium Study™* is now exclusively available through Business Valuation Resources, LLC. Subscribers may choose between an enhanced and easily searchable Web-based database tool or a binder of printed material. One important benefit to the Web-based version is the instant access to three years of back data allowing easy manipulation of the control premium and minority discount information needed. Data is organized by industry, SIC code, calendar quarter, and by individual business sale. The *Mergerstat/Shannon Pratt's Control Premium Study™* contains up to 52 data fields for each sold business. The Web site launched in February 2001 included approximately 2000 sold businesses. Each quarterly print publication contains details on approximately 250 sold businesses.

DISCOUNTS FOR LACK OF MARKETABILITY

Emory Pre-IPO Studies. "The Value of Marketability as Illustrated in Initial Public Offerings of Common Stock." John D. Emory, Sr., ASA. Emory Business Valuation, LLC. 611 North Broadway, Suite 340, Milwaukee, WI, 53202, 414-273-9991. This is a series of studies over time and published as nine separate articles, with most appearing in *Business Valuation Review* and the earliest in *ASA Valuation.* The most recent article studies only dot-com companies and was co-authored with John D. Emory, Jr. and F. R. Dengel III, and published in *Shannon Pratt's Business Valuation*

Update™. The studies analyze fair market value transactions of private company stocks that occurred within five months prior to the IPO. The tables show private transaction price, transaction type, public offering price, and discount from IPO price or premium over private transaction price (expressed as a percentage), as well as various other information. Beginning with the earliest, the time periods covered in the studies are: January 1980 through June 1981; January 1985 through June 1986; August 1987 through January 1989; February 1989 through July 1990; August 1990 through January 1992; February 1992 through July 1993; January 1994 through June 1995; November 1995 through April 1997; May 1997 through March 2000. The Emory Pre-IPO Studies are available at www.BVLibrary.com.

Restricted Stock Studies.   National Association of Certified Valuation Analysts. 1111 East Brickyard Road, Suite 200, Salt Lake City, UT 84105, 801-486-0600, www.nacva.com. This is a series of studies undertaken independent of each other, comparing private block sale prices of restricted stocks to same day public trading prices, with the differences considered proxies for a discount for lack of marketability. Beginning with the earliest, the names of these studies and the time periods they cover are: SEC Institutional Investor Study (1966-1969); Gelman Study (1968-1970); Trout Study (1968-1972); Moroney Study (1968-1972); Maher Study (1969-1973); Standard Research Consultants Study (1978-1982); Willamette Management Associates Studies (1975-1995); Silber Study (1981-1988); FMV Opinions Study (1979-1992); Management Planning Study (1980-1996); Johnson Study (1991-1995); and Columbia Financial Advisors Study (1996-1997).

DISCOUNTS FROM NET ASSET VALUE FOR LIMITED PARTNERSHIP INTERESTS

Comprehensive Guide for the Valuation of Family Limited Partnerships.   Partnership Profiles, Inc. P.O. Box 7938, Dallas, TX, 75209, 800-634-4614, available from www.bvresources.com. This book offers empirical support for valuing minority interests in family limited partnerships. Based on eight years' worth of partnership secondary market data collected by Partnership Profiles, this book's key premise is that discounts from net asset value are the result of the rate of return sought by an investor. The authors develop a methodology of deriving a risk premium to use in building up discount rates for real estate entities using REIT and publicly held real estate partnership return data. The book also includes all of the historical Partnership Profiles discount studies since 1992, the authors' articles on FLP valuation and the most important court decisions regarding FLP valuations reprinted from www.BVLibrary.com.

The Partnership Spectrum.   Partnership Profiles, Inc. P.O. Box 7938, Dallas, TX, 75209, 800-634-4614. Published bimonthly, available in print. This publication tracks the partnership industry, especially focusing on, but not limited to, real estate partnerships. The annual May/June issue is a compilation of empirical data concerning discounts from net asset value at which minority interests in partnerships, particularly real estate limited partnerships, trade in the informal resale market. The partnership data included in the May/June annual studies include value per unit, average trade price, average discount, distribution frequency, type of real estate, level of debt (low, high), and distribution rate. The other issues are valuable to the partnership industry, however, they are not predominantly data compilations. Information for each partnership includes specific property holdings, cash distribution history, debt levels, key operating statistics, and so on.

2000 Partnership Re-Sale Discount Study. Partnership Profiles, Inc. P.O. Box 7938, Dallas, TX 75209, 800-634-4614, www.partnershipprofiles.com. Published annually, available on CD-ROM and online. This study reports the price-to-value discounts at which minority interests in real estate partnerships traded in the informal limited partnership secondary market during the two-month period ending May 31, 2000. The study reports price-to-value discounts for each partnership included in the study, as well as average price-to-value discounts for the entire group of partnerships, and based upon (i) real estate type, (ii) degree of debt financing, and (iii) distribution history. Also includes a new price-to-value discount study on liquidating partnerships. The 2000 study comes with a 266-page print Special Addendum that details the FLP's properties, several years of operating statistics, property distributions and more. Similar studies are available for the years 1993 through 1999. As a bonus, this also includes a CD-ROM with the most recent Form 10K/annual report for virtually every publicly held limited partnership.

Minority Interest Discount Database. Partnership Profiles, Inc. P.O. Box 7938, Dallas, TX 75209, 800-634-4614, www.partnershipprofiles.com. Available on CD-ROM and online. This is a software database for business valuation professionals, real estate appraisers, and CPAs who need empirical data to support minority interest discounts when valuing family limited partnerships and other fractional interests involving real estate. This database includes data compiled since 1994 in connection with Partnership Profiles' annual *Partnership Re-Sale Discount Studies.* The software program includes an interface allowing appraisers to select the attributes that are comparable to the FLP or other minority interest being valued, and the database will locate and display those partnerships that match the chosen criteria. The partnership information can be downloaded into a spreadsheet for further analysis.

DISCOUNTS FROM NET ASSET VALUE FOR REITs AND REOCs

NAREIT 2001 Statistical Digest. National Association of Real Estate Investment Trusts (NAREIT). 1875 Eye Street, N.W., D.C. 20006, 800-3-NAREIT, www.nareit.com. Published annually, available on CD-ROM and online. This is a comprehensive resource for insight into the Real Estate Investment Trust (REIT), Real Estate Operating Company (REOC), and publicly traded real estate industry, providing a broad range of relevant data, including an overall industry profile, securities offerings information, and performance statistics.

Realty Stock Review. Rainmaker Publications Group, Bldg. II, Suite 222, 802 West Park Avenue, Ocean NJ 07712, 732-493-1999, www.realtystockreview.com. Published semi-monthly, available in print and online. Publishes data on REITs and REOCs (Real Estate Operating Companies) including estimated adjusted net asset values from investment analysts, benchmark returns such as from Morgan Stanley REIT Index, NAREIT Index, and the Wilshire Real Estate Securities Index. This publication also presents side-by-side analysis of more than 100 REITs and REOCs compared to one another on more than 12 variables, including: price, net asset value (NAV), premium/discount, debt, dividend, market capitalization, total return, and more. Types of property in the study range include apartments, factory outlet centers, office, industrial, self-storage, and more.

DISCOUNTS FROM NET ASSET VALUE FOR CLOSED-END INVESTMENT FUNDS

Barron's. Dow Jones & Company, Inc. 200 Liberty Street, New York, NY 10281, 800-544-0422, www.barrons.com. Published weekly, available in print and online. Presents data on closed-end funds, municipal bond funds, mutual fund performance averages, and indexes. For the closed-end funds the following data are offered: ticker, objective, reported, asset value, NAV, market price, premium/discount, 52-week average premium/discount, annualized market returns for the quarter, year, 3, 5, and 10-year, 1-year NAV return, dividend yield, expense ratio, phone number, and manager. The *Mutual Funds* pull-out section is published weekly with special quarterly guides containing data on more than 8,000 mutual funds.

New York Times. The New York Times Company, 229 West 43rd Street, New York, NY 10036, 800-NYTIMES (698-4637), www.nytimes.com. Published daily, available in print and online. The *Money & Business* section distinguishes among the following types of closed-end funds: separate general and specialized equity, preferred stock, world equity, convertible securities, bond funds, world income, national municipal, and single state municipal bond. Fund name, stock exchange, NAV, market price, and change are presented for each fund.

Wall Street Journal. Dow Jones & Company, Inc. 200 Liberty Street, New York, NY 10281, 800-JOURNAL, www.wsj.com. Published daily, available in print and online. Offers data on closed-end funds trading on the AMEX, NASDAQ, NYSE, NASDAQ small cap, and Chicago stock exchanges. The data includes yield change, 52-week low and high, dividend, yield, volume, close, and net change.

The Investor's Guide to Closed-End Funds. Thomas J. Herzfeld Advisors, Inc. P.O. Box 161465, Miami, FL 33116, 305-271-1900, www.herzfeld.com. This is a monthly research report containing trading recommendations on all closed-end funds in every issue. The August 2000 issue of the report contains a 61-page section of ten-year charts of premium/discount to net asset value from 30 June 1990 to 30 June 2000 for each closed-end fund (approx. 574 funds).

The Thomas J. Herzfeld 1997/1998 Encyclopedia of Closed-End Funds. Thomas J. Herzfeld Advisors, Inc. P.O. Box 161465, Miami, FL 33116, 305-271-1900, www.herzfeld.com. Provides a complete guide from the basics of closed-end fund investing to effective trading strategies for every risk level. The volume contains a complete statistical section comparing each fund by performance, expense ratio, income ratio, size, management, plus a full page of coverage for over 480 closed-end funds. It also includes 120 pages of historical charts of net asset value/price and premium/discount for all funds covered.

DISCOUNT AND CAPITALIZATION RATES

Appraiser News. The Appraisal Institute. 875 N. Michigan Ave., Suite 2400, Chicago, IL 60611-1980, 312-335-4100, www.appraisalinstitute.org. This is a source of equity yield rates for real property investments. These rates of return are typically based on transactions involving fee simple interests.

Cost of Capital Quarterly. Ibbotson Associates. 225 North Michigan Avenue, Suite 700, Chicago, IL 60601, 800-758-3557, www.ibbotson.com. This is a source of equity rates of returns on publicly traded companies in a wide variety of industries. Data are sorted by standard industrial classification (SIC) code.

Stocks, Bonds, Bills, and Inflation, Valuation Edition. Ibbotson Associates. 225 North Michigan Avenue, Suite 700, Chicago, IL 60601, 800-758-3557, www.ibbotson.com. Published annually, available in print. This is a source of equity risk premiums of publicly traded companies. This data is typically used in the capital asset pricing model (CAPM) to quantify equity rates of return specific to certain industries.

Korpacz Real Estate Investor Survey. Price WaterhouseCoopers, www.pwcreval.com. Published quarterly, available in print and online. This report is a source of equity yield rates for real-property investments. These rates of return are typically based on fee-simple transactions. The report contains industry standard up-to-date capitalization and discount rates and other cash flow forecast assumptions of active investors.

Real Estate Report. Real Estate Research Corporation. 980 North Michigan Avenue, Suite 1675, Chicago, IL 60611, 312-587-1800, www.rerc.com. This publication is a source of equity rates for real-property investments. These rates of return are typically based on transactions involving fee-simple interests.

Table of Cases

This table of cases includes court decisions on all topics discussed in this book and is divided into the following subjects: tax cases (includes gift tax and estate tax cases), Employee Stock Ownership Plan (ESOP) cases, dissenting shareholder and shareholder oppression cases, marital dissolution cases, and a bankruptcy case.

The full texts of all cases included in this Table of Cases are available to subscribers of BVLibrary.com.

GIFT, ESTATE, & INCOME TAX CASES

Adair v. Commissioner, T.C. Memo 1987-494, 54 T.C.M. (CCH) 705 (1987) 257

Andrews, Estate of v. Commissioner, 79 T.C. 938 (1982) 173

Barge, Estate of v. Commissioner, T.C. Memo 1997-188, 73 T.C.M. (CCH) 2615 (1997) 312, 313

Barnes v. Commissioner, T.C. Memo 1998-413, 76 T.C.M. (CCH) 881 (1998) 198, 221

Barudin, Estate of v. Commissioner, T.C. Memo 1996-395, 72 T.C.M. (CCH) 488 (1996) 66, 289

Borgatello, Estate of v. Commissioner, T.C. Memo 2000-264, 80 T.C.M. (CCH) 260 (2000) 172, 175, 242

Bosca, Estate of v. Commissioner, T.C. Memo 1998-251, 76 T.C.M. (CCH) 62 (1998) 222

Branson, Estate of v. Commissioner, T.C. Memo 1999-231, 78 T.C.M. (CCH) 78 (1999) 258

Brocato, Estate of v. Commissioner, T.C. Memo 1999-424, 78 T.C.M (CCH) 1243 (1999) 257

Busch, Estate of v. Commissioner, T.C. Memo 2000-3, 79 T.C.M. (CCH) 1276 (2000) 310, 311

Christie, Estate of v. Commissioner, T.C. Memo 1974-95, 33 T.C.M. (CCH) 476 (1974) 256

Church v. United States, 2000 U.S. Dist. LEXIS 714 (W.D. Tex. 2000) 290

Cloutier, Estate of v. Commissioner, T.C. Memo 1996-49, 71 T.C.M. (CCH) 2001 (1996) 175

Davis, Estate of v. Commissioner, 110 T.C. 530 (1998) 88, 239, 240, 241, 243, 248, 253, 257, 319

MARITAL DISSOLUTION CASES

Stayer v. Stayer, 206 Wis.2d 675, 558 N.W.2d 704 (Wis. Ct. App. 1996) 75
Tofte, In re the Marriage of, 134 Or. App. 449, 895 P.2d 1387 (Or. Ct. App. 1995) 204
Verholek v. Verholek, 1999 Pa. Super. 282, 741 A.2d 792 (Pa. Super. Ct. 1999) 74
Zoldan v. Zoldan, 1999 Ohio App. LEXIS 2644 (Ohio Ct. App. 1999) 246

BANKRUPTCY CASE

In re Frezzo, 217 B.R. 985 (Bankr. E.D. Pa. 1998) 75, 243

Appendix D

How Much Can Marketability Affect Security Values?

Francis A. Longstaff*

Journal of Finance, Volume 50, Issue 5 (Dec., 1995), 1767–1774.
Journal of Finance
© 1995 American Finance Association
© 2001 JSTOR

HOW MUCH CAN MARKETABILITY AFFECT SECURITY VALUES?

Abstract

How marketability affects security prices is one of the most important issues in finance. We derive a simple analytical upper bound on the value of marketability using option-pricing theory. We show that discounts for lack of marketability can potentially be large even when the illiquidity period is very short. This analysis also provides a benchmark for assessing the potential costs of exchange rules and regulatory requirements restricting the ability of investors to trade when desired. Furthermore, these results provide new insights into the relation between discounts for lack of marketability and the length of the marketability restriction.

The issue of how marketability affects the value of securities is of fundamental importance in finance. This has been dramatically illustrated by the recent collapse of several well-known financial institutions that were unable to sell investment assets quickly enough to meet unexpected cash flow needs. This issue has also become increasingly important to regulators, rating agencies, security exchanges, auditors, and institutional investors.

*The Anderson Graduate School of Management, UCLA. I am grateful for the comments of Michael Brennan, Julian Franks, Mark Grinblatt, Eduardo Schwartz, Jean-Luc Vila, and Pradeep Yadav and seminar participants at the American Stock Exchange (AMEX) Options Colloquium, Case Western Reserve University, the London School of Business, McGill University, the University of Strathclyde, the University of Toronto, and the University of Vienna. I am particularly grateful for the comments and suggestions of René Stulz and an anonymous referee. All errors are my responsibility.

There are many situations in which the marketability of a security may be restricted. For example, when an investor lends securities under a reverse repurchase agreement, the investor foregoes the right to sell the securities until they are returned—a lesson painfully learned by Orange County. For many investors, the marketability of initial public offering (IPO) shares can be temporarily restricted. This is because underwriters often pressure investors who are allocated shares in an IPO to refrain from flipping or immediately reselling the shares. This implicit restriction on marketability may explain a portion of the underpricing of IPOs. Another example is letter stock. This is stock issued by firms under SEC Rule 144 that cannot be sold by an investor for a two-year period after it is acquired. As shown by Silber (1992), letter stock is typically placed privately at 30 to 35 percent discounts to the value of otherwise identical unrestricted stock.

This article presents a simple analytical upper bound on the value of marketability. The intuition behind these results can best be conveyed by considering a hypothetical investor with perfect market timing ability who is restricted from selling a security for T periods. If the marketability restriction were to be relaxed, the investor could then sell when the price of the security reached its maximum. Thus, if the marketability restriction were relaxed, the incremental cash flow to the investor would essentially be the same as if he swapped the time-T value of the security for the maximum price attained by the security. The present value of this lookback or liquidity swap represents the value of marketability for this hypothetical investor, and provides an upper bound for any actual investor with imperfect market timing ability.

This analysis provides a number of new insights about how marketability restrictions affect security values. First, we show that discounts for lack of marketability can be large even when the length of the marketability restriction is very short. Second, the upper bound provides a benchmark for estimating the valuation effects of marketability restrictions such as circuit breakers, trading halts, and prohibitions on program trading. Finally, these results allow us to assess directly whether empirical estimates of discounts for lack of marketability are consistent with rational market pricing.

I. The Framework

We first describe the framework in which we derive the upper bound on the value of marketability. An important advantage of this framework is that we do not need to make all of the assumptions about informational asymmetries, investor preferences, etc. that would be required in a full general equilibrium model. The cost of this, of course, is that we only obtain bounds, rather than an explicit model of the value of marketability.[1] To make the intuition more clear, we focus on the simplest possible

---

[1]Mayers (1972, 1973, 1976), Brito (1977), Stapleton and Subrahmanyam (1979), and Boudoukh and Whitelaw (1993) present general equilibrium models of the returns on nonmarketable assets. Their results suggest that the size of the equilibrium discount for lack of marketability depends critically on how closely the optimal strategy approximates the buy-and-hold strategy.

framework in this section. This framework, however, could clearly be extended to provide tighter upper bounds.

Let V denote the current or time-zero value of a security that is continuously traded in a frictionless market. We assume that the equilibrium dynamics of V are given by the stochastic process

$$dV = \mu V dt + \sigma V dZ, \tag{1}$$

where μ and σ are constants and Z is a standard Wiener process. We also assume that the riskless interest rate r is constant.

Consider a hypothetical investor who holds the security in his portfolio, but is restricted from selling the security prior to some fixed time T. The value of this security to this investor equals the present value of a cash flow of V_T to be received at time T.[2] Now assume that this investor has perfect market timing ability that would allow him to sell the security and reinvest the proceeds in the riskless asset at the time τ that maximizes the value of his portfolio. Let M_T denote the time-T payoff to this investor if the sale could be timed optimally, where $M_T = \max_{0 \leq \tau \leq T}(e^r(T-\tau)V_\tau)$. As long as the investor cannot sell the security prior to time T, however, he cannot benefit from having perfect market timing ability.

This marketability restriction imposes an important opportunity cost on this hypothetical investor since the security position is only worth V_T to the investor at time T if he is restricted from selling, but would be worth M_T if he were allowed to sell earlier.[3] Thus, using a standard dominance or no-arbitrage argument, the value of marketability to an investor with perfect market timing ability is simply the present value of the incremental cash flow $M_T - V_T$ that the investor would receive if the marketability restriction were relaxed. Clearly, the value of marketability would be less for an actual investor with imperfect market timing ability. Thus, the present value of the incremental cash flow $M_T - V_T$ represents an upper bound on the value of marketability.[4]

This incremental cash flow $M_T - V_T$ can also be viewed as the payoff from an option on the maximum value (including interest from reinvesting the sale proceeds) of the security M_T, where the strike price of the option V_T is stochastic. Since $M_T \geq V_T$, this lookback option will always be in the money at expiration. Hence, $\max(0, M_T - V_T) = M_T - V_T$. Alternatively, the cash flow $M_T - V_T$ can be viewed as the payoff of a liquidity swap in which V_T is swapped for M_T at time T.

---

[2]Observe that nonmarketability is investor-specific rather than security-specific in this framework. This differs from the equilibrium models presented in Amihud and Mendelson (1986) and Boudoukh and Whitelaw (1993). Since the other investors in this market are unrestricted, derivative claims on V can be priced using standard no-arbitrage arguments.

[3]Note that M_T will generally be higher than the maximum value reached by the underlying asset price since it includes interest from reinvesting the proceeds of the sale.

[4]We are implicitly making the standard no-arbitrage assumption that the price V of the underlying asset is exogenous and is not affected by whether this hypothetical investor is restricted or not.

II. The Upper Bound

The present value of $M_T - V_T$ can be determined using standard risk-neutral valuation techniques familiar from option-pricing theory. Let $F(V, T)$ denote the present value of $M_T - V_T$. This present value equals

$$F(V, T) = e^{-rT}E[M_T] = e^{-rT}E[V_T],\tag{2}$$

where the expectation is taken with respect to the risk-neutral dynamics for V. Using the well-known density function for the maximum of a Brownian motion process in Harrison (1985), the expectations in equation (2) can be evaluated directly to give the following closed-form solution for the upper bound,

$$F(V, T) = V\left(2 + \frac{\sigma^2 T}{2}\right)N\left(\frac{\sqrt{\sigma^2 T}}{2}\right) + V\sqrt{\frac{\sigma^2 T}{2\pi}}\exp\left(-\frac{\sigma^2 T}{8}\right) - V,\tag{3}$$

where $N(\cdot)$ is the cumulative normal distribution function.[5]

The upper bound $F(V, T)$ is proportional to the current value of the security V. Thus, bounds on the value of marketability, or equivalently, bounds on the size of the discount for lack of marketability, can easily be expressed as a percentage of the value of V. It is readily shown that the upper bound is an increasing function of length of the marketability restriction T. In addition, the upper bound is an increasing function of the variance of returns σ^2. This is intuitive, since the more volatile the price of the security, the higher is the opportunity cost of not being able to trade. Taking the limit of $F(V,T)$ shows that the upper bound converges smoothly to zero as $T \to 0$.

This upper bound represents the largest discount for lack of marketability that could be sustained in a market with rational investors. If illiquid securities could be acquired at prices less than $F(V,T)$ below those of otherwise identical liquid securities, then arbitrage profits could potentially be achieved by holding nonmarketable securities and synthesizing marketability using derivatives.

This upper bound is illustrated in Table I, which reports the percentage upper bounds for values of σ^2 comparable to those for 6-month, 1-year, and 2-year Treasury securities. The percentage bounds for a 1-day nonmarketability period range from 0.053 to 0.210. The percentage bounds for a 5-day nonmarketability period are only about twice as large. This shows that the per-unit-time-period effect of illiquidity is largest for relatively small values of T. These results have important implications for the overnight and term repo markets, since the difference between the general and special collateral rates should reflect the value of the marketability foregone by lending the security.

Figure 1 graphs the upper bound as a function of the nonmarketability period for values of σ ranging from 0.10 to 0.30. This range of volatility is consistent with

---

[5] The first term in equation (2) equals e^{-rT} times e^{rT} times the expected maximum of the discounted process $e^{-rt}V_t$. This discounted process is a martingale with respect to the risk-neutral dynamics for V.

Table I Upper Bounds for Percentage Discounts for Lack of Marketability
The standard deviations σ = 0.0125, 0.0250, and 0.0500 correspond to the approximate historic standard deviations of returns for 6-month, 1-year, and 2-year Treasury securities.

Marketability Restriction Period	$\sigma = 0.0125$	$\sigma = 0.0250$	$\sigma = 0.0500$
1 Day	0.053	0.105	0.210
5 Days	0.118	0.235	0.471
10 Days	0.166	0.333	0.667
20 Days	0.235	0.471	0.944
30 Days	0.288	0.577	1.157
60 Days	0.408	0.817	1.639
90 Days	0.500	1.001	2.010

typical stock return volatilities. As shown, the upper bound is an increasing concave function of the length of the marketability restriction. In addition, Figure 1 shows that discounts for lack of marketability can be very large even when the duration of restricted marketability is fairly short. This can also be seen in Table II, which reports numerical values for the percentage upper bound using the same range of volatilities.

Figure 1 Upper bounds for percentage discounts for lack of marketability graphed as a function of the length of the marketability restriction period measured in days and for varying values of the standard deviation of returns denoted as sigma.

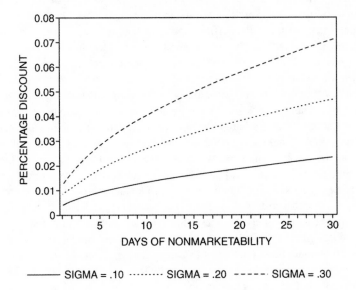

Table II **Upper Bounds for Percentage Discounts for Lack of Marketability**
(The standard deviations correspond to the range typically observed for equity
securities.)

Marketability Restriction Period	σ = 0.10	σ = 0.20	σ = 0.30
1 Day	0.421	0.844	1.268
5 Days	0.944	1.894	2.852
10 Days	1.337	2.688	4.052
20 Days	1.894	3.817	5.768
30 Days	2.324	4.691	7.100
60 Days	3.299	6.683	10.153
90 Days	4.052	8.232	12.542
180 Days	5.768	11.793	18.082
1 Year	8.232	16.984	26.276
2 Years	11.793	24.643	38.605
5 Years	19.128	40.979	65.772

Table II shows that the upper bound ranges from 0.421 to 1.268 percent for a 1-day
marketability restriction. The upper bound ranges from 1.337 to 4.052 percent for a
10-day marketability restriction.

The magnitude of the upper bounds for restriction periods measured in days or
weeks has important implications for equity markets, since there are many situations
in which the marketability of shares is restricted for a short period of time. For example, IPO underwriters often allocate shares to investors with the implicit understanding that the shares will not be flipped or immediately resold in the aftermarket.
Investors who violate this implicit understanding may be less likely to receive allo-
cations in attractive future IPOs. This implicit restriction on marketability may only
last for a few days or weeks, during which time the underwriter may engage in market stabilization efforts. Our results suggest that the cost to the investor of the temporary restriction on selling IPO shares could be fairly substantial given the fact that
the volatility of returns may be particularly high during this period.

These results also provide some measure of the potential cost to investors of impos-
ing market restrictions such as circuit breakers, trading halts, or prohibitions against program trading. Table II suggests that the potential cost of these restrictions could again be
very sizable. An important implication of this is that prices of securities in markets where
liquidity may be interrupted could be substantially lower than they otherwise might be
because of the expected costs of nonmarketability. Our analysis provides a framework for
evaluating the potential costs of different forms of exchange and regulatory requirements.

The upper bound can also be viewed as the maximum amount that any investor
would be willing to pay in order to obtain immediacy in liquidating a security position. Thus, this upper bound provides an endogenous measure of the largest possible
bid-ask spread or transaction cost for a security. In contrast, previous research on the
valuation of illiquid securities by Amihud and Mendelson (1986) and Boudoukh and

Whitelaw (1993) and on the valuation of securities in the presence of transaction costs by Constantinides (1986) and Vayanos and Vila (1992) takes the bid-ask spread or transaction costs for the security to be exogenous.

III. A Comparison

It is also interesting to compare the upper bound to empirical estimates of discounts for lack of marketability. In particular, much of the empirical evidence about discounts for lack of marketability focuses on the pricing of SEC Rule 144 restricted stock. This is stock issued by a firm that is not registered for public trading, but is otherwise identical to publicly traded stock. The primary limitation of Rule 144 stock is that the recipient cannot sell the shares for a two-year period. After two years, the shares become marketable, subject to several minor trading-volume limitations. Restricted shares are typically issued by firms via private placements instead of the usual public offering mechanism. By comparing the price at which the restricted stock is privately placed to the market price for the firm's registered shares, the discount for lack of marketability can be directly measured.

Pratt (1989) summarizes the evidence from eight separate studies of restricted stock. The median percentage discount found in these studies is approximately 35 to 40 percent. This range is fairly consistent across all of the studies summarized by Pratt. This range is also consistent with the results of a recent study by Silber (1992) who finds that the mean discount for lack of marketability is 34 percent in a sample of private placements of stock during the 1981 to 1988 period.

In order to make comparisons, Figure 2 graphs the percentage upper bound on the discount for lack of marketability for a wide range of volatilities. Assuming that the average standard deviation of returns for the firms studied by Pratt (1989) and Silber (1992) is in the range of 0.25 to 0.35, Figure 2 suggests that empirical estimates of the discount for lack of marketability closely approximate the upper bound. In one sense, this is a surprising finding since the upper bound was derived from the perspective of a theoretical investor with perfect market timing ability. These results, however, suggest that the upper bound may actually be a tight bound. Thus, the analytical results in this article may actually provide useful approximations of the value of marketability, rather than just serving as an upper bound.

IV. Conclusion

This article provides a first step toward developing a practical model for valuing liquidity in financial markets. The results of this analysis can be used to provide rough order-of-magnitude estimates of the valuation effects of different types of marketability restrictions. In fact, the empirical evidence suggests that the upper bound may actually be a close approximation to observed discounts for lack of marketability. More importantly, however, these results illustrate that option-pricing techniques

Figure 2   Upper bounds for percentage discounts for lack of marketability graphed as a function of the standard deviations of returns. The length of the marketability restriction period is two years, corresponding to the length of the marketability restriction for letter stock.

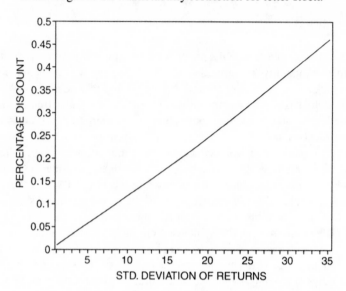

can be useful in understanding liquidity in financial markets and that liquidity derivatives have potential as tools for managing and controlling the risk of illiquidity.

References

Amihud, Y., and H. Mendelson, 1986. Asset pricing and the bid-ask spread, *Journal of Financial Economics* 17, 223–249.

Boudoukh, J., and R. F. Whitelaw, 1993. Liquidity as a choice variable: A lesson from the Japanese government bond market, *The Review of Financial Studies* 6, 265–292.

Brito, N. O., 1977. Marketability restrictions and the valuation of capital assets under uncertainty, *Journal of Finance* 32, 1109–1123.

Constantinides, G. M., 1986. Capital market equilibrium with transaction costs, *Journal of Political Economy* 94, 842–862.

Harrison, J. M., 1985. *Brownian Motion and Stochastic Flow Systems* (John Wiley, New York, NY).

Mayers, D., 1972. Nonmarketable assets and capital market equilibrium under uncertainty, in M. C. Jensen, ed.: *Studies in the Theory of Capital Markets* (Praeger, New York, NY).

Mayers, D. 1973. Nonmarketable assets and the determination of capital asset prices in the absence of riskless asset, *Journal of Business* 46, 258–267.

Mayers, D., 1976. Nonmarketable assets, market segmentation and the level of asset prices, *Journal of Financial and Quantitative Analysis* 11, 1–12.

Pratt, S. P., 1989. *Valuing a Business* (Irwin, Homewood, IL).

Silber, W. L., 1991. Discounts on restricted stock: The impact of illiquidity on stock prices, *Financial Analysts Journal* 47, 60–64.

Stapleton, R. C., and M. G. Subrahmanyam, 1979. Marketability of assets and the price of risk, *Journal of Financial and Quantitative Analysis* 14, 1–10.

Vayanos, D., and J. L. Vila, 1992. Equilibrium interest rate and liquidity premium under proportional transactions costs, Working paper, Sloan School of Management, MIT.

Internal Revenue Service Revenue Ruling 77-287

1977-2 C.B. 319; 1977 IRB LEXIS 258; REV. RUL. 77-287

July, 1977

Valuation of securities restricted from immediate resale. Guidelines are set forth for the valuation, for Federal tax purposes, of securities that cannot be immediately resold because they are restricted from resale pursuant to Federal securities laws; Rev. Rul. 59-60 amplified.

SECTION 1. PURPOSE

The purpose of this Revenue Ruling is to amplify *Rev. Rul. 59-60, 1959-1 C.B. 237,* as modified by *Rev. Rul. 65-193, 1965-2 C.B. 370,* and to provide information and guidance to taxpayers, Internal Revenue Service personnel, and others concerned with the valuation, for Federal tax purposes, of securities that cannot be immediately resold because they are restricted from resale pursuant to Federal securities laws. This guidance is applicable only in cases where it is not inconsistent with valuation requirements of the Internal Revenue Code of 1954 or the regulations thereunder. Further, this ruling does not establish the time at which property shall be valued.

SEC. 2. NATURE OF THE PROBLEM

It frequently becomes necessary to establish the fair market value of stock that has not been registered for public trading when the issuing company has stock of the same class that is actively traded in one or more securities markets. The problem is to determine the difference in fair market value between the registered shares that are actively traded and the unregistered shares. This problem is often encountered in estate and gift tax cases. However, it is sometimes encountered when unregistered shares are issued in exchange for assets or the stock of an acquired company.

SEC. 3. BACKGROUND AND DEFINITIONS

.01 The Service outlined and reviewed in general the approach, methods, and factors to be considered in valuing shares of closely held corporate stock for estate and gift tax purposes in *Rev. Rul. 59-60,* as modified by *Rev. Rul. 65-193.* The provisions of *Rev. Rul. 59-60,* as modified, were extended to the valuation of corporate securities for income and other tax purposes by *Rev. Rul. 68-609, 1968-2 C.B. 327.*

.02 There are several terms currently in use in the securities industry that denote restrictions imposed on the resale and transfer of certain securities. The term frequently used to describe these securities is "restricted securities," but they are sometimes referred to as "unregistered securities," "investment letter stock," "control stock," or "private placement stock." Frequently these terms are used interchangeably. They all indicate that these particular securities cannot lawfully be distributed to the general public until a registration statement relating to the corporation underlying the securities has been filed, and has also become effective under the rules promulgated and enforced by the United States Securities & Exchange Commission (SEC) pursuant to the Federal securities laws. The following represents a more refined definition of each of the following terms along with two other terms—"exempted securities" and "exempted transactions."

(a) The term "restricted securities" is defined in Rule 144 adopted by the SEC as "securities acquired directly or indirectly from the issuer thereof, or from an affiliate of such issuer, in a transaction or chain of transactions not involving any public offering."

(b) The term "unregistered securities" refers to those securities with respect to which a registration statement, providing full disclosure by the issuing corporation, has not been filed with the SEC pursuant to the Securities Act of 1933. The registration statement is a condition precedent to a public distribution of securities in interstate commerce and is aimed at providing the prospective investor with a factual basis for sound judgment in making investment decisions.

(c) The terms "investment letter stock" and "letter stock" denote shares of stock that have been issued by a corporation without the benefit of filing a registration statement with the SEC. Such stock is subject to resale and transfer restrictions set forth in a letter agreement requested by the issuer and signed by the buyer of the stock when the stock is delivered. Such stock may be found in the hands of either individual investors or institutional investors.

(d) The term "control stock" indicates that the shares of stock have been held or are being held by an officer, director, or other person close to the management of the corporation. These persons are subject to certain requirements pursuant to SEC rules upon resale of shares they own in such corporations.

(e) The term "private placement stock" indicates that the stock has been placed with an institution or other investor who will presumably hold it for a long period and ultimately arrange to have the stock registered if it is to be offered to the general public. Such stock may or may not be subject to a letter agreement. Private placements of stock are exempted from the registration and prospectus provisions of the Securities Act of 1933.

(f) The term "exempted securities" refers to those classes of securities that are expressly excluded from the registration provisions of the Securities Act of 1933 and the distribution provisions of the Securities Exchange Act of 1934.

(g) The term "exempted transactions" refers to certain sales or distributions of securities that do not involve a public offering and are excluded from the registration and prospectus provisions of the Securities Act of 1933 and distribution provisions of the Securities Exchange Act of 1934. The exempted status makes it unnecessary for issuers of securities to go through the registration process.

SEC. 4. SECURITIES INDUSTRY PRACTICE IN VALUING RESTRICTED SECURITIES

.01 Investment Company Valuation Practices. The Investment Company Act of 1940 requires open-end investment companies to publish the valuation of their portfolio securities daily. Some of these companies have portfolios containing restricted securities, but also have unrestricted securities of the same class traded on a securities exchange. In recent years the number of restricted securities in such portfolios has increased. The following methods have been used by investment companies in the valuation of such restricted securities:

(a) Current market price of the unrestricted stock less a constant percentage discount based on purchase discount;

(b) Current market price of unrestricted stock less a constant percentage discount different from purchase discount;

(c) Current market price of the unrestricted stock less a discount amortized over a fixed period;

(d) Current market price of the unrestricted stock; and

(e) Cost of the restricted stock until it is registered.

The SEC ruled in its Investment Company Act Release No. 5847, dated October 21, 1969, that there can be no automatic formula by which an investment company can value the restricted securities in its portfolios. Rather, the SEC has determined that it is the responsibility of the board of directors of the particular investment company to determine the "fair value" of each issue of restricted securities in good faith.

.02 Institutional Investors Study. Pursuant to Congressional direction, the SEC undertook an analysis of the purchases, sales, and holding of securities by financial institutions, in order to determine the effect of institutional activity upon the securities market. The study report was published in eight volumes in March 1971. The fifth volume provides an analysis of restricted securities and deals with such items as the characteristics of the restricted securities purchasers and issuers, the size of transactions (dollars and shares), the marketability discounts on different trading markets, and the resale provisions. This research project provides some guidance for measuring the discount in that it contains information, based on the actual experience of the marketplace, showing that, during the period surveyed (January 1, 1966, through June 30, 1969), the amount of discount allowed for restricted securities from the trading price of the unrestricted securities was generally related to the following four factors.

(a) Earnings. Earnings and sales consistently have a significant influence on the size of restricted securities discounts according to the study. Earnings played the major part in establishing the ultimate discounts at which these stocks were sold from the current market price. Apparently earnings patterns, rather than sales patterns, determine the degree of risk of an investment.

(b) Sales. The dollar amount of sales of issuers' securities also has a major influence on the amount of discount at which restricted securities sell from the current market price. The results of the study generally indicate that the companies with the lowest dollar amount of sales during the test period accounted for most of the transactions involving the highest discount rates, while they accounted for only a small portion of all transactions involving the lowest discount rates.

(c) Trading Market. The market in which publicly held securities are traded also reflects variances in the amount of discount that is applied to restricted securities purchases. According to the study, discount rates were greatest on restricted stocks with unrestricted counterparts traded over-the-counter, followed by those with unrestricted counterparts listed on the American Stock Exchange, while the discount rates for those stocks with unrestricted counterparts listed on the New York Stock Exchange were the smallest.

(d) Resale Agreement Provisions. Resale agreement provisions often affect the size of the discount. The discount from the market price provides the main incentive for a potential buyer to acquire restricted securities. In judging the opportunity cost of freezing funds, the purchaser is analyzing two separate factors. The first factor is the risk that underlying value of the stock will change in a way that, absent the restrictive provisions, would have prompted a decision to sell. The second factor is the risk that the contemplated means of legally disposing of the stock may not materialize. From the seller's point of view, a discount is justified where the seller is relieved of the expenses of registration and public distribution, as well as of the risk that the market will adversely change before the offering is completed. The ultimate agreement between buyer and seller is a reflection of these and other considerations. Relative bargaining strengths of the parties to the agreement are major considerations that influence the resale terms and consequently the size of discounts in restricted securities transactions. Certain provisions are often found in agreements between buyers and sellers that affect the size of discounts at which restricted stocks are sold. Several such provisions follow, all of which, other than number (3), would tend to reduce the size of the discount:

(1) A provision giving the buyer an option to "piggyback," that is, to register restricted stock with the next registration statement, if any, filed by the issuer with the SEC;

(2) A provision giving the buyer an option to require registration at the seller's expense;

(3) A provision giving the buyer an option to require registration, but only at the buyer's own expense;

(4) A provision giving the buyer a right to receive continuous disclosure of information about the issuer from the seller;

(5) A provision giving the buyer a right to select one or more directors of the issuer;

(6) A provision giving the buyer an option to purchase additional shares of the issuer's stock; and

(7) A provision giving the buyer the right to have a greater voice in operations of the issuer if the issuer does not meet previously agreed upon operating standards.

Institutional buyers can and often do obtain many of these rights and options from the sellers of restricted securities, and naturally, the more rights the buyer can acquire, the lower the buyer's risk is going to be, thereby reducing the buyer's discount as well. Smaller buyers may not be able to negotiate the large discounts or the rights and options that volume buyers are able to negotiate.

.03 Summary. A variety of methods have been used by the securities industry to value restricted securities. The SEC rejects all automatic or mechanical solutions to the valuation of restricted securities, and prefers, in the case of the valuation of investment company portfolio stocks, to rely upon good faith valuations by the board of directors of each company. The study made by the SEC found that restricted securities generally are issued at a discount from the market value of freely tradable securities.

SEC. 5. FACTS AND CIRCUMSTANCES MATERIAL TO VALUATION OF RESTRICTED SECURITIES

.01 Frequently, a company has a class of stock that cannot be traded publicly. The reason such stock cannot be traded may arise from the securities statutes, as in the case of an "investment letter" restriction; it may arise from a corporate charter restriction, or perhaps from a trust agreement restriction. In such cases, certain documents and facts should be obtained for analysis.

.02 The following documents and facts, when used in conjunction with those discussed in Section 4 of *Rev. Rul. 59-60*, will be useful in the valuation of restricted securities:

(a) A copy of any declaration of trust, trust agreement, and any other agreements relating to the shares of restricted stock;

(b) A copy of any document showing any offers to buy or sell or indications of interest in buying or selling the restricted shares;

(c) The latest prospectus of the company;

(d) Annual reports of the company for 3 to 5 years preceding the valuation date;

(e) The trading prices and trading volume of the related class of traded securities 1 month preceding the valuation date, if they are traded on a stock exchange (if traded over-the-counter, prices may be obtained from the National Quotations Bureau, the National Association of Securities Dealers Automated Quotations (NASDAQ), or sometimes from broker-dealers making markets in the shares);

(f) The relationship of the parties to the agreements concerning the restricted stock, such as whether they are members of the immediate family or perhaps whether they are officers or directors of the company; and

(g) Whether the interest being valued represents a majority or minority ownership.

SEC. 6. WEIGHING FACTS AND CIRCUMSTANCES MATERIAL TO RESTRICTED STOCK VALUATION

All relevant facts and circumstances that bear upon the worth of restricted stock, including those set forth above in the preceding Sections 4 and 5, and those set forth in Section 4 of *Rev. Rul. 59-60*, must be taken into account in arriving at the fair market value of such securities. Depending on the circumstances of each case, certain factors may carry more weight than others. To illustrate:

.01 Earnings, net assets, and net sales must be given primary consideration in arriving at an appropriate discount for restricted securities from the freely traded shares. These are the elements of value that are always used by investors in making investment decisions. In some cases, one element may be more important than in other cases. In the case of manufacturing, producing, or distributing companies, primary weight must be accorded earnings and net sales; but in the case of investment or holding companies, primary weight must be given to the net assets of the company underlying the stock. In the former type of companies, value is more closely linked to past, present, and future earnings while in the latter type of companies, value is more closely linked to the existing net assets of the company. See the discussion in Section 5 of *Rev. Rul. 59-60*.

.02 Resale provisions found in the restriction agreements must be scrutinized and weighed to determine the amount of discount to apply to the preliminary fair market value of the company. The two elements of time and expense bear upon this discount; the longer the buyer of the shares must wait to liquidate the shares, the greater the discount. Moreover, if the provisions make it necessary for the buyer to bear the expense of registration, the greater the discount. However, if the provisions of the restricted stock agreement make it possible for the buyer to "piggyback" shares at the next offering, the discount would be smaller.

.03 The relative negotiation strengths of the buyer and seller of restricted stock may have a profound effect on the amount of discount. For example, a tight money situation may cause the buyer to have the greater balance of negotiation strength in a transaction. However, in some cases the relative strengths may tend to cancel each other out.

.04 The market experience of freely tradable securities of the same class as the restricted securities is also significant in determining the amount of discount. Whether the shares are privately held or publicly traded affects the worth of the shares to the holder. Securities traded on a public market generally are worth more to investors than those that are not traded on a public market. Moreover, the type of public market in which the unrestricted securities are traded is to be given consideration.

SEC. 7. EFFECT ON OTHER DOCUMENTS

Rev. Rul. 59-60, as modified by *Rev. Rul. 65-193*, is amplified.

Appendix F

Securities and Exchange Commission Rules 144 and 144A

Rule 144

THIS SECTION IS CURRENT THROUGH THE MARCH 16, 2001
ISSUE OF THE FEDERAL REGISTER

TITLE 17—COMMODITY AND SECURITIES EXCHANGES
CHAPTER II—SECURITIES AND EXCHANGE COMMISSION
PART 230—GENERAL RULES AND REGULATIONS, SECURITIES ACT OF 1933
GENERAL

17 CFR 230.144

§ 230.144 Persons deemed not to be engaged in a distribution and therefore not underwriters.

PRELIMINARY NOTE: Rule 144 is designed to implement the fundamental purposes of the Act, as expressed in its preamble, To provide full and fair disclosure of the character of the securities sold in interstate commerce and through the mails, and to prevent fraud in the sale thereof * * * The rule is designed to prohibit the creation of public markets in securities of issuers concerning which adequate current information is not available to the public. At the same time, where adequate current information concerning the issuer is available to the public, the rule permits the public sale in ordinary trading transactions of limited amounts of securities owned by persons controlling, controlled by or under common control with the issuer and by persons who have acquired restricted securities of the issuer.

Certain basic principles are essential to an understanding of the requirement of registration in the Act:

1. If any person utilizes the jurisdictional means to sell any nonexempt security to any other person, the security must be registered unless a statutory exemption can be found for the transaction.

2. In addition to the exemptions found in section 3, four exemptions applicable to transactions in securities are contained in section 4. Three of these section 4 exemptions are clearly not available to anyone acting as an underwriter of securities. (The fourth, found in section 4(4), is available only to those who act as brokers under

certain limited circumstances.) An understanding of the term underwriter is therefore important to anyone who wishes to determine whether or not an exemption from registration is available for his sale of securities.

The term underwriter is broadly defined in section 2(11) of the Act to mean any person who has purchased from an issuer with a view to, or offers or sells for an issuer in connection with, the distribution of any security, or participates, or has a direct or indirect participation in any such undertaking, or participates or has a participation in the direct or indirect underwriting of any such undertaking. The interpretation of this definition has traditionally focused on the words with a view to in the phrase purchased from an issuer with a view to * * * distribution. Thus, an investment banking firm which arranges with an issuer for the public sale of its securities is clearly an underwriter under that section. Individual investors who are not professionals in the securities business may also be underwriters within the meaning of that term as used in the Act if they act as links in a chain of transactions through which securities move from an issuer to the public. Since it is difficult to ascertain the mental state of the purchaser at the time of his acquisition, subsequent acts and circumstances have been considered to determine whether such person took with a view to distribution at the time of his acquisition. Emphasis has been placed on factors such as the length of time the person has held the securities and whether there has been an unforeseeable change in circumstances of the holder. Experience has shown, however, that reliance upon such factors as the above has not assured adequate protection of investors through the maintenance of informed trading markets and has led to uncertainty in the application of the registration provisions of the Act.

It should be noted that the statutory language of section 2(11) is in the disjunctive. Thus, it is insufficient to conclude that a person is not an underwriter solely because he did not purchase securities from an issuer with a view to their distribution. It must also be established that the person is not offering or selling for an issuer in connection with the distribution of the securities, does not participate or have a direct or indirect participation in any such undertaking, and does not participate or have a participation in the direct or indirect underwriting of such an undertaking.

In determining when a person is deemed not to be engaged in a distribution several factors must be considered.

First, the purpose and underlying policy of the Act to protect investors requires that there be adequate current information concerning the issuer, whether the resales of securities by persons result in a distribution or are effected in trading transactions. Accordingly, the availability of the rule is conditioned on the existence of adequate current public information.

Secondly, a holding period prior to resale is essential, among other reasons, to assure that those persons who buy under a claim of a section 4(2) exemption have assumed the economic risks of investment, and therefore are not acting as conduits for sale to the public of unregistered securities, directly or indirectly, on behalf of an issuer. It should be noted that there is nothing in section 2(11) which places a time limit on a person's status as an underwriter. The public has the same need for protection afforded by registration whether the securities are distributed shortly after their purchase or after a considerable length of time.

A third factor, which must be considered in determining what is deemed not to constitute a distribution, is the impact of the particular transaction or transactions on the trading markets. Section 4(1) was intended to exempt only routine trading transactions between individual investors with respect to securities already issued and not to exempt distributions by issuers or acts of other individuals who engage in steps necessary to such distributions. Therefore, a person reselling securities under section 4(1) of the Act must sell the securities in such limited quantities and in such a manner as not to disrupt the trading markets. The larger the amount of securities involved, the more likely it is that such resales may involve methods of offering and amounts of compensation usually associated with a distribution rather than routine trading transactions. Thus, solicitation of buy orders or the payment of extra compensation are not permitted by the rule.

In summary, if the sale in question is made in accordance with all of the provisions of the section as set forth below, any person who sells restricted securities shall be deemed not to be engaged in a distribution of such securities and therefore not an underwriter thereof. The rule also provides that any person who sells restricted or other securities on behalf of a person in a control relationship with the issuer shall be deemed not to be engaged in a distribution of such securities and therefore not to be an underwriter thereof, if the sale is made in accordance with all the conditions of the section.

(a) Definitions. The following definitions shall apply for the purposes of this section.

(1) An affiliate of an issuer is a person that directly, or indirectly through one or more intermediaries, controls, or is controlled by, or is under common control with, such issuer.

(2) The term person when used with reference to a person for whose account securities are to be sold in reliance upon this section includes, in addition to such person, all of the following persons:

(i) Any relative or spouse of such person, or any relative of such spouse, any one of whom has the same home as such person;

(ii) Any trust or estate in which such person or any of the persons specified in paragraph (a)(2)(i) of this section collectively own 10 percent or more of the total beneficial interest or of which any of such persons serve as trustee, executor or in any similar capacity; and

(iii) Any corporation or other organization (other than the issuer) in which such person or any of the persons specified in paragraph (a)(2)(i) of this section are the beneficial owners collectively of 10 percent or more of any class of equity securities or 10 percent or more of the equity interest.

(3) The term restricted securities means:

(i) Securities acquired directly or indirectly from the issuer, or from an affiliate of the issuer, in a transaction or chain of transactions not involving any public offering;

(ii) Securities acquired from the issuer that are subject to the resale limitations of § 230.502(d) under Regulation D or § 230.701(c);

(iii) Securities acquired in a transaction or chain of transactions meeting the requirements of § 230.144A;

(iv) Securities acquired from the issuer in a transaction subject to the conditions of Regulation CE (§ 230.1001);

(v) Equity securities of domestic issuers acquired in a transaction or chain of transactions subject to the conditions of § 230.901 or § 230.903 under Regulation S (§ 230.901 through § 230.905, and Preliminary Notes);

(vi) Securities acquired in a transaction made under § 230.801 to the same extent and proportion that the securities held by the security holder of the class with respect to which the rights offering was made were as of the record date for the rights offering "restricted securities" within the meaning of this paragraph (a)(3); and

(vii) Securities acquired in a transaction made under § 230.802 to the same extent and proportion that the securities that were tendered or exchanged in the exchange offer or business combination were "restricted securities" within the meaning of this paragraph (a)(3).

(b) Conditions to be met. Any affiliate or other person who sells restricted securities of an issuer for his own account, or any person who sells restricted or any other securities for the account of an affiliate of the issuer of such securities, shall be deemed not to be engaged in a distribution of such securities and therefore not to be an underwriter thereof within the meaning of section 2(11) of the Act if all of the conditions of this section are met.

(c) Current public information. There shall be available adequate current public information with respect to the issuer of the securities. Such information shall be deemed to be available only if either of the following conditions is met:

(1) Filing of reports. The issuer has securities registered pursuant to section 12 of the Securities Exchange Act of 1934, has been subject to the reporting requirements of section 13 of that Act for a period of at least 90 days immediately preceding the sale of the securities and has filed all the reports required to be filed thereunder during the 12 months preceding such sale (or for such shorter period that the issuer was required to file such reports); or has securities registered pursuant to the Securities Act of 1933, has been subject to the reporting requirements of section 15(d) of the Securities Exchange Act of 1934 for a period of at least 90 days immediately preceding the sale of the securities and has filed all the reports required to be filed thereunder during the 12 months preceding such sale (or for such shorter period that the issuer was required to file such reports). The person for whose account the securities are to be sold shall be entitled to rely upon a statement in whichever is the most recent report, quarterly or annual, required to be filed and filed by the issuer that such issuer has filed all reports required to be filed by section 13 or 15(d) of the Securities Exchange Act of 1934 during the preceding 12 months (or for such shorter period that the issuer was required to file such reports) and has been subject to such filing requirements for the past 90 days, unless he knows or has reason to believe that the issuer has not complied with such requirements. Such person shall also be entitled to rely upon a written statement from the issuer that it has complied with such reporting requirements unless he knows or has reasons to believe that the issuer has not complied with such requirements.

(2) Other public information. If the issuer is not subject to section 13 or 15(d) of the Securities Exchange Act of 1934, there is publicly available the information concerning the issuer specified in paragraphs (a)(5)(i) to (xiv), inclusive, and paragraph (a)(5)(xvi) of Rule 15c2-11 (§ 240.15c2-11 of this chapter) under that Act or, if the issuer is an insurance company, the information specified in section 12(g)(2)(G)(i) of that Act.

(d) Holding period for restricted securities. If the securities sold are restricted securities, the following provisions apply:

(1) General rule. A minimum of one year must elapse between the later of the date of the acquisition of the securities from the issuer or from an affiliate of the issuer, and any resale of such securities in reliance on this section for the account of either the acquiror or any subsequent holder of those securities. If the acquiror takes the securities by purchase, the one-year period shall not begin until the full purchase price or other consideration is paid or given by the person acquiring the securities from the issuer or from an affiliate of the issuer.

(2) Promissory notes, other obligations or installment contracts. Giving the issuer or affiliate of the issuer from whom the securities were purchased a promissory note or other obligation to pay the purchase price, or entering into an installment purchase contract with such seller, shall not be deemed full payment of the purchase price unless the promissory note, obligation or contract:

(i) Provides for full recourse against the purchaser of the securities;

(ii) Is secured by collateral, other than the securities purchased, having a fair market value at least equal to the purchase price of the securities purchased; and

(iii) Shall have been discharged by payment in full prior to the sale of the securities.

(3) Determination of holding period. The following provisions shall apply for the purpose of determining the period securities have been held:

(i) Stock dividends, splits and recapitalizations. Securities acquired from the issuer as a dividend or pursuant to a stock split, reverse split or recapitalization shall be deemed to have been acquired at the same time as the securities on which the dividend or, if more than one, the initial dividend was paid, the securities involved in the split or reverse split, or the securities surrendered in connection with the recapitalization;

(ii) Conversions. If the securities sold were acquired from the issuer for a consideration consisting solely of other securities of the same issuer surrendered for conversion, the securities so acquired shall be deemed to have been acquired at the same time as the securities surrendered for conversion;

(iii) Contingent issuance of securities. Securities acquired as a contingent payment of the purchase price of an equity interest in a business, or the assets of a business, sold to the issuer or an affiliate of the issuer shall be deemed to have been acquired at the time of such sale if the issuer or affiliate was then committed to issue the securities subject only to conditions other than the payment of further consideration for such securities. An agreement entered into in connection with any such purchase to remain in the employment of, or not to compete with, the issuer or affiliate or the rendering of services pursuant to such agreement shall not be deemed to be the payment of further consideration for such securities.

(iv) Pledged securities. Securities which are bona-fide pledged by an affiliate of the issuer when sold by the pledgee, or by a purchaser, after a default in the obligation secured by the pledge, shall be deemed to have been acquired when they were acquired by the pledgor, except that if the securities were pledged without recourse they shall be deemed to have been acquired by the pledgee at the time of the pledge or by the purchaser at the time of purchase.

(v) Gifts of securities. Securities acquired from an affiliate of the issuer by gift shall be deemed to have been acquired by the donee when they were acquired by the donor.

(vi) Trusts. Where a trust settlor is an affiliate of the issuer, securities acquired from the settlor by the trust, or acquired from the trust by the beneficiaries thereof, shall be deemed to have been acquired when such securities were acquired by the settlor.

(vii) Estates. Where a deceased person was an affiliate of the issuer, securities held by the estate of such person or acquired from such estate by the beneficiaries thereof shall be deemed to have been acquired when they were acquired by the deceased person, except that no holding period is required if the estate is not an affiliate of the issuer or if the securities are sold by a beneficiary of the estate who is not such an affiliate.

NOTE: While there is no holding period or amount limitation for estates and beneficiaries thereof which are not affiliates of the issurer, paragraphs (c), (h) and (i) of the rule apply to securities sold by such persons in reliance upon the rule.

(viii) Rule 145(a) transactions. The holding period for securities acquired in a transaction specified in Rule 145(a) shall be deemed to commence on the date the securities were acquired by the purchaser in such transaction. This provision shall not apply, however, to a transaction effected solely for the purpose of forming a holding company.

(e) Limitation on amount of securities sold. Except as hereinafter provided, the amount of securities which may be sold in reliance upon this rule shall be determined as follows:

(1) Sales by affiliates. If restricted or other securities are sold for the account of an affiliate of the issuer, the amount of securities sold, together with all sales of restricted and other securities of the same class for the account of such person within the preceding three months, shall not exceed the greater of

(i) One percent of the shares or other units of the class outstanding as shown by the most recent report or statement published by the issuer, or

(ii) The average weekly reported volume of trading in such securities on all national securities exchanges and/or reported through the automated quotation system of a registered securities association during the four calendar weeks preceding the filing of notice required by paragraph (h), or if no such notice is required the date of receipt of the order to execute the transaction by the broker or the date of execution of the transaction directly with a market maker, or

(iii) The average weekly volume of trading in such securities reported through the consolidated transaction reporting system contemplated by Rule 11Aa3-1 under the Securities Exchange Act of 1934 (§ 240.11A3-1) during the four-week period specified in paragraph (e)(1)(ii) of this section.

(2) Sales by persons other than affiliates. The amount of restricted securities sold for the account of any person other than an affiliate of the issuer, together with all other sales of restricted securities of the same class for the account of such person within the preceding three months, shall not exceed the amount specified in paragraphs (e)(1) (i), (ii) or (iii) of this section, whichever is applicable, unless the conditions of paragraph (k) of this rule are satisfied.

(3) Determination of amount. For the purpose of determining the amount of securities specified in paragraphs (e) (1) and (2) of this section, the following provisions shall apply:

(i) Where both convertible securities and securities of the class into which they are convertible are sold, the amount of convertible securities sold shall be deemed to be the amount of securities of the class into which they are convertible for the purpose of determining the aggregate amount of securities of both classes sold;

(ii) The amount of securities sold for the account of a pledgee thereof, or for the account of a purchaser of the pledged securities, during any period of three months within one year after a default in the obligation secured by the pledge, and the amount of securities sold during the same three-month period for the account of the pledgor shall not exceed, in the aggregate, the amount specified in paragraph (e) (1) or (2) of this section, whichever is applicable;

(iii) The amount of securities sold for the account of a donee thereof during any period of three months within one year after the donation, and the amount of securities sold during the same three-month period for the account of the donor, shall not exceed, in the aggregate, the amount specified in paragraph (e) (1) or (2) of this section, whichever is applicable;

(iv) Where securities were acquired by a trust from the settlor of the trust, the amount of such securities sold for the account of the trust during any period of three months within one year after the acquisition of the securities by the trust, and the amount of securities sold during the same three-month period for the account of the settlor, shall not exceed, in the aggregate, the amount specified in paragraph (e) (1) or (2) of this section, whichever is applicable;

(v) The amount of securities sold for the account of the estate of a deceased person, or for the account of a beneficiary of such estate, during any period of 3 months and the amount of securities sold during the same period for the account of the deceased person prior to his death shall not exceed, in the aggregate, the amount specified in paragraph (e) (1) or (2) of this section, whichever is applicable: Provided, That no limitation on amount shall apply if the estate or beneficiary thereof is not an affiliate of the issuer;

(vi) When two or more affiliates or other persons agree to act in concert for the purpose of selling securities of an issuer, all securities of the same class sold for the account of all such persons during any period of 3 months shall be aggregated for the purpose of determining the limitation on the amount of securities sold;

(vii) The following sales of securities need not be included in determining the amount of securities sold in reliance upon this section: securities sold pursuant to an effective registration statement under the Act; securities sold pursuant to an exemption provided by Regulation A (§ 230.251 through § 230.263) under the Act; securities sold in a transaction exempt pursuant to Section 4 of the Act (15 U.S.C. 77d) and not involving any public offering; and securities sold offshore pursuant to Regulation S (§ 230.901 through § 230.905, and Preliminary Notes) under the Act.

(f) Manner of sale. The securities shall be sold in brokers' transactions within the meaning of section 4(4) of the Act or in transactions directly with a market maker, as that term is defined in section 3(a)(38) of the Securities Exchange Act of 1934, and the person selling the securities shall not (1) solicit or arrange for the solicitation of orders to buy the securities in anticipation of or in connection with such transaction, or (2) make any payment in connection with the offer or sale of the securities to any person other than the broker who executes an order to sell the securities. The requirements of this paragraph, however, shall not apply to securities sold for the account of the estate of a deceased person or for the account of a beneficiary of such estate provided the estate or beneficiary thereof is not an affiliate of the issuer; nor shall they apply to securities sold for the account of any person other than an affiliate of the issuer provided the conditions of paragraph (k) of this rule are satisfied.

(g) Brokers' transactions. The term brokers' transactions in section 4(4) of the Act shall for the purposes of this rule be deemed to include transactions by a broker in which such broker:

(1) Does not more than execute the order or orders to sell the securities as agent for the person for whose account the securities are sold; and receives no more than the usual and customary broker's commission;

(2) Neither solicits nor arranges for the solicitation of customers' orders to buy the securities in anticipation of or in connection with the transaction; provided, that the foregoing shall not preclude (i) inquiries by the broker of other brokers or dealers who have indicated an interest in the securities within the preceding 60 days, (ii) inquiries by the broker of his customers who have indicated an unsolicited bona fide interest in the securities within the preceding 10 business days; or (iii) the publication by the broker of bid and ask quotations for the security in an inter-dealer quotation system provided that such quotations are incident to the maintenance of a bona fide inter-dealer market for the security for the broker's own account and that the broker has published bona fide bid and ask quotations for the security in an inter-dealer quotation system on each of at least twelve days within the preceding thirty calendar days with no more than four business days in succession without such two-way quotations;

NOTE TO PARAGRAPH (g)(2)(ii): The broker should obtain and retain in his files written evidence of indications of bona fide unsolicited interest by his customers in the securities at the time such indications are received.

(3) After reasonable inquiry is not aware of circumstances indicating that the person for whose account the securities are sold is an underwriter with respect to the securities or that the transaction is a part of a distribution of securities of the issuer. Without limiting the foregoing, the broker shall be deemed to be aware of any facts or statements contained in the notice required by paragraph (h) of this section.

NOTES: (i) The broker, for his own protection, should obtain and retain in his files a copy of the notice required by paragraph (h) of this section.

(ii) The reasonable inquiry required by paragraph (g)(3) of this section should include, but not necessarily be limited to, inquiry as to the following matters:

(a) The length of time the securities have been held by the person for whose account they are to be sold. If practicable, the inquiry should include physical inspection of the securities;

(b) The nature of the transaction in which the securities were acquired by such person;

(c) The amount of securities of the same class sold during the past 3 months by all persons whose sales are required to be taken into consideration pursuant to paragraph (e) of this section;

(d) Whether such person intends to sell additional securities of the same class through any other means;

(e) Whether such person has solicited or made any arrangement for the solicitation of buy orders in connection with the proposed sale of securities;

(f) Whether such person has made any payment to any other person in connection with the proposed sale of the securities; and

(g) The number of shares or other units of the class outstanding, or the relevant trading volume.

(h) Notice of proposed sale. If the amount of securities to be sold in reliance upon the rule during any period of three months exceeds 500 shares or other units or has an aggregate sale price in excess of $10,000, three copies of a notice on Form 144 shall be filed with the Commission at its principal office in Washington, DC; and if such securities are admitted to trading on any national securities exchange, one copy of such notice shall also be transmitted to the principal exchange on which such securities are so admitted. The Form 144 shall be signed by the person for whose account the securities are to be sold and shall be transmitted for filing concurrently with either the placing with a broker of an order to execute a sale of securities in reliance upon this rule or the execution directly with a market maker of such a sale. Neither the filing of such notice nor the failure of the Commission to comment thereon shall be deemed to preclude the Commission from taking any action it deems necessary or appropriate with respect to the sale of the securities referred to in such notice. The requirements of this paragraph, however, shall not apply to securities sold for the account of any person other than an affiliate of the issuer, provided the conditions of paragraph (k) of this rule are satisfied.

(i) Bona fide intention to sell. The person filing the notice required by paragraph (h) of this section shall have a bona fide intention to sell the securities referred to therein within a reasonable time after the filing of such notice.

(j) Non-exclusive rule. Although this rule provides a means for reselling restricted securities and securities held by affiliates without registration, it is not the exclusive means for reselling such securities in that manner. Therefore, it does not eliminate or otherwise affect the availability of any exemption for resales under the Securities Act that a person or entity may be able to rely upon.

(k) Termination of certain restrictions on sales of restricted securities by persons other than affiliates. The requirements of paragraphs (c), (e), (f) and (h) of this section shall not apply to restricted securities sold for the account of a person who is not an affiliate of the issuer at the time of the sale and has not been an affiliate during the preceding three months, provided a period of at least two years has elapsed since the later of the date the securities were acquired from the issuer or from an affiliate of the issuer. The two-year period shall be calculated as described in paragraph (d) of this section.

HISTORY

[37 FR 596, Jan. 14, 1972, as amended at 39 FR 6071, Feb. 19, 1974; 39 FR 8914, Mar. 7, 1974; 43 FR 43711, Sept. 27, 1978; 43 FR 54230, Nov. 21, 1978; 44 FR 15612, Mar. 14, 1979; 45 FR 12391, Feb. 28, 1980; 46 FR 12197, Feb. 12, 1981; 47 FR 11261, Mar. 16, 1982; 53 FR 12921, Apr. 20, 1988; 55 FR 17944, Apr. 30, 1990; 58 FR 67312, Dec. 21, 1993; 61 FR 21356, 21359, May 9, 1996; 62 FR 9242, 9244, Feb. 28, 1997; 63 FR 9632, 9642, Feb. 25, 1998; 64 FR 61382, 61400, Nov. 10, 1999]

AUTHORITY

(Secs. 2(11), 4(1), 4(4), 19(a), 19(c), 48 Stat. 74, 75, 77, 85; secs. 201, 203, 209, 210, 48 Stat. 904, 906, 908; secs. 1-4, 6, 68 Stat. 683, 684; sec. 12, 78 Stat. 580, 84 Stat. 1480; sec. 308(a)(2), 90 Stat. 58 (15 U.S.C. 77b(11), 77d(1), 77d(4), 77s(a); sec. 209, 59 Stat. 167; sec. 3(b), 48 Stat. 75; sec. 308(a)(1), (2), (3), 90 Stat. 56, 57; secs. 2, 18, 92 Stat. 275, 962; secs. 505, 622, 701, 94 Stat. 2291, 2292, 2294 (15 U.S.C. 77c(b), 77d(1), 77s(a), 77s(c)); secs. 2(11), 4(1), 4(4), 19(a), 48 Stat. 74, 77, 85; secs. 201, 203, 209, 210, 48 Stat. 904, 906, 908; secs. 14, 5, 68 Stat. 683, 684; sec. 12, 78 Stat. 580 (15 U.S.C. 77b(11), 77d(1), 77d(4), 77s(a)))

Rule 144A

THIS SECTION IS CURRENT THROUGH THE MARCH 16, 2001
ISSUE OF THE FEDERAL REGISTER

TITLE 17—COMMODITY AND SECURITIES EXCHANGES
CHAPTER II—SECURITIES AND EXCHANGE COMMISSION
PART 230—GENERAL RULES AND REGULATIONS, SECURITIES ACT OF 1933
GENERAL

17 CFR 230.144A

§ 230.144A Private resales of securities to institutions.

PRELIMINARY NOTES:

1. This section relates solely to the application of section 5 of the Act and not to antifraud or other provisions of the federal securities laws.

2. Attempted compliance with this section does not act as an exclusive election; any seller hereunder may also claim the availability of any other applicable exemption from the registration requirements of the Act.

3. In view of the objective of this section and the policies underlying the Act, this section is not available with respect to any transaction or series of transactions that, although in technical compliance with this section, is part of a plan or scheme to evade the registration provisions of the Act. In such cases, registration under the Act is required.

4. Nothing in this section obviates the need for any issuer or any other person to comply with the securities registration or broker-dealer registration requirements of the Securities Exchange Act of 1934 (the Exchange Act), whenever such requirements are applicable.

5. Nothing in this section obviates the need for any person to comply with any applicable state law relating to the offer or sale of securities.

6. Securities acquired in a transaction made pursuant to the provisions of this section are deemed to be restricted securities within the meaning of § 230.144(a)(3) of this chapter.

7. The fact that purchasers of securities from the issuer thereof may purchase such securities with a view to reselling such securities pursuant to this section will not affect the availability to such issuer of an exemption under section 4(2) of the Act, or Regulation D under the Act, from the registration requirements of the Act.

(a) Definitions. (1) For purposes of this section, qualified institutional buyer shall mean:

(i) Any of the following entities, acting for its own account or the accounts of other qualified institutional buyers, that in the aggregate owns and invests on a discretionary basis at least $100 million in securities of issuers that are not affiliated with the entity:

(A) Any insurance company as defined in section 2(13) of the Act;

NOTE: A purchase by an insurance company for one or more of its separate accounts, as defined by section 2(a)(37) of the Investment Company Act of 1940 (the

"Investment Company Act"), which are neither registered under section 8 of the Investment Company Act nor required to be so registered, shall be deemed to be a purchase for the account of such insurance company.

(B) Any investment company registered under the Investment Company Act or any business development company as defined in section 2(a)(48) of that Act;

(C) Any Small Business Investment Company licensed by the U.S. Small Business Administration under section 301(c) or (d) of the Small Business Investment Act of 1958;

(D) Any plan established and maintained by a state, its political subdivisions, or any agency or instrumentality of a state or its political subdivisions, for the benefit of its employees;

(E) Any employee benefit plan within the meaning of title I of the Employee Retirement Income Security Act of 1974;

(F) Any trust fund whose trustee is a bank or trust company and whose participants are exclusively plans of the types identified in paragraph (a)(1)(i) (D) or (E) of this section, except trust funds that include as participants individual retirement accounts or H.R. 10 plans.

(G) Any business development company as defined in section 202(a)(22) of the Investment Advisers Act of 1940;

(H) Any organization described in section 501(c)(3) of the Internal Revenue Code, corporation (other than a bank as defined in section 3(a)(2) of the Act or a savings and loan association or other institution referenced in section 3(a)(5)(A) of the Act or a foreign bank or savings and loan association or equivalent institution), partnership, or Massachusetts or similar business trust; and

(I) Any investment adviser registered under the Investment Advisers Act.

(ii) Any dealer registered pursuant to section 15 of the Exchange Act, acting for its own account or the accounts of other qualified institutional buyers, that in the aggregate owns and invests on a discretionary basis at least $10 million of securities of issuers that are not affiliated with the dealer, Provided, That securities constituting the whole or a part of an unsold allotment to or subscription by a dealer as a participant in a public offering shall not be deemed to be owned by such dealer;

(iii) Any dealer registered pursuant to section 15 of the Exchange Act acting in a riskless principal transaction on behalf of a qualified institutional buyer;

NOTE: A registered dealer may act as agent, on a non-discretionary basis, in a transaction with a qualified institutional buyer without itself having to be a qualified institutional buyer.

(iv) Any investment company registered under the Investment Company Act, acting for its own account or for the accounts of other qualified institutional buyers, that is part of a family of investment companies which own in the aggregate at least $100 million in securities of issuers, other than issuers that are affiliated with the investment company or are part of such family of investment companies. Family of investment companies means any two or more investment companies registered under the Investment Company Act, except for a unit investment trust whose assets consist solely of shares of one or more registered investment companies, that have the same investment adviser (or, in the case of unit investment trusts, the same depositor), Provided That, for purposes of this section:

(A) Each series of a series company (as defined in Rule 18f-2 under the Investment Company Act [17 CFR 270.18f-2]) shall be deemed to be a separate investment company; and

(B) Investment companies shall be deemed to have the same adviser (or depositor) if their advisers (or depositors) are majority-owned subsidiaries of the same parent, or if one investment company's adviser (or depositor) is a majority-owned subsidiary of the other investment company's adviser (or depositor);

(v) Any entity, all of the equity owners of which are qualified institutional buyers, acting for its own account or the accounts of other qualified institutional buyers; and

(vi) Any bank as defined in section 3(a)(2) of the Act, any savings and loan association or other institution as referenced in section 3(a)(5)(A) of the Act, or any foreign bank or savings and loan association or equivalent institution, acting for its own account or the accounts of other qualified institutional buyers, that in the aggregate owns and invests on a discretionary basis at least $100 million in securities of issuers that are not affiliated with it and that has an audited net worth of at least $25 million as demonstrated in its latest annual financial statements, as of a date not more than 16 months preceding the date of sale under the Rule in the case of a U.S. bank or savings and loan association, and not more than 18 months preceding such date of sale for a foreign bank or savings and loan association or equivalent institution.

(2) In determining the aggregate amount of securities owned and invested on a discretionary basis by an entity, the following instruments and interests shall be excluded: bank deposit notes and certificates of deposit; loan participations; repurchase agreements; securities owned but subject to a repurchase agreement; and currency, interest rate and commodity swaps.

(3) The aggregate value of securities owned and invested on a discretionary basis by an entity shall be the cost of such securities, except where the entity reports its securities holdings in its financial statements on the basis of their market value, and no current information with respect to the cost of those securities has been published. In the latter event, the securities may be valued at market for purposes of this section.

(4) In determining the aggregate amount of securities owned by an entity and invested on a discretionary basis, securities owned by subsidiaries of the entity that are consolidated with the entity in its financial statements prepared in accordance with generally accepted accounting principles may be included if the investments of such subsidiaries are managed under the direction of the entity, except that, unless the entity is a reporting company under section 13 or 15(d) of the Exchange Act, securities owned by such subsidiaries may not be included if the entity itself is a majority-owned subsidiary that would be included in the consolidated financial statements of another enterprise.

(5) For purposes of this section, riskless principal transaction means a transaction in which a dealer buys a security from any person and makes a simultaneous off-

setting sale of such security to a qualified institutional buyer, including another dealer acting as riskless principal for a qualified institutional buyer.

(6) For purposes of this section, effective conversion premium means the amount, expressed as a percentage of the security's conversion value, by which the price at issuance of a convertible security exceeds its conversion value.

(7) For purposes of this section, effective exercise premium means the amount, expressed as a percentage of the warrant's exercise value, by which the sum of the price at issuance and the exercise price of a warrant exceeds its exercise value.

(b) Sales by persons other than issuers or dealers. Any person, other than the issuer or a dealer, who offers or sells securities in compliance with the conditions set forth in paragraph (d) of this section shall be deemed not to be engaged in a distribution of such securities and therefore not to be an underwriter of such securities within the meaning of sections 2(11) and 4(1) of the Act.

(c) Sales by Dealers. Any dealer who offers or sells securities in compliance with the conditions set forth in paragraph (d) of this section shall be deemed not to be a participant in a distribution of such securities within the meaning of section 4(3)(C) of the Act and not to be an underwriter of such securities within the meaning of section 2(11) of the Act, and such securities shall be deemed not to have been offered to the public within the meaning of section 4(3)(A) of the Act.

(d) Conditions to be met. To qualify for exemption under this section, an offer or sale must meet the following conditions:

(1) The securities are offered or sold only to a qualified institutional buyer or to an offeree or purchaser that the seller and any person acting on behalf of the seller reasonably believe is a qualified institutional buyer. In determining whether a prospective purchaser is a qualified institutional buyer, the seller and any person acting on its behalf shall be entitled to rely upon the following non-exclusive methods of establishing the prospective purchaser's ownership and discretionary investments of securities:

(i) The prospective purchaser's most recent publicly available financial statements, Provided That such statements present the information as of a date within 16 months preceding the date of sale of securities under this section in the case of a U.S. purchaser and within 18 months preceding such date of sale for a foreign purchaser;

(ii) The most recent publicly available information appearing in documents filed by the prospective purchaser with the Commission or another United States federal, state, or local governmental agency or self-regulatory organization, or with a foreign governmental agency or self-regulatory organization, Provided That any such information is as of a date within 16 months preceding the date of sale of securities under this section in the case of a U.S. purchaser and within 18 months preceding such date of sale for a foreign purchaser;

(iii) The most recent publicly available information appearing in a recognized securities manual, Provided That such information is as of a date within 16 months preceding the date of sale of securities under this section in the case of a U.S. purchaser and within 18 months preceding such date of sale for a foreign purchaser; or

(iv) A certification by the chief financial officer, a person fulfilling an equivalent function, or other executive officer of the purchaser, specifying the amount of securities owned and invested on a discretionary basis by the purchaser as of a specific date on or since the close of the purchaser's most recent fiscal year, or, in the case of a purchaser that is a member of a family of investment companies, a certification by an executive officer of the investment adviser specifying the amount of securities owned by the family of investment companies as of a specific date on or since the close of the purchaser's most recent fiscal year;

(2) The seller and any person acting on its behalf takes reasonable steps to ensure that the purchaser is aware that the seller may rely on the exemption from the provisions of section 5 of the Act provided by this section;

(3) The securities offered or sold:

(i) Were not, when issued, of the same class as securities listed on a national securities exchange registered under section 6 of the Exchange Act or quoted in a U.S. automated inter-dealer quotation system; Provided, That securities that are convertible or exchangeable into securities so listed or quoted at the time of issuance and that had an effective conversion premium of less than 10 percent, shall be treated as securities of the class into which they are convertible or exchangeable; and that warrants that may be exercised for securities so listed or quoted at the time of issuance, for a period of less than 3 years from the date of issuance, or that had an effective exercise premium of less than 10 percent, shall be treated as securities of the class to be issued upon exercise; and Provided further, That the Commission may from time to time, taking into account then-existing market practices, designate additional securities and classes of securities that will not be deemed of the same class as securities listed on a national securities exchange or quoted in a U.S. automated inter-dealer quotation system; and

(ii) Are not securities of an open-end investment company, unit investment trust or face-amount certificate company that is or is required to be registered under section 8 of the Investment Company Act; and

(4)(i) In the case of securities of an issuer that is neither subject to section 13 or 15(d) of the Exchange Act, nor exempt from reporting pursuant to Rule 12g3-2(b) (§ 240.12g3-2(b) of this chapter) under the Exchange Act, nor a foreign government as defined in Rule 405 (§ 230.405 of this chapter) eligible to register securities under Schedule B of the Act, the holder and a prospective purchaser designated by the holder have the right to obtain from the issuer, upon request of the holder, and the prospective purchaser has received from the issuer, the seller, or a person acting on either of their behalf, at or prior to the time of sale, upon such prospective purchaser's request to the holder or the issuer, the following information (which shall be reasonably current in relation to the date of resale under this section): a very brief statement of the nature of the business of the issuer and the products and services it offers; and the issuer's most recent balance sheet and profit and loss and retained earnings statements, and similar financial statements for such part of the two preceding fiscal years as the issuer has been in operation (the financial statements should be audited to the extent reasonably available).

(ii) The requirement that the information be reasonably current will be presumed to be satisfied if:

(A) The balance sheet is as of a date less than 16 months before the date of resale, the statements of profit and loss and retained earnings are for the 12 months preceding the date of such balance sheet, and if such balance sheet is not as of a date less than 6 months before the date of resale, it shall be accompanied by additional statements of profit and loss and retained earnings for the period from the date of such balance sheet to a date less than 6 months before the date of resale; and

(B) The statement of the nature of the issuer's business and its products and services offered is as of a date within 12 months prior to the date of resale; or

(C) With regard to foreign private issuers, the required information meets the timing requirements of the issuer's home country or principal trading markets.

(e) Offers and sales of securities pursuant to this section shall be deemed not to affect the availability of any exemption or safe harbor relating to any previous or subsequent offer or sale of such securities by the issuer or any prior or subsequent holder thereof.

HISTORY

[55 FR 17945, Apr. 30, 1990, as amended at 57 FR 48722, Oct. 28, 1992]

AUTHORITY

15 U.S.C. 77b, 77c, 77d, 77f, 77g, 77h, 77j, 77r, 77sss, 77z-3, 78c, 78d, 78 l, 78m, 78n, 78o, 78t, 78w, 78 ll(d), 78mm, 79t, 80a-8, 80a-24, 80a-28, 80a-29, 80a-30, and 80a-37.

Index